W9-AAI-097

PACIFIC OCEAN

SEA

HONSHU

SHIKOKU

KYUSHU

Mito

Tokyo

Atami

Oshima Island

Mt. Fuji ▲

Nagoya

Gifu

Toba

Ise

Nara

Osaka

Kyoto

Kobe

Wajima

Kanazawa

Takarazuka

Tottori

Yonago

Himeji

Okayama

Takamatsu

Matsue

Hiroshima

Oki Island

Yamaguchi

Fukuoka

Kumamoto

Beppu

Oita

Shimabara

Nagasaki

Miyazaki

Kagoshima

Ibusuki

SCALE

0   100   200 Miles

Robert Freese

THE
SILENT TRAVELLER
IN JAPAN

THE
SILENT TRAVELLER
IN JAPAN

記畫本日

Written and Illustrated by

CHIANG YEE

W · W · NORTON & COMPANY · INC ·

NEW YORK

COPYRIGHT © 1972 BY W. W. NORTON & COMPANY, INC.

First Edition

Library of Congress Cataloging in Publication Data

Chiang, Yee, 1903–
    The silent traveller in Japan.

    1. Japan—Description and travel—1945–
I. Title.
DS811.C44   915.2′04′4   75-116118
ISBN 0-393-08642-9

TO
YIAU–MIN

Contents

Plates in Color

THE
SILENT TRAVELLER
IN JAPAN

I

Prologue

"THE UNIVERSE is an inn for all creatures, while time is a passer-by from generation to generation. Our floating life resembles a dream: how long can we enjoy it?" Thus wrote Li Po, one of the greatest poets of eighth-century China. But the universe which Li Po conceived was within the frame of T'ang China, bounded by the Gobi Desert in the north, the Kunlun Range of the Himalayas on the west, and the China Sea on the east and south sides. To a Chinese of that time the universe was a limited region of the earth, and Li Po knew nothing of what was outside of it. Yet his words ring true in this twentieth-century universe which includes that limited region of eighth-century China. I feel fortunate to have been born into this twentieth-century universe and to have lived in an "inn" far bigger than Li Po's. And I am still one of the human family which Li Po knew, but he did not dream that this human family of ours would grow so enormously in numbers and would be joined by many other human families in other parts of the earth as well.

To enjoy life means to find interest in what one sees and understands throughout one's lifetime. The past thirty odd years of my life I have lived outside China, travelling round the five great continents and almost all the seven seas, though I cannot claim to have visited every single piece of land on earth. In my travels I have seen infinitely more things than Li Po ever knew of, and I have found more interest in life than those whose passing Li Po lamented in his short floating life. Above all, Li Po could never have had the slightest idea that the Chinese would win the reputation of being "heathens," "inscrutable people," and of the Western world. I used to be bothered by being called such names "wearing emotionless face," as I learned in my first few years of living in but eventually I laughed at them, for I remembered the ancient Chinese fable which has been handed down from the third century B.C.:

Yang Pu, the young brother of a noted Chinese philosopher, Yang Chu, went out one day in his usual light-colored gown. Suddenly a heavy rain poured down and he made a quick change into a dark gown. When he came back home, his own dog barked at him terribly, for it did not recognize him. Yang Pu became angry and wanted to hit the dog with his stick. Yang Chu saw what was happening and told his brother not to hit the animal, saying, "Just imagine that your own dog was wearing his white coat when he left home and came back in a black one. Wouldn't you be feeling surprised at such a change?"

After all, Yang Pu was the same Yang Pu before and after the rain, but his dog did not recognize the change of his gown from a light-colored one into a dark one. The Chinese in the East are the same human beings as the people of the West; only they are different in their rather flat facial structure and they speak a different mother tongue. Their different appearances should not have made them strangers to one another. I have tried to read a few of the early books on China and the Chinese written by Western writers who had spent a little time in the East and who had invented various names and expressions for the Chinese. This induced me to put down my own impressions of a number of places where I have been outside China. However, I have been brought up in the Confucian belief: 性相近習相遠 "Hsing hsiang chin, hsi hsiang yuan," which means "human beings draw close to one another by their common nature, but habits or customs keep them apart." I began to record my travels with the aim of searching out similarities instead of differences, although I could not help observing habits and ways of living very unlike those of the Chinese, for we have not all been born into similar climates and geographical conditions. My observations I set down in my Silent Traveller books on the English lakeland, London, the Yorkshire dales, Edinburgh, New York, Dublin, Paris, Boston, and San Francisco. As I did not write these books in my mother tongue for the Chinese to read, those outside the Chinese human family could read and criticize them. The books have been received favorably on the whole. Only a few critics have questioned why I did not try to deal with some bigger subjects, such as the history, thought, religion, politics, and social structures of each land. I must admit that I do not find I am able to comment on those aspects of Western life. Unlike many Western writers who spent some little time in China without even knowing the Chinese language and returned home to produce thick books on China's history, philosophy, religion, and political events, I still do not know much about the English Tories and Whigs, nor the American Republicans and Democrats, even though I have lived in both lands for many years and speak their language. Large subjects such as history, philosophy, and religion are as far beyond my reach as gold. When I thought of them, I could not help recalling another ancient fable of China:

Some thousand years ago in the State of Ch'i lived a man who had great interest in gold. One morning he went to the local market and fixed his eyes on the gold being sold in a shop. He rushed straight to the shop and grabbed the gold and ran away as fast as he could. But he was caught by the police, who interrogated him saying: "How could you take another's gold in bright daylight and in front of so many people in the market?" The man replied that he saw only the gold when he came into the market but did not see any people.

Like the man of Ch'i I was much interested in the gold, but I could not grab it as he did, for I saw many people around me. So my interest shifted to the people instead.

This new volume of *The Silent Traveller in Japan* was written with particular interest in the people of the land. However, there is a difference from my other volumes, each of which dealt only with a single city or region. This volume deals with the people of Japan in many cities, for I have made four visits to Japan in different seasons.

C. Y.

Columbia University
November, 1970

II

Various Phases of Tokyo

I HAVE PAID Japan four visits so far; each time I landed first at Tokyo and spent some days there before I travelled to other places. Indeed Tokyo is an incredibly large city with the largest population of any on earth. In 1858 it was reported to have a population of two million, but now it claims to have more than eleven million. The land has not expanded five times within a little more than one hundred years but the living space which used to have two people now must house eleven. It was a small village some two thousand years ago. Dokan Ota, lord of the area in the fifteenth century, built a fort on the site of the present Imperial Palace, which was then rebuilt into the Edo Castle in 1603, when Edo was made the administrative center by the first Tokugawa shogun, Iyeyasu. It has been growing enormously since the emperor Meiji moved from Kyoto to make Tokyo the center for the administration of all Japan in 1868.

I have found the present Tokyo very complex and quite sophisticated even in my four not-too-long stays. I might not have found it to be so complex and sophisticated had I not lived in Europe and America for more than thirty years. Tokyo is not only the national capital but is also headquarters of all trades, industries, and commerce. It is like parts of Washington and New York combined, including some parts of Chicago and San Francisco. In Tokyo I found similarities to what I saw in Paris, London, Berlin, New York, and even Peking or Nanking. However, the invariable Japanese face is to be met at every corner, though some younger people and a few middle-aged persons have dyed their hair brunette, reddish brown, or even pale yellow. My moments in Tokyo were filled with interest but I can only record them sporadically here.

The spacious plaza before the Imperial Palace caught my fancy at once and I went to stroll there again and again. Its spaciousness was enhanced by the massive green of the big area of Hibiya Park beyond the wide Uchibori Avenue. This must have been planned at the beginning of the Meiji era and I admire the foresighted city planner of those days. The plaza was divided into four squarish green plots with Mita Avenue going through parallel to the palace wall. On each of the green plots grow many twisted pine trees, which I found interesting because they look like the pine trees in many famous Japanese screen paintings. Screen painting is the chief flower of Japanese decorative art and I used to think that Japanese screen painters invented such twisted pine trees for their decorative purposes. But I now faced the real thing and could not help but feel more interested in them. Very few pine trees can be seen growing in any of the big capitals of the world. Only those in the Imperial Palace Plaza stand out distinctively.

Each time I strolled round the plaza, I found hundreds of cars moving fast along Mita Avenue in solid blocks. Mita Avenue with its fast-moving cars reminded me of an American expressway or highway, though one could wait to cross over it after a good while. I don't think Emperor Meiji ever imagined such a mass movement of traffic in front of his palace when he rode out on his white horse. I often stood watching the unruffled water surface of the palace moat. Occasionally some wild ducks came by, seemingly from nowhere, and the sound of their quacking seemed louder than that of the cars moving behind me. A strange feeling. One morning I saw a pair of beautiful white swans gliding along majestically toward Niju-bashi (Double Bridge). They enlivened the place and seemed to be on guard at the palace. I was curious at not having seen many pigeons in the plaza, unlike the great flocks of them in the big cities of Europe and America. Why? On the other hand I was told that on cold winter days the plaza would be full of white sea gulls that had come in to roost, but did not appear at any other time. That is why the Japanese call sea gulls capital birds. Again, I ask why so?

Instead of pigeons, a large number of people stood in front of the palace at all times. They arrived in groups, each led by a guide holding a small flag. Most of the people were women and children, and school boys and girls in their school uniform, and all gazed at the palace, open-mouthed, in awe. Nearly everyone had a camera and shot views of the palace walls from all angles. I was told that before the Second World War, though not so many came, those who did come would make a deep bow or a gesture of homage to the imperial occupants, and the palace guards would often shove them away to keep them at a good distance.

I once composed the following little verse:

Many twisted and rugged pines meet me outside
    the palace;
The spring water of the royal moat is warm,
    while the ducks float gracefully.
Masses of boys and girls gathered here like bees,
Stretching their necks at the imperial gate for a
    glimpse inside.

I was told that a part of the plaza ground became reddened with blood when a number of officers and soldiers committed hara-kiri (the Japanese traditional ritual suicide by disembowelment) in order to express their loyalty and patriotism after Emperor Hirohito's broadcast that Japan had surrendered in 1945. This could only happen in Tokyo. The blood stains have been wiped away and I found no trace of them.

My second frequented area in Tokyo is the Ginza. I found it easy to get there by riding on the subway from the Roppongi station. I went there for the first time in order to buy some paper from the Kyukyo Do Co. Ltd., a famous stationery house in Japan. No matter when I walked in the Ginza, I always encountered more people there than in Times Square of New York, except that in the evenings Times Square has more people strolling about and many of them speak foreign languages. But in the Ginza those who stroll about are all Japanese, with only an occasional Western face in their midst. The strange part is that they are almost all young people who seem to have little to do in the evenings and daytime as well. During my four visits to Japan, I saw four big buildings put up on each occasion; two of which were new department stores. There seems to be no end to new building. Construction has been going on here and there all the time. My friend Professor Ivan Morris, author and authority on Japan, wrote in 1964:

> *Plus ce change, plus la même chose.* My impression is that ever since the Meiji period Tokyo has been in an almost perpetual state of reconstruction, . . . and the only permanent thing about the city is that everything is changing: the old Greek saying that "all flows" seems peculiarly appropriate here. I find it hard to believe that there will ever come a day when this city will be completed, in the way (for instance) that Paris was completed some fifty years ago. The genius of Tokyo, like that of New York, lies in its impermanence; and, if one finds these two cities charming, that is surely an essential part of their charm.

The Ginza is said to have started in 1873 when two-story brick houses and brick sidewalks were constructed along both sides of Tokyo's first big street, from Shimbashi Bridge to Kyobashi Bridge. Now the brick houses have been replaced by skyscrapers of steel and glass and the sidewalks by concrete. There seem to be more large department stores here than in any other quarter, and always packed with people, nearly all Japanese. A typical sight in any of the big stores is a pair of beautiful ladies elegantly dressed, standing on either side of the escalator bowing to the patrons being carried upward, and in genteel voices murmuring a welcome to them. As the moving stairs rolled on, always filled with people and the young ladies bowing up and down all the while, it seemed to me as if they were inseparable parts of the escalator. My

A scene inside a Tokyo
department store

experience gave rise to the following verse:

My travelling feet are just on the moving stairs,
On both sides ceremonial bows cause me to won-
    der.
When I try to compose myself to return the bows,
I realize that I have long left the beauties behind.

行脚甫登自轉梯
兩傍揖讓費猜疑
衣襟重整峰回禮
早與伊人賦別離

The Japanese department stores seem to sell everything that could be bought in any American one. Out of curiosity, I asked Miss Michi Mori-guchi, daughter of Professor and Mrs. Shigeichi Moriguchi of Tokyo University, when they kindly invited me to dine in their home, if the modern ladies of Tokyo would be able to buy tanning lotion to rub all over themselves to make it appear as if they have only just returned from the seaside. She quickly answered, "Oh, yes, one can buy tanning liquid in almost every store in the Ginza." This surprised me very much, for I thought Japanese women took great care of their fair skins and that they loved to use parasols under the bright sun. Besides, the geisha girls would never touch the tanning lotion. Young Michi remarked in Japa-

Pachinko house in Ginza

nese, "We are not living in old Japan." As a matter of fact, her parents told me that she is a serious student of Kabuki and No drama. So I was wrong to think that there must be something which could not be bought in Tokyo.

Shoes were on sale in the greatest abundance—shoes of every kind and style in different materials. Once I discussed with Ivan Morris why the Japanese are so conscious of their footwear. On entering any Japanese house or inn the first thing one encounters is the rows of shoes. Before stepping inside, one is given a kind of shoehorn, some with long handles, for taking off or putting on shoes. The reason for removing shoes before entering is obvious; the beautifully laid *tatami* ("mats") on the floors should not be soiled. But Ivan has developed an interesting theory that by nature the Japanese have an instinctively unpleasant feeling about shoes, particularly those made of leather, for they think leather is itself distasteful, and in his experience he found that the Japanese are horrified and thoroughly upset if their foreign friends walk into their homes wearing leather shoes. He added that the Japanese created the long-handled shoehorn because they dislike intensely having their heads close to the shoes. But Mrs. Nobuko **Morris**, who is Japanese by birth, pointed out that the Japanese *kutsu* (adapted Chinese character) for shoes is one with a *leather* radical (a part of the design for the word) thus 靴 . I smiled, saying that the word is Chinese by origin. The Chinese must have produced footwear in leather for rainy weather since the olden days. I was interested to notice that few Japanese women wear high heels in the streets, though I could be wrong. I also noticed that Japanese women love to take off their shoes while travelling in the train. Some would even sit on the train seats with their legs folded under them, as if they were on their tatami at home.

Many people disagree with the changes that have taken place in Tokyo in modern times. But must we have a prenotion that Tokyo must be totally different from all the other cities in the world? Professor Meyer Schapiro gave me a copy of his interesting address, *The Role of Art in Contemporary Society*, which he made when he took part in the International Symposium on Fine Arts in the East and West in March, 1966, in Tokyo. In it he says:

> Art in the past served religion and tribe and state or gave dignity to a noble caste, while art today is pursued for its own sake, a purely personal creation and object of delight. . . . They (the artists of our century) have been the first to appreciate primitive and exotic arts of all types. . . . The goal of wider availability, with more discriminating experience, rests on faith in the capacity of educated free human beings to live better and to realize themselves more fully through beauty, understanding and good will.

Though he did not say in so many words that we modern men should make use of whatever is good in every land and experience to create a better way of life, he seems to think all the changes in Tokyo and in the modern Japanese art movement are a natural outcome of our century. Meyer and I sat together occasionally to discuss random art objects. Though he is a great authority on the history of Western art, his interest in Eastern art is equally strong, for he once studied under the great French scholar Professor Paul Pelliot, the expert on Eastern art, particularly Chinese art. Meyer also has a great interest in Japanese architecture, old and new. Many people have expressed displeasure at finding an Eiffel Tower in Tokyo, for they thought it spoiled the city skyline. Meyer did not seem to mind this much and even made a sketch of it. When he showed it to me, I was struck by his view of it from his hotel window and asked to borrow it for an illustration of a corner of Tokyo.

Professor Schapiro's sketch of Tokyo Tower

It was on the Tokyo Tower that I saw a notice one day of a newly established center for modern Japanese literature known as Kindai Nihon Bungaku Kan, which was to be opened to the public. I asked Mr. Yoshimaru Tadokoro, manager of Macmillan's Japan office, to go with me. We took a taxi and had to ask the direction several times as the rain was pouring down. Though Tokyo is modern, it is a city where a given address cannot be easily found even by the local taxi driver. Eventually we reached a private garden and walked along a long winding path to a brand new building. The young woman in charge of the exhibition was surprised to see us on such a wet day; we were the only visitors. The manuscripts by modern Japanese writers on display in the cases interested me greatly, though I could not read them. Many great names in kanji were familiar to me, for I have read their works in English translation and some in Chinese too. This center for modern literature is the first of its kind that I had come across anywhere in all my travels in Europe and America. Sei Ito, the chairman of the board of the center, had worked hard to obtain funds for this new building and it is a great triumph for him. He and Mrs. Ito looked very pleased when I told them that I had gone to see it.

The Itos live in Suginami-ku in an old Japanese-style house with an interesting garden. It is not far from the house of Professor and Mrs. Moriguchi. I have been in both houses and seen the real Japanese way of living. Mrs. Ito has many miniature trees and flowers in pots in their garden. The Moriguchis' garden contains a small pool with running water in which several red water lilies were in bloom. Both families carry on the tradition of their country and both hostesses prepared typically Japanese dishes. Their hospitality made me wish that I could entertain them all in China according to our tradition. Much to my regret, I could not reciprocate for the present.

I got to know Sei Ito better through a talk we had about his own writings. He told me that his discourse on Japanese literature was very similar to the work of Van Wyck Brooks on American literature. I then sent Sei Ito a number of books by Van Wyck Brooks, whom I knew from 1950 until his death in 1963. Through Ito I became more acquainted with the Moriguchis, for they have both come to Columbia University as visiting scholars at the same time.

One day Sei Ito wanted to show me something ultramodern in Tokyo as well as a very old-fashioned and typically Japanese place. He and his younger son Rei took me to the Hotel New Otani, where we went up to the rotating restaurant on the top story. This was reputed to be the only rotating restaurant in Japan at the time. We sat by a window gazing out, and while the room rotated very slowly, Sei Ito pointed out some interesting places around Tokyo. The whole round took about an hour. Afterward a taxi took the three of us to an old quarter of Tokyo where there were many old Japanese houses with tile roofs. I could not tell where we were. When we entered one of the houses, a beautifully shaped pine tree inside the small courtyard caught my eye. After we passed through a few narrow corridors, a middle-aged lady in kimono

Sei Ito

came to greet Mr. Ito happily. Then, pushing the sliding door to one side, she ushered us into a spotlessly clean room. Cushions and small seats with a back (a modern device) were already nicely arranged. I learned that this inn, called Fukuda Ya, was known to every man of letters in Japan and has catered only to literary people for almost a hundred years. Junichiro Tanizaki, Yasunari Kawabata, Naoya Shiga, and many others frequented this inn for their short stay and entertainment. Apart from being a literary landmark, it also has a reputation for fine food. This was immediately proved to be true. It was utterly unbelievable that one could find a place so absolutely undisturbed as the room in which we were sitting in the center of the densely populated city of eleven million people. Mr. Ito suggested to me several times that I add a volume on Tokyo or Japan to my Silent Traveller series of books. He seemed to have planned this for me so well.

At the end of the meal Mr. Ito told the proprietress, who came in to inquire whether the food had been satisfactory, that I was a writer, calligrapher, and painter. She was happy to know this and bowed again and again. She brought in a brush, ink, and inkstone with two pieces of paper already mounted on cardboard. I asked if she had any favorite Chinese poem that she would like me to write. With no hesitation she wrote down four lines. I wrote the T'ang poem on one paper and added a small sketch of a crane in flight on the other. A memorable moment for me. Very few Chinese innkeepers could remember any great poets' names, let alone poems!

Sei Ito, a most considerate person, said that there was still time for me to do some sightseeing and suggested that his young son Rei take his place as my guide. Rei led me afoot through many streets, wide and narrow, and squeezed by many people of both sexes who thronged the middle of the side streets. Young Rei told me with an amused smile that more came to Ginza night after night. Many frequented the coffee houses and bars, and many just walked here and there, for there was little space in their homes, just waiting until the time for going home to bed. Indeed, Tokyo is a terribly crowded city.

Presently we came to a small lane, lined on both sides with small square tables, on each of which stood a tiny kerosene lamp. "This is Tsuji-Uranai, or street of fortunetellers," Rei announced to me. He wanted me see it specially and very few foreigners knew of it. Tied to the front of each table was a piece of cloth with two kanji words, either 神易 *shen I* ("divine change"), or 周易 *Chou I* ("change Ching of Chou dynasty"), both referred to the famous Chinese book, *I Ching*, or *Book of Change*, an English translation of which was first published a few years ago. I saw a man with longish beard seated at one table facing two young girls and murmuring gently while pointing to something on the table. Two other fortunetellers were beardless, for they were women. Another young man in black kimono was leaning against the wall reading a book while waiting for some customers. I could not help speaking rather loudly: "How like those in Cheng-huang-miao (Temple of City God) in Shanghai!" I thanked Rei for guiding me to this interesting quarter of Tokyo, for it gave me an unexpected reminder of my younger days in Shanghai.

Meiji Jingu, or Meiji Shrine, is a twenty-minute taxi drive from where I was staying. Arriving at the main entrance, I followed a large throng of boys and girls and passed through an enormous torii, a cement structure, directly to the shrine. Going up a few stone steps to the courtyard, I saw people pulling the thick cord of a bell to make it sound, thus announcing their presence to the god who is in fact Emperor Meiji. Then they clapped their hands together and threw some coins into a wooden cabinet which was placed under the bell before murmuring some words as in prayer. I was interested to see the different ways people clapped their hands and later did a number of sketches from memory.

Clapping hands before prayer
at a Shinto shrine

Inside the shrine building a Shinto priest in white robes was reading a document while a young couple stood behind him. The young man was holding a baby of a month or so in his arms. Afterward the priest led the couple away to sign a paper. The ceremony seemed similar to the Western christening service, and it could have been that the birth of a baby was being officially registered. There has been no official registry in China, which causes great trouble for a Chinese to produce evidence of his birth when he goes to a Western country. Confucianism is not a religion, for it does not have a priest, bible, or preaching, or any regular services. The Confucian temple was built in commemoration of the greatness of the Chinese thinker, but it had nobody there to register births and deaths. Our births and deaths were registered in the family clan-book.

Meiji Jingu was specially built for Emperor Meiji and Empress Shoken and dedicated to them in 1920. Its precincts consist of more than one million square meters including the inner and outer gardens. From the courtyard of the shrine I found my way to the Meiji Jingu Treasure Museum, where articles belonging to the emperor and empress, including many robes and gowns, are displayed. I was most interested to find there a number of Chinese books such as *Jogun Seiyo*, *Karakogami*, *Shisho Shuchu*, and a few others from the royal collection. Both the emperor and empress were evidently well versed in Chinese. The books in the cases looked to be in very fine condition, though there was no indication when they were printed. Both the emperor and empress wrote poetry and examples of their work in their own handwriting were

Meiji Jingu

also on display. I then moved on to look at the Western-style oil paintings which depicted the events of the Meiji Restoration. One, entitled
Promulgation of the Constitution in 1889, showed the empress and all
her ladies in waiting and the wives of the ministers in long Western
gowns and the emperor and his officials all in tails. What a complete
change in outward custom! This all took great daring and courage to
accomplish in the face of the many die-hard traditionalists. I could
not help wondering how the emperor Meiji and the Japanese as a
whole had accepted the change so wholeheartedly. It could never have
happened in the China of a hundred years ago, for who could imagine
the narrow-minded Manchurian-born Chinese empress dowager Tzu Hsi
dressed in a long Western-style gown!

Emperor Meiji was the Japan-born god and all his ministers were
Japanese-born citizens. Their voices easily reached the ears of all Japanese, who followed their instructions as god's words without the slightest
hesitation. Emperor Meiji had not only a great aptitude for learning the
knowledge of the Chinese but that of the Western world as well. He had
the wisdom to accept the ideas of others and to cooperate with them.
Many rulers in the course of history failed to become great simply
because they were too stubborn and narrow minded. With the great lib-
eral-minded ruler Emperor Meiji many able men had the opportunity to

advance their ideas with imperial support and as a result Japan has become a great modern nation.

In contrast it was obvious that China could not undergo any reformation like Japan. The emperors of China never thought of doing anything for the people's good because they were in constant fear of being overthrown by the people they governed. This is because China's rulers since the seventeenth century were not Chinese but Manchurians. They never trusted the Chinese people from the time they took over the throne in 1644 and, suspicious of any movement started by the Chinese, they would crush it instantly without inquiring what it was all about. The emperor kept himself deep inside the enormous palace grounds in Peking and his voice would take weeks, even months, to reach the region in the south and other remote areas of China. Even if the people heard they would not obey without force and any kind of reform was impossible. The cruel treatment meted out by the Manchurian rulers was shown in the Literary Inquisition of Emperor Ch'ien Lung (1772–1788), when many innocent Chinese men of letters who had committed not the slightest offense were killed.

Then there was the case of Yen Fu, also known as Yen Yu-ling, who went to study at the British Naval College, Greenwich, a few years after Marquis Hirobumi Ito had spent a year in England. The latter returned to Japan and rose to be a great statesman, but Yen Fu on his return to China was forced to study the ancient Chinese classics by order of the empress dowager and Yen never passed the imperial civil service examination to obtain an important post in order to make use of his knowledge of naval matters. Yen eventually became an outstanding translator of works on Western philosophy and social sciences. China has had men just as able and progressive as the great Japanese scholar Yukichi Fukuzawa, such as K'ang Yu-wei and Liang Ch'i-chao, who had to run for their lives when their arrest was ordered by the empress dowager.

Yukichi Fukuzawa

The Chinese diplomat Huang Tseng-hsien (1848–1905) worked in the Chinese legation in Tokyo for many years during the Meiji period. He was greatly impressed by the achievements of the Meiji Restoration and wrote a detailed history of Japan in forty volumes in order to instigate a reform movement in China. But the book was not published for many years after Huang had returned to China. The Manchu rulers were always against foreigners, and even against Chinese who acquired the learning of other countries.

The Japanese had long used Chinese characters for their written records, and during the Meiji Restoration many Japanese scholars gathered together to work out the appropriate expressions in kanji for the newly introduced Western terminologies. Curiously enough, these new terms were then used by the Chinese at the beginning of the twentieth century and very many new terms in the pure and social sciences that appear in Chinese newspapers and books today have their origin in Japan.

One morning Professor Tokiomi Kaigo telephoned, offering to show me some places of interest in Tokyo. We had been fellow senior specialists at the East-West Center in Honolulu in 1967. I gladly accepted his offer and I proposed we find an old temple near Meguro station which still has a number of its once famous five hundred *arhats*, or Buddhist saints. I was told about it by Professor Bunji Kobayashi, who had written a detailed account of this temple for an architecture magazine, but I could not locate the place by myself. Professor Kaigo had not heard of this temple and was happy to find it with me. Our taximan was confident of his knowledge and landed us outside a temple called Meguro Fudoson, but it had no Hall of Arhats. None of the people, many of them quite old, who were sitting in the temple grounds could direct us to what we wanted to see.

After a while we went on our way along a narrow lane walking single file. One side of the footpath was lined with tombstones, most of them inscribed in kanji. One of them was painted red and stood out distinctly. It read: "Kansho Sensei," which means "Mr. Sweet Potato." It appeared that this tomb contained the remains of one Konyo Aoki, born in 1700, the son of an Edo merchant. He had studied Chinese classics under Todai Ito in Kyoto, then was employed as librarian to the shogunate government and later was put in charge of the government publications. He had been greatly grieved when he learned that many of the prisoners sent into exile and marooned in distant parts of the country where the land was barren, eventually died of starvation. So he took the seeds of sweet potatoes from Satsuma Province and had them planted in many other provinces throughout Japan. Later, when the crop of rice and other grains failed, the people were glad to have sweet potatoes to eat, for they were by then growing abundantly everywhere. Thus Mr. Konyo Aoki became known as Mr. Sweet Potato.

At long last we found the temple with the five hundred arhats. It is called Rakanji, or Arhan Temple in Edo, but no one was on hand to show us around. Apparently few people know of this temple. It was not frequented by visitors. We looked into the main hall but could see only a few of the five hundred arhats. We were about to leave when an old abbot appeared and beckoned to us. He became our guide and took us inside the main hall, where only some two hundred out of an original five hundred were left. Each of them had been carved by the Buddhist sculptor-monk Shuon in the seventeenth century. Having conceived the idea of carving them after his visit to the Rakanji Temple in Bungo Province on the island of Kyushu, he came to live in Edo (modern Tokyo) during the era of Teikyo (1684–1687) and lived in a very small temple in Asakusa. Without any means to pursue his art, he went out begging for alms as a mendicant priest in the daytime and carved at night. Before he had completed fifty of the arhats, his unconventional way of working became common talk in the neighborhood. Eventually the story came to the ears of Lady Keishoin, mother of the shogun Tsunayoshi, who, being a devout Buddhist, gave a sum of money to support Monk Shuon in his work; many others followed her example. In 1695 Monk Shuon completed the five hundred arhats. Our guide, the abbot, pointed out one statue of more than life-size, which represented the sculptor-monk himself. Several arhats were labeled with names in kanji; one of them is said to be that of Lady Keishoin.

It was a hot August day and the abbot invited us to his room for a cold drink. Before leaving, I asked the abbot for his name and he sat down to write it first in Japanese and then in Chinese. Unexpectedly he started to speak to me in fluent Chinese with a Peking accent. He told me he had lived in China for twenty years and was a naturalized Chinese, working as personal secretary to Marshal Chang Tso-lin. Since his return to Japan more than twenty years ago he had not met a Chinese nor spoken Chinese until this moment. A very happy moment for him. And I was happy to have met someone who could speak Chinese so well.

Professor Kaigo, triumphant at having found the temple of five hundred arhats, suggested taking me to see Sengakuji Temple in the suburb, where the famous forty-seven *ronin* were buried. The forty-seven ronin, he explained, were masterless samurai, who differed from the true samurai who were retainers working under a lord. Those who had no lord are called ronin. Some two hundred years ago the lord of these forty-seven heroes was wronged by another lord. So they became masterless and made a vow to avenge the one who had wronged their master. They planned and waited for two years before they could carry out their vow. Meanwhile the co-leaders, Oishi Kuromosuki and his son Oishi Chikara, with their forty-five followers disguised themselves and took up a life of debauchery and degradation in order that no suspicion would fall on them. Without warning one snowy night they raised a signal and all rushed into the evil lord's mansion, cut off his head, and carried it off to Sengakuji, where they washed it and placed it in front of the tomb of their dead lord as proof of their absolute loyalty. Everything was carried out as planned. They all knew that there was no escaping the consequence of their crime and all were prepared to meet an honorable death by hara-kiri in the end. The forty-seven heroes were buried together in the sideyard of the Sengakuji.

We went into the exhibition hall where the carved wood portraits of the forty-seven ronin were displayed with their respective robes, swords, and other belongings. Each face looked heroic, like that of an actor in the Kabuki play. Behind the exhibition hall and on higher ground were the forty-seven tombs. We walked up the stone steps and found a young woman selling packets of incense. We bought some, lit them, and placed them in the incense burners of each tomb one by one. I noticed that Oishi Chikara had been only fifteen years of age. Many were not much older. I also found another one named Tadeshiki Takebayashi, who was a descendant of the famous Chinese Confucian philosopher Mencius.

On our way down the steps Professor Kaigo pointed out the well where the head of the evil lord had been washed. The well has been specially protected by a stone wall and a wooden railing facing the footpath. This construction was paid for by the famous actor Otojiro Kawakami, who for more than ten years played the leading part in the Kabuki *Chushingura*, a play based on this story. This play was revived year after year and served to rouse the Japanese feeling of loyalty to their superiors.

To finish our morning excursion, we had lunch of sukiyaki at Chinya Restaurant at Asakusa. Chinya became famous for being the first restaurant to serve beef after the Meiji Restoration. During the Tokugawa isolation period, very few Westerners moved round the big cities, such as Tokyo and Kyoto, and there was no demand for beef. Besides, cows and oxen were used to plow rice fields and were not butchered for eating. In addition Buddhism prohibited killing animals. After the Restoration many Europeans came to live in Japan and beef was their staple food. Cattle were then bred and kept for food. In those days any Japanese who ate at Chinya would be termed "modern." It is only the beef served in Chinya that is "modern," for the interior arrangement with partitioned rooms and tatami floors is still in the old-fashioned Japanese restaurant style.

At the University of Hawaii I had met Professor and Mrs. Takeo Yazaki of Keio University and now they wanted to show me some of the unusual places in Tokyo. One afternoon, Mrs. Yazaki, with a Mr. Mitsuharu Kanbe, drove me to a distant Tokyo suburb where we found a secluded temple, Shendai-ji of the Tendai sect, built in A.D. 733. We walked up a footpath with tall trees lining both sides. The first building was a small hutlike structure surrounded by green bamboos with many sparrows fluttering about. Mrs. Yazaki remarked that this was typical Japanese scenery often painted by Japanese artists. Following many other people into the main hall of the temple, we came upon a small shrine set to the left of the central altar. In it was a beautifully sculptured wood statue of Buddha, similar in facial expression and gesture to the famous *Siddhartha* in meditation at Nara, though the legs of this one were not folded as in most Buddha statues. This statue, called Hakuō butsu, is seated with both legs straight down in the manner of Egyptian kings and queens.

By the side of the main hall was a small courtyard with an enormous

Hakuō butsu

spreading tree that greatly interested me. It looked like an American magnolia, but was labled "Tai-shan-mu," or wood of Tai-shan, or Mt. Tai. I wondered if this tree had actually come from Tai-shan in the province of Shantung, China. I tried to make a sketch of it, but in the small courtyard I could not see it in full view.

Pachinko players

A short distance outside of the main hall stood an eating place where many people were eating soba, for which this temple is very famous. Soba is a darkish green buckwheat noodle, known to be very nourishing, and served in a small bamboo basket. A huge waterwheel by the entrance was rotating and the stream which drove it added a pleasant atmosphere to the place. The inn is called Ikkyu-en, a name which reminded me of the famous humorous monk Ikkyu of Japan who was once ordered by the shogun Yoshimochi to catch a tiger painted on a screen. The shogun was testing his wit. Monk Ikkyu readily agreed and asked for a rope, which he held outstretched in front of the screen saying: "If you will drive the tiger out I am ready to catch it." He won.

Back in the city Mrs. Yazaki and I joined Professor Yazaki at the famous restaurant Hototogisu, which had been very popular in feudal days when many samurai came to rest after a day's hunting, particularly after hawk hunting. The three of us occupied a small spotless room facing a large open area planted with willows and pine trees. Quite a number of people in kimonos who had already finished dining strolled in the open space as they did in the old feudal days. Professor Yazaki said he had chosen Hototogisu for dinner because it was famous for its specially prepared food and had created many new dishes and made a speciality of vegetable dishes since the olden days. Each dish came one after the other in a beautiful porcelain bowl. I sampled one dish that tasted sharply of vinegar, which immediately made me ask my host and hostess whether the Japanese had a special term or expression for a hen-pecked husband. Mrs. Yazaki, with a broad smile, wrote the words down for me, *Kyō Sai Ka*, saying that this was a new term that did not exist before the war. I asked this question because it is well known that Japanese women are submissive to their husbands in all things. Just then a maid came to lay dishes before us—first before me, then Professor Yazaki, and Mrs. Yazaki the last. Professor Yazaki pointed out that it was the Japanese custom not to serve the lady first as in the West. We all laughed. The older generation sticks to this custom still, but the younger ones have made changes. I then told them why the vinegar had prompted me to ask such a question; it was because in China "to drink vinegar" meant "jealousy." Then I had to relate the story I wrote in my book *The Silent Traveller in London*:

It is said a well-known prime minister of the T'ang dynasty had never had any chance to let his ideas stray to pretty girls because his wife was furiously jealous. But the emperor recognized the great services he had done for the empire and thought he should have a joyful time in his old age. So he sent the abstemious minister two court girls because he had no son to carry on his family. The minister hesitated to receive them, and the emperor, on learning about his jealous wife, summoned her to court. Preparing a cup of poison on the royal table, the emperor asked the wife whether she preferred to drink the cup or to curb her jealousy. She made no answer but just went up to the table and drained the cup at one draught. The emperor shook his head, sighed, and said: "Even a man who has as great power as I have cannot deal with a woman's jealousy!" Afterward the liquid in the cup was found to be not poison but vinegar, so since then "drinking vinegar" has come to mean "jealousy." Another explanation for the term is that we generally call a jealous woman a roaring lion, because of her manner and voice, and we traditionally believe that a lion likes to drink a large quantity of vinegar.

When I finished my story, Professor Yazaki laughingly remarked that the expression "drinking vinegar" would not mean much to the Japanese, for they all love pickled foods, which are all vinegary.

One day Yoshimaru Tadokoro and I went to see a performance of the International Noh Drama Club at Nogaku-Do. It was a *kyogen* ("comedy") of the Izumi School, and *Kagekiyo*, a No drama of the Kita school. Yoshi was greatly moved by the steady action and subtle gesticulation and by the absolutely silent audience. Though I could not follow the chanting, each movement had its symbolic meaning. Afterward, pointing out the lines in English translation when Hitomaru says to her father, "Do you mean to treat me unfairly because I am a girl . . . because I am not a boy you can rely upon?" I remarked to Yoshi that I did not know that the Japanese also preferred sons to daughters. Yoshi laughed and said that in the feudal days the Japanese did, for they all expected their sons to become samurai.

Yoshi and I also went to see the ghost play *Yotsuya Kaidan* at Kabukiza. Mr. Tokiko Fukao writes:

A famous Kabuki actor

> *Yotsuya Kaidan,* Kabuki's most representative play, is a ghastly ghost story told in terms of jealousy, murder, and revenge. The story of Oiwa, a tragic heroine, and her ghost is not entirely without foundation. Sometime in the 1600s, Oiwa, daughter of Tamiya Mataemon, who lived in the Samoncho district of Yotsuya in Edo, died of jealousy over her faithless husband, and later came back as a ghost to haunt him, eventually causing his death.

I was interested to know that the actors, before performing this play, had first to go and worship at a shrine in Yotsuya, erected for the purpose of placating the jealous spirit of Oiwa. There were a lot of stage tricks

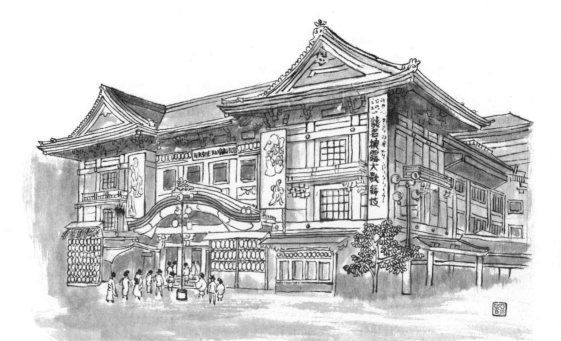

Kabukiza

and the ones who played the ghost roles had to perform acrobatics. So they went to pray for safety and protection from the spirit. Kabuki ghost dramas, I was told, were always played in summer so that the audience would be cooled by the chilling effect. At the end of the play I remarked to Yoshi that I did not feel any cooler and he replied with a laugh that he didn't either. Could it have been that the theater was air-conditioned and the stage was so brightly lit?

A ghost story at Kabuki theater, Tokyo

At the Shibuya railroad station there is a bronze statue of Hachi the dog. It has become a famous landmark in recent years. On another day Yoshi's sister Masako drove us to see it. Hachi belonged to a professor at Tokyo University and every morning the dog accompanied his master on his walk from home to the railroad station at Shibuya. There, every evening, was Hachi waiting for his master and the two returned home. This went on year after year. After the professor's death, Hachi continued to go to the station every morning and evening for several years more, till he himself died. The people who used this station knew the dog and to them his faithfulness to the professor became a legend. Eventually the monument was erected and it became known as a lovers' meeting place. When we three were examining the statue, quite a few young men and girls were standing round it talking and joking freely.

Hachi the dog

The young men had long hair similar to the girls and even their youthful faces could not help to determine their sexes. My friends informed me that they were Japanese hippies. I could not help but admire how fashions travelled so fast, but I doubt if we Orientals, Japanese and Chinese, could be real hippie-looking like the Westerners, for we cannot grow easily the bushy mustaches and beards.

From the dog statue we went to see the beautiful Koishikawa Korakuen Gardens. These were first laid out in 1629 by Tokugama Yorifusa and completed by his successor Mitsukuni. They now cover about seven-

Hippies

teen acres, less than one-third of its original sixty-three acres, owing to the encroachment of the city. It is still a big open ground for Tokyo. There is much to see and explore; its artificial hills, lakes, and streams, as well as its winding well-paved footpaths with stone patterns in Chinese style. The whole arrangement closely follows the Chinese principles of simplicity, suggestion, and imagination. It was said that the Chinese scholar Chu Shun-shui (1600–1682), who was staying with Lord Mitsukuni, had designed it.

Chu Shun-shui also designed the Confucian temple near Ochanmizu. To find such a well-designed and well-built Confucian temple outside of China uplifted my spirit in reverence for the great thinker of my country. I had a good look at the temple except for the main hall, which was closed each time I was there. I wrote the following verse, a semihumorous complaint to Confucius, for I had taught his classics ever since I left China:

You set up an Apricot Platform to teach long
   before I was born,
Neither could I enter the room nor climb up to
   the hall.
Now I have to keep saying "The Master says"
   year after year.
The most difficult part is to explain the meaning
   of "Shen chih shih."

Apricot Platform is the place where Confucius taught his students. Those who "enter the room" meant good students and those who "climb up to the hall" even better ones. "The Master says" is a phrase which repeatedly appears in Confucius's *Analect*. "Shen chih shih" was an expression by which Mencius praised Confucius as a wise man whose ideas marched with the time and suited all times. The amusing side of this verse is that I was not trained to teach the Chinese language at home but I now employ what I know of Chinese classics to teach Westerners who have become Confucius's fans.

From the Confucian temple I took myself for a long walk to the Kanda area of Tokyo. This is known as the center for bookshops, particularly many small and interesting secondhand bookshops where some long-out-of-print Chinese books might be found. Some bookshops sell foreign books, French literature, and German medical studies. The great center of learning, Tokyo University, lies nearby. I had a good look at the famous Red Gate which was built especially for the marriage of one of the twenty-seven daughters of the eleventh Tokugawa lord, who also had twenty-eight sons. This brought to mind a legend that said King Minos of Crete had more than eighty sons, and a Chinese ancient record stating that King Wen of Chou dynasty had one hundred sons. That was long, long ago. I don't know how the parents manage to look after a few young offspring nowadays. The Red Gate has long been the symbol of Tokyo University, where I proceeded to make a round of the campus. What attracted me most was the university garden with its deeply sunk lake surrounded by beautiful trees, grotesque rocks, and winding foot-paths leading up and down, which were not only a delight to the eye but also a help to the mind for clear thinking.

The big Sumida River runs through the city but it has never assumed so important a role as the Thames of London, the Seine of Paris, or the Tiber of Rome. Perhaps it was more prominent in the Edo days, but land in modern Tokyo is too precious and much of the river has been covered over with buildings. However, there are many famous bridges and I particularly wanted to see two of them. The first was Kototoibashi, which became known through one of the six great songwriters of Japan, Ariwara Marihira, a prince and writer of many love songs. He fell in love with the sixteen-year-old daughter of a powerful lord of the time. The lord wanted his daughter to marry the young emperor Seiwa Tenno, who was only nine years of age. She and her lover planned to elope but she was caught by her father's soldiers, and eventually became the empress and mother of Emperor Yozei Tenno. The young songwriter who loved her used to stroll along this bridge over the river and wrote the following lines:

> May I ask the world-renowned Miyakodori, birds of the capital,
> My love,
> Where is she?

The birds of the capital are the sea gulls. The expression "May I ask" is *kototoi* in Japanese. Thus the name of the bridge was later changed to Kototoibashi and the latter part *bashi* means *bridge* in Japanese. Thus the bridge is "May I ask Bridge." A confectioner near the bridge created a sweet called "Kototoi cakes," which were popular for a long time.

The second bridge was the Yodobashi, so named after the young bride who disappeared beneath it on her wedding day. Some five hundred years ago, Kuro Suzuki, a samurai, gave up his rank and came to live in the Nakano district of Edo. He was rich and soon owned much land in the area. But he was very mean and buried all his money in different parts of his land. As he could not do the work of burying money, he hired others to do so for him. As soon as the money was safely buried, he killed the worker and threw the body into the river beneath the bridge. It happened that his only daughter, Tsuyuno, fell in love with Kojire, a young man in the neighborhood. Kuro gave his consent for the marriage. A sudden thunderstorm raged in that area on the wedding eve and Tsuyuno disappeared mysteriously without a trace. Suzuki's neighbors believed that an enormous snake emerged out of the thunderstorm, entered Suzuki's house, and then dived under the bridge carrying off the young bride with it. This seemed to them to be a punishment for Suzuki's wickedness. Since then no young bride dared to walk over the bridge, which became known as the Sugaimizu-no Bridge. It was later renamed Yodobashi by Tokugawa Iyemitsu in order to wipe out the bad memory. But no trace of this bridge could be located when my friends took me round in search of it.

Kwannon Temple

Afterward, Masako drove Yoshi and me to see the big Kwannon Temple in Asakusa. Many people crowded the area and Yoshi and I were squeezing through an arcade lined with shops, while Masako had to stay in the car. I suddenly spotted a tall figure in black Buddhist robes, wearing a wide-brimmed bamboo hat and walking slowly, striking a small bell with his right hand while the left held an alms bowl. The

American Buddhist monk

perspiration streamed down his face, for he had on two heavy robes, a black one over a white, and the August day was very hot. Yoshi murmured that he was an American who came to live in Tokyo several years before and was converted to the Buddhist faith. He was studying in a university still.

We entered the spacious courtyard before the main hall of the temple. Many big candles were burning brightly, though I could not see the Kwannon statue inside. Apparently no big statue of Kwannon was enshrined here. This Kwannon-do temple, Sensoji, had its origin during the reign of the empress Suiko. The story goes that a samurai, Hashi Nakatomo, once was fishing with two of his retainers, Hamanari and Takenari, casting their nets in the river again and again, all day long, but failed to get any fish. They were about to haul in for the last time when they saw a gold image of Kwannon caught in the net. This gold image was soon enshrined in this temple, but it has never been shown to the public.

On a special evening, Yoshi and Masako insisted on having me to dine with them at Chinzanso, a very popular garden restaurant in Tokyo. We arrived about eight o'clock and first took a stroll through the garden, though it was impossible to distinguish anything in the darkness. Many heads and black bodies were moving here and there. Most of the strollers, like us, held small round paper lanterns, which provided just enough light to reveal the edge of the paths. We then reached a lake with artificial waterfalls pouring voluminously into it. Yoshi told me that it was still a part of the Japanese Bon Festival. After a round of the garden, we went into the big dining hall and were shown to our table. Actually it was not a table but we sat round a structure with a red-hot grill plate in the center with space around it to set dishes for each of us. A waitress in a darkish kimono brought bowls of thinly sliced meats, mushrooms, and vegetables, which she placed on the grill to cook. While we gave our chopsticks no rest, the maid continued adding meats and vegetables. Everyone in the hall ate in a similar way; each table had a maid to serve it. It seemed to me that Tokyo had much man power to spare, particularly plenty of women were willing to work. Yoshi gurgled, with a slice of hot meat in his mouth, that we were having a "Genghis Khan dinner." I said that in China we called it Meng-ku jou, or meat cooked in the Mongolian style. It was an interesting experience.

Before I left Tokyo for other cities, I wanted to find the tomb of the artist Katsushika Hokusai, who was not only well known in Japan but very much so in the whole Western world. I had seen a picture of his tomb in a book in a Tokyo bookshop, so I asked my friend Mr. Hsieh Kuo-tung, who teaches Chinese in a university in Tokyo, to go in search of it with me. Though Hokusai has been known to the Western art world for nearly a hundred years, no one in Tokyo seems to know the whereabouts of his tomb. With Mr. Hsieh's help in being able to speak Japanese, after two hours we eventually found a small temple, Seikyoji, at Matsugaya, I-chome of Taito-ku. A sign led us to a well-worn stone of darkish color with six kanji words engraved on it which in Chinese pronunciation reads "K'uan-hua-lao-jen-chih-mo," meaning "Mad-at-painting old man's grave." Two wooden boards were inscribed, one in English, the second in Japanese:

> Hokusai Katsushika was born in Edo in 1760 and died at a ripe age of ninety in 1849. He was a celebrated ukiyoye painter. His series of views of Mt. Fuji are favorites with foreign collectors.

The wording was as simple and humble as the grave. However, I thought a more impressive shrine could have been made for this illustrious son of Japan.

The Japanese called Hokusai a ukiyoye artist, the term used on his memorial tablet. Ukiyoye means "a floating world," that is, the depiction of human activities. In his prints the behavior and experiences of many types of people are portrayed with humorous touches. They were intended to entertain, for the medium chosen, the block print, was one suitable for popular circulation. They became known far and wide not only in the floating world of Japan but in Europe as well.

It was through Hokusai's work that Japanese art and literature began to be known to the whole world. Hokusai's wood-block prints were accidentally discovered by Félix Bracquemond, the Parisian engraver, in 1856, and they soon became his "breviary." They were then introduced to the impressionists by Mme. Soye and her husband in their shop, La Porte Chinoise, on the rue de Rivoli, in 1862. Manet, Gauguin, Duret, Degas, and many others, particularly van Gogh, were influenced by Hokusai's work. Japanese novels, poetry, and plays were gradually introduced to Europe at about the same time.

Monsieur and Madame Soye evidently started the fashion for collecting Japanese wood-block prints through selling things Chinese in their shop. However, Chinese works of art seldom depict all aspects of life—its complexity and pathos—with humor as Hokusai's prints did. This seems to me to be quite natural. The art of any culture represents the mind of the people who create it, as molded within the frame of its traditional thoughts and conventional ideas, which are in turn influenced by specific social, geographical, and climatic conditions. The Japanese, with a population densely packed on the four major islands, were bound to have closer contact with one another than the Chinese, who live spread out over a vast continental area. Thus all aspects of life aroused the emotions of Japanese artists and writers. The Japanese No and

Hokusai's tomb

Kabuki plays flourished continually; Lady Murasaki started early in the eleventh century to write a novel, *The Tale of Genji*; and Sei Shonagon brought out a diarylike novel, *The Pillow Book*, also in the eleventh century; by the time Katsukawa Shunsho lived from 1726 to 1792, uki-yoye composition was already in vogue in Japan.

Shunsho is regarded as the creator of the new type of actor prints. Hokusai first went to Shunsho to learn the design of theatrical prints and soon expanded his vision by his innate talent and urge to create. Hokusai in his lifetime created more than thirty thousand drawings and illustrations for five hundred books in addition to the many paintings in his inimitable style. From this record alone it would seem that he must have spent every minute of his life in designing and working. It is no wonder that he was called fanatic or mad old man.

China has not produced a man like Hokusai, nor indeed has any other country. Hokusai could be regarded as one of the most successful artists who ever lived in that he had all his creations printed in his lifetime, though he still, at the age of ninety, longed for a few more years to perfect his art. On the other hand, credit must be given to the stable social conditions of Japan that supported his aims. In the wood-block print he found the best medium to express his interesting mind and artistic insights on life, pleasing to himself as well as to others who saw the prints and collected them. The oil paintings of the West and the ink paintings of China could not be reproduced easily before the eighteenth century and were rarely found in other lands.

The making of wood-block prints was practiced in China as early as 593 for the circulation of the ink drawings illustrating Buddhist sutras. The use of engraved seals in bronze, stone, wood, and bone for stamps to signify authority probably date back even earlier, to the fourth and third centuries B.C. A need for circulating the sutras and Buddha's life story led to the invention of engraving Chinese characters and line drawings on wood in order to make multiple impressions. Thus printing was invented in China much earlier than in the West. However, the Chinese who wrote the characters or designed the line drawings were different persons from those who made the blocks and printed them. The Japanese wood-block print makers, particularly Hokusai, created the designs, engraved them, and printed them. In the Edo period Japan had a kind of wood-block print in which the basic design was printed in ink and then colors added by hand; this was called the Edo-e. (The last letter *e* means "painting or print" in Japanese.) Later, in 1764, Harunobu Suzuki started to produce multicolored ukiyoye by making several woodblocks for a design, one block for each color, and printed one over the other. From this point on, the Japanese engaged in block printing, continually perfecting the art until Hokusai entered the field. His artistic genius enabled him to make the fullest use of his engraving technique on wood, to the best advantage of an artistic rendering of the subject matter. He possessed the ability of designing, engraving, and printing and could adjust them in one way or another to bring out the best result. We need only to go through a few of Hokusai's prints to see how he constantly varied his technique and composition and ideas. Conservative as we Chinese were, it is sad for me to say that none of us who studied and lived in Japan over the years had thought of introducing Hokusai's block prints to China. I myself did not know of Hokusai until I went to live in Europe. Not a single print by Hokusai or any other Japanese artist-engraved piece could be found in the public or private collections in China. There has been a false assumption that most things Japanese came from China, which caused the Chinese to feel haughty and pay little heed to what the Japanese have achieved and perfected. Although a book of colored wood-block prints known as the *Ten-Bamboo Studio* did appear in the late sixteenth century in China, the subjects were all flowers and birds and they were done by two different hands—one an artist who painted and designed, while the other was the engraver and printer.

Mr. Kojiro Tomita and I were discussing the original drawings of Hokusai's *Day and Night* in the four seasons sketches at the Boston Museum of Fine Arts—now a great treasure. I noticed a big seal in red,

Pachinko players

which reads "Wu Ch'i Hua Shih Ko Shih Pei Chai Weng" in Chinese pronunciation. The first two characters *Wu Ch'i* mean "my wife" in Chinese and I was puzzled by this expression. But Tomita told me that the first two characters would be pronounced "Azuma" in Japanese, which referred to the eastern part of Japan in ancient times. Thus the big seal in red would mean "Hokusai, a painter of Azuma." So we should dismiss the notion that everything Japanese could be exactly like things Chinese, for even the same characters have different meanings in the two countries.

The ukiyoye print of Japan, with its special technique in design and color, in the hands of such a man as Hokusai was to be the forerunner for the spread of Japanese culture throughout the world. I therefore bow deeply with great respect to this illustrious son of China's closest neighbor!

III

Nikko's Attractions to Me

AN OLD FRIEND of mine, Yao Ko-neng, who had been living in Tokyo for a few years, rang me up. "I shall come to take you to see Nikko in the morning. Tomorrow, May seventeenth, is just the day to see Nikko," urged my friend. May always is a most agreeable month in this part of Japan and I yielded to his proposal.

A delicious morning dawned; bright sunshine, light late-spring air, a sky almost cloudless. A fresh yet delicate verdure of the countryside appeared as the train rapidly left the outskirts of Tokyo. Beautiful and attractive was the light showing through the young and fully grown leaves along the gray boughs of the trees which were at various stages of growth. There were distant hills which on one side were nearly clothed, on another were mottled with gray and green, and on yet another they were still perfectly naked, yellow and brown. Near the bottom of the hills stood some houses behind clusters of deep red azaleas, while tall feathery bamboos swayed and nodded. In the fields were many people, mostly women with white towels wrapped round their heads, bent over busy with their hands in the earth. The tops of several high hills still had strips of silver white snow streaking downward and the lofty Japanese pines, dim and dusky in the distance, stood out in the scene. Occasionally several black crows rose up from one field and flew to another, showing no fear of the scarecrows shaking in the wind.

A common sight in Japan's countryside

Such was the Japanese country landscape in May. I thought how appropriate was the name of the place, Nikko, in kanji meaning "sunlight." There was a great commotion upon reaching our destination. People streamed from the train in happy groups of all types and all ages—young and old, parents, children, friends. There were many different types of faces from Europe and America, and many different colors of hair, and the varied colors of the women's dresses. My friend with wide open eyes laughingly said to me: "You see everybody has come to see Nikko today!" With our crowd from the train the streets of Nikko had suddenly become Tokyo's Ginza.

Yao Ko-neng beckoned me to follow him along an avenue lined with tall old Japanese *sugi* (Japanese cedar or cryptomeria) trees. The trees reached upward so straight and high, standing closely together in neatly arranged rows as if they were soldiers of enormous height at attention watching us go by. This sugi avenue is a very impressive sight with its nineteen thousand trees extending for twenty-four miles. The trees had been planted more than three hundred years ago, when they were young, some mere shoots and sprouts. When the Toshogu Shrine, dedicated to Iyeyasu, the first shogun of Tokugawa, was being built in 1634, all the lords were ordered to contribute something to it. Lord Masatsuna Matsudaira was in charge of the construction but was poorer than many of the other lords and could not afford to make an expensive gift, so he devised the planting of the sugi trees as his contribution. Though the cost was little, the nineteen thousand trees took twenty years to plant. Although Lord Matsudaira might have imagined how fine and magnificent the sugi avenue would be when fully grown, he probably never realized that this avenue would stand here in his honor as long as the Toshogu Shrine remained.

We came first to one big torii and then another and soon we were standing before a five-story pagoda. Under the eaves of each story was a very elaborate wooden structure painted in greenish blue while the wooden balustrades were in dark red. A young Japanese guide was shouting stories about dragons and Buddha's bones to a crowded courtyard. But he did not explain why a Buddhist pagoda had been built within the precincts of a Shinto shrine. There were no pagodas in the grounds of Ise or Izumo or at any of the other shrines I had seen. However, much evidence indicates that Japanese Shintoism was very tolerant and gradually assimilated Buddhism and was even displaced by it without any rancor. No one knows when Shintoism and Buddhism began to amalgamate, but the presence of this five-story pagoda in the Toshogu Shrine could be a strong piece of evidence.

The area between the Yomeimon and Karamon gates was tightly packed with people. The bright sun shining on the gilded parts of the finely carved decorations on the Karamon gate so dazzled my eyes that I could not distinguish their shapes. Some of the people started to move and then the whole mass bolted out of the court like a huge jet of water. My friend dragged me through the throng, and finally the crowd came to a halt.

"The procession is coming," a young American girl shouted nearby, jumping with excitement. Someone said that the spirits of Iyeyasu, Hideyoshi, and Yoritomo had already been transferred to their respective portable shrines and would now take part in the procession. A number

Japanese spectators

of Shinto priests in white robes and black cone-shaped hats took up the
lead before a priest wearing a bright yellow robe and a tall black hat and
riding a dark horse, while four men dressed as the old retainers walked
in pairs on each side of the horse. Then came a long line of people
dressed in the different colored robes of the feudal samurai, then
priests—Shinto and Buddhist—and many common folk dressed in the
costumes of the Tokugawa era, some carrying swords, some in armor,
some holding spears, and some even with guns and rifles. Altogether
there were about a thousand people in the procession called Sennin
Gyoretsu, or procession of one thousand persons. I could not see very
well what was inside the portable shrine, but they might have been
carved wooden portraits.

I was interested to know that the other two powerful personalities,
Hideyoshi and Yoritomo, were also enshrined in Toshogu. From the
look of the stiffly starched, wide-shouldered costumes worn by the early
samurai, I wondered how they could fight the enemies so swiftly and
gallantly in the many battles waged in the course of Japanese history.

I admired how flawlessly the procession was carried out and what
skill there must have been to organize it from start to finish. The sys-
tem-minded Japanese, with their great sense for decoration and for
organization, were certainly the right people to do it. The Japanese are
so well experienced with festivals that a procession seems to them like a
natural happening. In China's two great capitals, Peking and Nanking,
there are mausoleums of our past emperors and empresses, but to hold
annual processions in their honor never occurred to the Chinese mind.
The reason must be because Chinese rulers were never deified, and also,
the Chinese have little interest in organizing pageantry. Though it is
true that in the early years of the Ch'ing, or Manchu, dynasty many
kinds of processions were held year after year, they were discontinued

after the T'ai P'ing rebellion (1850–1864) and the wars with foreign powers, particularly the opium wars with England (1840–1842 and 1856–1858).

The procession was a great show of Japanese pageantry which could not be easily matched anywhere else in the world. We returned to the Yomeimon and Karamon gates and examined the designs on the windows, doors, and other parts. I have never before seen such minutely detailed decorations and ornaments as those on the massive Karamon and roofs, yet they were finely finished down to the smallest detail. The stories used for the many decorations were chiefly drawn from famous Chinese novels such as *Feng-sheng-pang*, or the *List of Enfiefed Dieties*, and *Hsi-yu-vhi*, or *Journey to the West*, for which Dr. Arthur Waley translated an abridged version entitled *Monke*y. I thought the upper row of white figures above the door of the Karamon might represent the famous story of Ma-ku hsien shou, or the fairy Ma-ku dancing to celebrate the birthday of the Western Queen Mother in the Taoist paradise. Three other figures might represent three scholars—Su Tung-p'o, Huang Ting-chien, and Monk Fu-Yin tasting from a big vat of plum wine which all three felt was too sour. One of the most popular carved decorations at Nikko is *The Sleeping Kitten*, by the famous Takamatsu artist Hidari Jingoro (1594–1651), on the upper crossbeam of the entry to the main sanctuary. It is said to depict a Zen *koan*, which Dr. Daisetz T. Suzuki defined as "generally some statement made by an old Zen master, or some answer of his to a question," for example, "What about a sleeping kitten under a peony in bloom?" with the answer, "I would have nothing to do with it." I wondered why most of the decorations should have been based on popular Chinese stories and not on Japanese ones. My friend agreed with me that most of the fancy designs on the walls and doors, as well as beams and pillars, could have been influenced by Chinese late Ming art. The Chinese influence on the building of the Toshogu Shrine is most obvious. For instance, the Japanese Official Guide describes the Rinzo (Sacred Library):

> In front are installed the wooden image of Fudaishi (497–596), the reputed Chinese inventor of the revolving library, and his sons Fuken and Fujo. And on Yomeimon ("Gate of Sunlight") on the central beam in the front of the second story is a figure of a white dragon. The balcony on the upper story is flanked by a railing depicting a group of Chinese children at play. All the brackets supporting the balcony are designed in the shapes of peonies and lions, and between them are carvings of a Chinese prince, sages, and some Taoist immortals.

The Toshogu Shrine was built twenty years after Iyeyasu's death in 1616 and toward the end of the Ming dynasty when many more

Chinese, tradesmen and self-exiled scholars, came to live in Japan. Therefore popular Chinese stories and legends became well known in Japan and Japanese artists employed them for designs and decorations. It is little wonder that the plans for the construction of the Toshogu Shrine included decorations using many subjects from popular Chinese stories and legends. I must give a good word for the highly refined quality and finished touch that the Japanese craftsmen displayed in their decorations and ornaments on the Toshogu buildings.

One of Nikko's most talked-about carved decorations is the *Three Monkeys* near the top of a wall. Copies have been made in wood, porcelain, and bone, for sale not only in Nikko but almost everywhere in Japan. Foreign visitors have taken them home to all parts of the world. They are generally interpreted as "See no evil," "Hear no evil," and "Speak no evil" with one monkey with its two paws covering its eyes, another covering its ears, and the third covering its mouth. The interest in this particular carving is not for its artistic merit but for the meaning each monkey depicts. Most people thought the meaning came either from Indian philosophy or from China. I searched high and low and could not find any clue. Nor did Yao know its origin either. Finally I reached the conclusion that this was definitely derived from Chinese thought, actually from Confucius's sayings. In Confucius's *Analects* there is a passage translated by Professor James Legge (1815–1897) as follows:

> Yen Yuan asked about virtue. The Master said, "To subdue oneself and return to propriety is perfect virtue. If a man can for one day subdue himself and return to propriety, all under heaven will ascribe perfect virtue to him. Is the practice of perfect virtue from a man himself or is it from others?"
>
> Yen Yuan said, "I beg to ask the steps of that process." The Master replied, "Look not at what is contrary to propriety; listen not to what is contrary to propriety; speak not what is contrary to propriety; make no movement which is contrary to propriety." Yen Yuan then said, "Though I am deficient in intelligence and vigor, I will make it my business to practice this lesson."

Yen Yuan was considered one of the most intelligent pupils of Confucius. In my younger days in China everyone had to read Confucius's *Analects* as part of his early education, so all of us knew the *four nots*. As Confucius's classics were popular in Japan in the Tokugawa era, the artist who carved these three monkeys must also have known Confucius's four *nots*. As the fourth *not*, "making no movement that is contrary to propriety," was an action and could not easily be depicted in carving, the artist carved only three monkeys. It was an ingenious idea on the artist's part!

I myself had an experience connected with the four *not*s a year before I left China in 1933. I was then a civil servant in the capacity of a district governor of the Tang-tu District of Anhui Province. In those days a district governor acted also as a district magistrate to hold court. One day a member of the local gentry from the eastern part of the district who knew that I painted and was fond of collecting good paintings of early masters came to see me in my official residence. He brought four hanging scroll landscapes painted by the famous artist Hsiao Yun-tsung (early seventeenth century), born in Wuhu District next to Tang-tu. I found the four hanging scrolls to be genuine and I liked them very much, but they were rather expensive for me to buy. The visitor then insisted on my keeping the paintings for further inspection and went away. A little later I felt drowsy and went to lie on my bed for a while. When I woke up and before my eyes were properly open, I saw something obscurely lying on a small desk by my bed. It was the old-fashioned visiting card of my caller, a rectangular piece of red paper with three big Chinese characters in the middle "Wang Szu Fei" 王四非 or "Wang four nots." From my recumbent position the two characters "Szu Fei" seemed to have joined together into one character "tsui" 罪 , which means "fault" or "sin" needing to be punished. I at once got up sensing that something was wrong about my visitor. I asked myself why he had brought me the important paintings; perhaps something was on his mind to use the paintings as a bribe. So I at once sent a servant to take the four paintings back to him. In a month's time it became known that he had killed one of his peasant-tenants on the pretense that the peasant was a bandit. He was eventually brought to justice and punished.

Actually the area occupied by the Toshogu Shrine is not very big and the tightly detailed decorations and ornamentations seemed to be all cramped together under the massive foliage of the immense cedar trees. It was very oppressive, with little air circulating. An artistic composition without much space and air surrounding it cannot show up to the best advantage.

My friend then urged me to move on to see the bronze candelabrum under a gigantic cedar tree near a bell tower—presented by the Netherland government, which had also given a bronze lantern. These gifts were made in gratitude to the Tokugawa shoguns for allowing only the Dutch and Chinese to remain in Nagasaki when Japan was closed to foreign nationalities. We went on to see *Nakiryu*, or Crying dragon, which was painted on the ceiling of a temple close to the Yomeimon gate and which vibrated when Yao clapped his hands underneath its head. We then went to look around the shrine, the Treasure Museum, the Rinnoji

BYODOIN TEMPLE IN UJI, KYOTO

SWANS AND NIJU-BASHI, TOKYO

Temple, and then the Toshogu Shrine, where a number of Japanese women were kneeling in prayer and a priest was busy selling printed charms and incense. Later, with our shoes in hand we entered Futaarasan Shrine on the other side of the area. Two teen-age girls, dressed in white upper garments and crimson skirts and with long black hair hanging down their backs were each holding a *torimono*, or sword, in their right hand. They were dancing the Miko-Kagura dance while a priest blew the *fue*, or flute. Another girl, in a similar costume, was beating the *talko*, or drum. The dancers moved slowly, for the dance was said to be the one to comfort the divine spirits. After the dance the priest rose to distribute to all of us who watched the dance a small box containing a tiny lacquer sake cup. All worked out well according to the system, and what a system! Just think of the enormous number of tiny red-lacquer sake cups distributed each day!

From the Futaarasan Shrine we went to look at the Daiyuin Mausoleum, the mausoleum of Iyemitsu, grandson of Iyeyasu. Though a small building and comparatively simple in architecture, it seemed to have an immense number of gold sheets gilding the walls, pillars, eaves, tile-ends, and so on.

Coming out of the Toshogu grounds, we went to look at the red-painted sacred bridge, Mibashi or Shinkyo, both Japanese names with one meaning, "sacred" or "divine." Some twelve hundred years ago, Yao explained, the high priest Shodo (737–817), who was travelling around those parts, saw Mt. Nantai (formerly called Mt. Futaara) veiled with colored clouds and so mysteriously inviting he wanted to go to the top of the mountain but was barred by the terrible torrent of the river Daiya. He started to meditate and pray for help from the god. Suddenly an old man in white robes appeared coming from the other side of the river. The old man violently threw two enormous snakes—one red and one green—into the air. The snakes soon grew bigger and bigger and then bit each other's heads, joining to form a strong bridge. Priest Shodo walked on this snake bridge over to the other side and eventually managed to reach the top of the mountain. After many difficulties and hardships he constructed the Futaarasan Shrine on the top of Nantai-san. Though it has been rebuilt it still exists. On the basis of this legend, the Tokugawa shogun built this red-painted bridge in 1636, the same year the Nikko Mausoleum was completed. The bridge, being sacred or divine, was then reserved solely for the use of the shogun and imperial messengers on their visits to the shrine. It was destroyed by a terrible flood in 1902 but was rebuilt in 1907 at great cost.

My friend smiled and told me a story though he could not be sure of its authenticity. It was said that during his stay in Tokyo in 1879 General Grant one day came to see the Nikko Mausoleums. He and two of his personal aides strolled to the middle of this sacred bridge. When informed that it was reserved for the use of imperial personages only, General Grant immediately returned to the road, saying that he was not one to walk over the bridge. His prompt action was praised by many Japanese writers. General Grant was, after all, a human elected to the highest position in the huge country of America, while Iyeyasu was not only a most powerful shogun in Japan in the early days but is now regarded as a deity or even an incarnate Bodhisattva, for Emperor Gomizuno-o (1596–1680) conferred upon him the title Tosho Daigongen, or the East Illuminating Incarnation of Bodhisattva. This has puzzled my mind a great deal. As the Japanese ruler is a direct descendant of the Sun Goddess, he is himself a god and is invested with the power of endowing others with divinity. Iyeyasu's becoming an incarnate Bodhisattva explains why the five-story Buddhist pagoda was built in the main entrance.

We next boarded a motorcoach to Lake Chuzenji via the Irohazaka Driveway. The sun was shining brightly and the country air of the high mountains and hills could be no fresher and purer. The motorcoach tilted a little at each turn of the upward zigzag road while Mt. Nantai rose higher and higher in relation to our car. The Japanese driver was careful as he made each turn and my eyes could reach far and wide and way down below. There seemed to be several golf courses in Nikko and many golfers were on them. In the distance and far below, many trees in full dress were grouped together in small clusters here and there. Mt. Nantai now became more majestic than before as we reached Lake Chuzenji, which lies 4,194 feet above sea level. Before we came to the lake shore, the famous Kegon waterfall was pointed out to me, though I could not see its full beauty then. Yao said that we would see it again from another place. He also remarked that the fall became more famous after Misao Fujimura committed suicide there, having composed a great elegy while contemplating the ending of his life. Many have followed suit on the same spot!

We leisurely strolled round the lake and gazed at the scenery near and far. A number of cherry trees were still in full bloom while many petals were flying about as if to give the stillness of the balmy air a lively appearance. A few sailboats with white sails gleaming in the sun decorated the deep blue water and made the whole scene more attractive. During our walk we met a fisherman or two standing by the shore trying to catch something. I was told that this high lake did not have any fish, but the government now stocks it with carp, trout, and eels.

A sudden gust of wind nearly blew my friend into the water and he said that we had better see the best view of the lake and the waterfall from the observation point on Akechidaira. The ropeway took us up there in a few minutes. Oh, what a view it was! The blue lake was now below, and a deep ravine lay between us. The distant hills on the other side of the lake became pale blue and veiled in the late afternoon haze. The Kegon waterfall dropped down in a straight, pure white silver rope as if two angels held it tight at each end, having a tug of war. The roaring sound of the falls as it reached bottom could be heard so pleasantly, more so than when close at hand. The house roofs of Chuzenji Spa and other villages arranged so disorderly yet orderly; the luxuriant treetops by the waterfall, among the villages, and along the lake shore; the profusion of colors in different shades of green and purple with some red azaleas in bloom in some tiny corners; and above all the bright sunshine to light them all up and the unbelievably fresh combination of the mountain and lake at the very point where we were standing! Could any view be finer and more mysteriously beautiful?

Many famous poems on waterfalls by past great poets of China, Li Po, Tu Fu, Po Chü-i, came to mind, but none mentioned seeing an enormous lake above the waterfall as I witnessed now. The world-renowned Niagara Falls, though forceful and impressive, somehow did not give me the grand feeling I had expected, for I saw them from above at the same level as the edge of Niagara River, which looked placid and peaceful falling down below with no high mountains guarding it on either side to enhance its grandiosity. But the full length of the Kegon waterfall seen from a height seemed like a heavenly woven white silken rope of a magnificence fantastic beyond description. I just could not suppress my ecstasy but quickly composed a short verse:

A mirrorlike lake is lifted up, halfway reaching
    Heaven
The silvery falls come down into the great void.
Facing this absolutely wonderful scenery,
How many times have I met scenes like this in
    life?

Most unexpectedly a great rainbow arch appeared between us and Kegon Falls. At times it seemed to girdle the center of the waterfall, yet it did not look like a belt of color but masses of colored particles floating in the air, so ethereally unreal yet with something real in it. Its glittering splendor produced a rapture in us that was akin to fear. I looked at my

friend with a smile and thanked him again for the unforgettable trip. My
feeling for the whole day is summed up by these few lines of a piece of
English poetry:

> Passing from Italy to Greece, the tales
> Which poets of an older time have feign'd
> To glorify their temple, bred in me
> Desire of visiting paradise.

All Japanese caddies are girls

IV

Three Visits to Hakone

ONE DAY Yoshimaru Tadokoro suggested taking me to the hill resort Hakone. He came to fetch me and we caught the train on the Tokaido line to Odawara. We left Tokyo around six o'clock and it was raining hard when we arrived at our destination. We got a taxi and proceeded along a rather narrow road, one moment climbing up and next moment gliding down. I could hear the pouring rain and the chattering sound of the running stream alongside the road, but I could not get a glimpse of the scenery we were passing through, for it was pitch dark. After crossing several bridges the car stopped before a very modern looking hotel of many stories. We took off our shoes and a young maid in kimono led us to a big room with a low square table in the middle. Near the window with a step down from the floor was a rather high table and two chairs. Because I was not familiar with the communal bath, Yoshi very considerately told the maid to prepare water for me in the Japanese-type deep brick-tile bathtub in a corner outside the living quarter while he went out to have his bath with the crowd. Afterward we met for dinner in an enormous dining hall. On my way there, I passed many people, old and young, men and women, holding small towels, all going to the communal bath. After dinner I passed even more people also holding towels and going to the communal bath. As they all wore similar kimonos provided by the hotel, I could not tell whether they were the crowd that I met before or another lot. Yoshi laughed, saying that this could be the Japanese national weakness, for the Japanese just love to take baths, particularly the hot-spring baths. That was what they came here for. Some would take a bath every two hours or so if given the chance. In fact the communal bath here and in many other hotels nearby seemed to be on a twenty-four-hour shift. The hot spring is forever running. We walked through the gift-shop area, the game hall, the sports areas with bumper cars and other entertainments, as well as the main lounge where armchairs and drinking stands were all crowded with people, towels in hand, who seemed to be going to the bath again after having bought gifts or played some game. Or they might have just come out of the bath. The activities inside the hotel were terrific. I had not seen anything like it anywhere else. Curiously enough not a single European or American face was to be seen here in March. Yoshi, noticing my amazement at so much going on, said that I would find it the same in any other hotel at the many hot-spring resorts in Japan. It seemed to me that the spending capacity of the Japanese must be considerable, and Yoshi agreed that it had increased greatly after the war.

After a sound sleep we went down to breakfast and I met all the people again with towels in hand going to and coming from the bath. I wondered, do the Japanese bathe all the time at home?

Yoshi suggested for a change of scene a stroll outside the hotel which is named Kowaki-en. It stood in a lovely valley together with many other hotels. There were several swimming pools, some playgrounds, and many handsome old houses in Japanese style with nice footpaths for strolling around. Along the way were cherry trees with a number of blossoms already opened, and clusters of tall bamboos swaying their heads gently in the morning air, which was indescribably fresh and pure. All this gave rise to the following verse:

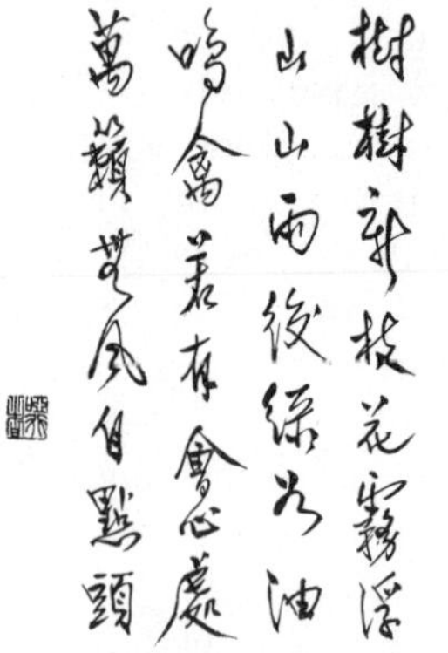

樹樹新枝花霧浮
山山雨後綠為油
鳴禽若有同心處
萬嶺芸風自點頭

The new branches of every tree have the flower
   mist floating over;
After rain hill after hill looks green as oil.
The singing birds seem to have the same thought as
   I;
Hundreds of bamboos nod their heads voluntarily
   with no wind stirring.

A most soothing moment.

Yoshi proposed we board the waiting bus that was to take us to the gap between the two big hills above Lake Ashi, popularly known as Lake Hakone, to see Mt. Fuji. The sun was still not out. The clouds became thicker and even turned grayish black at times. All the way the wind howled outside the bus windows. For about half an hour the bus drove between two massive black banks and then parked on a rather flat piece of open ground near a bus that had arrived just before us. But none of its passengers appeared to be getting out, and in fact the bus driver signaled he was about to start back. A young woman opened the door of our bus and got out but, unable to stand against the wind, she was instantly blown to the ground. The bus driver jumped down to pick her up. The rest of us all followed but the wind was too strong for any of us and soon we all returned to our seats. Masses of white clouds were rolling all around us and we could see only one or two yards away. I did not know where we were or where Mt. Fuji could be. So the bus returned to the valley. The clouds were dense only above the lake but did not come over the valley where the hotel stood.

Yoshi had to return to his office in Tokyo and we took a taxi down to the station. The car moved smoothly along the road alongside a rapidly flowing stream with high mountain slopes on either side. There were a number of paintable spots with some old Japanese houses and we stopped from time to time so that I could make some rough sketches. The route was most picturesque, with one panorama succeeding another, which made me regret not being able to see the whole Hakone range with Mt. Fuji rising in the distance. Yoshi was disappointed too, but said we must come again.

Not until two years later when I was about to leave Tokyo on my third visit to Japan did Yoshi take me to see Hakone again. It was a mid-September day—bright sunshine and reasonably warm. We took a different route, a train from Shinjuku station for Moto-Hakone, then changed to a small local train and again another change to reach a place where we rode on a cable car to the highest observation ground. People were already there; some were walking among the jets of white steam which rose at several points, some were strolling in the garden, and

Steam from hot springs

others were at the gift shops. Yoshi and I went to a teahouse, from which Mt. Fuji can be seen while one drinks tea or coffee. A young waitress shook her head saying to Yoshi, "Today too much fog and sunny haze are concealing Fujisan." I thought how elusive Mt. Fuji could be. However, it was bright where we were and our distant view reached even down to Lake Ashi. After a good walk around gazing in all directions for an hour, we rode the cable car down to the lakeside. It was quite a long ride and the hills seemed to be moving upward behind me while below I saw a beautiful school and a large football ground.

At the lakeside there was an office selling tickets for the excursion boats. We boarded one which had an upper deck from which we could have a good view all round. It is a beautiful lake, shaped like a Chinese calabash melon, a little more than five miles in length, a mile in width, and with thirteen miles of shoreline. The hills on both sides looked as though they were covered with a huge blue green silky veil, and the water of the lake was deep blue. As the hills and their reflection in the water moved toward us, their contour lines looked like the veins of two big slabs of marble joined together. At one point I was reminded of gliding down the river Rhine, and at another I might have been floating down the river Fu-ch'un Chiang of Chekiang Province in China. But when the brilliant vermillion-painted torii of the Hakone Shrine appeared on the lake shore to the left, I woke from my dream to find myself actually cruising on Lake Ashi.

I had been to Hakone Shrine two years previously. I had read that once there was a nine-headed dragon that molested the people on the western side of Lake Ashi. On seeing the people suffering so terribly, the priest Mangan recited a Buddhist sutra, caught hold of the spirit of the dragon, and tied it to a tree on the bank. The dragon was released only on promising to become the guardian deity of the lake and protect the safety of all those who travelled on it. A Dragon Festival was also to be held annually on the evening of July 31 to honor the dragon deity with an offering of fifteen hundred bushels of rice steamed with red beans. Two Shinto priests of the Hakone Shrine would take the steamed rice and beans in a boat and dump it in the middle of the lake, and they must not look back when they rowed ashore. If the rice sank to the bottom, it meant that it had been accepted by the dragon deity; if not, the dragon was annoyed by something or other, and the villagers who lived around the lake must take great care of themselves. During the evening of the festival, the villagers would hold a ceremony of offering the dragon deity lighted lanterns floating on the lake. What a marvelous sight that must be!

Leaving the torii, our boat passed by a high rocky promontory, on top of which stood a beautiful hotel with some Dutch-type windmills rotating high above the towers and on the water's edge four fountains spurted high in the air. Our boat continued on to the lower end of the lake, where we took a bus back to Tokyo. It had been a most enjoyable day, particularly the trip on the lake, though Yoshi was still a little disappointed, for he had wanted me to see Mt. Fuji from Hakone. I consoled him by saying that I had seen Mt. Fuji from Lake Kawaguchi when I stayed there on a previous trip.

When I made my fourth trip to Japan, Yoshi insisted on taking me to see the new country house which his brother-in-law, Mr. Akira Kitaoka, had recently built on a piece of land high above Lake Ashi. Yoshi and I took a bus to Hakone station and then went to the house by taxi. Mr. Kitaoka was detained at the office of his lens-manufacturing factory in Tokyo that day, so Mrs. Kitaoka received me politely with a deep bow together with their four sons, Noriaki, twelve, Tosiaki, nine, Hiroaki, seven, and Noduo, two and a half. Yoshi's younger sister, Masako, was there too. The main building was already finished and in use, but three laborers were there still working on the lawn. The house commands a wonderful panoramic view of many mountain ranges rising one after the other. Mrs. Kitaoka took the whole family and me to dine at the Kowaki-en Hotel, where Yoshi and I had been during my first visit. The twilight was lingering on and we had a good round of the hotel garden before we dined in an open-air dining area. Unlike my first visit, there were many foreigners in the hotel, chiefly from South America. After a sound sleep I woke up early next morning and Noriaki came to take me out on the road for a walk and to show me where Mt. Fuji was. Tosiaki and Hiroaki came along. The three boys walked in high spirit and kept on talking to me in fluent Japanese as if they did not know of my inability to understand them. Actually they knew that I could not speak their language, but their enthusiasm in trying to entertain me made them unable to be silent. I appreciated their kindness and lively manner greatly. Later on, Yoshi took the youngest, Noduo, to join four of us for a boat ride on the lake as well as a ride on the cable car. The hot sun lit up everything around the lake brightly. But the top of Mt. Fuji kept appearing in and out of the thick clouds all the while. Everyone of us enjoyed the short excursion, but I said to Yoshi that there was no snow on the top of Mt. Fuji. Yoshi laughed, remarking that it was now the height of the hot summer and that July and August were the two months when the snow was melted. Unlike the general belief, I realized that there are times when the snow does not stay on the top of Mt. Fuji.

Hakone is full of hot springs and was a popular Japanese resort before it became a great meeting place for Europeans and Americans. Many Japanese couples of all ages, particularly young lovers, have always come to spend their holidays in and around Hakone. There have been many interesting love stories about this area. I read about an unusual one that could have happened nowhere else but in Japan. A court warrior Yorimasa, whose home was in Hakone, fell madly in love with a lady of the court, Ayame, who happened to be a favorite of the emperor Toba. Yorimasa's behavior at court betrayed him and his passion became known to the emperor himself. Instead of showing furious wrath, the emperor asked gently if he was really in love with the Lady Ayame. How could Yorimasa answer? He was abashed and not a word could he say. Then the emperor ordered three court ladies, one of whom was Ayame, to be dressed exactly alike. The emperor said to Yorimasa: "I know you love Ayame. One of these three ladies is she; if you can find her she will be yours." Yorimasa, even more embarrassed, confronted with the ladies, wrote down the following verse:

Sadidare ni	Much water flowing over the stone walls
Numa no Ishigaki	Of the pond
Mizu koete	Caused by an early summer rain.
Izure ka Ayame	How is it possible to know
Hikize	Which is iris.

Ayame means "iris." The emperor, pleased with the poetic expression, took Lady Ayame by the hand and, with tears in his eyes, handed her to Yorimasa saying, "She is yours!" Japan had a generous and humane emperor and a general who was a poet!

Hakone is famous for two of nature's special creatures. The first is the *Hakone-sanshouo,* or Hakone salamander, found in mountainous localities. It is about five inches long and reddish in color with yellow stripes and brown spots. It does not like sunlight and always keeps in the dark. Many giant salamanders are found in different parts of Japan and they are edible. The Hakone salamanders are caught by the local people, who dry them in the sun for medicinal purposes. There is a small salamander, about one or two inches long, which Japanese children are encouraged to swallow live in the belief that it is a cure for nervous weakness and other illnesses. When a young child swallows a small live salamander he can feel it moving about in his stomach for a short time afterward.

The other creature is the long-tailed cock. Its tail feathers, fifteen to twenty-five in number, grow from eight to eleven feet long and occasionally to twenty-five feet or longer. I have seen these cocks in Japanese wood-block prints but missed seeing a live one in Hakone. The Hakone long-tailed cocks are said to have been developed by a Japanese farmer some one hundred and fifty years ago. They are bred now also at Miyanoshita and Nangoku in the Kochi Prefecture, but the Hakone

Long-tailed cock

cocks are still the most famous. They are said to live up to nine years, despite their difficulty in moving about.

Hakone is also noted for the many well-known Japanese writers who live there for the air, the mountains, the lake, and the hot springs; and it is not very far from Tokyo. Junichiro Tanizaki was one of these. Professor Donald Keene once gave a most interesting lecture on Tanizaki's foot fetishism and cracked many good jokes about the life Tanizaki led, for he always expressed his way of thinking differently from others. It is sometimes difficult to distinguish a Japanese face from a Chinese, but somehow I feel that Tanizaki had a distinctively Japanese face. There was a longer space between his nostrils and his lips; particularly with two curved lines from the nose to either corner of the mouth when the mouth was closed, he looked like a Kabuki actor on the stage. Tanizaki was living in Hakone when a disastrous earthquake occurred in Tokyo in 1923. Professor Keene told us that instead of feeling intensely grieved over the destruction and loss of life, Tanizaki was overwhelmed with joy about the future prospect of a new Tokyo which would become like Paris, London, Rome, and New York with many interesting buildings, wide avenues, lovely theaters, and many skyscrapers. Tokyo now is no longer the city Tanizaki knew but the Tokyo he dreamed of. He did enjoy seeing the new city, as he lived until 1965.

Junichiro Tanizaki

There have been fifty-three severe earthquakes in Japan according to the records. The first one occurred in the fifth year (286 B.C.) of the reign of the emperor Korei when both Mt. Fuji and Lake Biwa simultaneously made their sudden appearance. Despite so many disasters and calamities, Japan not only survived but progressed after each. Tanizaki's hope-for-the-best spirit is part of the Japanese national character.

I was surprised to learn from a Japanese book of the Japanese traditional belief that a huge catfish lives under the ground and every movement it makes causes a tremor of the earth. The fish has been under the control of a river stone, Kanameishi, beneath the Kashima Shrine in Hitachi Prefecture. I could not find any reference to the catfish-earthquake legend in any Chinese books, so I asked Professor Ivan Morris if he had come across it when he had lived in Japan, but the answer was negative. But a week or so later Ivan, in keeping with his reputation as a learned scholar, informed me with a wide smile that he had found a book about the subject. It was called *Namazu-E and Their Themes*—an interpretative approach to some aspects of Japanese folk religion—by Cornelis Ouwehand, published in 1964. *Namazu* means "catfish" in Japanese and *e* is a type of pictorial art in Japan. The book is an excellent study of the unusual subject with interesting text and thirty-one plates of catfish heads on human forms. Most of the plates were made from Japanese wood-block prints in a collection of eighty-

A Japanese namazu print

eight different namazu prints in the National Museum of Ethnology in Leiden. These prints seem to have been made after an earthquake. The author makes occasional reference to Chinese material on the subject, but I could not think of any Chinese story like it. The Chinese have been very fond of depicting animals in their artistic creations but never in any painting or sculpture did the ancient Chinese artists create bird or animal deities on human bodies, like some of the ancient Egyptian and Greek ones. So I tend to think of Chinese civilization as nonanthropomorphic.

Dr. Ouwehand mentioned many namazu legends and stories of Japan in his book and I quote the following one:

> The story takes place in Kashima shortly after the great Edo earthquake in 1855 and is told by an old man sitting near the hearth. In 1854, too, the first year of Ansei era, large parts of Japan had been ravaged by earthquakes. At that time the Kanto, and also Kashima, were spared, although light tremors were felt. Warned by the strange occurrence of a departure of the frogs (!) to safer places, people took the precaution of leaving their houses even though they could hardly believe that the Kashima god would not protect his own dwelling place. But then, who caused the earthquakes in other parts of the country? Could the Kashima god have been ill? It is indeed a matter of common knowledge that the Kashima god is not always at home; sometimes he is away, and even though at such times the Kashima-ishi will keep control of the monster-Namazu, the latter moves his feelers now and then and the small Namazu under him begin to stir. And are there not people who have seen the mysterious black Namazu-Otoko prowling about and manifesting himself? In the year 1855, when so many in Edo lost their lives in the great disaster, Kashima was again spared. Musing, the old man looks toward the ceiling, at the pothook with the wooden crossbar in the shape of a large Namazu fish above the fireplace, and all follow his glance. Suddenly the door opens. A black figure enters. The growling noise usually associated with earthquake is heard. But the old man calls out his conjuring words: "Watch out for the Namazu of the pothook!" and points to the entering figure with the iron fire tongs. The black, unwelcomed guest—none other than the Namazu-Otoko—is forced to leave the house without having done any harm.

According to Dr. Ouwehand, the Japanese believed in this kind of story long before the Edo earthquake. Apparently the catfish, like the Japanese badger or Chinese fox, can disguise itself in human form and cause great harm and disaster to mankind. There was recently an article in the *National Geographic Magazine* by Dr. Clarence F. Idyll about the walking catfish in Florida, which has been equipped by nature to survive on either land or in water. Each of the catfish's pectoral fins, used for steer-

ing and balancing in swimming, has a long stiff spine that can dig into
the ground and help balance and propel it while on land. The breathing
apparatus, too, does double duty. Elaborate organs behind the gills function much like lungs and enable the fish to breathe air for hours while
out of the water. So, how are we to deny the Japanese legend that catfish
did once walk like men? It was extremely likely that in the very ancient
days a catfish was seen walking during a great earthquake tremor. Thus
the spread of the Japanese legend.

Dr. Ouwehand describes how Drs. Hatai and Okubo of Tohoku University in Sendai tried to discover if the catfish has the power of foretell-
ing an earthquake. In their laboratory they set up barrels of water
containing namazu and subjected them to shock movement. The fish
were found to be extremely sensitive in their reactions. The experiments
revealed that in 80 per cent of the cases the fish reacted to the advance
indications of an earthquake registered fifteen hours later on the seismo-
graph. Both Dr. Hatai and Dr. Okubo concluded that a great many
phenomena, such as changes in composition of the water, changes in
water currents, underwater sounds, and electric radiation were perceived by the namazu by means of a very sensitive system of nerve cells
in the feelers and on the sides of the body. Only namazu possess feelers;
no other types of fish have them.

I chuckled to myself that in writing my experience in Hakone I did
not realize my mention of Tanizaki would have led me to touch the
problems of earthquakes in Japan.

Hakone's toyseller

V

Something Different from
Lafcadio Hearn's Days

MORE THAN forty years ago I read translations of Lafcadio Hearn's writings on Japanese scenes in a Chinese magazine. I began to like them, particularly the article "A Pilgrimage to Enoshima." Many things mentioned in the article were then beyond my comprehension, for instance the expressions "smell of the strong native radish," for the Chinese radish has little smell, and for *jinrikisha* China only had the word *ricksha* at the time, and so forth. In those days I was just beginning to learn the English alphabet and trying to find words in an English-Chinese dictionary. I even wrote a letter to argue with the translator about the expression "miniature shops," which, according to the dictionary, I thought should be translated as "toy shops" and nothing else, though I wondered why Japan had so many toy shops. When one is young, one can act impulsively. Though I liked Hearn's writings about Japan, I did not care much for his repeated use of words such as *little, small, dingy, tiny,* and *miniature.*

After more than forty years I had come to see Kamakura for myself. I did not arrive there by a jinrikisha but by an electric train early on a bright May morning. May has always been a favorite month for poetical description in almost every civilized nation in the temperate zones. In the mild climates May really unites all the soft beauties of spring with the radiance of summer and possesses warmth enough to cheer and invigorate without overpowering. Kamakura lies on the shores of Sagami Bay on the west side of the neck of Miura Peninsula, enclosed on three sides by ever-green hills and on the south by fine sandy beaches where the climate is always mild. On the way I saw masses of cherry blossoms still lingering on the trees while the fresh greenness of the pine needles was trying to brush away any fragments of mist in the air. The train carried a big load and upon arrival at our destination many passengers dashed to get on a bus and I followed them

Like Lafcadio Hearn I went first to see the big bronze Buddha. Unlike the time of Hearn's visit, now the wide road leading straight to the bronze Buddha was full of people, with a number of guides holding up small flags to lead the way for their respective groups. From down below and on the steps near the pedestal of the bronze Buddha it was difficult to get a full view of the statue without having somebody's head or limbs in the way. Time has indeed seen much change since Hearn's days. However, people, particularly the young ones, still climbed up the back of the Buddha to go inside it and up to his shoulders.

This big bronze figure was Amida, or Amitabha in Sanskrit, one of the Buddhist divinities. It was cast in 1252 by Ono Goroemon, a leading sculptor of the time, upon the order of Minamoto Yoritomo (1147–1199), who established his shogunate in Kamakura in 1192. The dimensions of this enormous bronze statue are approximately 42½

Big Amida

feet high, 97 feet around the base, his face is 7 feet 8 inches long, each eye is 3 feet 5 inches wide, the silver boss on his forehead weighs 30 pounds, and the total image weighs 94 tons. The figure was originally enclosed in a large temple, but this was damaged by a terrific storm in 1369 and the building was finally swept away by a tidal wave in 1495. What a colossal tidal wave it must have been to have come up such a long distance from the sea, which I could not even see from where I was standing by the pedestal of the big image. Perhaps in 1495 the seashore was not so far away as it is now.

It is said that Yoritomo was inspired by the great bronze Buddha erected in Todaiji Temple in Nara, and that he ordered this one for Kamakura slightly smaller in scale. The Nara image represents Buddha preaching, his right hand raised with its palm facing the audience while his left hand rests on his knee, but the Kamakura one represents Amida in silent meditation with both hands laid on the lap, palms upward and thumbs touching, with eyes half closed in complete contemplation.

Leaving the Amida image, I followed Hearn's footsteps to look at the "far-famed Kamakura temple of Kwannon"—Kwannon in Japanese, or Kuan Yin in Chinese, is the goddess of mercy. The temple, though large, was not dark. Many people strolled around with me to examine the eleven-faced gilt image of Kwannon, thrity feet in height, placed in the main hall of the temple. This image is said to have been carved in 721 by the priest Tokudo Shonin from one-half of a mighty camphor tree log over one hundred feet in length and is a duplicate of the Kwannon at the Hasedera Temple near Nara, made from the other half of the same log. A legend about it says that the Kamakura Kwannon was thrown into the sea near Osaka with a prayer that the influence of the goddess might save the souls of men from destruction at whatever spot the waves should wash the image ashore. After having drifted for fifteen years in the sea, it eventually came ashore at Yuigahama Beach at Kamakura in 736, where the temple was erected to enshrine it. The camphor tree has the natural quality of resisting blight and can last indefinitely.

Again I followed Hearn's example and went to see the holy island Enoshima. I reached the place called Katase and walked across Bentem-bashi—a concrete bridge now, more than a thousand feet long. While I was crossing, the water below flowed swiftly and the wind overhead blew deliciously. Nothing could be more welcome and revitalizing than the magic spell of the sea air after having been in the swirl of Tokyo life for days. Surely no concrete bridge like Bentembashi was here in Hearn's time, but he did not reveal how he managed to reach Enoshima. From the island end of the bridge I followed many others climbing upward and looked back to where I had just come from—the masses on the beach looked like piles of oranges and apples in a grocery, or colored balls in a department store. On the way up the hill one shop after another joined together lining either side of the road and people went in and out. The most popular items for sale in all the shops were sea shells and ornaments made from polished mother of pearl, decorations, jewelry, and many wares in porcelain and wood. I have always wondered how so many shops all selling the same things on the same spot could each make a living. The trees and plants surrounding the shrine looked luxuriously healthy in growth. The air inside the shrine was heavy and oppressive, so I went for a stroll round the edge of the cliff that was open to a view of the sea; the main part of the island is thickly wooded, though it is only a little more than a mile in circumference. The great expanse of the sea attracted me enormously—so wide yet so flat right to the distant horizon. And the magic translucence of the water seemed to have cast a spell on me. I remained there gazing at it for a long while.

While I was staring at the distant expanse of sea in another direction, a darker image like the back of an enormous whale appeared on the surface of the water far, far away; it must have been an island, though I could not tell its name. Far beyond this dark image and high above it there hung in the sky a silvery white cup in the shape of an inverted lotus leaf in an absolutely calm and restful attitude as if nothing could disturb it. It turned out to be the snowy top of Mt. Fuji, whose lower part was heavily veiled by the sunny haze and mist. I never imagined that I should see Mt. Fuji so ethereally beautiful from Enoshima.

I then went down to the Dragon Cavern. The steps downward were cut out of the pale yellow hard sandy rock joined by a long plank supported on a number of high, thick bamboo poles. The sacred cave, though deep, was not very dark, for many people had lighted candles in each hand. Nothing much could be seen except a vague image of Benten on the end wall. Minamoto Yoritomo, when he set up his shogunate in Kamakura, changed the small Buddhist temple into a shrine of Benten, whose Indian name is Sarasvati, an Indian goddess of art, literature, music, and eloquence. Dr. Haridus Chaudhuri, President of the California Institute of Asian Studies, tells me:

> Sarasvati (Benten) is the consort of Brahma (one of the Hindu trinity). So she is considered the goddess of all creative sciences and the origin of the intricate science of Indian music. She invented the Sanskrit language and the Devanagari script. She is the patroness of poetry and literature, of the arts and crafts.

That is why Enoshima is now known as the island of Benten. I first met the seven Japanese deities of good luck aboard a Japanese airplane, when a printed card about these deities was given to each passenger to bring him good luck. Of the seven deities, Dr. Chaudhuri had no specific information about when and how Benten, or Sarasvati, went to Japan from India.

Three others—Fuku-roku-ju, Jurojin, and Hotei—originated in China. From the fly duster held by Fuku-roku-ju, he could be Nü Tung-pin, one of the eight Chinese Taoist immortals. He was a T'ang scholar, wrote poems, and became a Taoist immortal who lived in heaven without need for human food. From time to time he came among men to try to save them from suffering and cured sick people by waving his fly duster over them. Nü Tung-pin also carried a dagger on his shoulder in the Chinese art representations of him, but the Japanese drawing of him does not show the dagger. Jurojin, who is always accompanied either by a crane or a stag, could be one of the three Chinese star gods, Shou-hsing, or Star of Longevity, derived from the story of the Taoist Paradise as the Old Immortal of the South Pole (Nan-chi-hsien-weng). He is always depicted in Chinese art-craft designs as an old man with white eyebrows, long white mustache and beard with an enormously high forehead, and usually wearing a yellow embroidered robe. He is accompanied either by a crane or stag and also a child, holding a rugged tree-root staff with a pair of peaches hanging from it. The Chinese used to display this figure in the house during the New Year Festival, and it also was presented as a birthday gift to people of over fifty years. Hotei is Pu-tai, which means "cloth bag" in Chinese. He was a Buddhist monk, said to be the incarnated Maitreya, or the contented Buddha. According to tradition, Maitreya was born in southern India of a Brahman family and his two epithets are *benevolent* and *Ajita*, or invincible. He is represented as the fat laughing Buddha. After having attained enlightenment, this T'ang monk used to carry an enormous white cloth bag and walk about in the streets, particularly in the market places, followed by a number of children, for he loved young people. He never buttoned his gown so his bare chest, his fat abdomen, and breasts were fully exposed. He seldom ate anything but he always looked robust and cheerful. The Chinese regard him as the god of contentment or the god of happiness. He is depicted in all kinds of Chinese art forms, in stone, jade, ivory, wood, and porcelain, in embroidery as well as in painting. In 1934 I made a painting of Pu-tai which was made into a print and has been in circulation ever since.

Both Ebisu and Daikoku appeared to be definitely of Japanese origin, though I don't know who they could be. Bishamon, clad in armor and holding a pagoda in his right hand as the Japanese deity of militarism, may have been derived from one of the four Indian deva kings. But how and when these seven deities were grouped together in Japan and for what reason would be very interesting for me to know. So far no one in Japan has given me an explanation.

Back again on the mainland, I took a taxi to visit the Tsurugaoka Hachimangu Shrine, which Hearn did not mention in his pilgrimage. Kamakura had been the Shogunate capital in the twelfth and fourteenth centuries and is reputed to have sixty-three Buddhist temples and nineteen Shinto shrines in the city and environs. No one would be able to see them all in one visit, but I had a reason for seeing this important place. The Official Guide describes this shrine as follows:

Tsurugaoka Hachimangu Shrine

It was founded in 1063 on another site by Minamoto Yoriyoshi (995–1082) and was removed in 1191 to its present location by Minamoto Yoritomo (1147–1199). The shrine is dedicated to the emperor Ojin, who reigned from 270 to 310. The existing buildings, dating from 1828, express the characteristic style of the Momoyama period (1573–1615), especially in their rich decoration in color and sculpture.

I did not come to see its architecture or sculpture, but to locate the spot where many notable heads had rolled on the ground during the Kamakura period in the twelfth and fourteenth centuries. A team of five men—a Mongol, a Korean, a Chinese, a Persian, and an Uigur Christian—sent to Japan by Kublai Khan, all had their heads chopped off somewhere in this neighborhood. Some years before this happened, the head of Yoshitsune, Yoritomo's most popular and active brother, was said to have been cut off here too, for Yoritomo had to get rid of him to protect his own power. But it was rumored around Japan soon after the execution that Yoshitsune had not been killed but had managed to escape and eventually reached Mongolia to become Genghis Khan. That was why the first ruler of the Mongols who became so powerful instigated his son, Kublai Khan, to invade Japan while Yoritomo was in power, to seek revenge. This was the rumor or legend prevailing at the time, which one may believe or not. In China long before the Christian era there was a legend about the disappearance of Lao Tzu, the originator of Chinese Taoism, who was said to have ridden away from China on an ox's back through the western pass and was never seen again. The legend said that Lao Tzu travelled to India and taught his principles and philosophy to Buddha, though he did not become the Buddha himself. There are similarities in these two legends. However, Genghis Khan seems to have become a household name in Japan, for in some street in every city of Japan one sees an advertisement on the wall: "Genghis-Khan-jo," meaning "Genghis Khan flesh or meat." A Chinese student, who finished college in Taiwan, came to do some research work in Japan and he complained to me in Tokyo that he never realized that the Japanese hated Genghis Khan so much till now, for he had seen everywhere that the Japanese wanted to eat Genghis Khan's flesh! There is a Chinese expression handed down from ancient days, "to eat the enemy's flesh" for revenge. So this young Chinese thought that Genghis Khan's son, having invaded Japan in the thirteenth century, was thus the arch enemy of the Japanese. He feared that he would not be able to study in Japan peacefully and planned to return to Taiwan immediately, and he said that his grandfather had never wanted him to come to Japan. But I tried to pacify him by saying that I never believed that hatred could last from generation to generation and that what the Japanese called Genghis Khan flesh or meat was a kind of meat dish which was known in China as Mongolian meat, meat cooked in Mongolian style. Thus can misconceptions arise through different interpretations of the same language.

After Yoshitsune's escape to the north of Japan, it is said that Yoritomo caught his young brother's mistress, Shizuka, a celebrated dancer of the time, in order to find out where her lover was. Later she was compelled to dance at the foot of the steps of the main hall of the Hachimangu Shrine to entertain Yoritomo and his wife.

Yoshitsune's prison

It was also in the courtyard of this very Hachimangu Shrine that the chief priest hid himself behind an enormous ginko tree, about twenty-three feet in circumference and seventy feet tall, waiting to assassinate his uncle Sanetomo, the third shogun of the Kamakura period. This is another story about Japanese Buddhist monks or Shinto priests who had become involved in politics. Very few of the Chinese Buddhist monks had shown a political connection in China's history.

Near the treasure hall is the lotus pond which was said to have been created by order of Yoritomo's wife, and when I saw it, a good many young buds were about to bloom. The healthy leaves of the lotus in the pond must have been growing for many generations since the twelfth century.

One of the main reasons I went to see the Hachimangu Shrine was that I wanted to imagine how the great Buddhist priest Nichiren presented his challenge to Hachiman, whom Nichiren stopped and called upon to save him when he was forced to ride through the streets to his appointed place for execution. The following are his words as translated from Satomi, "Japan Civilization," in the book *Sources of the Japanese Tradition*, edited by Professor William Ted de Bary:

> Oh, Hachiman! Art thou in truth a Divine Being. . . . When the Great Master Dengyo preached on the Lotus sutra, didst Thou not do homage to him by laying at his feet a gown of purple color? I now say unto Thee that I am the Only One whose life is the Lotus sutra. There is no fault in me whatsoever; I am proclaiming the Truth, for the sole purpose of saving the people who dwell in the land from sinking into the deepest of Hells on account of degrading the Lotus. If it came to pass that this land were subjugated by the Mongols, wouldst Thou, O Hachiman, alone with the Sun Goddess be in safety? Let me now say unto Thee that when our Lord Sakyamuni preached the Lotus, all the Buddhas gathered together from the ten quarters like unto a sun and a sun, a moon and a moon, stars and stars, mirrors and mirrors, and were ranged face to face with one and another; and with hosts of heaven within their midst, deities and saints of India, China, Japan, etc., present in congregation, all of them vowed to watch over who should labor to perpetuate the Lotus sutra.
>
> Now shouldst Thou come hither and fulfill what Thou has sworn. Why then comest Thou not to fulfill Thy promise! When I, Nichiren, this night shall be beheaded and shall have passed away to the Paradise of Vulture Peak, I shall declare unto our Lord Sakyamuni that Thou, Hachiman, have not fulfilled the vows. Therefore, if Thou fearest, tarry not, but do Thy duty!

How brave and great Nichiren was! His plea must have been answered, for the executioner failed to cut off his head. Hachiman and the Sun Goddess were certainly present to fulfill their vows! Many Christian theologists have condemned Buddhism as a negative religion while Christianity, they said, was a positive one. But if they had known what Nichiren did in his life, they could not very well have regarded Buddhism as a negative religion. Strangely enough, Lafcadio Hearn never mentioned Nichiren in his interpretation of Japan.

Once Professor Burton Watson and I compared the political system of the Japanese and the Chinese. Many people in the Western world have been curious as to why the Chinese had so many dynasties one after another while the Japanese continued under one family from the first emperor till the present day. I think the earliest Japanese tradition of rule by the direct descendant of the Sun Goddess has kept the Japanese family intact in its succession. All those first shoguns, no matter how powerful and clever they might have been, were not able to put aside the lineal emperor and ascend the throne themselves, for they knew that they were not the direct descendants of the Sun Goddess and therefore not able to have the confidence of all Japanese. The Japanese Buddhist monk Dokyo could easily have been put on the throne if the empress Shotoku had not had strong faith in the god Hachiman and in the Sun Goddess. I read that when the question of having the monk Dokyo as the emperor was put to the temple of Hachiman, the oracle of the deity was not actually revealed, but Wake-no-Kiyomaro (A.D. 733–799) reported to the empress the result of his mission in the following words:

> "In this country," said the oracle, "the difference between the ruling class and the ruled has been so distinctly established from the beginning that no one but a scion of the imperial family has ever ascended the throne. Hence, it is absolutely necessary that one from the imperial family be chosen as emperor. Should any one venture to violate this eternal order of Heaven, he shall immediately be cut off."

That was in the tenth century. No one dared again. If either of the three powerful shoguns—Yoritomo, Hideyoshi, and Iyeyasu—had been born in China, each could have set up a new dynasty. The earliest Chinese tradition has it that all the Chinese were the direct descendants of the Yellow Emperor, who was a man-emperor, not a ruler descended from a god or goddess. From the records dating from Confucius's days, if not earlier, China had a legendary ruler, Emperor Yao, who found his own son unworthy and left his throne to his minister who became Emperor Shun, who in turn was dissatisfied with his son and caused his minister to become Emperor Yü. All Chinese emperors have been very human from the very beginning of Chinese history. Mere human faith in ruling the masses could not prevent the rise of human lust for power. The result is that China changed dynasties from time to time. The Japanese expect to become a *kami* one day, but Chinese tend to dream at times of becoming the emperor. That is the difference between the Chinese and Japanese systems.

The sun was still high and bright when I left the Tsurugaoka Hachimangu Shrine, and, it being too early to return to Tokyo, I strolled back to the place where the big bronze image of Amida sits peacefully on its pedestal. I remembered seeing a sign "Museum of Modern Art" in the morning, and I went in. It is a modern two-story building with good walls and beautiful light to show up what is on display. A very well designed art museum, it has a good number of art objects—modern in treatment and in different mediums. Almost every one of the exhibits could be combined in any show in Paris, London, or New York, for they were all done in the Western manner with the Western technique and medium—a few in oil pigments and many with pen-and-ink, as well as some in crayon, none with Japanese brush and ink stick. The subjects were all abstract and nonobjective, nothing indicating their connection with Japan. In his interpretation of Japan, Lafcadio Hearn wrote:

Art in Japan is so intimately associated with religion that any attempt to study it without extensive knowledge of the beliefs which it reflects is mere waste of time. By art I do not mean only painting and sculpture, but every kind of decoration and most kinds of pictorial representation—the image on a boy's or a girl's battledore, not less than the design upon a lacquered casket or enameled vase—the figures upon a workman's tower not less than the pattern of the girdle of a princess—the shape of the paper dog or the wooden rattle bought for a baby, not less than the forms of those colossal Ni-O who guard the gateways of Buddhist temples.

Hearn might find it difficult to express his views on art in Japan if he were alive to visit this Museum of Modern Art only a minute or two away from the big bronze Amida image.

After a round on the ground floor and then upstairs, I leaned on the balcony railing on the second floor, watching two young ladies in bright-colored kimonos discussing the new lotus blooms in the pond— elegantly and leisurely. My sense for the place of art in our daily life was soon restored. Art is embodied in life. Life is not to be found outside Nature, and it is necessary to be in harmony with Nature before one's mind can swing in the peaceful rhythm of life. Art cannot become a universal mechanical means to fly every one of us to the moon, or even to Mars for that matter!

A common sight in Japan

Mt. Fuji from the Shore
of Lake Kawaguchi

THERE ARE many magic words in Japan—*torii, pagoda, geisha, sumo, hot springs, Ise, Mt. Fuji*—but the last is the most magic of all. Other countries can have hot springs, can build torii, pagodas, and even Ise-like cathedrals, and can also train geisha and sumo wrestlers, but only Japan has such a mountain as Mt. Fuji. Mt. Fuji has the real meaning of a magic symbol with a definite symbolic significance; it not only stands for Japan but also for the mind of Japan as well.

The word *mountain* has fascinated the Chinese since time immemorial, and the first one mentioned by name and the most important is Tai Shan. The first emperor of Ch'in, who lived in the third century B.C., united all the feudal states into the first Chinese empire, built the Great Wall, and climbed it to watch the sunrise. Tai Shan rises near the eastern coast of China in Shantung Province. Confucius was born there and mentions it in the *Analect*. Therefore Tai Shan becomes the best known and revered mountain to all Chinese who have read the *Analect*. I once made a secret wish that I would climb up to the South-Heaven Gate, through which I would go to the top of Sun-gazing Peak of Tai Shan to see the sunrise when I grew up. But I never did, for I never had the opportunity to go to Shantung Province before I left China. Besides Tai Shan there are many other higher and more famous mountains in China, such as Mt. Lu in my native province of Kiangsi, and Huang Shan, Yellow Mountain, in Anhui Province, as well as the four Sacred Mountains of China, but none of them can stand out as the only center to attract all Chinese for worship or for a life-gratifying satisfaction if one managed to climb up to the summit. But Mt. Fuji is unique in every way, for it is the whole of Japan. The uniqueness of Mt. Fuji is in its cone shape, its snow-capped summit, and in the fact that it can be seen from all over Japan. Mt. Fuji has not only provided a center for worship for all the Japanese throughout their history, but it also provides Japan with a symbol for her publicity, for it has all four characteristics described for a

Fellow travellers in a tour

symbol by Professor Tillich—picturesque quality, perceptibility, innate power, and acceptability as such.

I had seen Mt. Fuji in pictures, wood-block prints, and photographs before I went to Japan. Yoshimaru Tadokoro wanted me to see Mt. Fuji from Hakone and we went there twice; once it was hidden in heavy rain and the second time it was veiled in dense sunny haze.

I had been in Japan twice before and had left without having a good look at Mt. Fuji. Now I joined a tour for the purpose of seeing it. Our motorcoach moved out of Tokyo, passing through a suburb where the road was lined with ginkgo trees, and then stopped at the Satatsuki Silk Factory. We went in to look at the different textile designs for kimonos and silk materials and watched the women workers weaving them. Shortly we were summoned in to see a fashion show. Eight or nine young ladies came onto the stage one after the other, each in a different kimono. Though the colors and the designs on the textiles were different, somehow my impression was that there was little change in the dress design itself. Perhaps I do not know enough about Japanese kimonos, but, like Chinese ladies' dresses, I cannot find much variety in them. James Laver, an English fashion expert, once remarked that "a fashionable gown requires personality in the wearer: two equally charming models attired in equally fashionable outfits would give an entirely different impression." I am sure this applies to the Japanese kimono as well.

After visiting another famous silk-weaving shop in a country town, the coach moved on and we eventually reached Hotel Lake Kawaguchi for lunch. After lunch the journey was resumed and soon we passed through a big gray torii, signs proclaiming it was the gate of Mt. Fuji. Our spirits lifted, though the weather had become rather dull. The guide gave each of us a piece of paper with the song *Fujisan* on it. She asked us to sing together with her:

Fujisan	Mt. Fuji
Atama o kumono ueni dashi	Its head reaches above the clouds
Shiho-noyamao-mioro-shite	It surveys the mountains all round,
Kaminari-samao-shitani-kiku	It hears the thunder far below—
Fuji wa Nippon ichi no Yama	Fuji, the highest mountain in Japan!

(The translation by Ivan Morris.)

We were now up in the heights. Snowflakes were flying past the coach window. The cheerful air of the song was toned down by the chill sight of the snow. Outside were mostly leafless trees with their branches bent in the same direction and some had snow on them. As the coach moved higher up more clumps of trees appeared. They were lined up in vertical rows, and growing close together; they could not spread naturally and their trunks were twisted by the strong winds. More snow was flying and almost obscured the windows. At long last we came to a stop at the fifth station—a good way up the main mass of Mt. Fuji. The guide said that the climb to the top of Mt. Fuji started here, rather than from down below as people used to do years ago. Actually the season for climbing Mt. Fuji was still three months off. The snow was falling hard outside. Four other coaches had already stopped in the open space before two large gift shops, where one could also have something to eat and drink. Shortly the snow stopped and everyone was out with his camera. I walked over to the leafless trees and found them to be old birches with bright white trunks and branches. A few seemed very old and their rugged, twisted trunks were very beautiful in formation. There was plenty of snow on the ground. All we could see were the trees—the top of the mountain was blocked from view. I never expected to be in such a scene; we were still in the world of humans yet not quite so. Only the presence of the coaches and cars made the human world all too real. I found a small lane and walked along it. There I met two tiny boys, each not more than three years old, both busy building up something like a snowman by a red-painted torii. They looked up at me for a moment but soon turned back to carry on their work. Through the red torii a small shrine came into view with a pair of carved stone lions done in Chinese style and quite a big monument with three kanji words meaning "Monument to a Loyal Soul," though I could not find out who the person was.

It was getting dark. Two coaches had already started downward and ours soon followed. The wind became stronger and the snowflakes again struck noisily on the windows. Everyone inside the coach seemed to feel contented, for we did get some little way up Mt. Fuji. The coach then dropped me back at Hotel Lake Kawaguchi, as I intended to stay on a bit. A girl of fourteen or fifteen served me at dinner. She had a lovable face with apple cheeks and always received my order politely with a broad smile. She might have been a new graduate from the local high school and had learned a few words of English for the job. The food was good and it was a pleasant end to my day. I then composed two little poems while lying in bed before I dozed off:

First day of arriving near Mt. Fuji

Flying over hundreds of miles I came to visit Fu
　　Sensei;
A whole day cloudy and foggy, half a day fine.
How should I expect you to have snow obscuring
　　your true face?
Besides, the sound of wind mingled with the sound
　　of rain!

On the way back to Hotel Lake Kawaguchi

Wind harsh, sky low, and no break in the fog;
Dragon-twisted trunks of old trees grow in the
　　snow!
Still unable to recognize the face of Duke Fu;
Oh, the endless clouds fly and rain strikes at me!

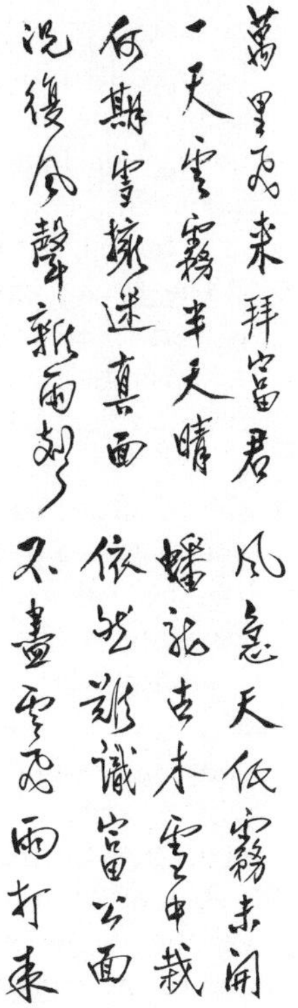

萬里飛來拜富君
一天雲霧半天晴
何期雪域迷真面
況復風聲新雨趣

風急天低霧未開
蟠虬古木雪中栽
依然難識富公面
不盡雲飛雨打來

The poems each contain only twenty-eight Chinese characters and I managed to incorporate in both five different natural phenomena—cloud, fog, snow, wind, and rain—an interesting attempt.

At breakfast I asked the young girl who served me again the way to the lakeside and she directed me to the back garden of the hotel. I crossed over a small red bridge and passed by a thatched cottage where the tea ceremony takes place and then came to the lake shore. I could see almost the whole of the fourteen thousand-acre lake and all the rolling hills on the other side—some with dark green patches of trees, some rather bare with sparse grass exposing the reddish soil of the hills. Though the sun was not out, it was a mild and peaceful scene. The surface of the lake was ruffled and a rather strong wind made a hissing sound in the leaves on the trees.

As I walked toward a village of many cottages clustered together, I saw directly facing me a little island and a small rowboat just coming from it. I learned that the island was named Unoshima, or Cormorant Isle, because of the many cormorants that come to it. On the island stands a small shrine dedicated to Benten, a goddess of beauty and music, like the one dedicated on Enoshima. I then walked along a strip of land that stretches out into the lake just behind the back garden of the hotel. It was covered with tall pine trees and I felt happy walking through the pine grove all alone. Reaching the tip of the land, I saw a couple lying on the pebbles and on the far side of the lake were some modern machines at work. A fisherman with a long fishing rod drifted in a boat in the center of the water. His silhouetted image and that of the boat, though so very small, enhanced the tranquillity of the scene.

The young smiling girl served me again at lunch. From her smile she seemed to be willing to talk to me, but my inability to speak Japanese rather embarrassed me. Afterward, I walked out toward the main road, and I strolled along meeting a few people on the way. Soon I entered a narrow but quiet street with nice shops. Coming out of the street I walked along the lake shore toward the station of the ropeway which took visitors up the hill for a view of Mt. Fuji. Unfortunately the clouds were very dense and nothing could be seen; so the ropeway was not operating. I then turned back to the footpath along the lake shore. Coming toward me was a man bent over under an enormous square box filled with some heavy load. He looked familiar to me, as I have seen many figures like him in old Japanese wood-block prints. But I could not help wondering why it was necessary for him to carry such a heavy load on his back in this modernized Japan!

A loud noise suddenly burst out not too far from where I was walking. Some five young boys were playing along the water's edge. One of the boys was wet and dripping. Two other boys helped him out of the water, while the last two carried some of his belongings. The sight made me wonder if there was a *kappa* in Lake Kawaguchi. I had heard many stories about kappa everywhere I went in Japan. Kappa is a strange creature, living in the waters of a lake, river, or sea. It would come to the shore and pull youngsters into the water and drown them. The strange part is that kappa never attacked adults. It was said that kappa was very fond of cucumber and before the summer season arrived, Japanese mothers used to throw cucumbers into the water in order to ask the kappa not to molest their children when they came to bathe. A story tells of a kappa who could walk like a human being, speak Japanese, and could even write. The most interesting description of kappa is in the book *Netsukes* by Albert Brockhous:

> *Kappa* is of pure Japanese origin. It is a fascinating animal, mostly depicted with a body resembling a tortoise, frog legs, and a monkey-

like head—on the top of which is a hollow which is filled with his water elixir of life. This creation, nevertheless, is "scientifically" described as a froggy creature four feet nine inches in height, and in 1830 was still caught in swamps. He falls in love, he is dangerous to young ladies, has a fighting spirit, but is ceremonious as a nobleman. Before engaging in a duel with a *Kappa,* a man is advised to request that the *Kappa* make a polite bow. The *Kappa* is such a gentleman that he will comply with the request of his adversary, but this causes the life-giving water to flow out of the hollow on his head so that he is easily conquered!

What a strange creature and what a fantastic tale! I thought that the boy who got himself so wet might have had a fight with kappa and won the battle. When I emerged from my thoughts, all five boys had disappeared. It had begun to rain; the wind blowing across the lake from the hills felt cold. I had been out for the whole day but still had no idea where to look for Mt. Fuji and was a little frustrated and disillusioned.

On the third morning it was dry again, but still no sun. I went down for breakfast earlier than the morning before. The same young smiling girl was there to serve me. When I was about to leave the dining hall, she hurried over and drew my attention to a window through which the sun was shining. I went over to the window and immediately opened my mouth and eyes wide. It seemed as though some heavenly being high above was trying to draw upward a colossal, dense, grayish white cloud cover from a huge stretch of ground. Inch by inch it rose. Underneath the clouds, there were some strips of silver shining and glittering. By and by more silverlike snow appeared while the cover of dense clouds seemed to be closing upon itself. I was now able to see about one-fifth of the conical mountain that I had come to see! There is supposed to be a goddess living right on top of Mt. Fuji. Was it she who drew up that cover of dense clouds a moment before? All the cloud mass which had covered the whole area a moment ago was now a large, furry white ball near the top of the conical mountain. It changed into a feathery white fish floating motionless by the summit of Mt. Fuji. Another feathery white cloud taking the form of an angel was playing with the fish, but the fish paid her no heed. Or was she dancing gracefully in front of the fish, which enjoyed watching the dance? The story from the favorite No play *Hagoromo* I had read in *We Japanese* by Frederic de Garis came true before my eyes.

A fisherman, Hakurin (White Dragon) by name, beached his boat at Miho-no-Matsubara, and while admiring the superb beauty of this bit of seashore and Mt. Fuji in the distance, he chanced to see a beautiful feather robe hanging on a pine tree branch. At the same time perfumed flowers fluttered down from the sky to the accompaniment of majestic music, which swelled as the blue waters of the bay swirled. The man took down the robe and was amazed at its magnificence. An angel appearing asked what he was doing with her robe. "I want to take it home, as it is so beautiful," replied the fisherman. "No, you may not do so. Please return it to me. Without it I cannot fly back to heaven." The argument continued thus until at last her appeals were effective, and the robe was given back. Instantly, the angel ascended to heaven, flying away over Mt. Fuji, fast disappearing toward the west. She was, however, good enough to perform a dance in midair in grateful recognition of the man's kindly act. This was the Hacoromo-no-Mai, a celestial dance.

What a piece of luck that I saw this dance not in the No theater in Tokyo but by the window of Hotel Lake Kawaguchi! I also thanked the young girl who guided me to see it.

I could no longer stay indoors, but went straight out and walked in the direction of Mt. Fuji. As I went along the main road it seemed that Mt. Fuji retreated. I soon reached a place where I could see the whole conical formation unobstructed by trees; its shape was not quite a cone but more like a slightly squashed Chinese coolie's hat with a very wide brim. The feathery white clouds were still around the top but were thinner.

I continued along this road and presently a loud-speaker sounded nearby. I had reached a village where a group of people stood around a well-dressed gentleman with a white flower in his buttonhole who was speaking loudly in Japanese. I guessed it was a local election day. Many women, old and young, came to listen intently and I was impressed by their orderly manner and civil conduct. This reminded me of when I was civil governor of Wuhu during the years 1928 and 1929, and China was supposed to be a republic governed by the consent of the people. Actually the Chinese countryfolk did not yet have any idea about the meaning of democracy. Most of them were peasants, retaining their fear of officials who in the past had generally oppressed them instead of helping them. I had to disguise myself so that they would not recognize me when I rode my horse round the countryside to talk to the people accompanied by two of my personal aides. If the people had known who I was, they would not have talked. What China still needed was to educate the masses. But from the scene in the village near Lake Kawaguchi, I could understand well why Japan was able to adopt the Western system so successfully; it was simply because the first object in the Meiji Restoration was to educate the masses and this popular education has achieved great wonders.

Shortly I left the crowd and turned to look again at Mt. Fuji. More snow now appeared on its peak, and the feathery white clouds hanging above were gradually thinning out and looked like smoke or steam spiraling upward. The scene recalled the following legend:

There was once the Lady Kaguyahime, who was an angel incarnate on earth. Her beauty was so great that she had many suitors, but not one, not even the emperor of Japan could win her heart. After living in the world of humans for many years she flew up to heaven one full-moon night. However, before she left she sent an elixir of life to the emperor, who had become so grieved over her loss and cared for nothing. Later the emperor sent a courtier to carry the elixir up to the top of Mt. Fuji and ordered him to burn the medicine there. Being the highest part of Japan, the emperor thought it would be near where Lady Kaguyahime lived—the moon. Therefore Mt. Fuji has had white smoke ascending to heaven ever since. The Chinese name for the elixir of life is "Fu Shih Yao" (弗 死 藥), or never die drug. That is why Mt. Fuji is so named Fu Shi, two Chinese characters pronounced in Japanese, meaning "never die."

According to the oldest Japanese belief, Mt. Fuji rose up at the same time as the land submerged to become Lake Biwa, about 286 B.C. There is another story about Mt. Fuji, told by Mr. Atsuharu Sakai, which I find rather disturbing:

It is said that the ancestral god, Mioya-no-kami, was making calls on a number of gods all over the country and happened to arrive at a place near Mt. Fuji at dark, so he asked the god of Mt. Fuji to accommodate him for the night. Just at that time the god of Mt. Fuji was so busy in the preparations of the local Good Crop celebration he could not manage to put the ancestral god up for the night. The latter became so annoyed that he denounced the god of Mt. Fuji for being so lacking in filial piety and declared that cold snow would cover its top throughout the ages, so that few people would climb up to offer food. That is why Mt. Fuji has always had snow on its top from that time on. The Mioya-no-kami then went to stay with the god of Mt. Tsukuba for the night and there he was treated most kindly and lavishly, and for that reason Mt. Tsukuba has many people climbing the whole year round.

But now the snow round the top of Mt. Fuji was shining brightly as if smiling with wide open eyes. It did not have any cold feeling for me at all at that moment.

On and on I strolled, looking at Mt. Fuji from every possible angle—sometimes as the background for a lonely house, sometimes at the head of a narrow street, and sometimes behind a single tree or a cluster of trees. Mt. Fuji stood there in great dignity and serenity with its benevolent conical form and glittering light shining all around it. Now

there were no feathery clouds around the peak, not the smallest wisp.
The entire sky was a vast sheet of azure with the perfect clear-cut shape
of Mt. Fuji standing out against it in a most unbelievable fashion. It was
as though I were looking at an enormous postcard. But a postcard scene
is generally lifeless, while here everything was alive. Mt. Fuji stood in
the distance like some living being sitting in the way a Japanese emperor
sits with his heavily starched kimono spread out in stiff lines all round
him. The snow on the summit sparkled in the sun all the while. Between
me and the mountain, trees were swaying, crows and sparrows were fluttering about, and people were walking. I believe some supernatural
being must reside at the top of Mt. Fuji or even far above it from
whence he is in complete control of all the activities down below.
Those activities seemed to be conducted under a divine spell, or else
why should all Japanese have had such great reverence for it all through
their history? Why is there an endless procession of climbers to its
summit year after year? There must be some invisible power attracting
all this activity to it. Without the climbers and the thoughts and the
reverence of all the Japanese, Mt. Fuji would be merely a big rocky
mound rising out of the land between Yamanashi and Shizuoka with no
living quality whatsoever. The first climber was the priest En-no-Gyoja
during the reign of the emperor Mombu. Women were not allowed to
ascend Fuji before the Meiji Restoration era and the first woman to
climb it was not Japanese but British, Lady Parks, wife of the British
Minister Plenipotentiary and Envoy Extraordinary to the Court of Edo,
in 1867.

Back into reality I found myself heading toward the group of houses
and shops on the north side of Lake Kawaguchi. Though I had walked
part way here the day before, something was different in the scene. The
long tassellike branches on some young willows were now greener in the
bright sun and two small cherry trees were in full bloom. It was a perfect day for walking, for it was neither hot nor cold—an ideal April day.
I managed to cross the busy road to a restaurant. After lunch I found
my way to the ropeway station. Other people had gathered and tickets
began to be sold. While the ropeway car was drawn gradually upward,
the lower part of Mt. Fuji seemed to grow bigger and rounder. In fact,
Mt. Fuji not only appeared to spread out its base, but also to lift itself
upward higher and higher as if it was about to stand up instead of sitting
down on the flat tatami like a Japanese emperor. When the car reached
the top of the hill, Mt. Fuji looked like a Kabuki actor in a massive colored kimono standing erect with raised chest and in a wide-spreading
skirt. It no longer looked to me like a squashed Chinese coolie's hat.

There was much to see from the top of the hill besides Mt. Fuji.
When I turned to look at Lake Kawaguchi it had become an odd-shaped

KEGON FALLS, NIKKO

MT. FUJI FROM HOTEL LAKE KAWAGUCHI

mirror, neither round nor squarish. Little Cormorant Isle had taken the form of a tiny cormorant gliding gracefully on the water. Many boats on the lake looked like insects crawling on the surface of a sheet of glass. The bright green willows and the white cherries dotting the shore road there gave a soothing feeling in the gentle spring breeze. After a good hour I rode the ropeway down and was amazed to see that all of a sudden everything had become pink and red from the slowly setting sun. The lower part of Mt. Fuji below the snow line, originally bare yellow brown soil, had turned deep crimson. It suddenly dawned on me that Mt. Fuji now looked like a chief priestess in a white blouse and a wide-spread scarlet skirt about to kneel down in front of the Jingu Shrine of Ise. There she was indeed. I felt so happy to have recognized what Mt. Fuji really was in its connection to Japanese Shintoism. What a great revelation that was to me! In bed that night I lay awake for a long while thinking about the day and composed the following two little poems:

Along the shore of Lake Kawaguchi

Along the lake the new willows dance in the wind;
All the way the cherry trees bloom at will.
Thinking of all my travels through the floating world,
I am now silently walking into the depth of Mt. Fuji.

Gazing at Mt. Fuji

Strolling aimlessly by the mountain lake of Kawaguchi,
"Oh, the head of Duke Fu is white on the horizon!"
Its graceful and refined air resembling the work by Wang Wei.
But why the sharp line and precipitous look? I had better ask Sesshu!

Actually the famous Japanese monk-painter Sesshu had not painted Mt. Fuji. Why hadn't he, as he had painted quite a number of Chinese landscapes?

About five o'clock I was awakened by a great noise outside. It must have been a wild and stormy night. Hail was falling, and thunder and lightning followed one another at short intervals. The joy I had experienced the previous day seemed enhanced by this sudden change of the weather. I could not sleep anymore but just lay in bed gratefully revisualizing the events of the day before.

A taxi came at ten o'clock to take me to Atami. Nothing was to be seen through the window, neither Mt. Fuji nor the hills by the lake, which had also disappeared. Not even the tall pine trees in the back garden could be singled out clearly. A high wind was blowing and rain dashed against the trees along the road. I did not know where we had been and where we were going. For an hour or so we drove along with dense white clouds all around. It was as though the driver and I were completely enclosed in a white tent riding a merry-go-round at an amusement park. Presently the driver stopped and suggested I get out for a look. Other cars were also there. The rain had ceased for the moment, but it was still heavily overcast. I joined the other people by a wall and could see the foot of a long sweeping range of hills stretching down to the sea and could make out the faint image of a long bridge. One of the other sightseers, an American, told me that this was Jukkoku Pass, or Ten-Province Pass, noted for its marvelous view in clear weather!

As the car approached the outskirts of the city of Atami, the clouds gradually dispersed and it rained no more. It seemed to be a tropical land, for I saw tall palm trees and cactus too. The climate had changed abruptly. Atami is by the sea. What a variety of weather I experienced in one day or, more exactly, only three or four hours. Before we reached Atami, I asked the driver to stop for a moment so that I could have a look at the small island called Hatsushima. It was too far away and I could not make out much of it. I had become interested in Hatsushima when I heard a legend about a beautiful girl of seventeen named Ohatsu, who once lived on the island. She fell in love with a young man of Atami who promised to marry her on condition that she cross over to visit him every night for a hundred nights. The girl's love for him was so strong she could not refuse his request and she made the crossing every night. But on the ninety-ninth night the little light on her small boat was blown out as she was crossing. Ohatsu soon lost her way and was later drowned. When the young man heard of her death, he shaved his head and became a Buddhist priest. I then composed the following little poem:

Two passions, one waterway, leave me wondering:
Why should there be one hundred times for
   evening meetings?
Hatsushima is as green as ever.
But nowadays the girls command their lovers
   to cross over to them!

兩情一水費疑猜
夕渡何須定百回
初島青々如往日
而今倩女雪郎来

VII

Nagoya and Ch'en Yuan-pin of Ming China

Nagoya Tower

MY FIRST visit to Nagoya was in the cherry blossom season, in the first week of April. Nagoya had suffered terribly during the Second World War, but now no war scars could be seen. I stayed at the Hotel New Nagoya, situated in a most modern, Western-style quarter, where the only indication that the place was in Japan was the shop signs in kanji and kana. Something new which I discovered was one long underground street lined on both sides with shops selling all kinds of goods.

As I walked along the widest street in the center of the city, I was most struck by a tall steel tower with some brilliantly colored and well-arranged flower beds in its front and rear. Nearby were two bronze sculptured, fully developed naked females of a Western type but with Japanese heads. This group was beyond my comprehension, and I thought the figures would have surprised Lafcadio Hearn, who described Japanese women as having a small physique. A sign in kanji, "The First Exhibition of the Oriental Art Association," written on a big white cloth banner was hanging outside a new building, so I went in for a look. There were more than thirty works on display, all painted in oil. Apart from one painting of a woman and child, the subjects were all landscapes, birds, and flowers. Technically all were handled in a rather conventional way of the Western impressionist and postimpressionist period. The Western style of painting in oils has long been practiced by Japanese artists from the early Portuguese and Dutch trading days. The first Japanese artist to use the Western technique and media in painting was Hiraga Gennai (1729–1780), who also gave lessons in Western-style painting to some of the local samurai in Akita. Since the Meiji Restoration days many Japanese have gone to Paris and Rome to study art. Quite a few established their names in the Western art world. It seems to me that there are more practitioners of the Western technique and media than otherwise in the present Japanese art world. It is no longer quite correct, however, to speak of Japanese painting as Western style, for it is actually a definite Japanese type of painting in oil by now.

The difference is only in the technique, for the individuality of the beauty and artistic value of a work still lies in the creator. I find that art is something very difficult to divide into schools and nationalities. It is the individuality of each work that counts. It may bring out a regional or provincial flavor, yet its greatest effect should be international. I do not indulge in the conventional form of art, for I think there is something more to be aimed at than the activity of mere imitation. Many people have adopted a sort of sneering attitude toward Japanese painting by implying that first it was an imitation of the Chinese and now of the West. I do not deny that Japanese artists have many, many imitative pieces, but there are also original pieces. Can we say that all American paintings are imitations of the French or the English?

The arts need patrons to grow and flourish, and happily Japanese painters, no matter whether they work in Western style or otherwise, are not lacking in patrons. Through my friend Yoshimaru Tadokoro, with whom I visited Hakone, I met his brother-in-law, Mr. Akira Kitaoka, a successful industrialist in the optical lens-manufacturing business, who has a great love for art and has provided financial support for young Japanese artists to study in Europe.

From the top of the Nagoya Tower I was able to locate the famous Nagoya Castle and I soon went down to have a look at it. Many branches of blossoming cherries and other trees within the castle grounds appeared above the walls to smile at the throngs streaming toward the castle. There is a waterless moat surrounding the castle and a few people were playing ball against the castle walls. Inside the castle grounds I saw a group of young students, boys and girls, around an elderly gentleman with a white mustache and long beard—possibly their

Cherry blossoms and Nagoya Castle

professor—who was pointing out the rocks which were arranged about the southern courtyard. I moved near them and wished that I could understand what the old man was saying about the rocks. I have always been crazy about artistic formations of natural rocks. An artistic eye is needed to find rocks like those used in many famous Chinese gardens instead of man-made sculptures, and many Chinese books have been written about rocks.

Then I strolled about examining the cherry trees. Each tree standing by itself reveals its individual character much better than when planted in masses. I made a few sketches of them, for each had a very distinctive shape, with different branches of varying lengths, twisted into different forms. I have seldom viewed flowering trees in such a healthy and happy state of being—not a single petal had fallen.

I heard many youngsters singing nearby. The song was familiar to me, for it was the popular cherry blossom song, which my friend Mrs. Nobuko Morris translated as follows:

Sakura, sakura,	Cherry blossoms, cherry blossoms
Yayoi no sorao	in the wide sky
Miwatasu ka kagiri	to the end of my view
kasumi ka kumoka	like mist, like cloud
nioi no izuru	but its perfume redolent
izaya izaya mini yukan.	Come, come let us go, give our eyes joy.

What a beautiful and gay feeling one has in this cherry blossom season in Japan! It is not surprising to find the close association between cherry blossoms and Japanese literature and art, particularly screen-painting, lacquer designs, and textile decorations. There must be an end-less number of romantic stories connected with the cherry blossoms too.

Gradually making my way toward the entrance gate of the castle, I passed by the dry moat outside the walls. In it were a number of deer playing and looking up at us as if expecting some food. The sight of their faintly spotted brown coats against the zigzag stone walls and the green grass was very interesting. I marveled at the exquisite grace of those slender legs treading so daintily. Presently I went inside the castle and the first thing I saw were the models of a pair of gold dolphins which are famous the world over. The female is 2.51 meters high and 1.95 meters round, and the male 2.59 meters high and 2.07 meters round. Both originals on the roof were made of pure gold weighing together 165.273 grams. The story goes that once someone, by flying an enormous kite, tried to hook one away but did not succeed. I heard that one of the dolphins was removed during the Meiji era to be sent to an exhibition in Vienna. When it came back the steamer *Nile* was wrecked on the Izu Peninsula and the dolphin was lost. However, it was fished up six months later. Most Japanese castles have two dolphins mounted atop their roof ends, but only those on Nagoya Castle are made of gold. The dolphins were generally believed to possess the power to protect the castle from fire. In the Christian religion the dolphin is a symbol of resurrection. From a distance the Nagoya dolphins looked like the dragons and phoenixes on the roofs of Chinese palaces, monasteries, and temples. The dolphin proves to be one of the things in which the Japanese did not follow the Chinese.

Climbing one flight of steps after another I reached the top floor, the castle's fifth story, called Tenshukaku. Though the history was not written up, I learned that the castle was originally built and completed in 1612 by order of Iyeyasu as a fortified residence for his son, Yoshinao, whose children continued to live there until 1868 when the Meiji Restoration began. The building was destroyed, together with the whole city of Nagoya, in the intense bombing of 1945. Only recently its reconstruction was finished at a cost of six hundred million yen, including the new pair of gold dolphins above the dungeon.

After coming down from the castle, I took a long stroll on the castle wall above the dry moat and could see many more cherry blossoms here and there, looking particularly fine and charming against the dark green needles of the pines. Later when walking in the northern courtyard of the castle grounds I found a group of strangely shaped rocks surrounding two small mounds called Crane Islet and Tortoise Islet. One rock was given the name of Tortoise-head rock, another Tortoise-tail rock, a third Phoenix-tail rock, and so on. They looked to me like centuries-old lava. Close to the castle wall a small camellia tree was in full bloom, the waxy red petals in circular shape loosely attached to the branches gave additional color to the whole scene. Most of the cherry blossoms were white, a special species indigenous to the Japanese soil. There are many species of cherry growing in Japan but many have been cultivated as ornamentals and do not bear fruit. China has one popular kind with pink blossoms, which grows in profusion at Hou-Hu, meaning "Lake at the Rear," in Nanking and is famous for the flowers as well as for their fruit. I knew both, for they are not far from the university where I studied for five years.

Making a turn, I came to the front of a building with a sign in kanji, meaning "Exhibition of Valuable Rocks," arranged by the Central Section of the Rock-finding Society in Nagoya. This attracted me immediately. This is not in the Western sense a society composed of those who are students or experts on mineralogy or geology. The rocks are collected not for their scientific structure or ingredients but for the aesthetic value of their natural shapes and formations. The Chinese men of letters and artists have long had great interest in collecting the natural rocks ever since the Sung dynasty (960–1279), if not earlier. We regard a beautifully shaped rock as "nature's sculpture." Not every rock possesses an interesting shape or form, which needs only be discovered by an artistic eye. None of these rocks must show any trace of being molded artificially by hand or mechanical means. They usually resemble a part of nature in miniature, such as a rocky cliff or a rocky hill. This kind of interest could have evolved after the development of painting pure landscapes in the annals of Chinese pictorial art. I have a few artistically shaped rocks in my possession so I went in the building for a look at the exhibits.

There were two hundred and forty-three pieces on display and each was owned by a member of the society. Many pieces had interesting names and many were named after animals and birds for their resemblances. A good few seemed to have been well polished. One rock was in the shape of Mt. Fuji with a part of white rock on the top like snow. Its exact likeness indicated some artificial touch which takes away its aesthetic value. Nevertheless I felt happy to have seen the exhibition and to know the existence of a rock-finding society in Japan. The next day I went to see the Atsuta Shrine.

Unlike my first visit, made without any idea of what I might see in Nagoya, my second visit had a definite purpose to find the tomb of a Chinese scholar, Ch'en Yuan-pin (1587–1671), who spent some ten years in the place. After a wash I entered the hall for a meal. Shortly a rather stout fellow came to ask to join me at my table. He told me that he came from Colorado and said laughingly that a big party had been arranged to see the Sex Shrine next morning. He urged me to go with him but I excused myself as I had fixed a visit to Kenchuji Temple. At the end of the dinner, he stood up and gave me a good pat on the shoulder, saying, "What can you see in a temple? You will miss a lot tomorrow, my boy!" He left still laughing. The worship of the male sex has been a cult in the world ever since prehistoric times, and there is an extensive literature on the study of phallicism in the primitive cultures of the world. Japan is not the only country that had this ancient cult. The ancestral worship in China might have developed from this cult and was long in existence before Confucius, who lived in the sixth century B.C. In the Western world there is a wrong conception that China's ancestral worship was started by Confucius. Confucius did not start it but he encouraged it by emphasizing filial piety and so forth. Indeed, Japan's ancestral worship has long been included in Shintoism and was not imported from China.

After breakfast I took a taxi to Kenchuji Temple and found myself in a big temple courtyard in which a number of fine trees looked healthy and bright in the brilliant August sun. The temple appeared well kept and some parts were being repaired and repainted, indicating it was a

wealthy precinct, but it was obviously not frequented by tourists. I was
the only one strolling around, trying, but in vain, to find the cemetery. I
could find no written information about the temple, nor was there anybody to whom I could make an inquiry. I began to feel a little vexed and
found some shade under a tree. The temple is not near any main streets,
so it would have been difficult for me to get a taxi back. After half an
hour I went to a side building, for the August sun in Japan can be hot.
Soon after, a middle-aged woman came out of the main building to put
on her sandals. I at once realized my mistake in standing indoors with
my shoes on, so I went out to the porch. A few minutes after she disappeared, a young monk with a close-shaved head and in very thin white
robes came along. He could not understand my question in English,
but later he pronounced the word *yes* when I showed him Ch'en
Yuan-pin's name in kanji. He then managed to let me know that Ch'en
Yuan-pin had lived in this temple for more than ten years, after he came
to Japan at the beginning of the seventeenth century. This meant that
the temple had been here for at least three hundred years. The young
monk knew that Ch'en Yuan-pin was buried in the temple cemetery
which was some distance away, but he could not explain to me how to
get there. He went inside to ask his master, or somebody else, and to
fetch a map drawn with a ball-point pen, but this latter was no use to me
for the names on it were written in Japanese hiragana. We stood facing
each other for a good while till I suddenly exclaimed the word *taxi*. Smilingly he nodded his head several times and went inside straightaway. In
about ten minutes a taxi appeared and the young monk hurried out

The tomb of Mr. Ch'en Yuan-pin

while I bowed to him in great gratitude. He had to explain where the temple cemetery lay in great detail to the young driver, who did not seem to have heard of the place before. From his unsmiling face I could not tell whether he was willing to go or not. However, we started out and drove right into the countryside along a good, straight road. The driver made several stops and got out to see if he could find the tomb. At long last we saw a number of people including a monk by the side of the road waiting for a bus. The monk knew the whereabouts of the cemetery and gave directions to my driver. The car soon left the main road and went up a side footpath; on reaching a field the driver called me to follow him. I found a big stone tablet with these few words in Chinese, difficult to decipher: "Ta Ming Kuo Wu Lin Pai Shan Ch'en Yi-tou Hsien-Sheng Mo," or The Tomb of Mr. Ch'en Yuan-pin of Hangchow of Great Ming. It was encircled within a square of stones in the midst of many other graves and could not be seen easily. Ch'en died in 1671. I wonder if any of his descendants in Hangchow of Chekiang Province knew his grave was here. It looked deserted but was not in too bad a condition considering it was three hundred years old. Indeed it should be considered remarkable that this tomb was still in existence and I felt gratified at having found it. I gave it a deep bow in accordance with Chinese custom before I left. Upon returning to the hotel, I gave the young driver some money and told him to keep the change. As a rule the Japanese taxi drivers do not take tips, but on my insistence, and as an expression of my gratitude for his help in finding Ch'en Yuan-pin's tomb, he accepted and went happily on his way.

Why should I have been so interested in Ch'en Yuan-pin's tomb? Dr. Shunzo Sakamaki, Dean of the Summer Session of the University of Hawaii, wrote a brief biographical account of the poet in *Eminent Chinese of the Ch'ing Period (1644–1911)* as follows:

Ch'en Yuan-pin (1587–1671) was a native of Hangchow, Chekiang. In the spring of 1621 he accompanied Shan Feng-hsiang, an official of Chekiang, on a journey to Japan to lodge a protest against piratical activities along the China coast. During his sojourn in Japan, Ch'en composed verses with Hayashi Nobukatsu (1583–1657) and others. He went back to China but in 1638 returned to Japan. Soon after his arrival in Nagasaki he fell ill, but later he secured a position with the Lord of Owari at a stipend of 60 *koku* of rice per annum. He produced one scholarly work on Lao Tzu, entitled *Boshi Tsuko*. Together with a priest, Gensei (1623–1668), he composed and published some eighty poems under the title *Gen Gen Showa Shu,* in 2 chuan. By introducing the poems of Yuan Hung-tao (1568–1610) to Gensei he indirectly made a valuable contribution to the development of Japanese poetry. In 1660 Ch'en's patron ordered a kiln to be built, and Ch'en manufactured a number of pieces of porcelain modeled after imported Annam ware and modified by his own original patterns. Later this ware was called gen-pin-yoki, i.e., Ch'en Yuan-pin ware. To Ch'en is also frequently ascribed the introduction of jujutsu. An anonymous work, *Kempo Hisho,* published some time before 1683, stated that jujutsu had originated in Japan following a conversation between Ch'en and three ronin regarding the Chinese method of seizing a man. This theory has since been widely accepted. However, careful investigation by competent scholars has disclosed the prior existence of a similar art known as yawara, and Ch'en probably should not be regarded as the founder of jujutsu, but rather as one who gave it the stimulus that inspired its later prodigious development. He died in 1671 and his remains were interred at the Kenchu Monastery in Nagoya.

From that brief biographical account, one can see that Ch'en was a person of versatile talent, discussing Taoist philosophy, writing poetry, making porcelain, and also understanding wrestling. In the sixteenth and seventeenth centuries Chinese scholars, like many earlier ones, seem to have been not only devoted to the study of Confucius's classics, but were also craftsmen.

Mr. Saburo Egami, manager of the Tourist Information Center, told me that the Kenchuji Temple of the Jodo sect was built in 1650 by Tokugawa Mitsutomo, a feudal lord of the Owari clan, in memory of Tokugawa Yoshinao (1600–1650), a son of Tokugawa Iyeyasu, and that a few pieces of gen-pin-yoki (or Yuan-pin ware) are in Japan, some of which are in the Tokugawa Art Museum in Nagoya City. But Mr. Egami thought that the Chinese kempo is a quite different thing from jujutsu, and that some arts resembling jujutsu can be traced back in Japan before Ch'en Yuan-pin's time. Though Ch'en Yuan-pin could not have had any association with the founding of jujutsu in Japan, I thought his knowledge of Chinese Taoism—Taoist philosophy, not Taoist religion—could have led him to practice *tai-chi-chuan*, a type of Chinese health exercise in which muscle movement and blood circulation is stimulated through the gentle, systematic wrestling of the limbs and body which can be practiced alone or with others. This was a Taoist invention and those in China who were interested in Taoism generally knew this art. It is different from the Japanese judo or jujutsu. Friends have taken me to see judo practiced and I found that the judo wrestler always aimed to throw his opponent down flat on the floor. The sumo wrestlers appeared in Japanese Shinto shrines long, long ago, and I was told that Emperor Shomu opened the first national sumo tournament in 728, which was long before the arrival of Ch'en Yuan-pin from China. I saw a sumo wrestling show in Osaka and found that way of wrestling could have led to the development of judo or jujutsu. I have read that there were women sumo wrestlers in Japan, who used to attract large

A sumo winner

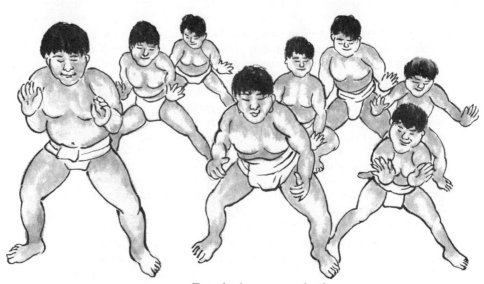

Exercise in a sumo school

audiences, for they wrestled half naked. Many blind men also wrestled in a sumo match. In 1822 there was a woman who wrestled with a bear in Nagoya. The Japanese sumo wrestler is a very unusual type of man, indigenous to Japan. They are usually well built, squarish shaped with strong limbs and plenty of flesh. How they could grow almost all alike puzzles me. Once I discussed my puzzlement with some Japanese friends, asking what does a sumo wrestler do after he finishes his wrestling career. Mr. Koide Jiro, editor of *The Rising Generation* magazine, told me smilingly that they were all wealthy and were never out of a job, for they could be instructors to the next generation, or become managers of one organization or another. Besides, they could all get the best-looking girls to marry them! We all laughed.

After seeing Ch'en Yuan-pin's ware in Nagoya, I learned that the mountain city Seto, where much of Japan's best ceramics have been produced for over seven hundred years, is within easy reach of Nagoya. I could not refrain from going to see Seto, for I had long heard of it. I was born in a city close to the world-renowned ceramic center of China, Ching-te-chen, where the imperial kilns were set up in 1004. Products of the kilns were shipped to all parts of the world from my native city, Kiukiang.

Many books in English on Chinese porcelain have mentioned Seto products; for instance, the late Robert L. Hobson of the British Museum wrote:

> The Chinese tea contests were adopted by the Japanese, who elaborated them into the curious ceremony known as *chanoyu*, which

later assumed a semipolitical aspect. The Japanese *cha jin* (initiates of the tea ceremony) have always prized the Chien Yao bowls (a type of ceramic produced in the province of Fukien, which is usually a dark soft brown black earthenware body and thick, lustrous, purplish black glaze, mottled and streaked with golden brown) to which they gave the name temmoku. . . . The tea-testing contests seem to have lost popularity in China at an early date, and late Ming writers took little interest in the partridge cups. . . . In Japan, on the other hand, the vogue of the tea ceremonies has continued unabated to modern times, and no doubt the Chien bowls were eagerly acquired by the Japanese aesthetes. Hence their rarity in China today. Moreover, the Japanese potters of Seto have copied them with astonishing cleverness, so that the best Seto imitations are exceedingly difficult to distinguish from the originals.

It was Kato Shirazaemon who first established a kiln at Seto in the reign of the emperor Juntoku (1197–1242) and produced some primitive unglazed ware. He then went to China in 1223 with a priest named Dogen of Echizen Province, and for four years studied the art of porcelain making. On his return to Japan he travelled far and wide over the country in search of better clay, but failing to find any superior to that at Seto, resumed his work there. He also brought some clay from China from which he made porcelain known as Toshiro-Karamono (chinaware of Toshiro). The ware made with Japanese clay after his return from China is known as Old Seto, and both it and the Toshiro-Karamono are very much prized. I think the Shino bowl, about which the Nobel Prize winner Yasunari Kawabata wrote again and again in his novel *Thousand Cranes* could have been a Toshiro-Karamono or an Old Seto. As the Japanese would pay any price for a Chinese Chien Yao bowl, it has become almost unobtainable in China in the past hundreds of years. The rise of the Seto ware, with its great achievement in imitation since the eighteenth century, was a natural outcome.

On a guided tour we went through three big ceramics factories including the best-known, the Noritake factory. We saw many beautiful modern products, but neither a piece of Toshiro-Karamono nor Old Seto was to be seen. Though I may be wrong to generalize, I think Japanese clay tends to give a lustrous, fish-belly-white tint to the products while China clay breathes a bluish hue.

Nagoya can also boast having another outstanding industrial art craft, Japanese cloisonné, or Shippo Yaki, through the establishment of Ando Cloisonné Company in the city. I am always interested in all types of art crafts and found my way there for a look. The Japanese word for cloisonné, *Shippo*, means literally "seven heavenly treasures," i.e., gold, silver, emerald, agate, coral, crystal, and pearl materials which are usually used. This art craft developed in Japan about the middle of the nineteenth century. Tsunikichi Kaji (1802–1883), the second son of a samurai living in the suburbs of Nagoya, first succeeded in making a small container, five inches high, after experimenting for six years. But the highly developed technique in modern Japanese cloisonné was the contribution of a German, Gottfried Wagner (1830–1891), who came to Japan at the time of the Meiji Restoration in 1868 and who perfected the technique and trained a few Japanese in the art. The grandson of Tsunikichi Kaji was actually the originator of the modern cloisonné technique when he became the chief artist for Ando Cloisonné Company in 1880. Nobody yet knows the place of origin and date of the earliest enamels, but it is believed that the technique of cloisonné enamels was invented sometime around the thirteenth century B.C., probably in Mycenaean Greece. The first evidence of Asiatic enamels lies in the copper cloisonné dish with Persian and Arabic inscriptions which contains a dedication to an Ortokid prince who reigned at Hsin-Kaifa (1114–1144). The earliest signed piece of Chinese cloisonné is reputed to carry the mark of Chih-Yüan (1264–1294 or 1335–1341, for there were two Chih-Yüan reigns in the Mongol period). It was through the Mongols, who ruled China then and had much communication and trade with the Middle East of the Arabs and Persians, that the technique of making cloisonné enamels came to the Chinese. But the best-known Chinese cloisonnés were produced in the reign of Ching T'ai (1450–1456), which became the celebrated name for this type of art craft. Many pieces of Ching T'ai cloisonné are in private and public collections. Some pieces of Ching T'ai could have gone to Japan, whose artists, probably including Tsunikichi Kaji, became interested in them. Thus the earliest Japanese workers in the art might have studied during the Ming period when there was more contact between the two countries. Though the Ching T'ai cloisonné became celebrated the world over for its artistic achievement, the Chinese craftsmen stuck to the old technique that they probably learned from the Arabs or Persians, that is, outlining the designs with copper or silver wire with no innovation. But the modern Japanese cloisonné has advanced so much as to give no indication of having wire outlines for the designs as in the old cloisonné. The enamels are used as a medium for freehand designs or paintings. The Ando Cloisonné Company produces seven types of cloisonnés: (1) Yusen Shippo—cloisonné enamels without lines, (2) Musen Shippo—cloisonné enamels without wire, (3) Zogan Shippo, (4) Saiyu Shippo—embossed metal and enameled, (5) Total Shippo—enamels with transparent insets, (6) Shotai Shippo—baseless cloisonné, and (7) Tomeiyu Shippo—transparent enamels. I was shown each type and could not help admiring the progressive and creative minds of the Japanese cloisonné artists who employ the cloisonné enamel not only to manufacture all types of utensils for daily use in a most attractive way, but have also manipulated their skills to produce pure art objects in cloisonné for aesthetic appreciation.

Most of the Chinese, old and young, as well as many Westerners, have the general notion that the Japanese learned many things from the Chinese and as pure copyists even topped them, but they never question the use the Japanese made of the knowledge they learned from other countries. This great point of their genius is one to admire, as is also the progress made by them. Owing to the tumultuous and chaotic conditions after China's defeat by the Western and Japanese powers, the Chinese cloisonné artists did not produce anything worthy of mention. Also, the Chinese were never receptive toward employing in their factories foreign artists such as the German Gottfried Wagner, who made his contribution to modern Japanese cloisonné. I, as one of the China-born Chinese, would never designate the Japanese as being copyists of China or the West, but admire the dexterity of their hands, their inventive minds, and receptive powers.

VIII

Shinto Dance at Ise

WHEN I WAS living in Oxford, England, I read Dr. Arthur Waley's translation of *The Tale of Genji*, in which was described an elaborate preparation to send the elder daughter of the emperor and empress of Japan to Ise to become the Virgin Priestess. I did not understand what all this was about. The name Ise had never entered my mind before. Now I was in Nagoya and heard of an excursion to Ise, so I joined the busload to go there.

It was a very fine mid-April morning. The bus stopped not far from the wide, long Uji Bridge over the Isuzu River. The river did not appear to be deep, for the pebbles at the bottom were clearly visible. We were told that every twenty years some old fir tree trunks would be drawn across this river from a nearby mountain by a large number of workmen dressed in bright green tunics and white robes on a day of special ceremony. The last ceremony had taken place only three years before, in 1966. Japan is indeed a country of ceremonies and festivals. Crossing over the bridge and passing through a big torii, I saw a few cherry trees in full bloom against the bright sunlight. They were so brilliantly white that they almost seemed to be cut out of paper, looking so unreal yet so real. Many people were scattered about a large open space which was enclosed by tall old trees, mostly Japanese cypresses. They seemed to dwarf all those walking along ahead of me. I paused to have a good look at the Shinto dancing platform, which had two big fanlike ornaments behind it. We then walked through the central pilgrimage road with tall trees lining both sides and a deep blue-and-green mountain range lying off to the right—most impressive and awe inspiring. Everyone was moving forward in the same direction. On the left were a few one-story houses, in one of which two young priests were selling illustrated pamphlets about the great shrine, colored postcards, printed Buddhist charms, and other souvenirs. As I continued the pleasant walk in the shadow of the tall trees which made me feel so infinitesimal and humble, my mind began to feel utterly cleansed. Shortly we came to another torii and, passing through, I followed a number of people walking to the right, where many women were bent over washing their hands in the

Washing hands in the Isuzu River

Isuzu River, which at that point is narrower and the water flowed swiftly and was very clear. This was the first stage in the pilgrimage: to purify oneself before reaching the shrine. Next we came to a trough of stone at which many long-handled wooden spoons were provided for pilgrims to wash their mouths by gargling the water. To the Japanese, water has long been considered a source of purity. The observance of cleanliness and the fear of contamination seems to be innate in the Japanese nature. Everyone performed this cleansing as a matter of course. My head had already been cleansed by the walk along the pilgrimage route under the tall trees, but I went to gargle like the rest. After going up a flight of rough stone steps and turning to the left, suddenly we were standing before the Ise Daijingu, or the Grand Shrine of Ise. A complete silence reigned over all of us. Not even an ant could be seen moving on the ground as I examined the pure white curtain hanging in front of the shrine. Only the imperial personages would ever be allowed to go beyond. As the shrine was recently rebuilt, all the wooden beams, pillars, and walls retained their newness and shone like pure gold, brightly in the April sun. They looked so sumptuously adorned yet in marvelous simplicity. Perhaps it was this splendid simplicity of construction and arrangement that held all of us in absolute suspense, indescribable awe, and inspiration. No one dared to move. Presently a gentle breeze went whispering through the trees just behind us as if singing a cheerful tune while the pure white curtain was blown open slightly. At once everyone, as though under an order, bent over a bit trying to see what was inside. Nothing but a pitch-dark line revealed itself, even blacker in contrast with the white curtain. Finally we moved over to a corner to look at the structure of the shrine and then walked along the fence on the rocky wall for a glimpse of the roofs of the shrines. They all have the great *chigi*, or horned roof beams, which are typical of Japanese Shinto shrine architecture. I could not understand why this simple construction and arrangement could have held the Japanese hearts for two thousand years or more and why it could still hold us speechless and motionless as we faced it. It is easier to work on elaboration and fine ornamentation but harder to achieve the awe-inspiring and aesthetically satisfying simplicity. The Ise Daijingu is a great example of such unmatchable excellence. Who was the first architect who planned such a simple construction?

We went on to see a few other buildings—one where a white-robed priest was supervising the lighting of the ritually pure fire for cooking the special food offering to the Sun Goddess, the storehouse for the rice grown in the shrine's own rice fields, the shrine kitchen, the shrine, and several lesser shrines. Actually the daijingu is a self-contained unit and a very well organized body with a long tradition which has carried on for almost two thousand years.

Professor Alexander Soper of New York University wrote about Ise:

> In the case of the best known, the imperial precincts at Ise, the traditional practice has been to reconstruct the entire complex in identical form every twenty years. All historical experience made it unlikely that this very expensive custom could have been carried out with anything like regularity, however, particularly during the long, medieval eclipse of the imperial house. At any rate the practice was instituted only in 685.

Though Professor Soper might have doubts about the regular practice in the early days, I am sure that it was done regularly from the beginning of the Tokugawa era till the present. I was told that the whole complex would be reconstructed in the next few years. It would be interesting to know whether the funds will be provided by the national treasury or from other sources. The immense amount needed for the reconstruction indicates how strongly the Shinto faith has taken hold in Japan. Moreover it is only the Japanese people with their innate sense for system and the keeping of festivals who could have kept such an institution in regular practice. This also helps me to understand why China has never set up a state religion. By now, everybody knows that Confucianism is not China's national religion, and there has never been a definite center for the worship of Confucius, whose tomb in Kufow of Shantung Province seldom received any imperial visits. The Confucian temples in the cities have no priests to conduct any services or any other festivals. When Buddhism came to China as a religion and more Buddhist monasteries were built in the fourth century, China was divided and in a great turmoil of futile strife. Those who suffered much mentally and physically sought sanctuary in Buddhism, but little attention was paid to its systematic development and financial organization. So Buddhism did not hold the Chinese very firmly and it suffered reverses from time to time. The Chinese Taoist religion came into being after the introduction of Buddhism but it also had no firm hold on all the Chinese, so there was no definite Taoist center in China for worship and no regular services have ever been held. As far as Chinese Christian converts are concerned, all the Chinese Christian activities have had to rely on financial support from outside and very little from China herself. I think the basic difference between the Chinese people and others is that they are fundamentally an agrarian people living entirely on what they can get out of the earth and have a rational way of thinking and a pragmatic attitude toward the land on which they live though they are religious in thinking like the rest.

Professor Alexander Soper had more to say about the Ise Daijingu:

> The so-called inner shrine, Naiku or Kodaijingu, is said to have been founded under Suinin, in the late third century A.D. The *Nihon Shoki* explains that in the reign of Sujun, his predecessor, an unexplained plague brought general panic. Ignorance made the emperor dread all unseen powers, even the formidable two who had hitherto been worshiped together in the great hall of his palace, his ancestress the Sun Goddess and the territorial god Yamato-no-Okunidama-no-kami. He removed their cults to a safe distance, while appointing his own daughter the chief priestess of a special shrine to the Sun Goddess. Under Suinin the latter was established permanently at Ise.

I am glad to know why Ise was chosen to be the safe center of the most sacred area for all Japan. Emperor Suinin could not have chosen a better center than Ise with sea in the front and Mt. Asama at the back. But many of my friends, including Professor Meyer Schapiro, and I questioned why Amaterasu-Omikami, the Sun Goddess, and not the sun god, should occupy the greatest dignity at the very center of the whole Shinto pantheon? In Chinese cosmology the sun is called T'ai Yang, or Great Yang—great male—and moon, T'ai Yin, or great Yin—great female—and partake of the Yin-Yang dualism. The sun and moon were always embroidered on the royal official robe of a Chinese emperor. It seems that the world over, the sun is a male god. But why did it become a goddess in Japan? Can this make us regard the Japanese as altogether a different species of human being, as they are descendants of the Sun Goddess? It is not irrelevant to point out that a Bodhisattva in India was a man who then came to China to become Kuan Yin, goddess of mercy, a female, who then went to Japan as Kwannon, still a female. Could it be that once the sun god stepped into Japanese territory it became a sun goddess in similar manner?

There was an ancient Ainu legend in which the sun was regarded as a female *kami* ("god") for she gave all the warmth and kindness to people, and the moon as a male kami because it is always cold and gave no life to anything. Matteo Ricci, an Italian Jesuit, in the late sixteenth century went to China. He reported that the main shrine at Macao was of the goddess of the sea, Ama, and that the Okinawan sea goddess was Ma or Ma-meko. Could these two indicate that Amaterasu was derived from them? But Amaterasu is a sun goddess, not a sea goddess. Some suggest that the ancient Japanese could have come from the southern tip of Korea, but the Koreans did not have the traditional legend of the Sun Goddess. However, though it is uncertain of how the Sun Goddess came to be the greatest ancestress of the Japanese imperial house, it is certain that all the Japanese from the ancient days have been sun worshipers, for their country's name in kanji, Nippon, means "the place where the sun rises." As Japan lies in the farthest eastern part of Asia, it is the general belief that the sun rises there. Though Japan has her rainy season as well as heavy snowfalls and typhoons, she enjoys more sunshine than many other places. That is perhaps why Japan enjoys a luxuriant growth of many important timber and flowering plants.

We were told that inside the Ise Daijingu there was no statue of the Sun Goddess, but three imperial treasures. The first imperial treasure is an eight-foot bronze mirror, or Yata-no-Kagami. The other two are a jewel and a sword. Three of them together signify "wisdom for the mirror, technique for the jewel, and strength for the sword." The sword at Ise was known to have the toki feather for decoration. The toki is a rare bird, found only in Japan (its scientific name *Nipponia nippon*) and is often called the Japanese crested ibis. I remember reading a story from a Japanese book entitled *Short Stories of Eminent Japanese in Ancient and Modern Times*, published in 1888, which tells roughly:

Yamatotake-no-Mikoto was the second son of the emperor Keiko. He was exceedingly bold and daring. In the twenty-seventh year of his father's reign a man named Kumaso Takeru headed a rebellion in the western quarter against the emperor, and the young prince was sent in charge of an expedition force to subdue him. When he reached the rebellion quarter, he disguised himself as a young girl and mixed with other girls to serve in the banquet to kill the rebel leader by a concealed dagger.

Some time after that event, the aboriginal tribes in the eastern provinces became insubordinate and caused much disturbance here and there. The young prince requested of his father to be sent to quiet them. The request was readily granted. He went first to the country of Ise to worship Daijingu (the Sun Goddess, the first ancestress of the imperial Japan). Then he paid a farewell visit to his aunt Yamato Hime, who was at the time a vestal virgin to the goddess Daijin. When the prince told his aunt of his mission, she kindly advised him and gave him, as a parting present, the divine sword—one of the three imperial treasures. The sword helped him to get out unhurt of a wicked plot by the treacherous chiefs.

Later the prince died at Nobonu in Ise at the age of thirty. The story does not mention whether the prince returned the imperial treasure sword, and I do not understand how the vestal virgin could give one of the three important treasures as a personal gift to her nephew. It is now known that the divine sword is one of the eight well known swords for the Yatsurungi Shrine at Atsuta Shrine not far from the city of Nagoya.

Shaking my head over the story about the divine sword, I went to join the rest of the party walking back along the pilgrimage route. The bright sun had attracted many more people to visit the Ise Daijingu. Presently we reached an open space where a stage was set up for the sacred Shinto dance. Many people were already sitting and standing before the stage. A sacred Shinto dance named Ranryo-o was going on. A dancer wearing a brilliant reddish brown robe and a dragon's head mask and with a long spear moving in both hands danced slowly while an orchestra was playing music to match the steps. I read that this dance originated in the story of the Chinese hero Lan-ling-wang or Ch'ang-kung (Chinese pronunciation) of the Northern Ch'i dynasty (sixth century), who was the fourth son of Emperor Wen-hsiang and who with five hundred men went to do battle against the army of the Chou house. He wore a mask and when he was badly pressed by the enemy he took it off and his soldiers seeing he was the prince dashed up to save him. So the great battle was won and everyone on his side was happy and sang a song of victory on their return. The song became known as Lang-Ling-Wang-ju-Ch'en-Chü, or the song of Prince Lan-ling entering battle. This song and dance have been lost in China for hundreds of years.

After the first dance there was a short intermission. Not having a seat, I moved round to the back of the stage and saw four actors in brilliant yellow brown silk robes with black headgear about to step on the stage. When the music began, the four actors came forward, made a ceremonial bow, and then stepped backward a bit, and continued with a slow movement of bodies and limbs. This sacred dance seemed to be the Manzai-Raku, which is said to represent the phoenix and is a prominent congratulatory dance. It lasted twenty minutes, a little longer than the first one, giving me time to make a series of sketches showing the postures of the dancers' bodies. While the dance was still on, white petals from the cherry trees were floating down, adding new color to the whole scene of the red-painted posts of the platform, the yellow brown silk robes, two highly decorated fanlike screens at the back, and the fresh green needles of the tall pines surrounding all. The most sacred dance, Yamata-Mai, peculiar to the Grand Shrine of Ise, was not performed on that occasion. Nor did I see the well-known butterfly dance, or Kocho, said to have been composed over a thousand years ago by Tadafusa Fujiwara for the emperor Uda. I was quite contented to have seen the two sacred dances. The sound of the wind in the trees reached us like a caress. What a peaceful, dreamlike place it seemed to be!

As we moved toward the first torii to cross the Uji Bridge, a gentle breeze was heading our way and under the bright warm April sun it produced such a soothing effect. Even with many people moving about I had seldom experienced such a tranquil scene before and I composed the following two little poems:

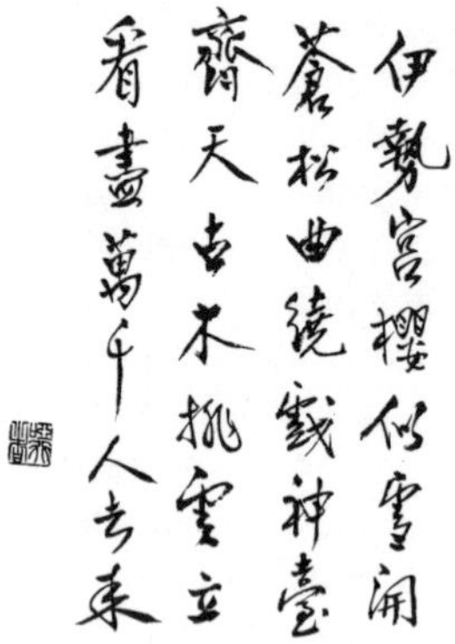

伊勢宮櫻似雪開
蒼松曲繞戲神臺
齋天古木挑雲立
看畫萬千人去來

Visiting Ise Daijingu

The Ise Daijingu opens to me with cherry blossoms like snow;
The green pines wind their way to surround the sacred dancing stage.
Those lofty trees, reaching the sky, stand together like masses of clouds,
Having observed thousands of people coming and going.

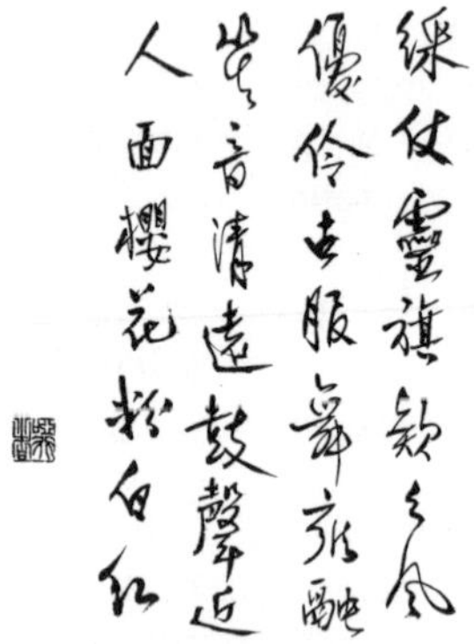

綠仗靈旗欸欸風
優伶古服舞�'融
芋音清遠鼓聲近
人面櫻花粉白紅

Witnessing the Sacred Dance

The decorated staffs with the divine banners sway in the wind gently,
The actors wearing ancient robes dance with grace.
The sounds of the bamboo pipes are pure in the distance while the drums sound quite close;
Human faces and cherry blossoms vie pink and white.

Leaving the Ise Daijingu, our bus went along the Ise-Shima Skyline Drive with the sea far, far away on one side and the high and thickly wooded mountains on the other, providing the eyes with a succession of many delicate tints vanishing into the distance and blending with the opalescent waters of the bay and the pale blue of the sky. The route is highly picturesque, one superb panorama succeeding another all the way.

Unexpectedly our bus stopped in an open ground. Our guide led us on foot to the Futamigaura Beach to see the Wedded Rocks, called Meoto-iwa in Japanese. The two rocks stood out from the shore; on the larger a torii was erected and a big straw rope around the top of it extended to the smaller rock to which it was also fastened. They were likened to the creators of Japan, Izanagi and Izanami. The rocks were

The Wedded Rocks

worshiped with a great ceremony each January 5 and a new straw rope replaced the old one every year.

On our way back from the beach we looked at an enormous stone frog supposed to be the frog deity. By it there was a water tank with wooden spoons for people to wash mouths and hands. Opposite the shrine were two small shops selling souvenirs of small frogs in gilt, silver, and porcelain. I bought a tiny gilded frog and also a porcelain one. I had seen carved wood frogs of different sizes in many gift shops in other cities and I can now understand why the Japanese worship the frog deity. My friend Ivan Morris told me that the sound of the Japanese word for frog can mean two things, "frog" and "to return." It has been a custom that when a Japanese went to war his parents or older relations would give him a small frog for a keepsake, to wish for the bearer's safe return. To remember the occasion I composed the following little verse:

The Frog Deity

One by one the cherry petals are flying in late
    spring;
They fly to the cloudy sky to vie with the setting
    sun.
After having seen the roped Wedded Rocks,
I also follow the others to buy a porcelain frog.

春深漸く萱櫻花
飛向白雪天閒晚霞
看罷繩牵夫婦石
也隨游伴買磁蛙

IX

Cultured Pearls and Toba

WITH THE bright sun gleaming on the hills, trees, houses, and roads, our bus made a slightly uphill journey and stopped in front of a modern building—the Toba Kowaki-en—for lunch. The hotel, built on an enormous rocky promontory, was a solitary structure commanding a wide view of the Ago Bay, on which a number of islets were scattered in an intricate pattern.

Presently we all went down to the ferryboat for Mikimoto Pearl Island. It was not a large island but the whole surface was well paved. Many nicely shaped pine trees were growing along the edge of the island and there were a few stone monuments; one carried an edict from Emperor Hirohito, praising the inventor's life work in perfecting the method of cultivating pearls, and another was a stone statue of the inventor, Kokichi Mikimoto. We went round the Mikimoto Pearl Hall, where a series of pictures on the walls told of the history and hardships Mikimoto had gone through in perfecting his method. In the middle of the hall were a number of stands and behind each sat a young girl to demonstrate a step of the work to us. She picked up an unopened oyster,

A girl trying to pick out a pearl

opened it, and then using a pair of pointed tweezers took out the already cultured pearl. At another stand we were shown how the pearls differed in color, slightly pinkish or grayish in shade, and at still another how a small hole was drilled through the tiny pearl. Around a long stand two young women were selling strand after strand of pearls. I then noticed a stand with the Mikimoto Liberty Bell, modeled after the Liberty Bell in Philadelphia, but encrusted with 12,250 Mikimoto cultured pearls. It had been shown at the New York International Exposition in 1939. I wondered at the time why Philadelphia's Liberty Bell had been chosen as the model and not something typically Japanese, say a Japanese stone lantern.

Kokichi Mikimoto, a native of Toba, when he was forty years old perceived the possibility of producing pearls artificially. He studied the subject deeply and established a farm for the culture at Ago Bay in Mie Prefecture. He put all the money he had into the work and devoted all his energy to it, but failed repeatedly. His relatives and friends laughed at his stupidity at trying to do the impossible, but none of this daunted him a bit. Eventually he succeeded in producing semispherical pearls in 1894 and was granted a patent two years later. Not satisfied with the result, he went on to perfect his method, and in another ten years he had produced cultured pearls equal in luster, odor, and shape to the finest natural pearls. He soon became the pearl magnate of Japan.

Mikimoto at first thought that a foreign substance had to be introduced into the oyster as necessary for the formation of the pearl, but his most important finding was when he later discovered that the pearl sac was formed spontaneously from a disease. Then he found a way to encourage the disease to spread and was able to produce more and more cultured pearls each year.

The present Mikimoto Company now maintains a pearl oyster farm at Gokasho Bay, Ago Bay, Basama Bay, Hikimoto Bay, Kata Bay, Omura Bay, Nanao Bay, Tanabe Bay, Yaeyama Island, Palao Island, and many other places. They claim to have cultivated altogether between three and four million pearl oysters annually. These pearls are sold all over the world.

Leaving the hall, we were guided to the Ama stand. Ama is the name for women divers, and we watched five of them dressed in thin white cloth with bare feet and a white towel round their heads dive from a boat, carrying a round wooden tub. Wearing goggles, each dived down deep to where they picked up the wild oysters from the ocean floor. All these wild oysters were then gathered together and put into the culturing cages, invented by Mikimoto, which were then hung from floating rafts to form the pearl oyster farm in the bay. These Amas were very swift in their movements and efficient in gathering oysters. It was obvious the bay was rich in wild oysters, but I could not help wondering why the divers were all women, and no men. In all my travels in Japan, women seemed to do all kinds of work: in the rice fields, on the farms, in the markets, in the department stores, in the hotels and inns, in all types of offices and shops, and on some islands there are naked fishing girls. Where are the Japanese men? Does Japan have more women than men?

I did not go back to the bus with the rest to continue the tour, for I had made arrangements to stay in Kowaki-en for the night. I strolled along a short narrow street, a part of the city of Toba, and noticed the shops on both sides selling all kinds of fresh seafood, which must have been local delicacies. I went into the small local zoological garden and saw a woman dive into a deep pool to feed the fish. At the corner which leads up to the Kowaki-en I was interested in an old Japanese type of house beside which was a rock monument with the kanji words Kadono Ikunoshin Sensei, who was evidently a noted personality. Immediately the well-known priest Toba Sojo came into my mind and I remembered reading about him. He was named Kakuyu, the former head of Enray-kuji Temple of the Tendai sect, and he retired and lived in Toba. He was an artist and loved to paint the local life and social conditions of the time with a broad touch of humor. Owing to the satirical manner of his painting, people loved them. His style became known as Toba-e. He once drew a picture of many rice bales being blown about in the air and the local people trying to hold them up. This was shown to the emperor Shirakawa, who summoned Toba Sojo for an explanation. It seemed that many people did not fill the bales with rice, which was supposed to go to the government in payment for tax, but with husks in order to avoid the payment. The people tried to hold on to them and not let them be blown away in order to cheat the collectors. The emperor was pleased with this discovery and proceeded to enforce the law for the payment with genuine rice. Toba Sojo, who died in 1146, was supposed to be the first caricaturist in Japan; nothing of the kind had appeared before his work. The two best known Japanese hand scrolls of animal caricatures, one about monkeys and frogs and the other horses and cows, were attributed to Toba Sojo. I am very fond of the monkey and frog scroll, which is in the collection of Kaoron-ji, Kyoto; no one could have painted it except a master. His lines are so free yet so sure and his composition so well balanced in spacing yet so original. With Toba Sojo's work for a precedent we can better understand Hokusai's humorous treatment of his subjects.

I boarded a small steamer for a cruise round the bay. Not too many people came on board and I found a good place on the upper deck. The steamer darted between the different islands, which seemed to rush aside

Kadono Ikunoshin Sensei

to make way for it. Many hawks and eagles were circling high above but not many sea gulls. Most of the small islands round Ago Bay are like round buns with pines and other trees on their heights and with brownish rocky bases at sea level; they are beautiful to see as a group. Our steamer moved close to the land that faces the rocky hill where the Kowaki-en stands. This now looked like a squarish white box stuck on a dark green carpet. When the steamer reached the center of the bay, I noticed three cormorants standing on a big rock close by and one was just swallowing a big fish. A few minutes later two of the cormorants dived into the sea for some more fish.

The sun was then setting and through the golden light over the sea, the islands, and the Kowaki-en on the top of the rocky hill, the whole scene appeared like a vision, unreal, when I stepped inside the building for dinner. I never slept sounder than that night at Toba Kowaki-en!

In the stillness of the bright sunny morning, under a blue sky of exquisite beauty, a rather dense haze had spread an ethereal veil over the bay with many of the islands obscured. After a while I located Mikimoto Pearl Island. On leaving Toba Kowaki-en I was still pondering over the cultured pearls. Pearls have been regarded as precious gems since time immemorial. Pearls in their real, natural states have always been rare, so they are precious. Since the invention of cultured pearls by Kokichi Mikimoto, pearls have not been considered so precious as before, yet they are still gems. Whenever the word *pearl* is mentioned to a woman or girl, her eyes suddenly become brighter and sparkling and an involuntary smile spreads over her face. Like all the women and girls in the world, Chinese women love pearls too. However, there is one story of a lady in Chinese history who had no love for pearls. It has touched me deeply. In the early eighth century Emperor Ming Huang dearly loved a court lady whose surname was Chiang (not the same as my surname). She so much loved the winter-plum blossom, which was called mei in Chinese, that the emperor enfiefed her as Lady Winter-plum, or Mei-fei. She was born in P'u-t'ien of Fukien Province and had been brought to the court by the famous eunuch Kao Li-shih. As soon as the emperor saw her, he was infatuated by her beauty as well as by her talent, for she was a poetess. She was the emperor's favorite for a year or so till the arrival of another lady, Yang Yü-huan. The latter soon took her place and Lady Mei-fei was then removed to an inner palace far from the emperor. Though the emperor was enraptured with the new favorite, who was soon enfiefed as Yang Kuei-fei, the renowned female figure in Chinese history, he thought occasionally of Mei-fei. Once the emperor sent her a tiny bushel of pearls. She returned the pearls to His Majesty with the following poem:

柳葉雙眉久不描
殘妝和淚濕紅絹
長門自是無梳洗
何必珍珠慰寂寥

My two eyebrows, like willow leaves, have long
    not been painted;
The remnants of my making-up mingle with
    tears to wet my red silk dress.
Within the tall doors I voluntarily neglect my
    hair and complexion;
Of what use are pearls to comfort my loneliness?

Ming Huang was a musician and loved the poem so much that he composed a melody entitled "Yi Hu Chu," or "A Bushel of Pearls." He ordered his court musicians to play and sing it. Unfortunately this piece of music has not survived for us to hear, for it is likely to have suffered much from the jealousy of Yang Kuei-fei. Thus, we see that pearls are not everything in a woman's life. Something else is more important!

X

Romantic Kyoto

EVER SINCE I read Arthur Waley's translation of *The Tale of Genji*, and also his abridged translation of *The Pillow Book*, it has puzzled me how Japan as early as the eleventh century could have produced two such unusually gifted women as Murasaki Shikibu and Sei Shonagon. These two women served in the same court and were deeply learned in Chinese studies, which at that time were still new to Japan. My puzzle is as follows. Before the tenth century China had already produced a number of gifted women writers and particularly in the T'ang court during the eighth century when Yang Kuei-fei was a great favorite of the emperor Ming Huang (713–756) and most of the hundreds of court ladies could be regarded as well versed in poetry and familiar with the writings of the great poets of the time. Before that, the powerful and gifted empress Wu Chao (624–705), unequalled in Chinese history before or since, published a hundred volumes under the title *Ch'ui-Kung-Chi*, and she was said to have suppressed men and promoted women in her palaces. Although many of those gifted women writers could have created something similar to what Murasaki and Shonagon did, they did not leave anything which we can admire and read in the present day.

I think the difference lies in the way of making use of the Chinese language, and also in the form of the literary work at which each aimed in her writing. Though both Murasaki and Shonagon knew Chinese, neither wrote their works in Chinese. It must be understood that the Japanese had adopted Chinese characters about the beginning of the fifth century, if not earlier. In those early days many Japanese took great pride in their knowledge of Chinese and wrote in the fashion of Chinese. Poetry and essays and even some official documents were entirely in Chinese. However, the Chinese language was not used by the Japanese women writing at the time, as Shonagon remarked in her *Pillow Book*.

Murasaki wrote fiction and Shonagon wrote a diary, both forms regarded as unprecedented in Japanese literature and which also had not ever been used in China at that time or since. The Chinese written language was invented to record things and events in very concise expressions and not for use in writing very detailed accounts or narratives, for there was no need for these some four or five thousand years ago. This original function of the Chinese written language seems to have been preserved well into the present day. If we look through the earliest Chinese records written in the oracle shell-and-bone scripts which existed in the sixteenth and seventeenth centuries B.C., we can see how the early Chinese recorded their answers to the king's question about whether there had been a good or bad harvest that particular year, with the simple character for *good* or *bad*. Though the actual characters for good harvest read "shou lien," in those early days not many characters were invented beyond those for simple expressions. If the ancient scripts could have been employed for more detailed descriptions, we would be able to know much more about ancient Chinese life. Thus the development of Chinese literature continued to show a preference for concise expression, and even in narrative works, the shorter they were, the better. In Confucian times, the book *Ch'un Ch'iu* was specially valued for its great care in the choice of single words and its wonderfully concise expression. By the time of the T'ang period countless books had been written and published by Chinese writers, generally written in the concise style, for the style of the newly translated Buddhist literature had not yet become popular among all Chinese. The emphasis on the concise arrangement of words, sentences, and paragraphs may account for the slow development of storytelling and fiction writing in China. If Murasaki and Shonagon had employed the Chinese written language for their writings, they could not have done much better than all the Japanese men did. Shonagon wrote, "Women's language was traditionally less influenced by Chinese and contained a much larger portion of 'pure' Japanese words and constructions." Therefore we must realize that Japanese literature has not worn a Chinese cloak after all.

Both Murasaki and Shonagon wrote about the intimacy between men and women in the Heian courts, but those events described could not have happened so easily in China's court. Though much political and romantic intrigue might have occurred then, no one would have dared to describe them in detail in writing. Confucius himself might not have intended to separate men from women in society, but the Han Confucianists had cut a deep moat between men and women since the third century B.C. The Chinese Confucianists, chiefly moralists, strictly upheld this separation. Owing to this strict custom, which was supported by law, the free dialogue between men and women progressed from a simple greeting to a few common remarks among persons of the same ranks and generations, and never developed into anything like conversational discussions or arguments for a plot of a lengthy story or a complete novel. Though *The Tale of Genji* is fiction, the un-Confucian conduct of the shining prince could not have been tolerated in the T'ang palace. Besides, the lady's chamber would be inaccessible to the prince or any man. For instance, the following song, which was sung by one of the ladies in waiting as described by Shonagon:

> Who shall share my bed tonight?
> Hitachi no Suke—he's my man!
> His skin is soft to touch,

could not possibly have been sung in China's court under the moralists' principles. Chinese men of letters, particularly the T'ang poets, could turn out verse after verse very quickly on any suitable occasion, but none of them wrote about any little incident as Genji did to many ladies. No doubt many books of T'ang poems had circulated in Heian Japan, which Murasaki and Shonagon must have read. Their genius and talent inspired them to incorporate poems in their prose writings, which made delightful reading. But I am not sure if Shonagon really knew many T'ang poems well. For instance, she wrote that "the parrot does not belong to our country, but I like it very much. I am told that it imitates whatever people say." This means that she did not know the following famous lines in a well-known T'ang poem by Chu Ching-yü:

Full of emotion and desirous to discuss the
    court matters,
They dare not talk in front of the parrot.

This poem touched on the subtle sentiment of two court ladies at the point of gossiping and also showed that there were parrots in the T'ang palace which could easily imitate people's remarks. These lines also indicate that little gossip prevailed inside the T'ang court. If Shonagon knew these lines, she would have undoubtedly quoted them, as she used many references before. The greatness of Ivan Morris's new translation of *The Pillow Book* matches that of Arthur Waley's *The Tale of Genji*, for both of which I feel nothing but admiration. Once I questioned the word *nightingale*, which appeared in Waley's translation several times. Mr. Sei Ito told me there were no nightingales in Japan and I agreed that there were no nightingales in China either. Only in well-known English poetry does the nightingale appear often. But what was that bird in *The Tale of Genji* exactly?

Anyone who has read the translations of Murasaki's and Shonagon's works would want to see Kyoto, though Kyoto has many other attractions as well. I for one went not only once but four or five times. Kyoto's attraction for me is its way of living from the Heian period to the present day. Kyoto is to me a romantic city overall—historically, politically, socially, as well as sentimentally. I do not lament changes, for I take change as a natural consequence of time. Once Professor Paul Varley quoted to me what was said in the *Chronicle of Onin*:

> The flowery capital which was expected to last for thousands of years has now become the lair of foxes and wolves. . . . Although there have been disorders and vicissitudes since ancient times, in this conflict of Onin even the Buddhist and imperial laws have been destroyed.

Much of the Onin war was fought within the confines of Kyoto, as Paul remarked, and it left the city an almost total ruin. This happened in 1467 and 1477. Thus not many of the things of the Heian period of the last part of the fifteenth century are in existence. But the rulers and people of Kyoto have kept reviving the past, though modified at times, in the best way they could. And new things were added. Kyoto has long been one of the show places of Japan. The rulers and the people of Kyoto have exerted their energy in a combined effort to keep this remarkable city alive all the time. This is the great spirit of Kyoto and also the great spirit of Japan. It is this spirit that I have gone to see in Kyoto again and again.

There are so many interesting centers to see in Kyoto. The well-organized people of Kyoto provide guides who can speak English and

Outside of the old Imperial Palace

even German if necessary, but not Chinese, which means that not too many Chinese have come to see this illustrious city. I did not ask for an English-speaking guide, nor did I join a tour chiefly for English-speaking visitors. I took the set tours arranged by the local authority probably for the Japanese themselves and completed their ten sets of tours on successive days, though it meant revisiting many places. I did not understand what the guides were saying or singing on the way. This has always been my bad habit, that before I travel to any new place I read nothing about it, for I want to get my own first impressions which would draw me back again. Of course this needs time, and time is a most important factor in our modern life. After having seen almost thirty different places in my several stays in Kyoto, I then tried to visualize them and read about them and then went to see some of them again. The impressions which came most vividly to my mind were of the old Imperial Palace, which we were not allowed to enter, for the present imperial heads were in residence at the time. But we managed to see something of it from the outside.

The second object that impressed me was the powerful panel painting of a hawk on a well-twisted branch of pine with emerald needles by Kano Tanyu at Nijo Castle. Tanyu's keen aesthetic sense for composition, with well-placed space and his shaping the pine branches to spread horizontally in a most natural manner while the hawk, naturalistically rendered, suggests its intention to fly away in the right place—a space in the golden background—interested me much. No one could deny that the group looked real, but its reality was heightened by the artist's strength, present even in a single needle of the pine. This is a typically Japanese creation and many of the Japanese long scrolls that illustrated *The Tale of Genji* and other narrative stories bear little Chinese influence. Though Tanyu's panel painting came from a long Japanese tradition in making screen-paintings, it was Tanyu who broke away from figure subject matter to a free, naturalistic rendering of nature's phenomena that made Japanese screen-painting famous in its own way. There are several other panel paintings in Nijo Castle painted by Tanyu's followers of the Kano school but none reached the greatness of Tanyu's work.

Nijo Castle was built in 1603 by order of Tokugawa Iyeyasu as his Kyoto residence. How often Iyeyasu stayed in Nijo Castle was not recorded; his days were chiefly spent in the Edo Castle (now the modern Imperial Palace in Tokyo) conducting the nation's affairs. Nevertheless he was known as one of the great patrons of art. His choice of Kano Tanyu to paint the great panels in the Nijo Castle showed his artistic taste and was the start of the Kano school of painting, the main product of the Tokugawa period.

Though the Onin war had almost wiped out every trace of the early landmarks of the city, I could not help wanting to locate the places where Murasaki and Shonagon actually lived and which they described in so much detail in the early eleventh century. I was advised that I would find some traces of them in the Heian Shrine, which is modeled on the old palace, rebuilt on the present site after the fire of 1788, and completed in 1790. The original palace built in 794 by the emperor Kammu, about which Murasaki and Shonagon talked often, was in the eastern quarter of the city, where the Heian Shrine now stands. I went there twice. The shrine, dedicated to the emperor Kammu and also to the emperor Komei, who was recently enshrined there, was built in 1895 to commemorate the 1,100th anniversary of the founding of Kyoto by the emperor Kammu. The Japanese Official Guide told me that the Shinden (main hall), Daigokuden (Great Hall of State), two towers, Otemmon (main gate), and Otorii (large ferro-concrete gate) are replicas on a reduced scale of the first Imperial Palace and are all brightly colored. Actually the last two words, *brightly colored,* as I looked at them had smashed into pieces my fancy imagination in trying to visualize how Murasaki and Shonagon carried out their royal service duties. These buildings gave me no illusions and I did not go inside. With white and red paint for the walls and wooden structures brilliantly lit by the sunshine, it looked so new and fresh as if it had been finished only a month or two before I came. The Japanese were reputed to be the great tradition lovers of the world, but I wonder why they did not leave something to refresh the memory of those who have so enjoyed reading Murasaki's

Lady Murasaki in the procession

and Shonagon's writings of the old Kyoto. However, I was told that the annual festival on October 22, dedicated to the shrine and called Jidai Matsuri, had the great feature of an interesting procession through the city, composed of groups dressed to represent different periods in the history of Kyoto including one for Lady Murasaki. Many participants represented the shogun's suite when he visited the Imperial Palace, and a procession of court nobles in the Fujiwara period (897–1185).

I could not be in Kyoto in October, but I was there in the cherry blossom season for a good round of the garden behind the shrine. Close by the back of the two wing buildings, the Soryu-ro ("Green dragon") and the Byakko-ro ("White tiger"), were a few skeleton structures of wood supporting a number of beautiful pink weeping cherries in full bloom. With the dark trunk in the center and the blossom-loaded branches drooping all round, they looked like some special cherry blossom umbrellas which shaded the Sun Goddess and her retinue ready for a great procession through the ancient city of Kyoto. I have never seen such beautifully shaped cherry trees blooming in their fullness. On one hand they were enhanced by the bright sunshine and on the other by the supporting vermillion pillars and the whitewashed walls of the Soryu-ro and Byakko-ro buildings close by the sacred lake, with well-trained pine trees here and there. I was told that there were several kinds of cherries such as Samei Yoshino, Yomazakura, and Atsumonozakura in this palace garden and some of them have been blooming in April and early May for the past eighty years.

After following some other visitors across the stepping stones in the lake I went to relax a bit in the covered bridge called Donobashi ("Bridge Palace"). I leaned on the window sill watching the large red and white goldfish swimming gracefully in the water while a number of ducks and their ducklings floated about quacking. Many students in their school uniforms walked through the long Bridge Palace without stopping. An elderly Japanese in black kimono was leaning against one of the pillars with his legs stretched out on the window bench. He had an interesting face with white eyebrows, white mustache, and long white beard and looked as if he had come out of a Chinese painting of the late Ming period. He kept smiling at me whenever I turned my head, and I thought he had taken me to be one of his fellow countrymen. So I stepped toward him and wrote a few words in kanji on a piece of paper explaining that I was Chinese. To my surprise he then wrote back on the same paper, saying "Eighty-one years of age, a merchant selling sport equipments, named Ezaburo Zushi, living at Sanzyo-sagaru, Nakagyo-ku, Kyoto." I gave him a good handshake and wrote again that I was admiring him for taking time for the quiet enjoyment of the lovely season in the holy garden. He returned me a compliment that there must be more beautiful places for quiet enjoyment in China. We continued our written kanji conversation for a while. It was an unexpected, unusual experience. I could not help admiring his leisurely pose in such a tranquil surrounding. His kanji writing strengthened my confidence in being able to travel through Japan without knowing the native language.

Murasaki Shikibu also spent some time in Uji where *The Lady of the Lake*, the seventh book of *The Tale of Genji*, was set. So I took myself to see the Byodoin Temple on the west bank of the river Uji. It was originally built as a villa for the prime minister Fujiwara Michinaga (966–1024) and was converted into a monastery in 1052. The main hall of the building, the Phoenix Hall, built in 1053, is still intact as an example of the best religious architecture of the period. The Onin war did not touch this section, which is a little way out of the city. The architectural plan of the building is said to be an exact copy of a T'ang pavilion of the Western Paradise, but I cannot vouch for this, for I do not remember seeing any building like it in my own country. The hall was designed to feature a phoenix, or ho-o, a fabulous bird of Chinese origin, in the attitude of descending to the ground, with the central hall for the body and the lateral corridors on either side for the wings and the rear corridor for the tail. Its architectural symmetry seen from outside as a whole with vermillion beams and pillars was most impressive. On the top of the central hall stand a pair of phoenixes, one male and one female, about to take flight. They were originally bronze but Professor Burton Watson told me that after having stood there for centuries, the bronze figures were replaced by a new pair carved in wood, for the air pollution in recent years was corroding the original pair, which are now well protected in cases as national treasures. I specially liked this building and its setting on the bank of the pond with many water lilies in bloom at its front, and beautiful pines on both sides, though I wish the pond could be bigger to give more air to the building. A large number of purple irises on the left completed the whole color scheme for a good painting for me.

From the Byodoin Temple I went to see the Ishiyama-dera Temple, where a small room is still preserved as it was when used by Lady Murasaki for the eighth full moon of 1007 to write her seventh book of *The Tale of Genji*. A few sheets of paper, ink, and a broken brush were there, as they were the materials used by that illustrious woman writer.

The interesting arrangement of various rocks on well-swept sand patterned with parallel wavy lines in the small garden of Ryoanji Temple caused many to halt their steps in awe and inspiration. I was no exception, though the whole layout was quite strange to my Chinese eyes. This is a Zen garden, or a garden representing Zen principles, long acclaimed for its simplicity, its aesthetic value of having so little yet

A monk lecturing in front
of the rock garden

meaning so much and its entrancing magic for meditation. I grant it all these things and I also admire the person who first devised it with white sand for its base, but to call it a garden requires a change in the usual definition of what a garden is. A garden to me generally means an enclosed place of ground devoted to the cultivation of flowers, fruits, or vegetables, or some ornamental ground used as a place for relaxation and enjoyment. This small plot of few rocks and sand at the Ryoanji Temple serves neither purpose. It can be regarded as an artistic creation with the ground for the canvas and the rocks and sand for the mediums instead of ink or color pigments. Its size must be limited, for it cannot be too small, which would have no meaning, nor can it be too big, which would destroy its function to entrance the onlookers and invite meditation. Being a purely aesthetic creation, it is understandable and appreciated for its attractive quality. The Chinese love to arrange some rugged-shaped, grotesque rocks in their gardens, as one can see from Chinese paintings by Sung masters (960–1279) and there are many famous gardens in China which still have natural rocks in their original settings. The Chinese seldom had any man-made sculpture in their gardens, for they thought of rocks as being the bones of the earth and possessing beautiful shapes as sculpted by Nature, thus avoiding any air of artificiality in the whole arrangement, as I mentioned in the Nagoya chapter. The Chinese prefer rocks that have been eroded by the action of water in rivers and lakes, and that have natural holes. The more solid forms of rocks, like those in the Ryoanji Temple, are seldom to be found in Chinese gardens. The Chinese plant flowers, fruits, or other plants by the rocks to enhance their naturalness. The rock setting on sand in the Ryoanji garden is a typical Japanese creation, not Chinese.

The Daisen-in Temple is a part of Daitokuji Temple, which is the headquarters of the Kaitoku-ji school of the Rinzai sect of Zen Buddhism. I visited Daitokuji Temple twice in order to see some special objects. One was the teahouse which Dr. Daisetz T. Suzuki described fully:

> Where a series of flagstones irregularly arranged comes to step, there stands a most insignificant-looking straw-thatched hut, low and unpretentious to the last degree. The entrance is not by a door but by a sort of aperture; to enter through it a visitor has to be shorn of all his encumbrances, that is to say, to take off both his swords, long and short, which in feudal days a samurai used to carry all the time. The inside is a small semi-lighted room about ten feet square; the ceiling is low and of uneven height and structure. The posts are not smoothly planed, they are mostly of natural wood. After a little while, however, the room gradually becomes lighter as our eyes begin to adjust themselves to the new situation. We notice an ancient-looking kakemono [meaning "scroll" in Japanese] in the above with some handwriting

In meditation

or a picture of Sumi-e type. An incense burner emits a fragrance which has the effect of soothing one's nerves. The flower vase contains no more than a single stem of flower, neither gorgeous nor ostentatious; but like a little white lily blooming under a rock surrounded by in no way sombre pines, the humble flower is enhanced in beauty and attracts the attention of the gathering of four or five visitors especially invited to sip a cup of tea in order to forget the worldly cares that may be pressing them.

I did not manage to see the inside of that teahouse, for it was closed. But I have been present at the tea ceremony, or *chanoyu* as the Japanese call it, elsewhere on many occasions. While watching the movement of the girls in geisha hairdress and flowing colored kimonos, it was a different world altogether. I talked with a number of young Tokyo friends in coffee houses and they all said that they preferred to drink coffee, for they could not afford the time to go through the tea ceremony. Yet there are still schools in Japan for training young girls to be tea hostesses.

An interesting point is that the northern Chinese call this special kind of beverage *cha*, so the Japanese call it *cha*, for Japan is close to Northern China. But the southern Chinese call this beverage *te*, so the English when they contacted China in Canton in the sixteenth century took the sound *te* to invent the word *tea*, which first appeared in English dictionaries in the late sixteenth century. As the English language is more internationally in use, so the world knows about *tea* instead of *cha*. I was told that the Uji area is the tea-growing center of Japan. But I don't know what kind of tea grows there; the Japanese green powdered tea used in the tea ceremonies is the bright green tea leaves dried and then powdered. One has to swallow the powder with the liquid. This green powdered tea, called *matcha*, was made by a method devised by the fifteenth-century Zen Buddhist priest Shuko, who was generally considered the originator of the Japanese tea ceremony. I don't remember this kind of powdered tea on sale in China and I came from a city surrounded by the tea-growing area and it was a center for all tea merchants. I have never drunk the green powdered tea in China, nor could I take it very well in Japan.

Another object I wanted to see in Daitokuji Temple was its treasure hall where a good many Chinese paintings by Sung masters are preserved. There used to be a whole set of Chinese paintings of five hundred arhats in Japan painted in A.D. 1178 by Lin Ting-kuei and Chou Ch'i-ch'ang. Each one depicted a group of five holy men as the principal theme. The whole set consists of one hundred hanging scrolls and they were taken from China to Japan in the thirteenth century and deposited at the Jufukuji Temple at Kamakura. Later they were transferred to Soun-ji at Hakone by the powerful Hojo family, which supported that monastery. Again they were removed by Toyotomi Hideyoshi in 1590 to Kyoto and were presented to Hokoji, a temple founded by him. Eventually eighty-two of the hundred became the property of Daitokuji, while two others are in a private collection. The remaining sixteen are now in the Boston Museum of Fine Arts. I often went to Boston to see them. Since I was in Kyoto I naturally wanted to see the eighty-two if possible. But an arrangement to see them could not be made in time. There are four other famous paintings by a Sung Ch'an master painter, Mu Chi, also in the treasure hall of Daitokuji; three of the four have often been reproduced in books on Chinese and Japanese art. In particular one of the four, an ink painting of six persimmons in monotone, has become specially famous, for it is widely reproduced in books on Zen Buddhism. Anyone who sees this painting cannot help admiring the artist's skill in applying the gradation of the ink colors on four of the persimmons while two have only a light contour line to suggest the shape of the fruit. The whole arrangement shows the dimension of each persimmon in relation to the others in an artless, perfectly simple composition. Each persimmon is placed in its correct position—no other arrangement could be better, and no other brush strokes need be added to express what the artist wanted to convey. Though so economical in strokes, it is full of feeling and meaning. Few writers have explained what the artist had in mind with this work, but everyone claims it as a Zen painting simply because the artist was a Ch'an master. I find the work to have a profound meaning. In it there are six persimmons. Six is a number often used in Buddhist sutras. The Chinese have long made use of written characters for pun symbolism. For instance, the sound in Chinese for *persimmon* is pronounced "shih." In Buddhism there is a phrase "lu shih cheng chiu": 六事成就 meaning the six things which enable a Bodhisattva to keep perfectly the six paramitas: (1) worshipful offerings, (2) study of moral duties, (3) pity, (4) zeal in goodness, (5) isolation, and (6) delight in the law. The character for *thing* is pronounced "shih," so this painting symbolizes the six particular things of Buddhism which the artist-monk had in mind. To me it suggests even better the Buddhistic "lu shih" 六識 耳識 目識 鼻識 口識 意識 觸識 arising from the six organs of the senses, which are ear, eye, nose, tongue, mind, and body. In other words the six organs produce the senses of (1) hearing, (2) seeing, (3) smelling, (4) tasting, (5) feeling, and (6) touching. The nothingness of Zen in Ch'an preaching is achieved through meditation, the aim of which is to be rid of all human emotions which could be caused by any of the six senses. The Chinese character for *sense* is also pronounced "shih," similar to that for *persimmon*. Therefore the six persimmons in this painting could mean "six senses" which the artist-monk meant to be rid of. I am very interested in this painting and have used it to illustrate Ch'an principles.

One afternoon Burton Watson and I went to see the Gold Pavilion of the Rokuonji Temple. We reached the place in rain, and it was packed with school boys and girls. We could not find a space from which to have a good view of the building and its setting, but Burton told me to look at one thing which I had not previously known about. It was the pine-tree boat, regarded as the best example of artificially shaped pines in the whole of Japan. The shape of a sailing boat was made of a single pine-tree boat, regarded as the best example of artificially shaped pines branch of a young pine had been bent at an angle to form the hull of the boat while the trunk was left to grow to form the sail. Later Burton took me up a winding footpath behind the Gold Pavilion and then crossing a small stream, I noticed a sign with three kanji words "Hu-Hsi Chiao," or Bridge of Tiger Stream. I made an exclamation of joy, saying that this was the name of a bridge high up on my native Mt. Lu. I related to Burton a story which my father told to me when I was a boy of ten and which was described in my book *A Chinese Childhood*:

The temple (Tung-lin-tzu) was very famous in China in the fourth century, when a scholar monk named Hui-yuan gathered eighteen other scholars and monks to form a Buddhist Institute which bore the name of Pai-lien-she (White Lotus Society). The best known poet of the time, Hsieh Lin-yun, was refused admission because his daily conduct was not above reproach. Another well-known poet, T'ao Chien (T'ao Yuan-ming), was offered membership but accepted only on condition that he be allowed to drink wine. Buddhist principles severely restricted the drinking of wine, but when T'ao Chien arrived at the institute, wine was served freely. The poet was a thoroughly Bohemian hermit. Sitting among the other members he would speak not a word, and no sooner was the wine jar empty than he went away. Nobody minded him. This group of scholars and monks discussed the principles of Buddhism and ultimately Hui-yuan became the head of a new school of Chinese Buddhism.

Hui-yuan made it a rule never to escort his friends over the wooden bridge Hu-hsi ch'iao, or Bridge of the Tiger Stream. Once, however, when he was escorting T'ao Chien and Lu Hsiu-ching, the three of them, lost in contemplation of the beauty of the evening, inadvertently strolled over the bridge and a long way farther. Then one of them remembered Hui-yuan's rule, and they all had a good laugh.

Burton has translated many Chinese poems and knows T'ao Chien's work very well and he joked that we two were now crossing over this very bridge. To commemorate our experience I wrote this verse:

The swinging branches of the trees vibrate in the
    wind as if welcoming us
The rainy footpath is secluded and clean, causing
    our feeling to become richer.
Are we the governor T'ao and Master Yuan of
    today?
I follow you, Burton, dashing over the Bridge of
    the Tiger Stream.

風枝搖曳似相招
兩徑清幽意特饒
陶令遠公今豈是
共君閣過虎溪橋

Burton is not a Buddhist like Master Hui-yuan nor am I the poet T'ao,
but we had the happy illusion.

    After passing the Bridge of the Tiger Stream, Burton told me that
there was a Rozanji temple in Kyoto. I was surprised to know of this
temple with the name of my native Mt. Lu and urged him to take me
there. The temple yard was not large, and presently a young woman
came to take our admission fee. After removing our shoes we went

Main entrance of Rozanji Temple

Murasaki Shikibu Koshi

inside. I looked at photos on the wall of the Devil Dance Festival for which the temple is famous. Later we went into the back garden which was of a good size with two tall pines standing in the center. A big stone stood under the pines on which were the kanji words "Murasaki Shikibu Koshi," the old site of the residence of Lady Murasaki. This interested me enormously, for neither of us had ever heard of it before. There were also two cemeteries with a number of tombs bearing the names of members of the royal family. Clearly the area is a part of the old Imperial Palace where Lady Murasaki had living quarters. Though she spent a month in the Ishiyama-dera Temple in Uji to finish the writing of one chapter, she must have spent a good part of her life here at the site of the present Rozanji Temple. Before we left the garden I made a rough sketch of the two pines for their shapes. The way they stood together reminded me of a famous Sung painting by the master Li Cheng.

During my third visit to Kyoto I had the great pleasure of meeting the head priest, Machida Chigen, of the Rozanji Temple, though we had corresponded before when I had sent to the temple my imaginary portrait of the Chinese monk Hui-yuan. We had a very enjoyable meeting, and from him I learned the following history of Rozanji interpreted by my friend Risaburo Murakami:

The founder of the temple was Genzan Daishi or Jikei Daishi, who was featured as the saint in the famous No play scene "Shikaibo." He was also the inventor of the *omikuji,* fortunetelling papers which are tied on the trees of many Japanese temples and shrines. This Rozanji used to be one of the largest temples in Japan situated on the Funao-kayama Hill. The hill was compared to Mt. Lu of China. In the thirteenth century, the then chief priest, Kakuyu, copied the Chinese priest Eon Zenshi of Lu-shan, who established the invocation society called White Lotus Society and Kakuyu constituted Japan's first Invocation Society, Rensha, in this temple. Later Japan's Rozan Invocation Society was transferred to Mt. Lu in China by order of the emperor Gokomatsu. After much trouble and civil strife among samurai, at the end of the sixteenth century the Rozanji Temple was moved to the present site. It was pure coincidence that a few years ago Lady Murasaki's relics were archaeologically located in this same precinct. Regarding the famous Bean-scattering Ceremony staged on February 2 or 3, Rozanji Temple was the originator. The founder of the temple, Genzan Daishi once offered the Buddhist service for three hundred days on end in the imperial family. One day there appeared three devils—the Red Devil, the Blue Devil, and the Black Devil. These three devils represented three important causes of human agony—avarice, jealousy, and complaint respectively. But the head priest, Genzan Daishi, drove them all away with his religious staff. Thus on February 2 or 3 the Setsubun Festival was held with the Buddhist religious service while the three devils, dressed in red, blue, and black respectively, came to dance and the priest threw the beans to chase them away amid the noise of drums and other musical instruments. As it has been held annually, it has become the famous Devil Dance Festival.

I had thought some Japanese must have gone to my native Mt. Lu when the emperor Gokomatsu ordered Japan's Rozanji Invocation Society to be transferred to China and I wish I could find the names of those Japanese monks. I wonder why Lady Murasaki's relics have only been located in recent years and not before if the Japanese themselves are so interested in their most-gifted lady writer of the early eleventh century.

Everyone told me that I was lucky to be in Japan during April and May—the cherry blossom season. Indeed, I did see how the cherry trees began to bloom, how they were in full glory, and how their petals drifted in the air like red and white snowflakes. According to the Japanese legend, the cherry was first named after the mythological goddess, Konohara Sakura Hime, said to be the granddaughter of Amaterasu-Omikami, the Sun Goddess of Japan whose shrine is at Ise. *Konohara* and *sakura* mean cherry and the flower of the tree respectively. This mythological goddess was enshrined on Mt. Fuji. Though it grows on almost every plain and hill in Japan, the cherry grows best on Mt. Yoshino in Nara Prefecture, where thousands of trees grow and bloom together like a mountain range under pink and white snow. Nevertheless, cherry blossoms have a close association with the city of Kyoto. It is said that the first cherry tree to be transplanted was brought to Shisenen Palace in Kyoto in 960 and the greatest and grandest cherry-viewing party ever staged was given at Daigo by Hideyoshi Toyotomi on March 15, 1598, three months before the famous host died.

It could have been for this reason that Miyako Odori, or Cherry-

A lane near the Pontocho
Kaburenjo Theater

Girls playing their samisen

blossom Dance, was staged every year in Kyoto and nowhere else. I was fortunate to have been in time for the first show of the ninety-ninth annual performance. The title of that year's dance was "Ishin-sono-Zenya," or "The Dawn of the Meiji Restoration." I found myself in the Pontocho Kaburenjo Theater in the Gion area a little ahead of the performance. People were streaming in after me. Every corner of the auditorium had an artificial twig of cherry blossoms made of pink paper for decoration. Many in the audience wore kimonos of different shades of colored silk; there were also a few American and European faces. The program was made up of dances by the geisha of Pontocho. It is said these geisha dances were first staged in 1872 and continued year after year. But why it was announced as the ninety-ninth performance I did not know. A number of geisha holding their samisen (a three-

Girls playing small drums and flutes

stringed musical ins rument) were sitting in the Japanese fashion on the right balcony which joined the stage, while another group holding their small drums were on the left balcony.

First, came a dance drama based on the celebrated drama *Semimaru* by Chikamatsu Monzaemon, which took place in the times before the dawn of' the Meiji Restoration. The hero was a legendary figure—an imperial prince of the Heian period—who counting on his good looks was known as a great lover who besides being unfaithful to his consort had an affair with a lady in waiting named Basho and also fathered a child born by a Princess Naoshime. His consort and the lady in waiting joined in prayers to the god of jealousy to put a curse on Naoshime. The two women each have three lighted candles on her head and each holds a baby doll in her arms as if carrying out a secret rite at a shrine. Unfortunately they are discovered by a retainer of Semimaru, the hero, and in the ensuing chase the consort falls into the river and is rescued by a local squire. It so happens that the hero escaping pursuit after eloping with Naoshime is himself in the same house with the wife of the squire. So the whole scene changes into a rather comic situation, though the atmosphere of the drama was serious while the two women are quarreling. Then the hero becomes blind and later a monk and, being a noted composer of *biwa* music, then devotes himself to composing for the Japanese lute, *biwa*, which the Chinese called *p'i p'a*.

After the drama came the dances to illustrate the dawn of the Meiji Restoration which began in Kyoto in 1868. It was divided into five different scenes from spring when cherry trees were in full bloom, then summer, autumn, and winter and again in cherry blossom time at its highest glory for the end. The backdrop changed accordingly to indicate the different seasons. The whole show reminded me of the English pantomime season at Christmas time, though here musical instruments were played in each scene. One thing that interested me particularly was the geisha girls impersonating men's parts.

After the show masses of the people streamed out like fish, yet the atmosphere was quiet and orderly as if I was in the midst of the early Heian days. I noticed several geisha and maiko girls in their full costumes and typical hair styles walking among the crowd and I could see their rather thickly powdered faces looking as if they belonged to a special species of human being. This is a typical sight that can only be seen in Japan. However, I felt that somehow I knew the hair style of those geisha and maiko girls well, for they looked similar to those of the women musicians in a Chinese painting by an unknown artist of the Five Dynasties (907–960) in the Palace Museum collection of Taiwan, and also of the women ironing silk in a painting by Emperor Hui Tsung (reigned 1101–1125) in the Boston Museum of Fine Arts. Can we say that the hair styles of the modern geisha and maiko girls in Kyoto could have been influenced by the early T'ang or Sung China? The interesting part is that there are Japanese girls who still retain their early hair styles while the modern Chinese girl does not. The ukiyoye or Japanese color block prints started in 1764, which is a little more than two hundred years ago. Many geisha and maiko girls of the present day could be identified with the early ukiyoye prints by their hair styles and also by their kimonos. To revive and make a reproduction of the past seems to me to be the actually intended business of Kyoto and of Japan. This is why Kyoto remains the show place of Japan, for it has reproduced the past so well that we are all attracted here to see it.

The Japanese kimono is not quite similar to the ladies' dresses of T'ang China, nor those of Sung or Ming China if we make a careful comparison of what the geisha or maiko wears today with T'ang figurines or with those ladies in the Sung and Ming paintings. The strange part of the Japanese dresses is that all geisha and maiko girls have a wide robe gathered into the waist with a big piece of brocade in different colors and designs hanging down the back; the Chinese women had nothing like this since the T'ang days. I could not help composing the following rather lighthearted verse:

香滿京都十二橋
春光冶蕩不勝嬌
胸前雲錦背團繡
誰道人間鬭細腰

Fragrance fills Kyoto over all its twelve bridges,
The gaiety of the spring light is heavily loaded with charming flirtation.
A cloudy brocade on her bosom and a round embroidered ball from behind;
Who says that this human world is competing for a slender waist?

According to Chinese history in the fourth or third century B.C. there were many court ladies who died of starvation from trying to keep their waistline as slender as possible, for the King of Ch'u was known for his special love of the slender-waisted ones. Another thing that interested me was the footwear of the maiko girls, for they wear high-soled *ohobo*, which contradicts what I said about the Tokyo girls not caring to wear high-heeled shoes.

The Gion area is a special quarter of Kyoto having its own type of two-story houses with wooden-lace fronts lining both sides of the rather narrow streets. The layout of Kyoto city was said to be based on that of Ch'ang-an, the famous Chinese capital of the T'ang period. I have never been to Ch'ang-an in Shen-si Province and cannot say whether the old residence quarter outside the ancient palace is in fact similar to the Gion center, but I remember that some houses with two low stories in Soo-

Houses in the Gion area

chow, Hangchow, and in the southern part of old Nanking are somewhat similar, though the Chinese houses are usually built of bricks, not wood. Many two-story houses on one side of Kamo River with the geisha or maiko girls leaning on the wooden railing on the upper story reminded me very much of those houses along the river Ch'in-huai on the southern part of old Nanking. Nanking was a famous capital during the whole epoch of the Six Dynasties (220–589) and that part of the river Ch'in-huai was lined with the houses of courtesans. The many beautiful and gifted courtesans attracted wealthy folk and men of letters to spend a gay life of entertainment with music, songs, and wine as much or even more, one imagines, than the geisha girls at Gion during the Heian period, although those geisha and maiko girls were not exactly courtesans.

Many beautiful stories and poems have been written about the river Ch'in-huai, on which flowery boats carrying poets, singsong girls, and banquet tables moved slowly up and down the river. The gaiety of life of those early days in Nanking has been handed down to the present, though conditions are far different from what they used to be. When I was a college student in Nanking, a few friends and I once hired a boat with wine, food, and musicians to glide on the river, but the dirty look of both shores, the smelly water, and the dilapidated railings and walls of the houses from which beautiful girls could easily fall at any moment rather disgusted me. I went there in order to see how the gay life, as described in Chinese stories and poems, might have been conducted in those early years, but I got no illusion at all. Here in Gion of Kyoto, though it may have been modified somewhat, I can imagine the way of life that has been led since the Heian days. Here, as I said at the beginning, everyone seems to be intent on contributing his or her effort to keep the past of Kyoto alive. This is a well-organized business that has kept modern Kyoto still the old Kyoto.

One evening my friend and colleague, Professor William Ted de Bary, translator of *Five Women Who Loved Love* by Ihara Saikaku and the author of many other books, asked me to dine with him and his wife, Fanny. It so happened that Ted was spending his sabbatical-year leave in Kyoto writing a book and I had been spending mine touring Australia and New Zealand and was then arriving in Kyoto for a short stay. It was a rainy evening. Ted and Fanny took me to a modern Italian restaurant close to Kamo River. Though modern and Western in style, the restaurant had a neat and cosy arrangement which seemed to fit into that quarter of Kyoto very well. After a good talk about our experiences, particularly my trip to New Guinea and North Borneo and also good Italian food and wine, we three went to stand on the balcony and to gaze at a small boat moving slowly under the rain. My thoughts went straight back to river Ch'in-huai for a moment and then to some of Hokusai's wood-block prints. The following verse came to me in the end:

夜靜春深加茂川
分明一幅北齋畫
憑欄同看雨中船
共話京都別有緣

A talk together in Kyoto is an unusual treat;
By the railings we gaze at the boat in the rain.
This is exactly a piece of Hokusai's work,
In the quiet evening of a late spring by river Kamo!

Professor Masao Abe
in meditation

Among all the places I have seen in Kyoto, my experience up on Kiyomizudera-ji still lingers in my mind vividly. It was Professor Masao Abe of Nara Gakugei University who urged me to spend a day there when I went to see him in his Kyoto home one rainy night. Professor Abe and I met in New York on several occasions. He is a great disciple of Dr. Shin-ichi Hisamatsu, a noted Zen master in Kyoto and a famous modern Japanese calligrapher. The Kiyomizudera Temple is built on a promontory at the western foot of Higashiyama Hill, on higher ground unlike the other temples on the plains. The first structure was made at the beginning of the ninth century but the present one, dating back to 1633, is a replica of its main hall. Though the temple itself was on higher ground, the main hall was higher still, built on many stilt poles of solid wood joined together to support the wide wooden platform, with wooden railings all round. From there I enjoyed a far more extensive panoramic view of the city than from the metal tower near Kyoto station. The beauty of this view is the sight of the temple standing above all the different kinds of trees in many shades of fresh green, with cherry blossoms here and there appearing among them. There are well-paved stone steps, and a number of Japanese women in colored kimonos dotting the scene everywhere; the whole view was an unforgettable one. Every part of the temple grounds interested me as I walked about, and I made a few rough sketches here and there in order to illustrate the views I failed to describe in words.

Though June is supposed to be a rainy month in the Tokyo and Kyoto areas, I got a greater share of rain in April when I was in both places. One morning when I came out of the Sanjusangendo after a good look inside, I was met by a torrential rain. Not a car was moving about. A boy of fourteen or fifteen suddenly walked over from the other side of the street and offered to share his umbrella with me, for he must have seen how completely drenched I was. I was greatly touched by his kindness and thought that, after all, Mencius was right in saying that human beings are born good.

When I left the hotel after breakfast it was very fine; I explored a number of places: the famous Kyoto lacquer works and also the Manjudo goods in Pottery Lane. Then I tried to find a man who was known to be still making replicas of the brushes which were used in China by the T'ang calligraphers, examples of which are in the collection of the imperial treasures in the Shosoin, Nara. This type of brush is described as one with an ivory-tipped bamboo handle with leopard marks, and a bamboo cap bound with bark strips—the handle is 20.3 centimeters long; diameter, 1.85 centimeters; and length of cap, 7.7 centimeters. This brush was called in Chinese Ch'ueh-tou-pi, or Sparrow-head brush, for the hair was shaped like the head of a sparrow. But I failed to find the person. My experience tells me that Japanese addresses are not arranged in sequence of the number. It is difficult to find an address in Tokyo and Kyoto.

I have always been interested in how things were made by noted craftsmen. I spent much time in locating them in my years in Europe. When I heard of Nishiyama, a small village by Lake Yodo in Kyoto, known as a center for making good Japanese samisen, I went there to see how it was made.

As Lake Yodo is very close to Lake Biwa, which is famous as a holi-

Kiyomizudera Temple

day resort, I made a good round of the many small huts along the lake shore of the latter. My inability to speak Japanese did not help me to gain an inside look at the samisen-makers in Nishiyama. However, I learned the local legend that the bottom of these two lakes, Biwa and Yodo, are joined into one. But the water level of Lake Yodo is fifty meters higher than that of its neighbor, Lake Biwa. Why is it so? The legend says it is because all tears of sorrow flow into it. Therefore the strings of Nishiyama have better tones because they are dyed in this water of sorrow. Based on this legend, a most outstanding Japanese movie was made in 1966. It relates the story of a young girl, Sabu, daughter of a poor farmer, who came to work in the Momose household in Nishiyama and fell in love with a coworker, Ukichi. But Sabu's beauty soon attracted a local famous samisen virtuoso who wanted to teach Sabu to play the samisen. The famous samisen master eventually wronged her just before her beloved Ukichi returned from the war front. They met but soon Sabu disappeared. Ukichi found her dead body and wrapped it well, then threw her body and himself into Lake Yodo and drowned. This is a double suicide drama, as most Kabuki plays were. I saw this movie. The story is a typical Japanese tragedy, but it is better than the common double suicide in the Kabuki plays, with their unhealthy emphasis on the charms of prostitutes and the nobility of the young men who elected to commit suicide with the prostitutes of their choice.

Arashiyama, a popular hill resort with a river flowing below, is not far from the city of Kyoto and I had an enjoyable visit there. I learned of Arashiyama from the following poem, which was written in the Chinese manner of four seven-character lines by the Japanese scholar Yoda Gokkai (1833–1909) in 1878:

松翠花紅微雨中
嵐山面目幾渾是
綺羅散畫寂痕雲
一道溪聲萬壑風

All the way the sound of the stream with wind from everywhere,
The wearers of beautiful silks are no more and hardly any trace of their shoe prints.
The face of Arashiyama seemingly familiar,
In the gentle rain among the green pines and red blossoms.

The rough translation into English is mine. The poet also said that the local people considered it better to see Arashiyama on a rainy day than on a fine one, and better to see it from a boat than while walking. One morning Miss Junko Nagatsuka, an artist and music teacher whom I had met in Nagasaki a month earlier, came with me to spend a few hours in Arashiyama. We got there in bright sunshine. All the way the artificial paper blossoms attached to every telephone post were breathing an air of gaiety. Many people were already walking on the well-paved promenades along the river and many were sitting at the windows of the restaurants while others were about to embark in boats, a good many of which were already moving on the river. I suggested taking a boat but Junko hesitated for a moment. I assured her that I had lived in Oxford for more than eleven years and that everyone who had ever lived in Oxford knows how to row a boat. She knows some English and consented to get in a boat with me. Unlike the river Isis at Oxford, which is quite narrow but not deep, the river Oi is wide and the water flows quite fast. Many boats including ours were going in the same direction. Each boat has a wooden canopylike structure to keep off the hot sunshine. While I rowed backward in the Western manner, our boat soon gave a big jump and Junko showed signs of being greatly frightened, for a motorboat manned by a young man struck the stern of our boat. I soon put our boat on course again, and we came to a part of the river where a number of wooden structures were set up along the bank facing Arashiyama Hill. Each structure had a roof shade underneath which many people were sitting or lying in all manner of poses while eating and drinking; the sight of their leisurely manner enhanced the tranquillity of the whole area. We now reached the narrow upstream part of the river. As very few boats moved upstream through the fast flowing water among the rocks, we turned back to our starting point. We went on shore to have a Japanese meal in a restaurant where we could sit by an open window and watch the people walking by and look across to a leafy hill with all kinds of trees in dark and fresh green, with here and there massive balls of pink and white cherry blossoms, all vaguely outlined and indescribably pleasing to the eyes.

Afterward we walked to the long bridge and saw a number of large pines twisted by the wind into interesting shapes; crossing over the bridge, we strolled along the footpath which was cut along the hillside. This footpath must have been there since the Heian days if not earlier, though neither Murasaki nor Shonagon seemed to have ever come over this area. However, one incident connected with Arashiyama and the river Oi interested me particularly. I read that in 1701 the noted painter Ogata Korin was at a picnic party at Arashiyama with a number of his friends at which they staged a most sumptuous repast, each member of the party providing some unusual, extraordinary dish. Japanese men were good cooks in those days and the picnic party turned out to be a contest of fine cooking. It was said that Korin, as a painter very fond of using rich color and particularly gold for the background of his screen paintings, produced his food wrapped up in big bamboo leaves specially decorated by him with gold. After eating and drinking, the party became hilarious and Korin tossed all the gold bamboo leaves into the river, where they floated like myriad twinkling eyes under the bright moon. What a wonderful sight it must have been! However, the authorities in Kyoto thought this wasteful performance had violated the law of 1698 forbidding common people from using gold and silver and they banished Korin from the capital. So he went to live in Edo, where he produced many important works.

It had begun to rain. A good many people were fishing along the river edge with rods, but none of them caught anything while we were near them. The sun had disappeared and the wind over the river ruffled its surface into constant motion. Walking underneath the big branching trees on the slope of the hill which stretched to cover the footpath, I felt quite cool on the warm May afternoon. Junko said that Arashiyama itself is the name of the hill, on which grew pines, cherry, and many other kinds of trees which she could not name, and it is known to be the best scenic spot for cherry-viewing parties in spring and for seeing scarlet maples in autumn. The latter is called Momiji Matsuri, or Maple Festival or Red-leaf Festival, and is held on the second day of November. Up on top of the hill is Iwatayama Monkey Park, where a good many monkeys are kept, but we did not have time to see them. On our way back I felt glad to have been to Arashiyama in the cherry blossom season, and remembering the boating episode, I composed the following verse:

不 忩 打 嵐
妨 爾 槳 山
汽 浪 中 默
艇 花 流 默
出 驚 春 一
蒼 女 四 水
頭 伴 浮 悠
　　　　悠

Still, still is the hill of Arashiyama and leisurely, leisurely flows the water;
Splashing the oars in midstream I see spring floating on all sides.
Suddenly the jumping foam startles my lady companion.
Not knowing a motorboat came round ours.

Each time I had come to Kyoto I had missed seeing Professor Kojiro Yoshikawa of Kyoto University. He is a great scholar of Chinese studies in Japan and for many years had been either teaching, writing, or lectur-

ing. Now he seems to have become busier since his retirement. We had
met at Columbia University on several occasions when he was a Japanese scholar in residence for a year. This time I wrote to tell him that I
would be coming to Kyoto again. He came to my hotel that day with a
mutual friend of ours, Professor Lien-sheng Yang of Harvard University, who had just come from a conference in Taipei and was on
his way back to Cambridge. Three of us sat together for a good, happy
exchange of greetings. Professor Yoshikawa wanted to show me his
Kyoto and asked if I had any special place to go to. I left it to his choice
and we three went in his chauffeured car to see Wan-fu-Szu. This temple
interested us, for it was built in a pure Chinese style of architecture by a
Chinese scholar-monk named Ingen, or Yin-yüan, of the Huang-po sect.
He was born in Fukien in 1592 and died in Kyoto in 1672 at the age of
80. During the early years of the Tokugawa period, the shogun wanted
to invite some learned Chinese monks to Japan to build temples and
requested the Chinese scholar-monk, Ichinen, who was the abbot of
Sofukuji Temple in Nagasaki at the time, to find some for him. Ichinen
then wrote to Ingen, and with much persuasion Ingen came to Nagasaki
in 1654, with his disciples Dokuchi, Dokutan, Beian, and Sokuhi. Not
until 1658 did he meet the Tokugawa shogun who gave him the present
site on which to build a temple. In 1660 Ingen finished the building, a
complete replica of one in Foochow in Fukien Province, and he himself
became the first abbot of it. From the first to the thirteenth, all the
abbots were Japanese-naturalized Chinese scholar-monks, who were not
only masters of Chinese Ch'an Buddhism of the Huang-po sect, but
several were good painters whose influence on Japanese painting of the
Nagasaki school was considerable.

Ingen's remains are kept here

After entering the spacious courtyard in front of the main hall,
Professor Yoshikawa asked if we found the whole arrangement very
Chinese. Lien-sheng Yang pointed to the footpath on which we were
walking. Its decorated square stones in the row were very Chinese in
style and looked like those footpaths in the notable gardens of Soochow
and Hangchow in China. I was very interested in seeing so many beautiful and healthy tall pine trees growing in the courtyard and other parts
of the temple grounds. After my exclamation about them, Professor
Yoshikawa remarked that one could not find any beautiful Japanese
scenery without pine trees. Having passed through the main hall and a
few smaller halls, I admired some of the couplets engraved from Ingen's
original calligraphy, which were hanging on the big pillars. Ingen was
known as a great calligrapher in his time.

Later we went to see the cemetery in which both the enemy and the
Japanese dead were buried together—a great idea from the time after the

Russo-Japanese War. The day was fine, neither hot nor cold, but this temple was not thronged with tourists as are many other temples in Kyoto; the reason, I was told, was that the Rinzai sect of Zen Buddhism dominates nearly all temples in the city while the followers of Huang-po sect are few. Only we three were there that day. There was an unusual quietness inside the temple, as in many big Chinese monasteries that I used to visit in China.

Professor Yoshikawa inscribes
a brick tile

When we came out of the main hall, someone in the front hall asked us to buy a brick tile as a contribution to the repairing of the temple. Each of us bought one and wrote our names in kanji on them. The question then was where should we go to have a good lunch. Professor Yoshikawa said that the restaurant opposite the entrance of this temple was famous for its vegetable dishes, the recipes having been handed down since Abbot Ingen's days, but an arrangement for a good vegetable meal had to be made a few days ahead. Nothing could be done in a hurry. So Lien-sheng suggested we go to Chung Hua Lou, where he had dined before. When we reached the place, it did not seem to be in operation. However, a young woman led us upstairs and in time some interesting dishes were produced for us. After a good round in the temple on a fine day with interesting companions and agreeable talk, we three were ravenous.

Though I differ in some ways with those who claim Kyoto to be a mirror of China, I must say that there are many things in Kyoto which are undoubtedly Chinese and with the Chinese characters as their background. Much of the temple architecture and garden arrangements have a Chinese flavor. Chinese Ch'an Buddhism, particularly the Rinzai and Huang-po sects, floats in the Kyoto air. Above all, the Department of Chinese Studies in Kyoto University, which has been led by Professor Yoshikawa together with Professor Ogama Tamaki, and now has a number of notable Japanese scholars of Chinese, has long been known as the chief center for Chinese studies in Japan. Apart from many Japanese scholars, Western scholars of Chinese studies have all felt that they have to spend some time at Kyoto University before they can claim to be scholars of Chinese. This is largely due to the great achievement of Professor Yoshikawa's work in his own Chinese studies. I bow to him more than forty-five degrees! Before he left Columbia in 1965, he gave me a set of his publications in Chinese, which he entitled in a very modest way *Chih-fei-chi,* or *Collected works of knowing wrong* or *A collection of acknowledged faults.* Though the phrase "Chih-fei" came from Han Fei Tzu, a Taoist philosopher, I was specially touched by it, for it could have come from a line of writing by a great Chinese poet,

T'ao Chien, who happened to be born in my native city in the fourth
century. I then wrote the following verse to Professor Yoshikawa:

In life the difficult thing is to know what has been
    wrong;
After having finished reading this collected work
    of *Knowing what has been wrong,* my senses
    spiral into infinity.
How far did the fisherman's song enter the river-
    let?
The cold cloud above at the end of the year is
    standing still—not flying.

歳暮寒雲静不飛
漁歌入浦深何許
讀罷知非此意微
人生難而是知非

In the third line I use the Chinese poet Wang Wei's meaning about the
mystery of life, which could be as subtle as the trailing sound of the fisherman's song on its way to entering the riverlet farther and farther, and
the fourth line I adopted from Professor Yoshikawa's own with a change
of the last word *drifting* into *flying* for the purpose of rhyme, and
because I also meant that I have come to a point where I understand "to
keep still," as I have reached the age of being able to do so.

    Though it would be too long for me to describe all that I did in Kyoto
on my several visits, I can sum up my feeling about it as a very feminine
city. It has many attractions to hold its visitors, like a young lady with
her hairdo, her dress, her manner of movement, and her soft voice
pleasing to everyone, but with a strong character persistently having her
own way, though with taste. While in Kyoto I met a few young natives
of the city who demanded that Kyoto be made modern, saying that if
Tokyo could be so modern why couldn't Kyoto. But I think a lady must
have her hairdo, her new dress, her graceful manner of movement, and
also her soft voice to keep her alive, so the people of Kyoto all work
persistently to keep its past alive. So I asked the young ones if they
wanted Kyoto to wear a miniskirt, or if she should stand in the center of
the city like the nude figure outside of the big greenhouse in the Kyoto
Prefecture Botanical Garden. Indeed, Kyoto to me is a great feminine
city, unlike any other city in the whole world, for none could have kept
its past alive as Kyoto has. With such a spirit as Kyoto has, I don't think
it will ever change much from what I know of it now. It is romantic in
every aspect!

A nude figure in Kyoto's Botanical Garden

XI

Yang Kuei-fei and Yamaguchi Prefecture

AMONG ALL the famous Chinese poets, particularly those of the T'ang period (618–960), Po Chü-in, or Hakurakutan in Japanese, has become the most familiar to the Japanese from the tenth century if not before. His name was practically a household word in Japan for centuries, though this may not be so nowadays. Perhaps his long poem *Ch'ang hen ko*, or *Song of Everlasting Regret*, describing the romantic figure Yang Kuei-fei's love for the Chinese emperor Ming Huang has made Hakurakutan so well known. Both Murasaki and Shonagon mentioned Yang Kuei-fei in their writings, for Yang Kuei-fei was regarded as the most admired beauty in China of her day. Japan has taken her name, Yo-ki-hi, to mean "beauty" in her dictionary. My friend and colleague, Professor Yoshito Hakeda, once showed me a photograph of a wood-carving representing Yang Kuei-fei as Kuan Yin in Chinese, or Kwannon in Japanese, the Buddhist goddess of mercy, which is in Sennyu-ji Temple, Kyoto, and urged me to go and see it when I went to Japan. This, I did. The carving was in the Temple of the Bubbling Spring in the southeastern part of Kyoto. A pamphlet there described the figure as follows:

> The Yang Kuei-fei Kwannon, enshrined in this temple, is a lifelike statue of Yang Kuei-fei commissioned by the emperor Hsüan Tsung (Ming Huang) of the T'ang dynasty in China. It was brought here in 1255 by the Japanese Tankai. This figure is celebrated as one of the most beautiful pieces of Buddhist sculpture in Japan.

As the wooden sculpture was placed on a pedestal within a small shrine high above the altar with silk curtains on both sides, I could not get close enough to study it as a work of art. As far as carved wood portrait is concerned, China's T'ang artists did not show much excellence. Yang Kuei-fei died in A.D. 756. Whether this statue was a good likeness, or was sculptured from life, or how it came into the hands of the Japanese priest after some four hundred years were questions which nobody could answer for me. Nevertheless, this carved Kwannon under the name of Yang Kuei-fei helped to make the beautiful Chinese woman known to the Japanese.

The great interest in this beauty of China has raised a good belief that Yang Kuei-fei had actually died in Japan. Her tomb is in the Yamaguchi Prefecture, I was told repeatedly. I remember reading a Chinese book entitled *Cha-p'o-chi* by Yü P'ing-po, published in 1928, which mentioned that Chou Tso-jen, brother of Lu Hsun, received a photograph of a tomb from a Japanese friend and Mr. Yü proceeded to discuss in detail how eventually Yang Kuei-fei was thought to have died in Japan. While I was visiting Japan for the fourth time, I was given a colored map issued by the local authority of Yamaguchi Prefecture on which Yang Kuei-fei's tomb was specially marked as an object of sightseeing interest. So I decided to go there for a look. I proceeded from Kumamoto to Asa, where I took a local train to Nagota-yumoto, staying at the Shirokiya Grand Hotel. The hotel's young proprietor, Mr. Seiji Shiroki, could speak some English and was most helpful. After dinner, he came to discuss in detail my trip to Kuzu, where the tomb is located, and I asked him then to book a taxi. To my great surprise in the morning, he told me that he would drive me there himself—it was quite a long journey taking an hour each way—not only that, he also asked a friend of his to go with us as well as a young lady who studied English at the local university and who would act as interpreter. He also arranged for Mr. Sukenari Miyazaki, a local author who has written much about Yang Kuei-fei in magazines, to meet us there. A most thoughtful and enterprising young hotel proprietor!

As the car moved along the country road at a steady pace we chatted a bit. I could not take my eyes off the pleasant country scene with its beautiful rice fields and clean, neat farmhouses, looking healthier and wealthier than the countryside of other prefectures I had seen. When we reached our destination, Mr. Sukenari Miyazaki was already there to receive us with a welcoming smile. He then led us up a number of stone steps to a small Buddhist temple named Nison-in, where the chief priest, Chimen Tadato, showed us a well-preserved manuscript, *Engi*, in which was something about Yang Kuei-fei's tomb. Although it was written in Chinese, I glanced through a few pages quickly and did not find any clear point about how Yang Kuei-fei came to die in Kuzu. Neither the priest nor Mr. Miyazaki could say when the *Engi* was made. But Mr. Miyazaki did remark that the legend which the *Engi* deals with is mentioned in a work called the *Bōchō Fūdo Chūshin-an* (a local gazetteer of the Yamaguchi area), which was compiled during the Edo period and published around 1840, so it is clear that at that time the legend was already in existence.

Then the priest took us to look at two small Buddhist statues, well-carved, which were proclaimed as national treasures in this temple. Afterward, we all walked down from the temple hall to the cemetery, in the middle of which was Yang Kuei-fei's tomb, specially pointed out to me. It was a stupalike erection with no Chinese characters nor Japanese writing on the large round stone in the center of it. It was surrounded by many small tombs in similar stupa-shape. I was told they were the tombs of her servants and retinue. But I don't remember seeing any T'ang tombs in China like this stupa-shaped one. I only wished my friend Mr. Lee Chia could have managed to come with me, for he could have then discussed the matter with the priest and Mr. Miyazaki in Japanese.

The big one is Yang Kuei-fei's tomb

The late Professor Herbert A. Giles gave an account of Yang Kuei-fei in his *Chinese Biographical Dictionary* based on Chinese history:

Yang Kuei-fei, died A.D. 756, was the daughter of an official named Yang Hsüan-yen, who had been president of the Board of War under the emperor Jui-Tsung, and had been ennobled as duke. Her personal name was Yü-huan. In 735 she became concubine to Prince Shou, eighteenth son of Emperor Ming-Huang; and three years later, upon the death of the reigning favorite, she passed into the harem of the father. She was surprisingly lovely and specially noted as being the only fat lady among Chinese historical beauties. Her influence soon became paramount. She herself received the title of Tai-chen. . . . In 745 she was raised to the rank of kuei-fei, and it is under this title that she is usually known. After an unparalleled career of luxury and extravagance, she fled with the court in 756 at the approach of the rebel An Lu-shan. But on reaching Ma-wei the imperial soldiers rose to revolt and demanded vengeance on the family of Yang. The emperor was forced to order the eunuch Kao Li-shih to strangle his idolized concubine (some say she was hanged on a pear tree).

Ma-wei is a small city in the western part of Shensi Province, far inland on China's northern plateau. The Japanese story is that though strangled or hanged, she did not die at once, but later on crawled aboard a boat which was driven by a typhoon to Japan. It is difficult to see how she could have crawled far enough to reach a boat on the Yellow River, not to speak of the time it would take for the boat to drift to the mouth of the river and enter the China Sea, there to be caught up in the typhoon. Owing to the great beauty of Hakurakutan's poem in describing the matchless loveliness of Yang Kuei-fei and the emperor Ming Huang's unwavering love for her, many legends and stories have arisen. But it has always surprised me that not a single Chinese Confucianist including the Confucian scholar, Hakurakutan himself, ever raised a word against the emperor who took his eighteenth son's girl for his idolized favorite. Sometime later I met Professor E. G. Pullyblank, an expert on the history of the An-lu-shan rebellion in T'ang China, who told me about a Japanese poem written in Chinese style about Yang Kuei-fei in *Kyū-shū*, published in 1964. This is how I translate it into English:

離魂倩女謫扶桑　私是馬嵬泉下魄　筆妙脂粉奈斷腸　風流脂粉又紅妝

Elegant in her rouge and her red gown,
She is lovely as a Buddhist goddess but bears a
  broken heart.
Though known as the ghost below the spring of
  Ma-wei,
Her wandering soul has come to be banished in
  Japan.

A poem like this indicates that the legend has been popular among Japanese men of letters and this poet indicates that he believes it.

After lunch I wanted to see Akiyoshi Cave, the second largest in the world after the Mammoth Cave in Kentucky. It is not too far from Nagota-yumoto. Again, Mr. Shiroki had offered to take me there, for he had to go to the capital city of Yamaguchi for business and Akiyoshi Cave was on the way. After a pleasant forty-five-minute drive, he dropped me at the entrance to the cave, telling me he would return at

Akiyoshi Cave

five o'clock to pick me up. The sun was shining brightly and hot. A long chain of people was entering the cave and many more continued to arrive. I joined them and was astonished to find myself in such an unbelievable long, cool cave. We walked on and on along the well-protected footpath, sometimes in the center of the cave, sometimes close by the wet walls among stalactites and stalagmites, and sometimes passing round rocky columns. Electric lights here and there lit descriptive labels such as the "Rock of Great Buddha," the "Umbrella Icicles," the "Central Pillar," the "Big Mushroom," the "One Hundred Dishes," the "Golden Pillar," the "King of the Cavern." The extent of the cave was beyond my estimation and it took me twenty minutes to walk back to the entrance.

From Akiyoshi Cave, I took a taxi to see Akiyoshi-dai, a great limestone plateau covering 150 kilometers and dotted with many grayish white rocks of various sizes. I saw a few wildflowers hidden among the rocks and several young girls sketching and painting by some trees. The edge of this huge expanse was beyond my sight. Apparently many of the rocks in the Akiyoshi Cave and outside were marble, for I found the short street lined with gift shops selling marble objects as souvenirs.

At exactly five o'clock Mr. Shiroki returned and suggested showing me yet another interesting place not far from his hotel. We went past his hotel on the other side of Nagato City and over the big stone bridge to Ohmi-jima Island. It was getting dark as we walked up to see the beautiful seacoast, which was dotted with many marvelous rocks rising sheer from the water, some of which have been tunnelled by the waves. I gladly followed him up step by step. Along the way and at every turn, most beautiful sights appeared, rocks or islets of many different shapes broke through the sea surface as if competing with one another to charm. Some rocks had great holes, worn by the waves for centuries, large enough for a boat to pass through. None of the many rocky islets had any trees growing on them. They presented a new loveliness, so different from any other seacoast of Japan. On the footpath we encountered a rock by the edge above the sea and saw three kanji characters, "Hekikaidai," engraved on it by Prince Hashimoto Isamu. Mr. Shiroki told me that the present emperor Hirohito had recently sent an artist here to make sketches so that he might paint the scene on the walls of the new palace. An admirable taste!

Mr. Shiroki and I then had a good Chinese dinner in the city of Nagato. On our way back he told me that Yamaguchi Prefecture was closely linked with Japanese history, for she had produced many noted generals and prime ministers. The present prime minister, Mr. Sato, was born in Yamaguchi. I asked if the Yamaguchi ladies were noted for their beauty. Mr. Shiroki was not sure of this, but I encouraged him by pointing out that the great beauty of China, Yang Kuei-fei, had come to die there. This amused him. I had never before in my travels met so generous and kind a hotel proprietor as Mr. Shiroki.

A country house in Yamaguchi Prefecture

XII

Cherry Blossoms and Deer in Nara

LIKE EVERYBODY else, I have long known that the cherry blossom is the
symbol of Japan, but only recently I learned that a special species called
yaezakura—double cherry blossom—is the symbol of Nara. As the Japanese proverb says, *Ima no hitohari, nochi no tohari,* which means one
stitch now is better than ten stitches afterward. So since I was in Japan
in the cherry blossom season, I went to see the symbol of Nara without
delay. Why had yaezakura become the symbol of Nara? I was told that
the tenth-century Japanese poetess Tayu Iseno wrote of "Inishie no
Nara no miyako no yaezakura," or "Double cherry blossom in the old
capital of Nara," when she was standing in the courtyard of Kofukuji
Temple. The empress Ichijo, wife of Emperor Jotomonin whom Tayu
attended, liked the particular tree and ordered it to be planted in the
garden of the court. Apparently there was only one tree of this kind
growing there at the time. When a monk of the temple prepared to dig
up the tree for transplanting, the local residents became furious and pro-
tested to the temple authorities against the removal. The temple officials
would not stop the digging, for they wanted to comply with the
empress's wish even if they had to die in carrying it out. These distur-
bances around Kofukuji were soon reported to the empress. Instead of
becoming angry with the people, she admired their affection for the tree,
like her own, and she gave a part of her own land to the temple to raise
funds for the conservation of the tree. And the beautiful yaezakura tree
was adopted as the symbol of the ancient capital.

On my arrival in Nara it was raining heavily. At the Nara Hotel I was
given a room with a window overlooking the Sarusawa Pond, in which
the reflection of a tall pagoda shimmered and vibrated with the raindrops. Despite the rain I went out to Kofukuji, which was within easy
walking distance. Shortly after I reached the temple grounds the rain
stopped. The courtyard before the main hall and the famous five-story
pagoda was quite spacious. Many cherry trees were in bloom among
many tall pine trees, but none seemed to have double flowers. No one I
met could tell me where the double cherry blossom was to be found, for
either they were visitors like me or they had not heard about the symbol

of Nara. Perhaps the ancient double cherry tree from the tenth century was not in the city. Then I moved toward a large group of people in front of the five-story pagoda. Most of the faces were Western, and I remembered it had been said that Nara was more international than Kyoto. A number of young Americans and Europeans were feeding some tame deer which roamed freely about the open ground. A good few were clinging round the youngsters begging for food. Suddenly I heard a loud voice in English from a young Japanese guide, saying: "You must have seen the five-story pagoda in Nikko or Tokyo! It is said they were used as graves for the monks. At first the graves were just high piles of soil. Later the Chinese created the pagoda to contain Buddha's bones. We Japanese followed the Chinese in building pagodas. But I say I can't believe they all contain Buddha's bones, for there are so many pagodas in Japan." All his audience roared with laughter, but no one realized that there was a Chinese in their midst. Everybody knows that Buddha was born in India and died in India, so his bones could not have been buried in China. And the Chinese did not create the pagoda, its origin was in India. There are indeed many pagodas in Japan, and one can see them standing out almost everywhere on the three big islands except Hokkaido. For myself I have always regarded the square-shaped five-story pagoda as the very symbol of Japan, far more so than the cherry blossom or any other object. Cherry blossoms can grow in other lands and are just as glorious as they are in Japan, for instance the cherry blossoms in Washington, D.C. But nowhere else can one find the true square planned five-story pagoda. Korean and Chinese pagodas are quite different in shape from the Japanese ones, though they all derived originally from Indian stupas—the Buddhist monument of tumulus form containing relics—which probably developed from a pre-Buddhist burial mound. The Indian king Asoka (273–232 B.C.) was the first to start the building of the stupas. The young guide was correct in doubting that the Buddha's bones could have been buried in so many Japanese pagodas, for none of Buddha's bones came to Japan. But when Indian Buddhism came to China, the Indian type of monument came too. The Chinese artists or architects might not have seen an original Indian stupa and so created a structure according to the descriptions they had heard—the round body of the stupa became angular with curved roofs from the Chinese palace buildings. At first the Chinese pagoda was built for the purpose of containing the bones of the dead abbot and other monks with their relics, for each pagoda was closely attached to the temple or monastery. There are still a few early Chinese pagodas built in the sixth and seventh centuries in existence, square in shape with three or five stories, but they were built of brick or stone, whereas the Japanese are all of wood. Most Chinese pagodas are hexag-

SHINTO DANCE AT ISE

DEER IN NARA

onal or octagonal in plan with seven, nine, or thirteen stories. There are wooden or stone stairs inside Chinese pagodas and visitors can climb up to the top for a panoramic view of the city. There must be stairs inside Japanese pagodas, but I never saw anyone being permitted to enter.

Presently the young guide took his group inside the main hall of the Kofukuji Temple and I followed him round. The dry-lacquered statue of Rahora interested me, for the artist had created such a benevolent face as if full of pity for all mankind. Later I noticed on the west of the main hall a most beautifully shaped Hokuendo, an octagonal hall—the best type of all octagonal halls I saw in Japan. None of those visitors led by the guide came to see it and they all soon disappeared from my sight. I then returned to stroll round the mirrorlike Sarusawa Pond, looking through the long hanging willow branches to glimpse the five-story pagoda and its reflection again before I went to the hotel for supper and rest.

Next morning was fine and warm. It took me no time to walk to the Todaiji Temple. As soon as I set foot inside the Daibutsu-den, or Hall of the Great Buddha, the young Japanese guide and his group appeared there too. One of the middle-aged Americans in the group asked him in a loud voice, "Who is this big guy here?" "That is the biggest guy in the whole world," the guide shouted back to him. He must have been familiar with American slang and used the word *guy* in order to please his customers. He naturally drew laughter from the rest of his party. He then related how the great Buddha had been cast in bronze by the order of Emperor Shomu in 735, when the whole country of Japan was suffering an epidemic of smallpox with many deaths. The emperor decreed that this colossal statue should be made to ward off the disease. It required five hundred tons of brass and the statue was erected on this very spot by connecting the castings piece by piece. It measured 53.5 feet in height and the face alone was 16 feet long with a nose 1.6 feet long and hands 6.8 feet. At this point, the guide stopped and told a story: "A few months ago, actually at Christmas, three or four wild guys who had had too many drinks, climbed up on the left hand and danced happily. It was near dusk and not many people were about. Later their noise was heard by the temple authorities and they were caught by the police. Though they had a good time there, they must have felt tired and went to have a good rest in prison!" This caused another shout of laughter. The guide must have prided himself on his sense of humor and had been making great efforts to hold the interest of his group. Immediately someone asked, "What did the fellows drink, sake or beer?" The guide did not give a straight answer, saying, "We young people don't like to drink sake, for we are supposed to sit on the floor to drink it. We young people are not used to sitting on the floor. If we drink too much sake we

Dancing on the palm of the
Great Buddha

feel headachey and dizzy till the next morning. We like drinking beer and whisky. . . ." He kept talking his own way, disregarding all the questions poured over him by his party. Only then did I realize that some modern young Japanese do not go in for the older customs which their forefathers followed.

I then left the crowd and entered the Nigatsudo, or Second-month Hall, to look at the famous statue of the eleven-faced Kwannon. As the temple was founded in 752 by the priest Jitchu, the statue must have been carved at that time, though little is actually known about its history. I then moved on to Sangatsudo, or Third-month Hall, which was built in 733, nineteen years earlier than Nigatsudo, and considered the oldest structure on the Todaiji ground still intact. Many other Japanese temples suffered damage or were destroyed completely by fire at one time or another, for they were all built of wood. This small temple was also called Hokkedo and has been an important object of study by students of early Oriental architecture. It contains some special items for study too, for it has a group of statues of the mid-Tempyo period, as the late curator of the Boston Museum of Fine Arts, Robert Treat Paine, wrote:

The impressive central image is a figure of Fukukenjaka Kwannon in the dry-lacquer technique. The eight arms, the perforated sun-ray aureole, the elaborate crown with its solid silver image of Amida, once stolen but fortunately in place again, and the canopy inset with bronze mirror betray the complex taste of the Nara period. Minor accessories preserved in the Shosoin reflect the same liking for elaborate, almost fussy detail. This is the oldest statue of Fukukenjaka Kwannon, a deity popular in Tempyo time who helped believers to keep away from evil karma and aided those who were sick and suffering. The involved iconography prepared the way for the "secret teaching" doctrines which became so popular in the ninth century. Other statues pointing ahead to the same development are the thousand-armed Kwannon of Toshodaiji, and in the Hokkedo the Shukongojin, the vajra or Thunderbolt Holder whose angry features are used to symbolize an inner benevolence. . . . It housed besides the dry-lacquer figure of Fukukenjaka Kwannon dry-lacquer images of Benten and Taishakuten, the four Guardians, and the two Kongorikishi, fierce-looking protectors of Buddhism better known as Nio. In 743 a great vegetarian entertainment was held at the temple to show reverence to the Konkommyo Saishoo. The sutra, which mentions the gods Benten (Brahmi), Taishakuten (Indra), Benzaiten, and Kichjoten, supplies the basis for the iconographical grouping. But today the two figures of Benten and Taishakuten standing immediately on either side of the central Fukukenjaka are clay images. The Hindu gods Brahma, lord of the world, and Indra, chief of the gods, were introduced into Buddhism at an early period, for the Buddha was teacher of both gods and men. The sculptures have also been identified mistakenly as Nikko and Gakko, the gods of sun and moon.

Years ago I had a talk with Paine about the Chinese and Japanese Buddhist sculptures and he urged me to go and see some of them in Nara.

On my way to lunch I could not help pondering over the enormous image of Buddha in bronze constructed by order of Emperor Shomu. He might have thought the bigger the size the stronger the Buddha's divine influence could be. Could he have seen some record or heard that there were enormous rock images of Buddha carved outside the famous Chinese caves of Yunkang and Tun-huang and adopted this idea? In his time this huge bronze image of Buddha was regarded as without precedent. It is still the largest Buddha in the world. Curiously enough I found the following passage in the English translation of a Chinese classic, *The Life of Hsüan Tsang*—The Tripitaka-Master of the Great Tzu-En Monastery, compiled by Monk Hui-li:

> To the northwest of the Nalanda Monastery was a large temple, more than 300 feet high, built by King Baladitya. . . . Further to the northwest was the place where the four past Buddhas had sat, while to the South of this place was the bronze temple built by King Siladitya. This latter was unfinished. It would have been more than 100 feet in height according to the plan. . . . At a distance more than 200 paces to the east of the city stood an image of the Buddha made of bronze. It was more than 80 feet high and could be housed only in a tall building that had six stories. This image was made by King Purnavarman of the old times.

Hsüan Tsang (600–664), who left China in 627, reached India in 633 and returned home in 645 after visiting and studying in many parts of India. The above quotation came from Hsüan Tsang's own writing. He must have seen the unfinished bronze temple and the eighty-foot high bronze image of Buddha erected in India before 749, so the fifty-four-foot bronze Buddha in Nara is not the biggest one in the world. However, the big bronze Buddha of Nara is still intact. This remains the legacy of the emperor Shomu and the pride of Japan.

The most memorable deed in the Nara period was performed by the pious and benevolent lady, the dowager empress Komyo, wife of the emperor Shomu, when she presented all her late husband's "treasures" to the temple of Todaiji. The authorities then constructed a special building to house them known as Shosoin—one of the most fabulous treasure houses in the world. Shosoin is a large rectangular log cabin with long logs piled one upon another with no windows and with the floor resting high above the ground on a number of sturdy posts. It is said that the interior has always remained dry; when it rains heavily the logs swell to close up any slight crevices and thus prevent any wind or

Shosoin

dampness from entering, but when it is dry and fine the logs shrink to leave space for ventilation. How scientifically it works and how did the designer who created the log cabin know this effect? No one is allowed to enter this building, but a number of its treasures are selected to be shown to the public for a few days in October each year. I never happened to be in Nara at the time of this exhibition, but I have seen many publications and catalogues that list many interesting objects in the collection. Many of them came from China and India and throw much light on the eighth-century court life not only of Japan but also of China and India.

I did not come to Nara merely to see the double cherry blossoms but with the earnest intention of seeing two famous temples, Horyuji and Toshodaiji, both reputed to be representative works of Chinese T'ang architecture. After having seen the Daibutsu-den and Shosoin in the morning, I took a taxi to Horyuji in the afternoon. On entering the main entrance I saw a large group of high school girls and a few boys standing on the steps with their teachers having their photographs taken with the temple building as background. The temple grounds are spacious, in which are the main hall, several smaller halls, and the elegant square five-story pagoda. The general layout produces an atmosphere of being within the quietude of a Chinese monastery, though our Chinese monasteries do not have the many stone lanterns, which are typically Japanese. I then looked at the smiling face of the central statue of Shaka Triad, a bronze of the Asuka period (623), and also gazed at the bronze halo and screen of the late Asuka period in the nearby Tachinbana Shrine, but it was not easy to distinguish all the details. Presently I moved into the back courtyard, where I found a young artist sketching by a small pond. When I walked up to him, he was kind enough to show me what he was sketching. It was a one-story building with whitewashed walls and wooden supporting pillars, which I took to be the living quarters of the monks. The different trees growing here and there with their leaves bright green directly against the sun and the top of the five-story pagoda in the distance combined into a composition for a picture. The young student-artist could not speak English, nor I Japanese, so we just smiled to each other and waved hands on parting! I climbed up to the Yume-dono (Hall of Dreams). It has an octagonal shape like the one at Kofu-kuji but this one is said to be the oldest and finest of its kind in Japan, dating back to the middle of the eighth century. A sign with the words "in memory of Langdon Warner" caught my eye and I tried to locate the monument but in vain, and there was nobody about to help me. I then walked along a narrow stream bordered by many trees, including a few cherry trees with bright red blossoms—a kind that I did not know. As it is far from the center of the city and near the foot of a hill, there was an unusual tranquillity in the air. I strolled slowly along, thinking of my meeting with Langdon Warner in Boston in 1946 directly after the war. He had then retired from his position as the curator of Oriental Art in the Fogg Museum but he had done much to arouse people's interest in Japanese art through his writings and lectures. Japanese scholars had evidently felt so grateful that they erected a memorial to him. But I had not realized that it was here in Horyuji.

Presently I returned to Kondo, or the Main Hall, to look again at the bronze Shaka Triad, for many of the visitors had now left. I moved around slowly and remembered Professor Peter H. Lee of the University of Hawaii, editor-translator of the *Anthology of Korean Poetry*, telling me:

> In Kondo of Horyuji the Shaka Triad was the creation of Kuratsu-kuri-otori, a grandson of the Pakche national named Shiba Tasshi. And the Kudara Kwannon carved out of one straight tree trunk with a pair of most elegantly elongated legs which serenity was also transmitted by a Pakche artist of ancient Korea.

Then I had a look at the famous murals which were said to have been based on an original sketch of a Koguryu (a part of ancient Korea) monk named Tamjing. They are only replicas, the originals having been destroyed by fire. Actually the murals show considerable influence from the frescoes of Ajanta in India. Again I saw the Tamamushi Zushi, the beetle-wing shrine which has pictures on four sides—they were all of colored lacquer. Although this kind of design is called *T'ang ts'ao,* or Chinese drawings of Six Dynasties, it is a technique which had been

Kudara Kwannon

used in Korea. Robert Paine said that the cypress wood of which the shrine is made, however, is of a type found in Japan, but not in Korea. It is clear that many Koreans must have settled in Japan in those early days and must have been employed to carry out most of this work, according to the method they had learned in China; and it is unlikely it was done by Chinese. It can certainly be said that there are more Korean influences in Horyuji than Chinese.

After studying the three Buddha statues in the Lecture Hall, I strolled out by the pond in front of the Shoryoin, or Sacred Spirit Hall, for Prince Shotoku, the founder of Japanese Buddhism. Indeed, though Buddhism had its Indian origin, Chinese Buddhist architecture shows no Indian influence at all. China has created a Buddhist architecture of her own, similar to the design of her palace buildings, which indicates how conservative is the Chinese mind. Japanese Buddhist temples with their curved roofs definitely show a Chinese influence. As in Kyoto, there are numerous Buddhist temples in the city; Nara is known to be very much like a Chinese city.

Though Prince Shotoku was regarded as the founder of Buddhism in Japan, he did have some difficulty in getting his way. Legend says that he was able to speak words distinctly when only a few weeks old. He was known as Prince Umayado No Oji, or Prince of the Horse-stable Door, because his mother gave birth to him soon after she passed a stable. After the death of Prince Shotoku's father, Emperor Yomei, the empress dowager was made the sovereign of Japan under the new name of Empress Suiko. She appointed Prince Shotoku as heir apparent to the throne and a regent. Prince Shotoku acted wisely as a great statesman and originated a code of seventeen articles for the government of the nation which were the first written laws of Japan. He erected many Buddhist temples and propagated Buddhism throughout the country. He died in A.D. 620, just at the beginning of the T'ang dynasty in China, and never ascended the throne, for the empress Suiko outlived him.

I remember reading a Chinese record telling how in the third month of A.D. 608 the ruler of Japan sent a letter to the Chinese emperor Yang-ti, as coming from the emperor of the Rising Sun to the emperor of the Setting Sun to inquire about his health. The letter seemed to have been drafted by Prince Shotoku. If he was well learned in Chinese classics and literature he must have known that "From the Rising-up one to the Going-down one" implied an insult to the Chinese. The Chinese history recorded that when Emperor Yang-ti received this letter he was so annoyed that he decreed that letters from foreign barbarians, if impolite, should not be reported to him.

Prince Shotoku (573–621), who founded the Horyuji temple, was not only regarded as a great patron of Buddhism, but also of Japanese art, religion, and culture in general. It has long been thought by many that Japan was highly influenced by the Chinese civilization and had taken almost all its culture from China. At first glance many aspects are undeniable but, to my way of thinking, this could be misleading. It is clearly recorded that in 594 the Koguryu monk Hyeje became tutor to Prince Shotoku. This means that the prince received his knowledge of Chinese and Buddhism from a Korean scholar who must have been extremely learned to have influenced the prince so deeply and converted him so strongly to the Buddhist faith. In the beginning of the seventh century, another Koguryu, named Hyegwan, came to Japan where he founded the Japanese Madhyamika, or Three Sastra Sect. Professor Peter Lee of the University of Hawaii told me:

> Buddhism had been transmitted to Japan in 552 from Pakche, one of the three kingdoms in Korea together with Silla and Koguryu. Pakche contributed most of the formation of Japanese culture. The traffic began in the latter part of the fourth century when Pakche sent scholars Ajiki and Wani to transmit Chinese writings and classics. Wani introduced the *Analects* of Confucius and the *Thousand Characters*. Besides Buddhist scholars and monks and some muicians, artisans, painters, brickmakers, and shipbuilders also came to Japan from Pakche and those helped to dig lakes and dikes and to construct reservoirs. In 601, the Pakche monk, Kwalluk, introduced calendars and books on astronomy and geography. In Japan, those learned Pakche people were known as Fuhite, and the artists were known as Tehito. The Pakche doctor Tongnae became famous, and his descendants all lived and practiced in Naniwa (modern Osaka). The wife of Emperor Kammu (782–805) was a Pakche national.

From what I saw of the works done by the Pakche builders, carvers, and artist-painters in the Horyuji Temple, together with all these facts which I have learned, it seems to me that the Koreans should take the credit for having introduced Chinese civilization to Japan. Our forefathers did nothing about it. I have never learned from any Chinese source that Korea produced so many great scholars, skilled craftsmen, and artists, who carried the characteristic Chinese civilization to Japan in the sixth and seventh centuries. I think most of the credit for the spread of Chinese culture in Japan should go to the early Korean immigrants. At any rate the world should know that the Japanese took over Chinese civilization from the Koreans, not from the Chinese directly.

I then gave the Shoryoin a deep bow to express my reverence for the Prince Shotoku before I strolled round the right side along the edge of the pond. I noticed an old tree with the main part of its trunk all crooked and rugged yet having a number of new branches with young leaves shining green against the sun; it was so old that it could have

An old tree

been planted in those early days when Horyuji was first built. Its aged look intrigued me and I began to sketch it from several angles. Later a simple verse came into my mind, which I roughly translate as follows:

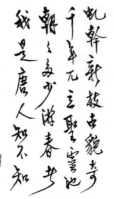

Dragonlike trunk with new branches, its antique
  face is intriguing;
Standing over a thousand years before Prince Shotoku's shrine.
Day after day how many people have come to visit
  this place,
Do you know me, I wonder—a man of T'ang?

The Japanese in the old days always called the Chinese men of T'ang.

From the pond off toward the left, passing through the Todaimon, or Big East Gate, and then the Shikoyakumon, or Gate of Four Legs, eventually I saw a sign hanging from the door, bearing the words "Chuguji Temple." A woman made a sign to me not to enter, but I pointed to my watch that it was not yet five o'clock. She realized that I was a visitor who could not speak Japanese and let me in to see the hall where the famous statue of Siddhartha, or Kwannon, was sitting in meditation in an absolutely unperturbed pose in the center. I knew before I came that it was carved from bare camphor wood and was not lacquered, yet the whole body seemed to glow and illuminate every corner of the hall. I was the only one there, standing dumfounded and hardly daring to breathe lest the image be disturbed by my presence. But not the slightest expression altered; the gentle inward smiling continued to impart a sense of having been enlightened. I moved very slowly around it, amazed at how the artist could have conceived such a figure in his imagination. Professor Peter Lee did tell me that this statue was also the work of Kuratsukuri-otori, as was the Shaka Triad in the Kondo and the Kudara Kwannon. I began to see in the rather rectangular face of this seated statue quite a similarity with that of the Kudara Kwannon, though the latter did not have such a gentle and soft smile. This is the only statue of Buddha or Bodhisattva that wears nothing on the upper part of the body, not even a necklace or bracelet. It was a young body, full of deep feeling and lovableness. It wore a long flowing skirt draped like that of the central figure in the Shaka Triad, which seemed to me to resemble very closely the drapery of some early Chinese Buddhist stone sculptures of the Northern Wei period (386–557). The greatness of this statue lies in its simplicity.

Siddhartha

When I came out of the hall I stepped into the courtyard of the next building, but the women would not allow me to proceed, for there was a wedding party in progress. I learned later that Chuguji is a nunnery. The nuns must have looked after that statue of Siddhartha, or Kwannon, day and night, dusting and polishing it all the time for hundreds of years.

The Toshodaiji Temple bears the Chinese name "T'ang Chao-t'i Szu," clearly indicating that this temple must have been modeled upon a Chinese one of the T'ang period. *Chao-t'i* is from the Sanskrit *caturdisa,* which means "belonging to the four quarters, that is, the Samgha or Church or name of a monastery." This is the only Buddhist temple with the word *T'ang* for its qualification in Japan; it was, in fact, founded by a Chinese priest, Chien Chen, or Gangin in Japanese pronunciation, in 759. Chien Chen was born in 688 and was ordained a monk at fourteen at the Ta Yun Monastery in Yangchow of Kiangsu Province. He later went north to make further study of Buddhism in Loyang as well as in Ch'ang-an under many famous priests. Apart from his knowledge of Buddhism, he excelled in the study of Chinese architecture and also in medicine. Within ten years he became widely known as the leader of the Chinese Buddhist religion. In 733 the emperor Shomu Tenno of Japan sent the priest Eiei of Kofukuji Temple and Fucu of Ra-an-ji to invite Chien Chen to come to Japan. At that time the sea voyage was dreaded by many. Chien Chen had no response from his disciple so he decided to lead the expedition himself. He made preparations with the help of the two Japanese monks and gathered more than a hundred and eighty persons including artists, jade carvers, wood and stone engravers, and embroiderers and bought a large ship for the trip. Unfortunately they encountered a strong wind and the ship ran aground on a small island. They suffered hardship; the winter of 743 was an especially bitter one. In the first month of the following year they had the boat repaired and started out once more to sail for Japan, but again the boat struck a hidden rock and was wrecked only a short distance from land. A number lost their lives. Chien Chen and a few others were without food for three days and nights. Eventually some fishermen rescued them and brought them to Ningpo in Chekiang Province. Chien Chen stayed at King Asoka Monastery at Ningpo for a year, then made a third attempt but failed again. He then went round preaching at different monasteries and tried to reorganize a party for Japan for the fourth time, still without success. But Chien Chen, though now aged sixty-one, never swayed in his determination to go to Japan. He continued to make plans, against the opposition of his disciples, who feared for the life of their devoted master, and eventually they set out for the fifth time. In 748 this time they encountered a typhoon and their troubles were worse than ever. The sailors lost control and just let the boat drift. They had no proper food but chewed some uncooked rice to stem their hunger. For fourteen days they managed to survive, and then their boat touched the shore of Yai-hsien on Hainan Island, the southernmost part of China. Chien Chen became blind, while his Japanese disciple Eiei fell gravely ill. Before he died, he said to Chien Chen: "I desired to assist you, Master, to spread teaching, but my life is coming to an end. I still hope you will carry the Vinaya sect to Japan and become its first patriarch there, though I may not live to see it I shall die without regret." Chien Chen was very touched by his devotion and wept bitterly. Another five years slipped by, but in 753 Chien Chen received the help of the Japanese envoy to the Chinese palace and decided to embark on the sixth attempt to reach Japan. His Japanese disciple Fusho happily came to join him and on the envoy ship they reached Japan at long last. Most of the people whom he originally planned to bring with him had died; only a handful remained—Fusho, Pu-chao, Shitaku Szu-t'o, and two or three others.

On Chien Chen's arrival at Nara, the Japanese court from the emperor down to the humblest subject gave him a great welcome and treated him as the most honored foreign guest with the deepest reverence. He first stayed at Todaiji and preached the Vinaya school, or Ritsu sect, of Buddhism, stressing the *sila* (Sanskrit for "commandment discipline"). At first most of the learned Japanese monks declined to receive ordination, for a Japanese could become a monk simply by vowing his devoted faith before the great statue of Buddha. The Chinese way of ordination includes the painful practice of burning brands, up to nine in number, on the top of the shaved head. There was some debate about the ordination in the ceremony but the Japanese monks were won over, so it is said, after a lengthy exposition by Szu-t'o. I would like to know if the Japanese monks were indeed ordained in the Chinese way during the eighth or ninth century, for there are no Japanese or Chinese records about it, nor have I seen a Japanese monk with ordination scars on his scalp. I consider this a stumbling block to making Buddhism a state religion in China, though there are no doubt other reasons. The practice of Chinese ordination is still carried on in many monasteries; I witnessed the ceremony in a Chinese monastery in Singapore a few years ago.

Though completely blind and at the age of sixty-six when he arrived in Japan, Chien Chen greatly influenced the Japanese. He did not know Japanese but did all his teaching in Chinese. In those days most of his Japanese audience must have known Chinese well enough to understand him. There was no record saying that he had an interpreter while he preached. He was born in Yangchow, the northern part of Kiangsu Province, where the people speak a dialect slightly different from the Peking dialect, or the so-called Mandarin dialect. His pronunciation of many Chinese characters could have been incorporated into the modern Japanese pronunciations of similar kanji words such as the word for *three* as "san," that for *mountain* as "zan," and that for *death* "shi." Despite his blindness, Chien Chen was asked to check the many translated sutras printed in Japan and he made corrections in them from memory. It is said that he also co-operated with his disciples in preparing the engraving of three sets of sutras for printing in Japan, some ten years earlier than the world-renowned oldest printed book, *Dharani sutra,* printed in Japan in A.D. 770. Also, many of his medical prescriptions were incorporated in Japanese medical books. After a short stay in Todaiji, Chien Chen, from the imperial purse and by public donations, was provided with the land and money to start building the Toshodaiji Temple of T'ang to serve as the headquarters of the Ritsu sect of Buddhism in Japan. He and his disciples, Szu-t'o among them, designed and built twelve of the present temple buildings—the Kondo, the Lecture Hall, the Hall of Royal Portraits, the Hall Manjusri, the Hall of Ti-tsang, or Jizo, the bell tower, and others. In addition, some of his followers who were sculptors created the main statue of Buddha, the thousand-armed Kwannon in the Kondo, and other statues. Chien Chen can be regarded as a perfect scholar in many branches of learning and one who had been responsible for bringing so much of things Chinese—art, medicine, and painting—to Japan.

The thought of the hardships he suffered in all six attempts to reach Japan and of his immovable determination in carrying out his desire, as well as his powerful personality, filled me with awe as I made my way to the Kondo of the Toshodaiji Temple. Both sides of the main footpath were lined with tall pines, maples, and other trees, which seemed to enhance the stillness of the atmosphere. Had it not been for the Japanese stone lanterns in the courtyard before the steps, I should have felt I was walking in a Chinese monastery on Mt. Lu or in Hangchow. The cloisters, with massive wooden pillars, reminded me of my homeland, where many big temples have just such a cloister round the hall for strolling to and fro and for meditation. The ceiling, made of wooden pieces arranged in many squares like a checkerboard, was very Chinese in style. What interested me were the slightly squarish faces of the dry-lacquered main Buddha in the center and of the thousand-armed Kwannon on the right and of another Buddha on the left, which resemble the northern Chinese faces, squarish with a heavy chin, unlike those rectangular faces sculptured by the Pakche artists in Horyuji. On careful investigation of the whole temple I found two small log cabins similar to the one at Shosoin, and I took them to contain treasures for a similar purpose, though I don't remember seeing any log cabins inside any Chinese monastery. The log cabins for treasures would be a Japanese creation. There was also a small stone monument with the following words in Japanese engraved on it and translated as follows:

> If you only allow me,
> I will willingly wipe
> Salt tears from your eyes
> with these fresh leaves.

Chien Chen

"Chien Chen, founder of the Toshodaiji Temple, is said to have lost his sight on his way to Japan on account of the salt that got into his eyes while he endured seven different trials on the sea. After bowing devoutly before his statue, I wrote . . ." This passage comes from Basho's book *The Narrow Road to the Deep North and Other Travel Sketches*, translated by Nobuyuki Yuasa.

There is a handscroll, more than fifty feet long, depicting the six attempts of Chien Chen to reach Japan, painted in 1290, but I could not see it, for it was kept in the treasure log cabin. The stone-piled platform with three stories not far from the main hall interested me intensely, for this was where the practice of sila, or commandment discipline, was performed, and I tried to imagine Chien Chen being present there. I also noticed that at each end of the top roof of the Kondo was a shibi, not in the form of dolphins like most Japanese castle roofs. At the end of my visit to Toshodaiji, I thought to myself with amazement, "How much one man like Chien Chen could do even when he had no sight!"

Close by was the Yakushiji Temple, built in 680 representing the Fa-hsiang, or Dharmalaksan sect. The faces of the three Buddhas in the Kondo are slightly rectangular, suggesting the Asuka period. I particularly liked the Yakushiji pagoda, Japanese style of five-stories, with its wooden beams and pillars all painted Indian red, not vermillion, and its walls white. All the other buildings in the Yakushiji Temple grounds are painted similarly and together they breathed a harmony. Their dull red color gave them an air of peacefulness and an antique flavor. Inside one of the small halls a monk was seated chanting a sutra while beating a wooden fish. The sound of the chanting was very similar to that of a Chinese monk in China. I then found a small hall, in the center of which was a stone, its top side well polished and engraved with the designs of the soles of Buddha's two feet. Thus it was called Hall of Buddha's Feet.

I enjoyed my visits to the Toshodaiji and Yakushiji temples, for I was one of the very few visitors there and I could move about freely anywhere I chose. But on my way up to the Kasuga Shrine I found innumerable sightseers on the stone steps. Not only that, but many deer began to follow me round, sometimes thrusting their heads toward me, licking my hands, and sometimes even treading on my feet. Deer are a typical sight in Nara. I have read that the remotest ancestor of the Fujiwara family, the god Amenokyane-no-Mikoto, to whom a shrine is dedicated, once rode on a deer and from that time the deer was regarded as a sacred animal, roaming about freely and becoming very tame once the antlers are cut off. An annual dehorning of deer takes place at Kasuga Shrine in mid-October. I was told that there used to be deer everywhere in Japan, but now they are only found in Nara and Hokkaido. The Japanese, particularly the Ainus of Hokkaido, not only eat their flesh but also use their fur for clothing. I must say that I like to paint deer, for I am interested in their slender legs, elegant manner of walking, their intelligent heads, and brilliantly alert eyes. I never came so close to deer as I did in Nara and I spent a good deal of my time sketching them. The leaping of the deer and their fast running movements may have inspired the well-known deer scroll by Ra Waraya Sotatsu (1576–1643) in the Seattle Museum of Fine Art. This could have been painted when more deer were about in Japan. There are many other Japanese painters, such as Ganku and Tsusen, whose deer paintings tend to be naturalistic and who could have been influenced by the work of Shen Chüan, or Shen Nan-pin, a Chinese painter who spent three years teaching painting in Nagasaki from 1696 on.

Another typical sight in Nara is the stone lantern. The higher up I climbed to the Kasuga Shrine, the more stone lanterns appeared. Eventually the vermillion-painted shrine came in sight with its whitewashed panels. No other Shinto shrine that I have seen was painted so brilliantly. Many more lanterns, now in metal, were hanging from the walls. There are two thousand stone lanterns and a thousand metal ones. I was told that they would be lit up, one by one, on August fifteenth, the Bon Festival, and the spectacle must be lovely.

There are far too many objects to be seen in the Nara National Museum on a brief visit. Apart from many permanent exhibits which belong to the museum, a number of exhibits came from other collections and are changed from time to time. The pottery model of a five-story pagoda of the Heian period excavated at Shizuoka Prefecture interested me, for it resembles pottery models of Chinese Han-dynasty towers, though the latter are less elaborate, as there is a thousand-year difference. Several of the old pottery tiles and brick captured my attention, as well as the old manuscripts and two of the sixteen arhat paintings dated from the Chinese Southern Sung·period and signed Lu Hsing-chung, a painter whose work I had not seen before. But the really good items in this museum are the many carved wooden or dry-lacquered statues of Buddhas and Bodhisattvas, and especially the four deva guardian kings. Though they have been inspired by Buddhism and are most likely based on the type of Chinese Buddhist statue, I think the Japanese Buddhist sculptors have developed in their art, particularly in wood and lacquer, a style of their own, starting in the Kamakura period. They showed particular dexterity in woodcarving and as a rule achieved fine and well-finished products. Those four deva guardian kings each had a different expression and gesture, and I was specially interested in examining the grain of the bare wood texture appropriately arranged for heads, shoulders, and chests of the statues of Mahakala, or the great black deva, of the boy Zennishi Doji, or Kumara, or Makorataisho, and many others. They were neither painted nor lacquered, with the definite purpose of showing how excellently the wood had been selected and arranged. This reminded me of Chinese jade carvers who, with a good piece of jade, uneven in color as all large pieces are, would spend days

Carved Buddhist images outside the town of Usuki near Oita

or even months planning how best to arrange the colors to suit and har-
monize with the object they were going to carve. One can see many
good examples of Chinese jade carving in many big museums of the
world including those in Japan.

The Japanese sculptors have carved many fine likenesses of well-
known monks, which have been set up in different temples. The carving
of the abbot of Toshodaiji Temple may have been the first example of
these. In all my travels in Japan, I have not seen a good Japanese Buddhist sculpture in stone, nor any caves with stone carvings like the Yunkang and Tun-huang caves of China. I did see a number of Buddhist
images carved into the stone cliffs just outside of the town of Usuki, not
far from Oita, but the sandstone did not help the artists to produce great
works of art.

In the main hall of the Nara Hotel hangs a long vertical scroll of calligraphy in Chinese characters written by a noted Japanese calligrapher
consisting of the following poem by a poet-monk, Su Man-shu:

On the pavilion in spring rain I play shakuhachi
   so,
And wonder when I can return to watch the tide
   at Chekiang.
In straw sandals and with a tin bowl, no one
   knows me;
Which number of the cherry blossom bridge am
   I crossing in Japan now?

春雨樓頭尺八簫
何時歸看浙江潮
芒鞋破鉢無人識
踏過櫻花第幾橋

Mr. Su was born in Yokohama not far from Tokyo, of a Japanese
mother and a Chinese father who was a businessman there. Being half
Chinese and half Japanese, he was not well received by the clan of his
father's family. After his father's death, his mother went back to Japan.
However, his elder half-brother, a pure Chinese, treated him very kindly
and supported him financially. So he continued his study with no break.
He received his education both in Japan and China and became a
learned scholar; he was also a brilliant linguist, knowing Sanskrit and
English, had translated a number of Byron's poems into classical
Chinese, and had also written many original poems and a novel. He was
also a painter and made a number of paintings in Chinese traditional
technique with some Japanese touches, which have been reproduced in a
book. Through his writing and painting he made many good friends

among the circles of Chinese men of letters. In Tokyo he associated himself with the revolutionary movement led by Dr. Sun Yat-sen at the beginning of this century. Being romantic by nature, he led a romantic life and then became a Buddhist monk; he died young, just a little over thirty. How many talented men like Mr. Su endured the sad life suppressed by unreasonable traditions and distasteful racial discriminations! Since Su had no connection with Nara, I had no idea that I would find his poem during my stay there.

Back lane of Toshodaiji

XIII

Takamatsu Port of Shikoku

A HEAVY MIST lay over the banks of Kobe Harbor when I went on board a steamer for Takamatsu on Shikoku Island. Not many buildings could be seen clearly; only the Kobe metal tower showed a pale reddish outline. The sun had long left Kobe for some other place. The rain that had begun gradually became heavier and heavier. Many passengers, including a large number of school girls and boys, were already occupying most of the seats. I managed to find a space for standing. It was odd to hear a band playing "Auld Lang Syne" after the steamer started to move. Soon we were passing through the strait between Awaji, the largest island in the Inland Sea, and the shores of Honshu. There was a constant commotion on the steamer, for the youngsters kept moving from one side to the other. None of them could see much in the heavy rain. The water surface was choppy, but the steamer, owing to its considerable size, was steady. Gradually it sailed so close to a big rocky islet that the pine trees on it could be counted one by one as we passed slowly by. The mist began to lift and the rain stopped. In the distance the sun cast a shaft of light like a searchlight. Actually the ray did not really move, but it looked to be mobile on account of the movement of our steamer. We could now see much farther and I drew a deep breath as I faced the wide expanse. There was an indescribable pleasantness in the air. More small islands appeared, and then disappeared as the steamer moved away. On a few of the islands people could be seen moving about. Then a big commotion started on the steamer; we were soon to land at Takamatsu!

The school children filed out first. Then there emerged from the cabins a number of men and women all dressed in white—kimono and leggings of white cotton; white *tabi,* or socks; white *teko,* or fingerless gloves, that only cover the back of the hands; and, on their heads, small shallow cone-shaped bamboo or palm hats. Many had a long stick or staff in their hands. They were Buddhist pilgrims, or *Ohenro-San.* These pilgrims would make a series of visits to every one of the eighty-eight temples which were either built by or associated with the great Japanese monk, Kōbō Daishi, who was born some thirteen hundred years ago in

A Buddhist pilgrim

Byobuga-ura not far from the present Takamatsu. In his younger days and after his return from his two-year stay in China, Kōbō Daishi walked almost everywhere on Shikoku Island and had left legends behind wherever he had been. His greatness in Japanese Buddhism is immeasurable and his name has become inseparable from Shikoku. Japanese pilgrims go to Shikoku as others go to Mecca or Jerusalem. It is said that fifty thousand or more pilgrims annually come to do the round of the eighty-eight temples on Shikoku and they usually make a start at Ryozenji Temple in Tokushima Prefecture and finish at Takamatsu. In the old days most of the pilgrims made the round on foot; now some take advantage of busses and cars. When I gazed at these pilgrims in their white dresses, a kind of uniform, I became more assured of the Japanese innate sense for system and organization. And they move about in groups, unlike the Chinese, who move about singly or at most in their own family unit.

Takamatsu looks quite a busy port, used as a transfer point by travellers to Honshu for Tokyo and other big cities. Some of the passengers from our steamer went on to another steamer and some boarded busses. A guide rounded up twelve of us and took us in three taxis to the Shin-Tokiwa Inn, typically Japanese in style. Several maids in kimonos saw that we changed our shoes for slippers and then led us to our respective rooms. In mine there was a hanging scroll with a poem in kanji written by a Japanese whose name was unfamiliar to me, though the calligraphy was quite good. The sun never came out on our arrival at Takamatsu, though there was no more rain. The twilight was dull outside my window. Soon we assembled for dinner in a hall at two tables. I found the food good, particularly the fresh seafood, though a stout American declared that the portion in each dish was far too small. He seemed to have missed his steak terribly. A small palm tree was growing in a pot in the hall and two small cacti in a tiny porcelain bowl suggested that the climate here was mild. In fact it is said to be subtropical.

Next morning the sun had already risen quite high in the sky when we finished our breakfast and climbed in the bus outside the inn. The air, the sight of a few tall palm trees, the sunshine, and the scents from flowers somewhere seemed to go slightly to our heads; we all looked exhilarated. A girl guide began to sing a local song as did those on many bus trips I took in Japan. It seems that to be a guide in Japan, a girl must not only have good looks and the ability to take care of all her charges, but also must have a good voice for providing entertainment on the way. Luckily Japan has many good-looking girls who seem to be born singers. And apparently each place in Japan has a traditional folk-song. As soon as we got down from the bus, one of our group saw two Japanese carrying a palanquin, somewhat like a Chinese sedan chair,

A palanquin

and he wanted to try it. The two Japanese carriers probably never experienced such a heavy load and swayed the palanquin quite a bit with their mouths wide open gasping for breath. I walked with the rest of the party and passed by a few shops, two of which were selling interesting rocks and I chose two small pieces to add to my collection.

We were now on the Yashima Plateau. The guide took us to a point where a low wall was built along the mountain edge and some stone benches were placed about. This celebrated beauty spot is a somewhat long and narrow tongue of land stretching westward into the Inland Sea. Two high mountains on both sides—deep green against the azure sky—caused a narrow strip of sea in between them to become deeper blue. Faint images of a few islands lying far away beyond the tip of the tongue of land gave me a feeling of infinity and of something which was invisible, mysterious, and supernatural. An elevating and exalting sight indeed!

From this high ground I looked vertically down on a number of scattered houses and part of a beach, as well as two or three pole-studded weirs for catching fish, crabs, and crayfish near the shore. There was such an uncanny stillness in the morning air at that moment—a sharp contrast to the days when Taira-no-Munemori, chief of the Taira clan, fled from Kyoto, taking the infant emperor with him to Yashima in 1182. This tranquil spot saw a great, bloody battle then. "At Yashima they [the Taira clan] enlisted the services of several lords in Shikoku and in the San-yo district," says the Japan Official Guide. "Thus strengthened they transferred their headquarters back to Jukuhara, Kobe, but were again compelled to flee . . . and to take refuge for the second time at Yashima." Professor Edwin O. Reischauer wrote in *Japan, Past and Present*:

> Meanwhile the remnants of the Minamoto family slowly recouped their fortune in their old family stronghold in eastern Japan. Eventually the Minamoto felt themselves strong enough again to challenge Taira supremacy, and in a bitterly fought war between 1182 and 1185 they completely crushed the Taira faction. The Taira leaders either were killed or committed suicide, and the new boy emperor who was the grandson of Kiyomori (first head of the Taira clan) perished with his Taira relatives in the final days of the war.

I learned that in April, 1185, the final battle took place at Dan no Ura Bay, east of Shimonoseki, where the Heike (Taira clan) fleet was annihilated. Naturally nearly all the Taira warriors were drowned or killed. Since 1185, some tiny crabs which appeared in Dan no Ura with some strange marks resembling human faces on their upper shells have been called Heike-gani, or Taira crabs. The local people believe that the crabs are the wraiths of the Taira warriors who died at that place.

Presently the guide came to herd us into the bus again. On the way downward we got out at a gate which led us to the Ritsurin Park. We walked along the footpath in the northern part of the park after having crossed two small stone bridges and I looked at the many red and white carp, a typical Japanese speciality, in the ponds, where the water was exceedingly clear and all the fish seemed to be playing with tiny pebbles. Many beautifully shaped pine trees were grouped together all about the place. Rocks of various sizes with veins of different colors were well arranged naturally beside the ponds. In the southern part of the park we came to the Kikugetsutei Teahouse, by the side of which was a pool with the poetic name "Moon-Scooping Pool." This name could have been derived from the following two lines of a Zen poem:

 Scooping the water, the moon is in my hand; Playing with flowers, my dress is full of scent.

I made a rough sketch with two rocks in an enclosure not far from the teahouse. The park was formerly the seat of the Matsudaira family and was laid out on the grand scale, having six ponds, thirteen hills, numerous bridges, and countless pine trees and rocks. It also has an art gallery and a small zoological garden, but we had no time to visit them. After we left the park we were shown, in a narrow street, an inconspicuous tombstone of Hidari Jingoro (1594–1651), who carved the Red Gate at Tokyo University, also *The Sleeping Kitten* at Nikko Toshogu, and the climbing dragon at Ueno Park, and he was as well the designer of the escape tunnel from the Edo Castle.

The famous bonsai, or miniature trees, from Kinashi not far from Takamatsu have not only been supplied to all parts of Japan for centuries but are now transported to the whole world. The Onago-Dori, or long-tailed cocks, are specially raised in Nangoku, a city in the southern part of Shikoku, where the crops of mandarin oranges are plentiful enough to provide for the demands of other Japanese cities. The guide also told us that two great modern leaders, Ryoma Sakamoto, who took an active part in effecting the Meiji Restoration and who was the founder of the Japanese navy, and Count Taisuke Itagaki, founder of Japan's first genuine political party, were both Shikoku-born, and both contributed much to the modernization of Japan. Thus Shikoku had a great share in the building of modern Japan.

There are two castles on Shikoku, Kochi Castle and Matsuyama Castle. The latter is considered the best preserved of all castle buildings in Japan, for it has not suffered much damage since it was originally built more than three hundred and fifty years ago. I did not have the chance to see it, but my friend and colleague Professor Martin Wilbur told me how he and Mrs. Wilbur went to see it in 1962.

Around Matsuyama city is a flat plain, but there is one peak about eight hundred feet high, arising abruptly from it. In the sixteenth century the Lord of Matsuyama, Kato Kiyomasa, built this castle on the top of the peak. A very large area surrounding the peak was also moated and walled, big enough that now it contains a park with several athletic fields within. On the pinnacle is a white three-story castle that commands a magnificent view of the close and the surrounding plain.

We ascended the peak by cable car, which took about five minutes. Our landing point was a large area surrounded by a sheer clifflike wall dropping down thirty or forty feet. From this area we wound our way up to higher levels, passing between rearing walls on a narrow, twisting approach road. After passing through several gates, each protected by battlements and doubling back and forth, we finally reached the eminence on which the castle itself stands. Even the castle can be entered only by two successive gates within walls. For an army possessing only primitive muskets, bows, and small cannon to reach the castle through the maze of walls and gates and narrow approaches must have been an almost impossible undertaking. The smallest of the stones from which the walls were made were two or three feet on a side, but some measured from seven to ten feet long. It must have been a killing job to drag those rocks up the steep hill and lift them into place in the walls. Yet they were marvelously fitted together and formed a nearly perpendicular face.

Once in the main gate of the castle you are still only in a sort of dungeon from which you must climb a steeply inclined ladder. Here you come out on the lowest of the three stories. The windows are set with loopholes for firing down upon the platform on which the castle rests. The timbers holding up the bottom story were huge, perhaps two feet in diameter. The three main floors of the castle are devoted to exhibits of arms, armor, and objects of daily use, presumably of the sixteenth and seventeenth centuries. The chambers get smaller as one goes up, each next floor being achieved by a steep ladderlike set of stairs. The view from the top is grand, out across the busy city of Matsuyama to emerald rice fields and mountains beyond.

Most of the Japanese castles on Honshu are new replicas in concrete, for their original structures were either destroyed by fire or war. The Genji-Heike War from 1182 to 1185 does not seem to have touched Matsuyama.

An interesting legend was told me about Matsuyama when the great monk Kōbō Daishi visited a place nearby more than a thousand years ago. There was a pigheaded and greedy man called Uemon-saburo. When Kōbō Daishi was going round from house to house, as many Buddhist monks do begging for alms, he came to Uemon-saburo's with his bowl to ask for rice. Uemon-saburo flew into a great rage and knocked the bowl to the ground, breaking it into eight pieces. Soon afterward, some unusual happenings took place in Uemon-saburo's house: his eight sons died one after another in strange circumstances. The local people began to regard this as a severe punishment from Buddha for Uemon-saburo's uncivil act toward Kōbō Daishi. Uemon-saburo became aware of this punishment and immediately shaved his head, put on a monk's robe, and went on a pilgrimage murmuring all the time a prayer for forgiveness for his former rude behavior. On the last pilgrimage he died. Soon after his death, the wife of the local lord Kono gave birth to a child holding a small stone in his tender palm with the word *Uemon-saburo* incised on it. So this tiny baby became known as Uemon-saburo reincarnated and his rude behavior was forgotten.

XIV

The Floating Shrine of Miyajima

HIROSHIMA WAS on the list of a tour I joined for a visit to Miyajima. I was told that the floating shrine at Miyajima could be easily reached by a ferryboat from Hiroshima, but I had no idea that we had to spend a day and night in the city. Hiroshima has been in my mind the saddest spot in the modern history of mankind, since the first atom bomb was dropped there in 1945. A dry day greeted us upon our arrival and we were installed in a beautiful, spacious hotel with modern facilities. There was no sign of the bomb's scar to be seen, nor any sadness in the air. It is a completely new metropolis in the midwest of Japan.

After a good midday meal, we were taken to see the so-called Peace Park and the Peace Museum, which displays many documental records of the horrible destruction and mass killing caused by the atom bomb. I was much dismayed by the sight of them. For the past thirty odd years I have expressed a strong belief in my writings that we are now living in a much saner age than before. From history we learned of the Roman emperor Nero's enjoyment of the slaughter of people by wild beasts, the incessant political assassinations of medieval Europe, the black-slavery period, the Spanish conquistadors' suppression of the American Indians, the British settlers hunting the aborigines on the island of Tasmania off Australia, the Mongolian, as well as the Manchurian, massacres of the Chinese when each came to rule China, and so on. Those killings in the past took place over days, months, and years. Now an atom bomb can destroy thousands and thousands of lives in a few minutes. Are we really saner now than before?

Only one bomb scar, the skeleton of an industrial building, stood out by the other side of the river. Can it become a modern ruin?

Next morning a heavy mist covered all the surroundings and it was rather chilly for mid-April. It had begun to rain when we went to Miyajima-guchi to board the ferryboat. It was shaped like a dragon with its head at the bow and tail at the stern, which reminded me of the Dragon Boat Race Festival of my younger days in China. It was still raining gently when the boat left the shore. The raindrops produced myriads of jumping pearls on the water's surface. We were moving toward the mys-

The ferryboat shaped like a dragon

terious bluish green mass of hills. They looked so inviting I stared ahead with unusual expectation. Presently an indistinct reddish object seemed to emerge from the water. It was a wooden structure, painted red and erected in the sea near the shore like a gate for our boat to go through. Gently our boat moved closer to the enchanted island; it did not go through the red gate but to a landing stage not far from it.

We were right inside the morning mist now. The hills stretched far on both sides. The haze of shimmering luxuriant woods that spread all around the foot of the hills sparkled with a confusion of colorful tints. The top of a Japanese pagoda lifted its head in pride above the trees and house roofs. We landed and were led through a narrow street lined with gift shops, each of which had sprays of red paper cherry blossoms hanging outside. The tips of a few real cherry trees were actually in bloom among the rain-washed green needles of pines. The narrow street, already crowded, now became filled to overflowing with the addition of our party. There was much activity and a cheerfulness filled the air despite the wetness of the road. We were on Miyajima Island, one of the three most scenic spots of Japan.

After a few short turns we walked around the base of the five-story pagoda. Then we moved on to the Thousand-Mat Pavilion, so called because it is supposed to contain one thousand Japanese floor mats, but the guide told us that there were in fact only 450 mats, some of which were now wearing out. This pavilion was said to have been built by Toyotomi Hideyoshi, the soldier-hero of Osaka Castle, with the wood from one single gigantic camphor tree. Hideyoshi used this pavilion as his staff headquarters during the invasion of Korea in 1588. There were also thousands of rice scoops inside the building, each of which was inscribed with the donor's name. Soldiers who were quartered here to await transportation to the Sino-Japanese War offered their rice scoops to the gods as a kind of prayer for victory and safe return. Being a China-born Chinese who as a schoolboy had read much about the great injustice wrought on the Chinese by the Japanese during the Sino-Japanese War, I naturally did not like being reminded of this piece of

The narrow street

past history and was surprised to find this holy place having some connection with the war against my native country more than seventy years ago. I had never imagined that Shinto gods would have so much to do with wars, just as it surprised me to find Jesus Christ connected with European wars such as the Crusades. Neither Buddha nor Lao-Tzu nor Confucius had any share in wars!

Shortly I came face to face with the enormous structure of the famous red torii standing firmly in the sea a little distance from the shore, which I had called a red gate. It is the biggest torii in the whole of Japan, 53 feet high with a 77-foot crossbar and the huge pillars 33 feet around the base. This huge camphor-wood torii which rose out of the sea about 530 feet from the shore was erected in 1875. The late Mock Joya mentioned that the lower portions of the high pillars were replaced in 1951 by new camphor wood. Nevertheless, the original lower portions of the first pillars had stood in the water for seventy-six years at least.

Camphor was recorded as having been in use in the Western world as early as the sixth century B.C., and it was doubtless utilized in the Orient long before that. The botanical name for the tree is *Cinnamomum camphora,* and it is native to Formosa, China, and Japan. I came from Kiangsi Province, China, where *Cinnamomum camphora* grows abundantly and there is a big town named Camphor Town, for it was the

Walking toward the Itsukushima Shrine

center of the camphor trade. Kiangsi Province has been famous for centuries for its camphor wood cabinets and chests; camphor is particularly valued because it can keep furs, woolens, and silks free from insects. But I had not heard before that camphor wood could be kept in the water for many years. I admire the person who thought of using this wood in erecting such an enormous torii offshore which has become one of the best-known landmarks in Japan and also a great emblem for Shintoism.

Walking away from the torii toward the Itsukushima Shrine, I passed by a number of stone lanterns and reached a big platform where a Shinto dance, *Kagura,* was taking place with many people standing around watching in complete silence. A Shinto dancer was dressed in an ancient costume of embroidered silk and was wearing a rather fierce-looking mask, as in the dance I saw at Ise, while four Shinto priests dressed in white silk robes and black caps were playing musical instruments. Two played bamboo flutes, the third had a drum, and the fourth a Chinese *sho* or *sheng*. Afterward I went to see another stage, on which a Kabuki play was being performed. The audience was sitting cross-legged on the floor of a long corridor-shaped structure. All their shoes were lying by the walls. I watched the acting from the opening in the wooden frame and took out my little sketchbook to make some rough sketches of the audience. Their different poses suggested to me that the Japanese in the early days must have sat in like manner to watch the Kabuki plays.

Many other people were walking to and fro in other corridors and galleries which stretched over the water on both sides of the shrine. When the water rose with the incoming tide the entire edifice looked as if it was floating on the sea. It was a very unusual piece of architecture and Japan has no other establishment like it. This Itsukushima Shrine was said to have been discovered in A.D. 811 and was dedicated to the

Audience watching a Kabuki play

three daughters of the Shinto god Susano-o-no-Mikoto—the princesses Ichikishima, Tagori, and Tagitsu—by the first Taira clan about the twelfth century. The whole building rested on stilts driven into the sea bottom. It seems that the sea around this part of Miyajima is quite shallow; and probably in the most remote days Miyajima Island was a part of the mainland of Honshu. The Ondo Strait between the mainland and Miyajima is said to have been dredged by Taira-no-Kiyomori, great head of the Taira clan in the twelfth century, and he erected the enormous torii at the same time, which has been rebuilt eight times since.

A very interesting tale about the origin was related by the late Mock Joya in his *Things Japanese* as follows:

> Once when he [Taira-no-Kiyomori] was visiting the shrine, he saw a very beautiful girl, whom neither the shrine priest nor others on the island knew. Kiyomori was much attracted by her and asked her to marry him. The girl, who was as beautiful as a goddess, replied that she would marry him if he constructed a new shrine building in one day. As Kiyomori was determined to marry her, he immediately set himself to the task of constructing a magnificent new building. As he applied his ax on timber, the flying wood chips turned into thousands of carpenters who eagerly started to build the shrine. The sun began to set, and Kiyomori waved his fan to stop it from going down. The sun stayed still and permitted him to finish the great building in one day. Kiyomori told the girl that now she must be his wife as the shrine was erected as promised and waited for her in a boat. But the girl climbed up the great torii in the sea and, turning into a dragon, jumped into the sea. In surprise Kiyomori sped his boat from the island, but the dragon followed him. As he reached Ondo he glared at the sea and prayed to stop the dragon from catching him. The current started to move rapidly toward the pursuing dragon. It could not swim speedily against the strong current so Kiyomori managed to escape. The current caused by Kiyomori still flows rapidly at Ondo.

The tale helps to explain why the shape of a dragon was chosen for the ferryboat. In China there are many tales about dragons, but none of them had a dragon transformed into a beautiful girl.

Coming out of the Nio-mon, a gate on the west side, I followed a few people to the Treasure Hall and had a look at many important objects—a good number of them labeled "Important Cultural Properties." Two young children came to drag their mother away. I was curious to know what interested them and left the hall too. It turned out to be the Miyajima Aquarium. I could not help admiring the Japanese organizing ability in providing interests for old and young even in these places of popular pilgrimage. As Japan is surrounded by the sea, the Japanese have a great interest in fish, and an aquarium seems to be most popular in many places. I have seen several and could not resist visiting this one. The small glass tanks along the walls had a different arrangement inside from any others that I had seen elsewhere. Mirrors were fixed on the backs of the tanks which reflected the small fish swimming through the coral and seaweeds with unusual depth and a new dimension not seen in the ordinary way. A most ingenious device!

While on the ropeway to the summit of Mt. Misen I had a bird's-eye view of the layout of the Itsukushima Shrine, which looked like a toy building in Japanese style floating inside the semicircular recess of Miyajima Island. No one had yet discovered the actual origin of this floating shrine, but the one who conceived the idea of building it on the incoming tide must have been a genius.

I then followed the others walking to the small red torii leading to the small shrine of Yama-no-Obasan, who, we were told, was "an Old Lady of the Mountain" and a witch. I could not think why an old witch should have a shrine built right on the highest point of the mountain. Did the Shinto gods in Itsukushima Shrine approve of her existence above them? Not far from the summit stood a Buddhist temple, called Gumonjido, said to have been found by Kōbō Daishi on his return from China in the ninth century. But my friend Professor Yoshito Hakeda, an authority on Kōbō Daishi's lifework, told me to have some reservations whenever I saw temples connected with the great Japanese priest.

The air on this mountain top was exceedingly fresh and clear and my view extended even to the hazy-looking city of Hiroshima and many scattered islands in the Inland Sea far away on my left. The sun was still high and the sky blue. The slopes all around Mt. Misen were thickly wooded with pines, cypresses, and Japanese cedars packed together, which shaded part of the Itsukushima Shrine down below. A number of blooming cherry trees were interspersed with the dense green foliage here and there. The unruffled beauty of the deep blue sea seemed to enhance them all clearly. A revelation and a harmonious, romantic, and poetic sight altogether. When I came down I tried to find a way of staying overnight but there was only one inn and that was already completely full. I was unable to witness the evening sight as my friends Professor and Mrs. John Rosenberg had done. John told me his impression as follows:

> Miyajima is the Delos of Japan, a sacred island on which, until the Meiji Restoration, birth and burial were forbidden. Even now the dead are buried on the mainland, across the narrow strait of Ondo. The ancient religious prohibition seems to exert its effect still, for on stepping ashore one feels a sudden suspension of time, a cessation of all the frenetic building and unbuilding that mark contemporary Japan. . . . Like all sights in Japan, the shrine has its special moment

for being seen but the ideally right conditions are hard to come by, since they involve a rare conjunction of sun, moon, tide, weather, and season. Only the last was mistimed for my wife and myself. We were living on the island in midsummer and hence had neither the cherry blossoms of April nor the foliage of autumn. But all else was perfect one extraordinarily calm evening, with the twilight sky radiantly clear and flushed by the sun which had just set over the mainland, directly opposite the shrine. The tide was at full so that the shrine, reflected in the russet-tinged water, appeared to be floating like some giant water lily silhouetted in the bay. As I glanced from the sunset opposite us to the hills directly behind, a full, pale moon was rising over the mountain sacred to Itsukushima. Moonlight and sunlight fused in a luminous arch over the shrine.

What an impressive experience this must have been! Although I missed that particular sight, I did enjoy my April day on Miyajima.

On our way back the tide was just moving in slowly and a faint mist was rising to veil the hills and trees. Inside the ferryboat a Japanese guide who could speak some English was telling his group that the population on Miyajima had never been very big, owing to the limited space for building. With the prohibition of birth and burial on the island still in practice, fresh settlers seldom came. I thought it was an ideal quarter for retirement, though the guide mentioned tourists were visiting in increasing numbers every year. I looked back to where we had come from and noticed that Mt. Misen and its surroundings were all veiled in mist. Everything I saw had become unreal, yet they were real in my mind. It also began to rain again. The whole scene looked like a rainy landscape such as were painted by the Sung master Mi Fei. However, something was not quite the same. So I composed the following verse:

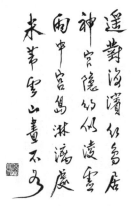

Facing the red torii by the seashore,
A Shinto shrine seemingly afloat.
The mist, the wet look of Miyajima Island in the
    rain,
Even Mi Fei's cloudy landscape is no match to
    this!

XV

Hells and Monkeys of Beppu

BEPPU IS KNOWN all over Japan for its hot springs which number 1,877 with a daily flow of 47,000 tons of hot water, far more than anywhere else in the country. As it lies at the eastern tip of Kyushu, there are many routes to Beppu from other parts of Japan by railway and steamer. But there is no direct route from Hiroshima, so I had to go by train, which took more than five hours. I did not mind the long ride in the train, for my lingering thoughts over the saddest disaster of an atom bomb in Hiroshima were gradually dispersed among the mountains, rice fields, and the coastal scenery along the way. Only by bus or slow train can the general look of the countryside be properly savored. It was still twilight when I got down from the train at Beppu station. At Suginoi Hotel I was received by a young maid in kimono. I had Western food for dinner and made a tour round the hotel afterward. It was a thoroughly modernized building with all the modern facilities, a big wing for entertainment, indoor sports, and all kinds of amusements, and a large room where all sorts of local products and gift souvenirs could be bought. A long corridor led to a separate section of rooms arranged completely in Japanese style. Many Japanese, especially those born in the late thirties and forties, are accustomed to the Western way of comfort, yet many still prefer the traditional way in which they were brought up.

In the main hall, as a decoration, there are five artistically shaped rocks of considerable size, each on a well-polished lacquer stand, which interested me very much. This kind of decoration would not be found in any big hotel in Europe or America. These rocks might have been obtained locally, but they each had a distinctive color and shape.

Already many visitors were in the hotel. Many had changed into kimonos and had a towel in hand for a bath; some looked to have already had their baths. I returned to my room and changed for a bath too. The hot spring bath really soothed every muscle and I completely relaxed in bed for a sound sleep.

Next morning was bright and calm. I got up, still much relaxed, and found the sunshine outside the window most dazzling. After breakfast I went on the roof of the hotel for a panoramic view. Everything was lit up crystally clear, and the air was fresh. The masses of rooftops beyond the water of the bay stretching a good way away from where I stood must be the city of Beppu. When I turned around, I saw a long range of hills and at the base of the hills there rose up directly from the earth a number of jets of white steam. Hot water must have been running swiftly beneath the ground under my feet when I came down for a stroll toward the hills. Most of the people in the hotel had already left either for sightseeing or some other activity. A number of bright-colored flags were flapping on the amusement wing of the hotel as if a big festival was to begin.

I walked toward some fields but found no rice growing in them, only some cabbagelike vegetables. Perhaps the hot water under the earth did not encourage rice growing. In one of the fields two women were at work tidying up the hedges. Passing by several columns of white steam, I came to a two-story country house in the old Japanese style. It looked to be a most desirable spot for comfortable living.

Later I walked back to a cement bridge, with a stream flowing far down below it. On both sides of the bridge were hotels and inns. I was told that there are three hundred hotels and inns in Beppu. How they all could sustain themselves day after day throughout the whole year is a wonder to me.

After a good lunch at the hotel I joined a sightseeing tour. The first stop was at a pond called Chinoike-jigoku, or in kanji blood-red hell, where the water was crimson with hot steam rising up and had a temperature of 168°. Someone remarked that an egg could be cooked in the water. Then we came to Bosu-jigoku, or head-shaved monk's hell, where muds of various colors bubbled and blew upward. I did not see what it had to do with the well-shaved head of a monk. The third one was Oni-yama-jigoku, or demon's mount hell, where in two or three pools a number of live, dark-colored alligators with spotted backs swam about.

The fourth stop we made was at Umi-jigoku, or sea hell, which is the largest pool of all, deep green with a temperature of 194°. On the pool floated masses of water-lily leaves and flowers in full bloom and many giant Mexican water-lily leaves as big as small round table tops. In the distance rose clouds of white steam. The fifth stop was at Tatsumaki-jigoku, a garden with a stone structure in a narrow recess, where every thirty minutes a geyser shoots up water to a height of three or four feet.

Beppu is famous for its hot springs not only in quantity but because of their many colors, such as bright red, dark green, yellow, navy blue, cobalt blue, and pure white. Cotton textiles said to have been dyed in these pools can be bought as souvenirs. The mineral qualities of Beppu's hot springs are varied as well, including alkaline, sulphur, iron,

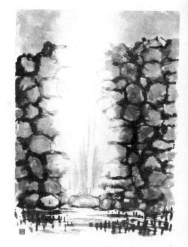

Tatsumakijigoku

and carbonated baths, efficacious for various ailments. In Japan there is a common belief that a disease will prove fatal if it is not treated by baths at a hot spring, sometimes five or six times a day, for three cyclic periods of seven days in three consecutive years. The Japanese think hot springs possess supernatural power to cure diseases; they call a hot-spring bath *kamiyu,* or divine bath.

The Japanese expression jigoku, if written in kanji, would be pronounced "ti yu" in Chinese, meaning "hell." The Chinese expression "ti yu" was invented when Indian Buddhism was introduced to China. The following description comes from Fa-Hsien's records of the Buddhist countries when he travelled to India from 399 to 414:

> When King Asoka was a child in a former life, while playing on the road he met Sakyamuni Buddha begging for alms. Delighted, he offered the Buddha a handful of earth, which Buddha took to spread on the ground where he used to walk. As a result of this good deed, the child became king of the iron-encircled hills where the wicked are punished.
>
> "What place is that?" he asked his ministers.
>
> "That is where Yama, the king of the spirits, punished the wicked," they told him.
>
> On hearing this, Asoka reflected that if the king of the spirits could make a hell to punish the wicked, why could not he, a ruler of men, make a place of punishment for criminals?
>
> So he asked his ministers: "Who could make a hell for me and take charge of punishing evildoers there?"
>
> Thereupon the king sent his ministers out in all directions to look for wicked men. Eventually they found a man by the side of a pond who was tall, strong, and swarthy, with yellow hair and blue eyes. He could catch fish with his feet and make birds and beasts come when he called; but then he shot, not sparing a single one. Having found the man, they sent him to the king.
>
> "Make a square enclosure with high walls," the king charged him secretly. "Plant it with a profusion of flowers and fruit trees and build a handsomely ornamented bathing pool, so passers-by will be eager to look inside. Make the doors and windows strong. Whenever anyone enters, put him to every torture you can devise and do not let him out again. Even if I should enter the place myself, you must torture me as well, and never let go. Now I appoint you the keeper of this hell.

To the Chinese then, a hell is a place for all kinds of torture, where no one wants to enter, and the keeper is a strong man with yellow hair and blue eyes and fierce looking, as depicted in many ancient Chinese figurines. But what sort of a king was Asoka, who could give the keeper such power to torture anyone whether he deserved it or not! Because of this, the Chinese dislike, and even dread, to mention the term "ti yu,"

RITSURIN GARDEN IN TAKAMATSU, SHIKOKU

THE FLOATING SHRINE OF MIYAJIMA

and there is nowhere one could see these characters put together in China except inside a temple where a hall of hell was constructed. But for the Japanese *jigoku* seems to mean something quite different, not a place to be dreaded, but a place one could purposely enter to cure his illness and come out a better man!

At any rate, I had had enough jigoku in the past few hours, and when it was announced that we would go to see the Takasakiyama monkeys, I was more than delighted. After the bus stopped we had to climb a good many stone steps to where forty or fifty monkeys of both sexes and all ages were kept. Though most of them stayed within the two enclosures, a few climbed outside, for there was nothing to prevent them from doing so. Two adult monkeys were climbing in a big tree in the center of the open ground. Nearly all the visitors crowded round the enclosure offering peanuts. The guide gave a loud warning to all of us to beware of the monkeys' mischievousness, for they would tear pockets, paper, and leather bags. The monkeys walked, ran, leaped, and bounded over the rocks completely at will. Two or three sat together helping each other search for lice, and the babies always clung to their mother's chest. Young ones not yet full grown were most playful and active. These monkeys appeared to belong to the family of Indian rhesus like those on the Rock of Gibraltar, but they had strange bright red faces. When I first saw a Japanese painting of a monkey by the noted painter Tsusen, I thought the artist had purposely put rouge on its face, for I had never before seen a monkey with a face that color. The bright red faces showed up clearly among the green leaves of the trees and the gray rocks. Nearly every one of the monkeys, including the little newly born ones, had the same rouged face. Monkeys of any species are comic enough, but with their rouged faces, particularly on the males, they are even laughable. I composed a little poem about it:

My mind is cleansed and scents come from all
　　around;
With a carefree feeling, and tasting every phe-
　　nomenon my thoughts become unusual.
If the male monkey, too, uses rouge on his face,
What can a girl monkey use to gain a lover?

The Japanese seem to have extended their energies to protect nature's specially endowed plants, birds, and wild animals, including those red-faced monkeys. At Kyoto University primate experts have made studies of the country's five thousand monkeys, and in recent years they found a good number of the red-faced monkeys that had branched off from the main stock and managed to survive the snowy months of the severest winters on a rugged, windswept peninsula of northern Honshu. A photograph of these monkeys showed that despite the harsh existence in the freezing wilderness, they retained their rouged faces exactly like those I saw on Takasakiyama. It is not known exactly how and when these red-faced monkeys started living in Japan. Traditionally there is a little taboo about speaking the Japanese word for monkey, *saru,* particularly to businessmen, stock speculators, gamblers, and restaurateurs, for *saru* also means "to go away" in Japanese and no businessman wants to hear "go away"! This is another example of pun symbolism in Japanese. There must be many Japanese words or expressions like this. The Japanese also commonly believe that the monkey possesses the power to keep off evil spirits, thus creating a demand for small monkey toys made of cloth, wood, or other material.

XVI

Kumamoto and Its Neighboring Cities

ONCE OUT OF the city of Beppu, the bus was soon running smoothly on the beautifully paved Yamanami Highway. There were blue hills all round with massive groups of green trees and patches of yellow and brown here and there. The expanse was enormous and the eye could reach quite far. However, there was no sign of crops; nor did any simple country house come into view. It took nearly an hour to reach a place called Yufuin Plateau with Mt. Hane seen behind some clouds. After another short ride, we all got down from the bus to have a look at a most beautiful, deep blue lake called Oda. A high mountain rose far behind, which took on a purple hue under the bright sunshine and blue sky. The water surface was like a huge mirror. On the other side a piece of land stretched out into the lake and a modern building of many stories stood there alone making the area resemble someplace in Switzerland. If I had heard correctly, this lake is the natural reservoir for the electric generating plant supplying power to the whole island of Kyushu. From Lake Oda we drove on for another hour, past many cattle grazing on the low hills. A dazzling sight was a hill half covered with wild azaleas in full bloom. The bright red and pink backed by dark green slopes and yellow soil with a black eagle circling above provided a most satisfying color scheme. After a further quarter of an hour the bus reached Makinoto Pass, and a vast valley of fertile-looking, well-cultivated flatland with clusters of houses here and there came into sight. We all got down for a view from an observation point. It was a rare, clear day and we could see far and wide.

On the move again, I could see far, far ahead of us massive white cloudlike balls rising up into the sky against a background of huge, bare brown gray mountains. Someone said that that was the still active volcano of Aso and that was where we were going. Presently the bus stopped at a big flat space scooped down from the highway and I saw a good many fine horses with men on their backs galloping happily round and round there. The horse is not a native animal of Japan. My mind went back to a story I read. In 1613, Lord Masamune Date of the Sendai clan sent Rokuyemon Hasekura as his envoy to Europe. He bought a number of good stallions there, but when he returned he could not keep them. It was the isolation period when Japan would have nothing to do with foreign countries. So Hasekura set the horses loose and drove them out of Sendai. The stray horses were then caught by the Nambu clan, and today the best horses of Japan are bred in Nambu. Perhaps the horses I saw had been bred there. But why would people come a long way to amuse themselves with the horses, far away from any habitation?

Again we were on the move. Shortly we passed a small conical hill, somewhat similar to Mt. Fuji though with no snow on its top, but it had a small crater and a footpath leading up. This was probably the hill

Aso crater

called Aso-Fuji. After another thirty-minute drive, we reached the ground outside the Aso crater. My friend Mr. Makoto Yamazaki wrote to tell me that Aso is the general name for five volcanic peaks, of which Nakadake (altitude 1,323 meters) is still active, and Kishimadake (1,321 meters), Eboshidake (1,337 meters), Takadake (the highest peak, 1,592 meters), and Nekodake (1,433 meters) are all extinct.

The Aso and Nango valleys are two extensive plains, containing three towns (Ichinomiya, Aso, and Takamori) and also three villages with a total population of 66,500. These plains, surrounded by mountain chains, were originally the crater of the volcano, 23 kilometers in length from north to south, 16 kilometers in width from east to west, and 255 square kilometers in area—the largest crater in the world. This crater-land could have been the vast valleys of the very fertile-looking flatland which I had seen from Makinoto Pass.

We were now facing the crater of Aso, which was still active by the side of Nakadake Peak, and occasionally black smoke rose up amidst the white vapor as if a storm was about to break through. The crater looked to be divided into several parts. I moved round the rim from the active part of the east side where I saw two professional photographers with their cameras ready waiting for customers. I began wondering if they could have much business nowadays when I saw a large group of school children coming up to the rim—there were hundreds of them in a long line, each wearing a red school cap and each with a camera of one type or another. Half closing my eyes, I saw a long string of large red beads joined together suddenly hanging in the air against the white vapor as the dark school uniforms mingled with the black lava earth. A very strange sight which could only be seen in Japan.

Before we left the Aso crater rim to return to the bus, I stepped aside to take a look at the small shrine, newly painted, nearby. Could this be the shrine for a Shinto deity who looks after the crater? According to the legend, the original shrine was said to have been founded around A.D. 100 and dedicated to Takeiwatatsu-no-Mikoto, who first settled in this region with his consort. What did they do when Aso erupted for the first time? There are recent records of the Aso eruptions in 1933, 1953, 1958, and 1961–1962.

We left Aso crater while the sun was still shining brightly. While we were moving along, gradually but surely the bare hills and fields on both sides changed from their dry look into the green of living growth. The view of the country became grander and more magnificent as we moved on. Rows of houses appeared and among them the Kumamoto Castle, a modern concrete building, stood out. It was originally built by the first lord, Kiyomasa Kato (1559–1611), the famous general who achieved much in the invasion of Korea under Toyotomi Hideyoshi. Being a grave and pious man, he kept up until death his loyalty to the family of his first lord Hideyoshi without wavering. This did not please the first Tokugawa shogun, Iyeyasu, who succeeded Hideyoshi, so Kato suffered in the later years of his life. Little of the old castle remains, for it was almost completely destroyed during a strange historical event two hundred years later. Then Saigo Takamori, one of the great three who laid

Saigo Takamori's monument
in Ueno Park

the foundations for the establishment of the Meiji Restoration, led a Satsuma rebellion against the government and besieged the castle for fifty days, which caused its destruction by the government army. However, the Japanese honored Saigo Takamori's great deeds for the country and ignored his senseless part in the rebellion and erected a bronze statue of him in Ueno Park, Tokyo. It is difficult not to be reminded of Takamori's connection with Kumamoto Castle when visiting it.

I looked inside the new castle, which has not become a museum as have most of the other castles. Being concrete, this new castle looks very solid and strong. Walking through the many pine trees on the castle

Stone monument commemorating the emperor's visit

ground, I noticed a stone monument commemorating the visit of an emperor to the castle. I thought this to be Emperor Meiji, who might have come to see it after the death of Saigo Takamori. Later on I came to a stone enclosure containing a small shrine with many lighted candles and incense burning; it seemed to be a popular center for worship. But I could not find any sign and wondered if it was the Kato Shrine. Presently three people appeared, apparently mother, father, and a teen-age daughter. The mother wanted to go in to burn incense and light a candle

White geese in Suizenji Park

for worship and the father was urged to follow, but the daughter pulled
at the father's sleeves trying to persuade him not to enter. This performance went on for several minutes. Though I could not understand what
they were saying, I guessed that this could be a typical happening in
Japan between the old and the young, what is known as a generation
gap. Similar happenings took place in China for years.

Not too far from Kumamoto Castle, the Suizenji Park still had blossoming cherry trees, fresh green pines, and red azaleas round the large
crystal clear lake Ezu-ko. The lake was said to have been laid out in
1632 by Gentaku, a Buddhist priest, under the direction of the lord of
the villa of the Hosokawa family, who succeeded the Kiyomasa Kato
family in controlling the area. While we were there, many activities were
going on in the park. A few people were trying to erect poles to hang the
big black and red carp for the Boy Day Festival. A number of people
were throwing food to feed many large Japanese gold carp under a stone
bridge. I noticed two pairs of snow white geese with red beaks leisurely
gliding over the water, turning their heads from one side to the other.
They added a lively color to the whole scene. At the same time they
reminded me of our greatest calligrapher, Wang Hsi-chih (321–379),
who had a special love for white geese and for a snow-white goose he
would always be glad to exchange a piece of his calligraphy, which has

long been regarded as an important treasure in China. So I composed the following little verse:

水荼池裡雨雙鵝
鳧游隨意擻輕波
慇夢一至右軍筆
不換名書王右軍

Two pairs of white geese on Ezu-ko Lake,
Gracefully and carefreely create ripples on the water surface.
Pity I cannot write as well as Wang Hsi-chih,
No exchange could be made between them and a piece of famous calligraphy!

Nearly two years later I was again in Kumamoto on my way to see Amakusa. At first I flew from Osaka to Kagoshima, then took a taxi, and again changed for a bus to Ibusuki. As it lies on the southern tip of Kyushu, it is in a semitropical zone and was quite warm when I arrived near the end of August. I stayed at the modern Ibusuki Kanko Hotel. It has a spacious lounge with Western furnishings, arrangement, and decoration. One exception is the Japanese-type hot-spring bath. Among the shopping quarter many local gifts and souvenirs were for sale including many tropical plants. While having dinner I noticed a thick forest of tall palm trees stood behind an open-air dining hall where a floor show was taking place with Hawaiian hula girls and Hawaiian music and songs. The atmosphere was Waikiki completely transplanted.

Next morning I joined a bus tour round Mt. Kaimon (called Satsuma Fuji), Lake Ikeda, and Nagasakibana. A sudden heavy rain did not help us to see much. On our way back the bus stopped at a small garden, called Wedding Botanic Park, along the bottom of a hill. It was so named, for all the trees there were planted by newly-weds at the time of their wedding. The garden authority has a place to perform the wedding ceremony with a Shinto priest and gives the couple a printed certificate with the couple's signatures on it, after which they are led to the garden to plant a tree. Their names are also attached to the tree. In years to come they will return to look at their tree and recall their wedding day. I was told that this botanic garden was doing a thriving business and many young couples wanted to hold their wedding ceremony here if they could afford to come from other parts of Japan. Ibusuki Kanko Hotel is the only modern place nearby to stay. So the garden and hotel operate a joint concern. This is another example of Japanese genius and enterprising spirit which has no tradition attached to it.

From Ibusuki I went to spend a night at Shiroyama Kanko Hotel. My room had a window directly facing the still active Sakurajima Volcano and Kinko Bay and I watched the white smoke rising up continuously and growing bigger all morning. After that, I caught a bus to Kirishima and the proprietress, Mrs. Marijunko Yano was very kind to ask her daughter Mikiko to drive us to see the Kirishima Jingu, dedicated to Ninigi-no-Mikoto, the divinity who came down to Japan to start the imperial line and who was the only one not to attend the Shinto gods' conference at Izumo in October. We also had a good drive round the Ebino Kogan Heights and I saw many, many beautifully shaped old pine trees, which are famous on that highland area. I vow to go back there again to paint all the pines, if possible.

Next day I took the Miyazaki Kotsu Bus for Miyazaki, where I saw the Children's Land, the Cactus Park, and also the Aoshima Islet. This tiny islet, not more than a few square acres, was connected with the mainland by a small bridge and a long footpath. I walked over there and found little access to the islet, for it was fully covered by the luxurious Japanese fan palms and many other tropical, as well as subtropical, plants with only a small open space to establish a miniature shrine. The guide told us that the geological formation of this islet was of great interest to geologists. All around it were the most strange-looking rocks or big rocky slabs piled up one after the other, like waves but immobile. They were created by the sea's erosion of an unusual outcropping of rocks. They are called the Ogres' Washboard. In fact, the entire coast of Miyazaki is full of Ogres' Washboards. I don't remember ever seeing any of this type of wavy-shaped coastal rocks before. Nature provides unexpected phenomena for us to continue learning. Indeed, our great philosopher Chuang Tzu of the fourth century B.C. was right to say, "Life has a limit but knowledge none."

Carved monkey above the cave
in Dogashima

Later I went to take a look in Haniwa Park, where the paths were spotted with hundreds of replicas of Haniwa clay sculptures from the grave mounds of Japan. The *kofun*, or burial mounds, of the third to seventh centuries, were centered at Saitobaru, which has six hundred ancient mounds, not far from the city of Miyazaki. But I could not find any explanation for the Haniwa clays.

My stay in Miyazaki led me to the following legend:

The mythology of Japan starts with the world being formless. Out of this formlessness came Izanagi-no-Mikoto (a male) and Izanami-no-Mikoto (a female). Together they spawned innumerable deities, among them, two of primary importance.

Amaterasu-Omikami, the Sun Goddess, who founded the Japanese imperial family line, and Susanowo-no-Mikoto, younger brother of the Sun Goddess, who is the weather god, unpredictable and mischievous. The Sun Goddess gave birth to Ameno-Oshihomi-no-Mikoto, who married Akizu-Hime and sired Ninigi-no-Mikoto.

Ninigi was sent down to Japan by his grandmother, the Sun Goddess, and from then on the imperial family line was continued on earth. Ninigi wed Konohanasakuya-Hime, who gave birth to Ho-Ori-no-Mikoto, and here the story takes an interesting turn. Ho-Ori married Toyotama-Hime, who came from the sea. After giving birth to Ugayafukiaezu-no-Mikoto, she returned to the sea and sent her sister, Tamayori-Hime, to care for her son. Ugayafukiaezu grew up and married Tamayori, his aunt. She bore him a child who became the first emperor of Japan, Jimmu Tenno.

Mythologically, Miyazaki Prefecture is where Japan had its beginning. But why is there nothing to indicate that the first Japanese government was set up there? Ugayafukiaezu's taking his aunt for his wife is contrary to Confucius's idea of five human relationships, by which members of the parents' generation could not marry members of the children's generation. Perhaps this is why Confucianism has never set deep roots in Japan.

After a good stay in Miyazaki I left for Kumamoto and Amakusa.

A beautiful scene along the coast of Kagoshima

XVII

The Battle of Amakusa-Shimabara

LEAVING KUMAMOTO by motorcoach with a number of American tourists, I heard one lady declare loudly, "I have been in Japan for a month and I have seen enough Japanese castles—this castle and that castle; I am tired of the word *castle* now!" She must have come all the way from Tokyo on the main island of Honshu, and almost every city has a castle. The coach moved fairly slowly along the shore. I saw that the tide was way out and on the flats many local people of all ages were bent over, picking up shellfish.

Shortly I was the only one to leave the bus and I took the ferryboat for Shimabara. Shimabara lies in the south of Japan and the climate is mild. We passed numerous small islands and after the boat was docked, I took a taxi to Shimabara Kanko Hotel. It is a modern establishment with a small swimming pool in the courtyard. After a simple meal I sat down by the swimming pool gazing around. Pines and other trees, including several slender palms, were planted along the side of the courtyard open to the sea. A few gas lights on poles were erected between the

Garden of Shimabara Kanko Hotel

palms. I was told that there were ninety-nine islands in Shimabara Bay, most of which were formed of lava from the eruption of Mt. Bizan in 1792. From where I was sitting in front of the hotel I could see the silhouettes of three islands with a few fishing boats near and far against the sunset. The sea was very silvery; the sky gradually made its slow change to pale pink and then pink. A dark-colored eagle came circling above the three islands as if inspecting the area. Later the following verse came into my mind:

孤鷹伴我共徘徊
九十九洲三入目
紅破天涯霧漸開
漁身點點日邊來

The fishing boats, one by one, coming from the place of the sun
The red pierces the horizon to clear the fog.
Of the ninety-nine islands three are in sight,
A lonely eagle shares with me the idea of wandering at will.

No one in the hotel could understand English, so I could not find out much about Shimabara. The city was a good way from where I was staying, so I went to bed early in order to reserve my energy for the next day.

In the morning I could see a castle from my window, and soon I found my way there. It was not a big castle nor an old one, but in the second story there were a number of oil paintings depicting the battle

Scene from the roof of Shimabara Kanko Hotel

between the Japanese Christian converts and the government forces and
the siege of Hara Castle; also one showing the Dutch naval vessel *de
Ryo*, hired by the shogunate government forces to bombard Hara
Castle—426 shells were fired during the battle. These paintings
reminded me of what I had read about the Christian suppressions and
the Shimabara Rebellion. Hara jo, or Hara Castle, located at south
Arima on the Shimabara Peninsula, is the relic of the famous Amakusa-
Shimabara Rebellion of Kan-ei 14 (December 1637). The boy-general,
Amakusa Shiro Tokisada, only sixteen years old, led a Christian revolt
against the tyrannical rule of the shogunate. The government forces
suffered setbacks during their initial attacks. Finally 100,000 men were
ordered to encircle the castle. With the aid of the Dutch ship, they
poured cannon fire on the castle for sixteen days. Though the besieged
were suffering from lack of food and ammunition, it took three more
days of desperate fighting before the castle fell. All the survivors were
then massacred except one who recanted. He was Yamada Yomosaku, a
Christian painter who betrayed the rebels.

That was Japan's most tragic event of the early seventeenth century.
Actually Christianity came to Japan with St. Francis Xavier in the
1540s and the Christian missionaries converted many influential Japanese daimio, including the powerful Konishi, and continued in the
land for almost ninety years till 1637. The root went deep enough and
they must have been a well-organized body. In his book *The Christian
Century in Japan*, Professor C. R. Boxer wrote:

> Whatever the real or ostensible cause of the rising, it speedily as-
> sumed a religious character once it had taken hold. The insurgents
> used banners with Portuguese inscriptions such as "Louvado Seia O
> Santissimo Sacramento" (Praised be the most Holy Sacrament), and
> shouted the names of Jesus, Maria and Santiago in their attacks. They
> announced their open adherence to the Christian faith and proclaimed
> their intention to live and die in it.

The strange part is that the Japanese people are known to be very religious as a whole, and most devoted to their rulers, to their national
Shintoism, and also to Buddhism. Yet despite their deep native faith
they could completely change over to a new faith with similar devotion
and could even sacrifice their lives for it. This is new knowledge to me. I
think the Japanese are far more religious than the Chinese. There has
never been a Chinese Christian martyr and there was therefore no saint
in China. Also China never had a religious war. In the year 845 the
emperor Wu-tsung, much encouraged by Confucian scholars and
influenced by Taoist priests, decreed the destruction of 4,600 Buddhist
monasteries and over 40,000 temples, and 265,000 monks and nuns
were compelled to return to normal life in society. No organized rebel-

lion was ever staged. Though Japan had adopted the T'ang culture with enthusiasm, the Japanese do not seem to have taken Chinese Confucianism to heart. Prince Shotoku did not encounter much opposition from Mononobe-no-Moriya and built many Buddhist temples and spread Buddhism all over Japan as a state religion equal to Shintoism. In China, Buddhism has encountered much difficulty trying to overcome the deeply rooted Confucianism, and so it never became a state religion for the Chinese. According to Confucius's disciple, Tseng Shen, "a man's body, limbs, hair, and skin were bestowed by his parents and he should not harm them"; it was unthinkable that anyone could sacrifice himself for a faith while his parents were still alive. This will explain why no one was known to have died for his Buddhist faith during the persecution of T'ang Wu-tsung in the mid-ninth century.

Mr. Saburo Egami of the Japan Tourist Information Center told me that the present Shimabara Castle, where I saw the paintings, was rebuilt in 1964 as a replica of the main donjon of the original Shimabara Castle, or Moridake Castle, which was constructed in 1618 by Matsukura Shigemasa, a feudal lord. This is not a replica of the Hara Castle, which was destroyed at the time of the Rebellion of Shimabara in 1638.

Foundation of the ruined Hara Castle

Only the ruins and site mark the place today where the castle stood in the suburbs of Shimabara. He also told me that the small bowerlike structure in front of the present Shimabara Castle is a monument to the war dead after the Boshin War—a war waged between the loyalists and

The landmark of the ruined Hara Castle

the supporters of the shogunate near Shimabara in 1868 and at the beginning of the Meiji Restoration.

Shimabara suffered two great wars within a little more than two hundred years. But my interest was much greater in the Christian revolt because of its leader, the boy-general Amakusa Shiro Tokisada. So I decided to learn something more of him when I went to Japan again. I went to Kumamoto from Miyazaki and caught a bus, passing over the recently built five bridges, for the city of Hondo. In the lounge of Amakusa Kokusai Hotel there was a small replica of the boy-general, but no one could tell me why he was chosen to lead the revolt. Then the hotel manager introduced me to one of his staff, Mr. Teishi Matsuoka, who could speak some English and would show me round the whole island of Amakusa, where St. Francis Xavier was supposed to have first set foot on Japanese soil. A car was hired and Mr. Matsuoka took me first to see the Senninzuka, meaning "Tomb of a Thousand Souls," a monument to those who fell in the Amakusa-Shimabara Rebellion. Then we had a look at the Christian cemetery and entered the traingle-shaped gate for a look inside the small museum where all the Christian relics of the rebellion days were kept. To my surprise I saw in a case an old book of the Chinese version of the New Testament which was printed in Amakusa. It was said that in 1592 the Jesuit fathers erected a college and printing press in Kawa-ura. The press was an annex to the college and the Japanese who worked in it had accompanied a delegation to Europe and studied printing in Portugal. They began printing books in Chinese characters. I wondered how the first Chinese translation came here. Another surprise for me was two small statues of Kwannon, wearing a Christian cross round her neck. During the persecution, Japanese Christians used Kwannon to remind them of the Blessed Mother. How interesting that

The tomb of a thousand souls

the goddess of one religion could become one for another. In the yard before the museum stood a large statue of the boy-general, who died on this island. Still nothing could tell me why he was chosen to take the lead. However, I read the following account:

> Matsukura, in Shimabara, literally taxed his people out of existence. In a time of poor crops and famine he invented taxes no one had ever heard of before; birth and death dues, taxes on hearth, door, and window. Failure to pay was punished by torture and death. On one occasion, when the daughter of a village headman had been publicly burned to death, her father, aided by the other villagers, set upon the tax officials and killed them. Conditions were no better in Amakusa.
>
> Finally, a group of samurai, based in the Amakusa islands, decided to resort to arms. To unify the people and put the spirit into them, they chose a lad of sixteen, Shiro Tokisada, and set him up as a heaven-sent leader. He is better known as Amakusa Shiro.
>
> After some initial successes in the field the rebels fortified themselves in Hara Castle. Superior government forces, aided by Dutch cannon, made three futile attacks on them. The castle was taken on April 11, 1638, after a three-month siege. Amakusa Shiro and thirty-seven thousand of his followers were killed, among them fourteen thousand women and children.
>
> The Amakusa-Shimabara Rebellion was in fact a peasant revolt against misgovernment. Matsukura was held responsible in Shimabara

and forced to die by seppuku. Terasawa was relieved of his governorship in Amakusa and committed suicide.

Nevertheless, the Tokugawa government gave out that the revolt was Christian-inspired and used it as an excuse to intensify the persecution.

After all, it was not a religious war, but a protest by Christian and non-Christian alike against the gross misrule of two daimio and a demand for basic human rights.

We then motored along the edge of the island for about two hours and came to a fishing village of Sakitsu, where in 1569 Father Almeida, the Portuguese Jesuit, crossed over from Nagasaki and began to preach. After a visit to the small church we found a tiny eating place for lunch. Afterward we found another church in Oe, which itself has been a Christian village for centuries. The Oe church, built on the crest of a hill, was rather secluded but bigger than the Sakitsu church. Inside of both churches there are no pews but the floors are spread with clean tatami for the local Japanese to sit on while attending the service. An unusual experience for me.

Amakusa Shiro Tokisada

XVIII

The Little Love Shrine on Unzen

AGAIN A DELICIOUS morning: bright sunshine, a sky almost cloudless, and a fresh, yet delicate, verdure on the roadside trees and in the fields. I caught a local motorcoach to Unzen from Shimabara. Shimabara is a port for boats to other cities of Kyushu, while Unzen is a resort with a number of hotels and a few shops. After an hour's pleasant ride, I settled down at the Unzen Kanko Hotel for lunch. The establishment is in Western style somewhat like an old English golf club of two stories, or some hotel at Eastbourne or Bournemouth in England with wooden balconies in parallel rows. But the English seaside between the end of April and the beginning of May could be wet and cold; here in Unzen it was warm and everything looked glossy in the sun. In the front of the hotel was a kind of Japanese-styled landscape garden. I went out for a stroll. There was a stillness in the air, under a fine azure sky of exquisite beauty; here and there along the borders of the road some little wildflowers showed up above the green grass. Very few people were about. Almost every building was either a hotel or an inn. I then entered a courtyard before a shrine. Two young workmen in white shirts and pants and wearing white caps were eating their box lunch happily.

Later I went through a big gray torii and realized that it was an Inari shrine. It was dedicated to the goddess of rice, Princess Ugatama, and was guarded by a pair of fox statues, When I saw the fox guard at a shrine for the first time, I could not understand their significance, for Chinese temples or any official office only have a pair of stone lions, a male and a female with a cub, as guardians, never foxes.

Curiously enough, it is said that the Inari shrines in Japan were actually started by someone of Chinese descent in 711—Iroko of the Hata family, who had abundant rice and paddies piled up and who built a shrine at Fushimi, near Kyoto, in honor of Princess Ugatama ("Barn spirit"). This example was then taken up all over Japan. No such shrine has ever been built anywhere in China. As one of the great agrarian countries of the world, China has many small shrines dotting the countryside, dedicated to the god of earth for having looked after the crops. Inside the small shrine there are usually two clay figures, the god of

The gray torii to the Inari shrine

earth and his wife. Many of these shrines are merely rough structures and often in very poor condition. In contrast each Japanese Inari shrine is an impressive structure with fox guardians and one or more red-painted torii standing one after the other in front. The Inari shrine is a Shinto establishment.

Presently I walked past a local giftshop where there was a group of young school children. All tried to help me when I asked where I could catch a bus for Nita-toge. Two younger boys even came to stand with me at the bus stop to see me on to the bus. I thanked them and thought they understood that simple English expression since we waved to each other. The way seemed endless, as the bus kept rounding the hill slopes, first one way and then another. A new view opened at each turn, a fresh combination of glade, path, and thicket. The crows, the sparrows, the swallows, the butterflies, and some small clusters of wildflowers appeared here and there. This part of the land used to be a volcanic crater many, many years ago, so many patches were bare except for isolated rocks and broken trees. Some places were almost all clothed with green grass, other places were mottled gray and brown, and yet still another place was still perfectly naked with lava sand. Presently the girl guide in the bus started to sing the popular folk song "Cuckoo" and asked the passengers to join in. As they were nearly all Japanese, they sang in chorus as if a large number of cuckoos were calling at the same time.

There was an interesting long strip of red along the lower part of the hill, composed of masses of red azaleas in full bloom, which, mingled with the blue sea of the Shimabara Peninsula, made a kind of ethereal layer in the air—a most enchanting sight. Azaleas in Chinese are called tu-chuan-hua, which means "cuckoo flower," for they bloom at the time when the cuckoo sings loudest. There is a Chinese legend about cuckoo the bird and cuckoo the flower. In Taoism every kind of creature, plant, and even insect has its leading spirit living in heaven. Once the spirit of cuckoo the bird committed a crime in heaven and was condemned by the Queen Mother to the severest punishment, which was to come down to live in the human world until harvest time, when he could go back to heaven. So the cuckoo bird came to the human world at the start of spring, crying all the way to hasten the crops to ripen so that he could go back to heaven. The sound of "cu-ckoo, cu-ckoo" resembles an expression in one dialect, "kuai-kuai fa ko," meaning "quick, quick, open the buds!" The bird sings at first slowly and intermittently and afterward continually, and then in a rush as if he can hardly wait for the crops to become ripe. In the late spring or even in June and July its sound becomes harsh, for it has exhausted all its tears and its blood drops over the countryside and turns into cuckoo flowers. In many parts of China azaleas grow wild, and on my native Mt. Lu there is a great ravine covered with wild azaleas which was called Chin-hsiu-ku, or brocade ravine.

I thought the girl guide sang the cuckoo song most appropriately for the azaleas that I saw on the hill. Our bus came to a stop at the rather rugged part of the mountain where the ropeway starts for going up to Mt. Yadake. There was a small observation platform with a metal railing built on a promontory still higher up, reached by a flight of stone steps. I stood there on high ground for a good while and my eyes commanded a magnificent panorama of the Chijiwa Bay, the mountain ranges one upon another, the distant villages large and small, the soft green golf courses, and the tangled masses of the azaleas in bloom far, far below. Several hawks or kites were circling in the air not far from where I was standing and one flew so close that I could see its sharp eyes staring as if deliberating who we might be. This grand and memorable view was greatly enhanced by the majestic performance of the sun, which lit up every corner. I enjoyed being able to contemplate the beauty of nature from such a high point and felt lucky to have picked a day with a spotless sky. On the way down from the upper platform I saw a small shrine rather in need of repair a little distance from the footpath. It was explained to me that this was a shrine dedicated to the god of love, for Unzen is known as a great resort for honeymooners. There were two pairs of young people close to the shrine for a look. As I had no reason to stop there, I followed the ropeway down to the bus stop. Many more crows appeared around the dry bushes. They were quite big, almost as big as the Welsh ravens in the British Isles but I could not understand why they should be around this rather bare mountain.

Not one pine tree could be seen, but several Japanese cypresses with masses of dark green leaves on their yellow white branches and trunks showed up distinctly in the area. The way down was full of interesting views and surprises as had been the case on the ascent. It was now late afternoon; the thin clouds had gathered into a veil and low canopy, and the setting sun gleamed underneath with a vague, blood red glare, and the crimson rays spread upward with a lurid and portentous grandeur, a subdued and dusky glow, like the light reflected on the sky from some vast conflagration. What a contrast from a few hours before and what a poetic change of views to be seen in a single trip!

A small observation platform
right on the top

XIX

Discovery of the West via Nagasaki

NOTHING IS MORE enjoyable than an unexpected encounter! I heard that my friend and colleague, Professor Donald Keene, had just arrived in Tokyo. I caught him on the telephone before he left for his Japanese house on a mountain outside Tokyo and suggested luncheon together. He came at the suggested time and took me straightway to a Szechwan restaurant in the Rappongi area not far from where I was staying. He then quickly wrote down three Szechwan dishes. When the food came, each dish was delicious, tasty, and a little spicy, as most Szechwan food is. While we ate he talked leisurely and gave me useful hints on how to read modern Japanese literature, particularly Japanese fiction, poetry, and drama. As he speaks and writes Japanese fluently, many Japanese have already taken him to be a Japanese. Apart from his many publications on Japanese literature, recently he went with a group of Japanese men of letters to represent Japan at an International Conference on World Culture in Trinidad. Like many Japanese scholars his interest in Chinese literature and the Chinese way of living, particularly food, is great.

After lunch Donald asked me to go with him to see the Spring Exhibition on Nagasaki, its history illustrated with pictures and art objects. When we reached a tall, modern office building where the exhibition was held, we found that it had ended the day before. Donald was rather disappointed, for he had ordered a photograph from the exhibition for his new book. A few days later he showed me his copy of the catalogue of the exhibition and many of the illustrations in it interested me greatly. One picture of a Chinese wearing the Manchu petty official's costume and dancing with a Japanese lady in flowery kimono, painted by Jo Girin, made both look emotionless and rather comic. Another picture, showing seven Dutch traders dining sumptuously around a table of Western-style food with two Japanese maids and a Chinese in a long gown as servants, was painted by Kawabata Keiga. Both Japanese painters made the same mistake as the early Chinese painters who showed Western eyes rather small and Oriental like. From 1641 to 1854 only the Dutch and Chinese were allowed to stay in Japan and mostly had to

A Chinese dancing with a
Japanese girl

confine their stay to Nagasaki. Another picture in the catalogue that interested me was of a porcelain plate from the Hui-shan kiln; for the design it had two camels, one with uplifted head and the other grazing. I had not seen a similar design on any other Chinese plate before. I thanked Donald for my first introduction to Nagasaki and knew that I would have a lot of things to see there.

On a fine April afternoon I caught a motorcoach from Unzen to Nagasaki and arrived there just about six o'clock. I was shown into a comfortable room in the Nagasaki Grand Hotel and then served a Western-style dinner. The smiling young lady at the desk told me that she had been studying some English in college. She suggested many things that I could see the next morning. It was still bright outside and the weather was mild and dry, so I stepped out of the hotel for a stroll. I walked along one side of the main street and looked at the shop windows, which contained mostly sweets, fish, and leather goods. Turning into a side street, I found many old Japanese houses along one side and a large number of tombstones along a slope on the other. Toward the end of the hilly road was a nice-looking house with its main entrance wide open to reveal a spotless interior and two young women in kimonos, highly painted and with elaborate hairdo like the maiko girls in Kyoto, both smilingly bowed to invite me to go in. I thought they must have been welcoming somebody walking behind me, so I moved on without acknowledging them. Just before I came down the street again, the scene was repeated at another house with two similar women in kimonos and highly painted faces giving me a sign of welcome. I shook

Two drinkers

my head and moved on. Facing me on the other side of the street was a torii-like structure with five kanji characters meaning "Tonza, Street of Joy." It intrigued me and I went over. It was like a confusion of small, narrow streets intertwined together, and on both sides, lined closely, one beside another, were all kinds of little drinking places and bars. Their shop signs extended overhead as if to cover the skyline. It was getting dark now and each shop sign was lit up to show the inscriptions either in kanji, or in hiragana, with some decorations in different colors giving a typically Japanese flavor. I just could not understand how each of these bars could have enough customers to make them pay. Around the corner, at the meeting of two narrow streets, two men in black kimonos, one older than the other, came out of a bar very unsteady on their feet. They were singing and talking as they walked along. The older one suddenly hit the wall and slid down to the ground, falling flat, while the younger man with his fumbling hands tried to hold him up. A girl of about twenty dashed out of the bar to help. No sooner had the older one managed to stand than all three of them fell down together. The young girl's face was perspiring. I did not know what else to do, as I was standing some distance away, but to take out my little sketchbook to make a quick sketch. Presently they all got up and moved on. While I was still strolling from one narrow street to another, my mind was full of the comic scene which I had just witnessed, and I remembered the following T'ang poem by an anonymous poet, which I translate roughly:

The dog is barking outside;
I know that my love has come.
Putting on my shoes I go down the steps,
"Oh, my wretched one is drunk tonight!"
I support him to enter the bed curtain;
He shows no wish to undress.
"Well, let him be as drunk as he will,
It's better than sleeping alone!"

I could not help smiling as I wondered if the beloved ones of these two drunken men would feel the same when they got home. We know how much the history of mankind has changed, yet human nature shows little difference from one place or time to another. Soon I was walking behind a row of stalls which sold fruits and some candies or such things. Each of them was small and cramped. In one I saw a middle-aged woman sitting cross-legged on a flat space which seemed to be her bed, closely reading a magazine under a kerosene lamp when no one was buying her wares. I thought of how different life could be from one person to another and of this woman's eagerness to read in such circumstances. I

Sake drinkers

would find hardly any Chinese woman of the same age, even a well-educated one, who would try to read so eagerly. To me the amazing achievement of Japanese civilization is the very low percentage of illiteracy. The proportion of the reading public in Japan is far greater than in any other country in the world that I know of.

After I had had breakfast the next morning the young lady at the desk helped me get a taxi to take me to see the Sofukuji Temple. It is a famous Chinese temple built by the Chinese of Nagasaki in the early seventeenth century. The numerous Chinese who lived in Nagasaki during the persecution of the Christians by the Tokugawa shogunate became afraid that they would be mistaken for Christian converts so they collected money to build this Buddhist temple in order to indicate they were Buddhists. The Chinese who had come to live in Nagasaki were traders, most from Fukien Province of south China. The founder of the Huang-po sect of Ch'an Buddhism lived on Huang-po Mountain of Fukien and the sect was flourishing there in the seventeenth century. So these Fukien Chinese in Nagasaki invited I-jan, the most noted Ch'an monk of the time, to come and build their temple in 1629.

Sofukuji Temple has red-washed walls and a Chinese-style structure. Step by step I climbed to the temple court before the main hall. There a small structure housed an enormous brass boiling pot four feet in height and three feet in diameter. I was intrigued and wanted to know what it was. The Chinese words on it were not easy to decipher. A young Japa-

Entrance to Sofukuji

An enormous brass boiling pot

nese lady was sketching nearby, so I went to talk to her. She knew some English and found the information for me. The big pot had been used by Priest Sengai to boil rice gruel for the hungry populace during the great famine of 1680. His good deed was remembered with gratitude by the presence of this pot preserved in the temple. The young lady told me that her name was Junko Nagatsuka and she had come to spend two days in Nagasaki with her father. She would be going back to Kyoto in a few hours. We then walked round to have a look at the main hall and other parts of the temple.

Twenty-six Japanese Christian martyrs

Afterward I suggested to Miss Nagatsuka that she come with me to see the Peace Park and also the place associated with Madame Butterfly. She accepted my invitation willingly. I made a sketch there of the monument in memory of twenty-six Japanese Christian martyrs. We went to Glover House, where many people were already moving around and looking at the bas-relief of Madame Butterfly on the wall, and the well-laid out garden with many azaleas and lilies in bloom. The house was under repair so no one could go inside, but we both stood on the balcony to gaze at the beautiful harbor and the interesting Nagasaki Bay. The bronze bas-relief on the wall of the house was of the Japanese lady who played the role of Madame Butterfly for twenty years or so and stayed in the Glover House for a while.

Madame Butterfly

After having seen Miss Nagatsuka back to her father for Kyoto, I went for a walk along the promenade of Nagasaki Harbor. While trying to read the words on a pedestal on which a cannonball was placed, I saw an elderly Japanese gentleman wearing an English type of bowler hat. He looked to be right out of the Meiji period and I made a quick sketch of him.

That evening I decided to go round to the good Chinatown in Japan for a Chinese meal. The taxi driver took me to Hamanomachi and put me down at the entrance to a small street and pointed in the direction I should take for Shinchi, which is the Japanese for Chinatown. I soon saw a number of shop signs with typical Chinese names. Most were restaurants. I stepped into one of them. Somehow Shinchi was quite different from the Chinatown of, say, San Francisco or New York. The reason is that the Chinese in San Francisco and in other American cities came chiefly from Canton or Kwangtung Province on the south China coast when they were driven by a great famine to America as laborers. The Chinese who came to Nagasaki were chiefly traders from Fukien Province and some from Chekiang Province. Though Fukien is a neighboring province to Kwangtung, it is closer to Japan; and Chekiang Province is even more so. The Fukien and Chekiang people came as traders to Nagasaki and settled in the place and some married the local girls. One of the most illustrious sons of these mixed marriages was Coxinga, whose father was Fukien-born and whose mother was a lady of Tagawa family in Hirado. It is said that in 1624 Coxinga was born by the side of a big rock while his mother was collecting clams on the beach. That rock is still in existence as a monument to him, for he later grew up to wage war against the Manchurians when they tried to overtake the Ming dynasty. Though he won many battles, he later was overwhelmed by the great odds and had to retreat to Amoy and finally drove the Dutch out of Formosa where he established himself as King of Formosa. He died on May 1, 1662, at the age of thirty-eight. His life story

An elderly Japanese by a cannonball monument

has been told in French, Dutch, and particularly in Japanese. On the first day of the eleventh moon of 1715 a new play called *Kokusenya Kassen*, or *The Battle of Coxinga*, specially written by Chikamatsu Monzaemon, was performed by the puppets at the Takemoto Theatre in Osaka and scored a great success. It was performed every night in Osaka for seventeen months and was also adapted for performances in several theaters in many of the chief cities of Japan. The audiences became known as the Coxinga-mad public and Coxinga rapidly became a household name in Japan. Donald Keene ascribes the reason for the success to its patriotic appeal, its exoticism, and the quality of the writing. He says that almost every Japanese could recite the *Michiyuki* in the fourth act, which began with a passage: "For the Chinese style of hairdress they use Satsuma combs; for the Shimada style of hairdress they use Chinese combs. Thus are Yamato and Cathay united." This implication had a natural, automatic appeal to the Japanese. I myself think Coxinga lived in Japan as a young boy during the feudal period and had no doubt been much influenced by the life stories of many samurai and that his later development in becoming a brave young general in the seventeenth century was a natural result. While the play was running in Japan so successfully in the eighteenth century, the Manchu rulers in China naturally had not allowed it to be translated and circulated among the Chinese.

During the troubled years just before the Manchurians destroyed the House of Ming and established the House of Ch'ing, many learned Chinese scholars and monks left China for Japan, simply because they did not wish to live or serve under the Manchu rulers. These Chinese generally landed in Nagasaki first and remained there. What interested me in Shinchi was a special Chinese-Japanese dish called *champon* with chicken cut in small pieces, cooked in Fukien style mixed with noodles and mushrooms and bamboo shoots. I found it quite good, and better than the Chinese-American dish chop suey. While eating, I looked at the big photographs on the walls, one of Peiron, Nagasaki's boat race festival, which generally takes place in mid-June, and another of the Chinese Dragon Dance on October seventh to ninth. The waiter had much to say about these two photographs for he had taken part on each occasion. Both could have originated with the early Chinese who came to Nagasaki and reenacted the Chinese festival of Dragon Boat Race on the fifth day of the fifth moon of the lunar calendar, which commemorates the death of Ch'u Yüan, the great Chinese poet of the fourth century B.C. The October Dragon Dance is the real Chinese dragon dance and the dragon lanterns held by the participants looked exactly like those I saw in Hangchow. They could have been constructed by the Chekiang-born Chinese in Nagasaki. It is interesting that both Peiron and the Dragon Dance have become annual events in Nagasaki.

Chinese dragon dance

My purpose in visiting Nagasaki's Shinchi was not merely for a Chinese meal nor to see how the Chinese lived in Japan's most popular seaport. I had read that Shinchi was the piece of land first assigned for a Chinese settlement by the Tokugawa shogunate in 1689, a few years after the Dutch settlement. I wanted to find the house of Shen Chüan, or Shen Nan-pin, who in 1696 was invited to teach Chinese painting in Nagasaki. Before Shen Chüan, there existed a Nagasaki school of Chinese painting. This school of painting was divided into two periods in the Japanese history of art. The early period was initiated by the Chinese Ch'an monk Ichinen Shoyo who came to Nagasaki in 1645 and became the abbot of Hinfukuji there. Ichinen, who was born in Jen-ho of Chekiang Province, left China because he did not want to live under a Manchu ruler. He was a good painter, teaching Chinese painting, particularly Buddhist subjects, whenever he was free from religious service. Two talented pupils of his, Sokushi and Ippi, were the leaders of the school for a long time. Then came the Chinese painters Hayashi Rozan, Yu Ruttoku, and the monk Shinetsu, whose pupils were Kitajima Setsuzan and Ike-no-Taiga. However, Shen Chüan's pure naturalism in rich color suits the Japanese taste and temperament. His works were chiefly flower and bird subjects as well as trees and large animals like tigers and deer, seldom pure landscape or figure painting. He had many talented pupils at the time and his styles are still practiced.

As the Japanese adopted the Chinese written language for their early records and expressions, and later added the hiragana and katakana of their own, they used the same type of brush and ink for writing as the Chinese. It was only natural that they would employ the same medium and technique for their artistic expressions too. With the continuous presence of many good Chinese painters in Nagasaki in the seventeenth and eighteenth centuries, the influence of Chinese painting permeated the Japanese artistic outlook—similar to the influence of Italian painting on the European artistic outlook.

While so much was going on in the study of Chinese painting under Chinese painters, some keen Japanese scholars began to discover Europe and expressed overwhelming enthusiasm for Western perspective and the use of light and shade to build up the solid form of the object they were painting. For instance, Shiba Kokan (1738–1818) first learned to paint in Chinese style but when he was thirty he eagerly switched over to learn Western methods from Hiraga Gennai in 1763 and soon excelled in painting Mt. Fuji in oils, about which he wrote the following theory:

> What is remarkable in painting is that it enables one to see clearly something which is actually not there. If the painting does not truly portray a thing, it is devoid of the wonderful power of the art. Fujisan is a mountain unique in the world, and foreigners who wish to look upon it can do so only in pictures. However, if one follows only the orthodox Chinese methods of painting, one's pictures will not resemble Fuji, and there will be none of the magical quality in it which painting possesses. The way to depict Fuji accurately is by means of Dutch painting.

He held that Western oil painting was "an instrument in the service of the nation" with its educational value. Many young Japanese journeyed from different parts of the country to learn the Western type of painting in Nagasaki at the time when the power of the Tokugawa shogunate began to decline. Shiba's teacher, Hiraga Gennai, was the first artist to have painted in a thoroughly European manner, though Okumura Masanobu (1686–1764), a print maker, and Maruyama Okyo (1732–1795), a follower of Shen Chüan, had both adopted the European perspective principle for their work earlier. Hiraga Gennai even went to teach the daimio of Akita, Satake Yoshiatsu (1748–1785), and Matsudaira Sadanobu sent a protégé to Nagasaki in 1799 to learn art directly from the Dutch. It soon became a vogue for people to collect the Dutch type of paintings and many copied them. It is a great pity that no great Dutch painter of note went to Nagasaki at the time.

I marveled at the Japanese eagerness to learn something new and their diligence in making full use of their new study when I compared the identical period and identical happenings in China. When the Italian Jesuit Giuseppe Castiglione arrived in Peking in 1715, he was twenty-seven and, being an accomplished painter and architect, he managed to have an audience with the Manchu emperor K'ang-hsi, to whom he showed his oil paintings of stories of Christ's life and also models of cathedrals and churches. Though he came to China definitely assigned to missionary work, he was immediately summoned to the court and the emperor appointed him as Hua-yuan-Kung-feng, or Artist-in-waiting at the Academy of Painting, for the emperor liked his work and found the figures in his paintings lifelike. He must have had the consent of the pope, for he lived and painted in the Peking palace until he died in 1766 at 78 years of age. How many works he must have turned out, for he had no worries about the supply of material and the problems of living, for everything was provided. From the pope's point of view and that of all in the Catholic world in Europe, with his direct access to the emperor's court he could have forwarded the missionary work easily, but he tried or could do nothing. What is so curious to me is that in all those fifty-one years and with his almost daily contact with other Chinese painters in the court, not one Chinese painter showed any enthusiasm for the Western type of painting which Castiglione represented, while Hiraga Gennai and Shiba Kokan, on their own, tried to learn the Western technique. Castiglione served three reigns from Emperor K'ang-hsi to his grandson Emperor Ch'ien Lung. Though the young emperor Ch'ien Lung also took great interest in Castiglione's work, he later persuaded and even ordered Castiglione to put his Western material and brushes aside and learn how to handle the Chinese brush and to paint in the Chinese manner on silk as well as on paper. He had to comply with the emperor's wish and learned to paint in the Chinese manner, producing more than a hundred works now in the collection of the Palace Museum at Taiwan. They show a distinct Castiglione school of painting in China's annals of art. It did arouse a few followers at the time, but most Chinese artists carried on their tradition as before. None of them became a Hiraga Gennai or Shiba Kokan.

The Portuguese took over Macao before they went to Japan. Though the Portuguese, together with the Dutch and British, tried hard to trade with China as they did with Japan, they did not succeed. However, the Chinese emperor decreed that foreigners might unload and load goods along the strip of land along the Canton River. Foreign men could land and stay for a while but no foreign women were allowed on shore.

George Chinery, born in London in 1774, with the well-known English painters, Turner and Girtin, studied under Sir Joshua Reynolds at the Royal Academy. In 1795 he moved to Ireland, where he married a wealthy woman, Marianne Vinge, by whom he had a daughter and son. But Marianne was always interfering with his work, so he was always on the move, though wherever he went she would go to join him. In 1825 he eventually found his sanctuary in south China and lived in Macao for the next twenty-seven years. He made trips eighty miles up the Pearl River to the stretch of land where trade was allowed for the foreigners and if there was a rumor of Mrs. Chinery's impending arrival, he retreated upstream to Canton, where foreign women were not allowed. In Macao between 1825 and 1846 Chinery reached the peak of his career and painted portraits for a living, landscapes for pleasure, and sketched continuously. Though he was there many years and his works circulated, not one single Chinese artist was known to have come to him for lessons in Western methods of painting. The Chinese are a most conservative race. Nor did Chinery's name ever appear in any Chinese book on art. George Chinery was a talented artist and had he gone to live in Nagasaki instead of Macao how much his personal influence could have affected Japanese art!

As I have said before, there is something more in art than imitation. Gennai and Shiba did not make such big names for themselves in the history of Japanese art, but their enthusiasm and eagerness to learn Western art methods extended their interest to other Western subjects, such as science, geography, medicine, and banking, thus laying the foundation for the Meiji Restoration, which achieved startling results and raised Japan into the company of other modern nations. Those who became interested in things Western under the strict Tokugawa shogunate's isolation policy, particularly after the 1637 Christian persecution, needed strong wills and great courage to find their way to Nagasaki without getting into trouble. Western studies carried on in Nagasaki had to be under some disguise in those days. No Japanese was allowed to leave the country, but some swam out in Nagasaki Bay and climbed aboard foreign ships begging to be taken away. The Englishman Glover of Nagasaki's Glover House smuggled out the first Japanese students to study in England. No foreign books were available for study. Yukichi Fukuzawa, the great master of enlightenment in the Meiji era, explained how he had begged to see a wonderful book on physical sciences and had copied the whole of it, over a thousand pages, in two days, with the help of a few friends. Japan's modernization and great achievement in industry and many other things did not come by an easy route. Japan has many admirable people whose enthusiasm and eagerness in pursuit of learning, and the use they make of what they have learned to improve what they already have, must be highly recommended.

I asked Donald Keene how he discovered Japan. It started twenty years ago. Since then, Donald has turned out book after book on Japanese literature, novels, stories, poetry, drama, and anthologies as well as copious essays and lectures. He has identified himself completely with the Japanese, but his discovery of Japan has been of even more benefit to those outside Japan than to himself. By his discovery of Japan, I have myself discovered that Chinese and Japanese are not quite the same by nature. As Donald says in his book *The Battle of Coxinga*:

> Japan had never seriously considered herself the center of the universe and the fountainhead of all civilization, [so] she was readier to take up foreign ways and wares than was China. . . . The Japanese were also quick to approve of Portuguese cooking, and tempura, a standard Japanese dish of today, dates from the same time [the sixteenth century], when Dutch wares enjoyed great popularity; there are eighteenth-century prints which show fashionable demimondaines wearing sashes of Dutch calico over their splendid silken robes. The wealthy merchants of Osaka were willing to pay tremendous sums for anything unusual, whether it was a strange animal or a European scientific instrument.

This can be easily seen in what has happened in the big cities of Japan. I have seen many young people having their hair dyed brownish red or even blonde. In Tokyo and Kyoto almost six or seven out of ten girls, including some middle-aged females, dyed their hair red or dark red. However, both the Japanese discovery of Europe and Donald Keene's discovery of Japan did not come the easy way. And I had to go to Nagasaki to make my own discovery.

America met Japan

X X

The Mongols and Hakata

IT WAS A dull gray late-April morning, with a dewy feeling in the fresh air, but not windy, when I reached Hakata with its many Western-style buildings. I did not expect to see such a modernized city. Hakata Bay was the first strip of Japan's coastline to be invaded by foreign vessels from China in the thirteenth century. This outlet at Hakata was Japan's only contact with the outer world in the early days. However, Hakata joins with Fukuoka as an important center for the political, economic, and cultural development of western Japan and they prosper from iron, steel, and other heavy industries and from chemical plants. It took me three and a half hours to go by train from Nagasaki and settle myself in the Hakata Nikkatsu Hotel for lunch. I came to see this place for its past history as well as for its present appearance.

It is said that Fukuoka Prefecture was the first to accept the ancient Chinese civilization as introduced through the Koreans. I went to find the remains of the Tofuro, which was the local government office thirteen hundred years ago, but very little of it remained. The taxi driver then took me to the nearby Dazaifu Tenmangu Shrine, which was dedicated to the great Japanese scholar and statesman, Sugawara-no-Michizane. I had read about Michizane in the *Short Biographies of Eminent Japanese in Ancient and Modern Times.*

He was the third son of a councilor of state named Sugawara-no-Koreyoshi and was born in the twelfth year of Showa (A.D. 845). From his youth, he exhibited extraordinary talents. He was a man of erudition, and very skillful in composing Chinese poetry. During the Jogwan (A.D. 859–876) he distinguished himself as a learned scholar and able statesman. Afterward in the first year of Shotai (A.D. 898), when the emperor Daigo ascended the throne, the retiring emperor advised the sovereign to entrust all important affairs of his government to Sugawara-no-Michizane, because, in knowledge as well as in age, that statesman was the first among all the officials. His advice had in view the lessening of the influence of the haughty Fujiwara clan. The emperor Daigo consequently called Michizane into his presence and made known to him his wishes. The statesman, seeing the impracticability of the measure, positively declined the offer. Fujiwara-

no-Tokihira, a young and haughty minister, and colleague of Sugawara, hearing that the emperor had made such a worthy proposal to
Michizane, became very jealous of him. There was likewise another
distinguished officer by the name of Minamoto-no-Hikaru, who had
been a rival and enemy of Michizane. These two formed an intrigue
and slandered him to the emperor saying that he was plotting a con-
spiracy. Sugawara-no-Michizane was at once degraded, and banished
to the province of Tsukushi at the western extremity of Japan. The
ex-emperor was greatly astonished at the report of this sad affair. He
went at once to the imperial palace to intercede for Sugawara with the
emperor. But Tokihira ordered the guards not to open the gates to anyone, as it was night. Being thus unable to enter the palace, the ex-
emperor with tears returned to his own palace. When Michizane was
in office, he wrote a comprehensive history of Japan, called *Ruiji Ko-
kushi,* which is still extant although some parts of it are incomplete.
Before he was banished he was employed in the composition of
another historical work called *Sandai Jitsuroku* (Genuine Records of
the Three Reigns), with the cooperation of some other scholars,
among whom the bad minister Tokihira was also reckoned. However,
when the work was finished, his name was not mentioned among the
writers of the work. Two years were passed in his place of banishment. In the third year, he died in the midst of great indignity—at the
age of fifty-seven. His death occurred in the third year of Enki (A.D.
903). After his demise, the imperial city was visited by several calamities. The capital city and the emperor's palace were burned down by
fire kindled by lightning. The young minister, Tokihira, his enemy,
died of a singular disease. It was then generally believed that those
calamities had been caused by the angry spirit of the illustrious exile.
The emperor consequently restored this distinguished man, though
dead, to his former office and rank. He was afterward deified, under
the honorable name of Tenman Dai-Jizai Itoku Tenjin—
Heaven-pervading Almighty and All-glorious God. His chief temple
was built at Kitano near the capital. Afterward he was promoted to
the first rank and to the highest office by the emperor Ichijo. Since
that period he has been worshiped throughout the empire as the god
of literature and penmanship. Scarcely is there a town in which his
temple is not seen.

I have a little argument with the writer of the above story. I don't
think Sugawara-no-Michizane's spirit became angry and caused those
disastrous calamities, for he showed no grievances during his years of
banishment. Those calamities might have been caused by the anger of
many other gods who did not agree with the treatment that Sugawara
received.

I became interested in Sugawara as the god of penmanship because of
my interest in Chinese calligraphy. In the long history of China many a
great scholar was wronged in his lifetime and was greatly revered after

his death, but none of them ever became a god, though some temples were built to commemorate their work at the places where they had lived.

Before entering the Dazaifu Shrine I went through a big bronze torii, then crossed the bridge, and went through a two-story gate. Outside the small oratory was a rather big tree in full leaf with a label in Japanese, "tobi-ume." The taxi driver tried to explain the meaning to me but I could not understand his rapid Japanese. However, I guessed what it meant, for I had read that Sugawara-no-Michizane was very fond of ume (really *mei* in Chinese but most Westerners translate it to mean "Japanese apricot") and wrote a poem about it when he was only eleven, as translated by Burton Watson:

Kochi fukaba nioi okoseyo	When the east wind blows,
ume-no hana aruji nashitote	Send your fragrance, flower of Ume.
haru na wasureso	Never forget spring even though your master is gone.

Jumping ume

It was said that this particular ume tree was formerly planted in Sugawara's residence in Kyoto but it moved itself one night to this place to follow Sugawara into exile. Therefore it remains outside this oratory and blooms every year. The Japanese words *tobi-ume* mean "jumping mei tree." This is one of the most poetic legends that a winter plum tree followed its beloved poet into exile. The Chinese poets and artists have expressed their great love for this tree through their poems and paintings but there has been no other story like this one.

Being the seat of the god of literature and penmanship, the Dazaifu Shrine received annually thousands and thousands of young students who came to worship and pray for success in their scholarship and calligraphy, for they left a number of brushes and inks hanging in the shrine. I wonder if modern Japanese students of the sciences and of European languages would come to do so too.

Next I visited Ohori Park, which lies west of Hakata station and has a big lake with a number of small islands joined by bridges. Many people were boating as the wind ruffled the water surface creating many ripples, which gave the illusion of the boats rocking up and down. I walked to the end of an island where a small bowerlike structure stood. A young Japanese sailor in uniform must have sensed something different about me, for he came over and spoke to me in English. Being a typical sailor and tending to be worldly and talkative, this young man had a lot to tell me, particularly about the girls of different places. Though he looked young, he had been to Hong Kong, Bangkok, Rangoon, Saigon, and Kuala Lumpur. He said that Hong Kong girls had slender waists and small feet, Bangkok and Rangoon girls were too Buddhistic and had big feet, and Malayan girls were too Islamic with big feet also. I did not know what he meant by girls being Buddhistic and Islamic. Though irrational, it is interesting that he did not say that Hong Kong girls were Confucianistic. Apparently the girls of Hong Kong whom he met were not altogether Chinese. This casual talk implies something of racial differences. "Japanese girls love to wear Western-style hats," continued the sailor, "while Chinese girls don't like to wear anything on their heads. This may be because the Japanese girls are accustomed to have a broad style of hairdress like the geisha girls, but Chinese girls do not have that habit." He seemed to be quite observant and I had never thought of this reason.

It was still early for dinner, so I lingered outdoors for a stroll along the main street of Hakata. Though most buildings looked very Western, the goods sold in the shops were all very Japanese. Apart from the small gifts and local candies, the prominent items for sale were footgear including colored slippers of all kinds, though most of them are now made of plastic and no more *geta* ("wooden clogs") or *zori* were seen about. As I have mentioned before, no other people in the world care so much about their footgear. In addition, Hakata has one famous product for sale. These are the Hakata dolls of all kinds and of all sizes. Those beautiful and lovable dolls are in the forms of various characters of No plays or Kabuki plays, geisha and maiko girls with different hairdos and in different kimonos, and many others representing the different walks of life of Japan! Though produced as general goods for sale and not ranked as art objects, each doll shows the great dexterity of the Japanese hand; each is made with meticulous care and faultlessness. I looked in several doll shops and examined each doll carefully. Nothing could have won my admiration more for its finished technique.

Perhaps the English word *doll* is not the exact equivalent of the Japanese expression *ningyo*, for the latter is used as a charm or symbol and not really as a plaything. The ningyo was originally made of twisted straw or crudely carved wood in the early rural days and used as a charm to keep off evil influences or against insects that might destroy crops, or cause sickness, or fire, and so on. Gradually it came to be made by skillful hands with good taste. From the seventeenth century onward it developed in the first part of the Tokugawa period. Not only were the dolls made with refined technique but they were also made in many different forms to represent figures in different occupations. People would buy them for their children to play with and also for indoor ornaments. There were a number of dollmakers who made big names for themselves, some of whom were born in Hakata and started their life work there. Thus Hakata became known all over Japan and also to the world through many foreign tourists who took the dolls home.

Chao-Hun-Pei

Late-April weather in Japan can be quite fickle. Yesterday was quite dull though without rain but this morning was sunny and bright. When I went to see the monument commemorating the Mongol invasion, I took a taxi to the main entrance of Higashi-koen, or East Park, and walked across a wide, flat open space with clusters of trees, conspicuously tall pines, here and there. First I reached an enclosure of low stone walls with a few monumentlike stones. Straight through from this enclosure was a stone platform with an impressive bronze statue of the emperor Kameyama in full court dress and traditional imperial hat, looking aloof with a commanding view over all the surroundings. Various colored flowers were planted around the stone plinth in the Western manner, neat and patterned. Not far from this bronze monument I saw two stone monuments with words in kanji on each, one of which had three big kanji characters Chao-Hun-Pei 招魂碑 or Summoning the souls monument, which could mean the summoning back of those souls lost in the fierce resistance to the Mongol invasion. Around this part of the park many women were busy clearing the grass and tidying up generally. They were preparing for a big festival about to be held for the followers of the Nichiren sect. A number of kanji words were written on a white cloth banner hanging in front of the bigger bronze statue of the Buddhist monk Nichiren. Many other banners with kanji words were flapping in the wind. There were two newly constructed stands with a person in each selling printed charms and other objects while another person registered the adherents of the Nichiren sect who were to attend the ceremony. A man and a woman with their hands clasped together were murmuring and praying in front of the Nichiren statue. I have mentioned Nichiren in the chapter on Kamakura, but his stormy life and great achievement impressed me greatly.

Born a sickly son of a fisherman's family of a humble origin and of the Sudras, the lowest caste, Nichiren grew up robust with a strong mind. After studying and training at the great monastic center of Mt. Hiei, he found the Truth in the Buddha Sakyamuni's teaching in the Lotus Sutra and established a Buddhist sect based on the Lotus Sutra as the key to everything. He even regarded himself as the reincarnated Bodhisattva of Superb Action, who was to be a stalwart pioneer in propagating the Perfect Truth. Not content with attacking other Buddhist sects as being false, he was so outspoken on the decadence of the government authorities that he was condemned to death, but the blade of the executioner's sword was struck down miraculously by lightning, so his life was saved and he was banished to live on Sado Island. In 1272, still in exile, he warned the government about the impending Mongol invasion and prophesied that a divine wind would come to wipe out the Mongol invasion fleet. All turned out to be true. This big bronze statue of Nichiren erected in the East Park in Fukuoka seems appropriate.

In my talks with Burton Watson on Japanese historical figures, I remember remarking that it was a great wonder that Japan had produced two of the greatest Buddhist figures within four hundred years, Kukai, or Kōbō Daishi, and Nichiren, one a descendant of an aristocratic family and the other a poor fisherman's son. Burton said that surely China with her long history must have had people like Nichiren from very humble origins. My answer was that China did produce many great men from very humble origins, particularly those first emperors of each new dynasty, for they were merely brave and cunning military-minded men with the driving force to gather large masses of people under their control. Quite a few great Chinese scholars, too, have risen from very humble origins. After they proved themselves to have a great talent for learning, the Chinese by their pragmatic nature could seldom go beyond Confucian principles and they could not attack others as Nichiren did. Besides, the Chinese always inclined to lead their lives as down-to-earth men while the Japanese seem to have had hopes of becoming *kamis*, or gods, in the end. Like many others, both Kōbō and Nichiren were gods in their lifetime as well as afterward, for they could lead the Japanese masses, who by nature were all believers in kamis. Large masses of Chinese seldom followed a leader for long, simply because the bulk of them were peasants, illiterate and ignorant of anything other than their own rice fields. If either Kōbō or Nichiren had been born in China with the ambition to achieve what they had in Japan, I am not sure they would have received the same high respect that they did in Japan. Japan is much smaller than China. Owing to many natural disasters—earthquakes, volcanoes, typhoons, floods—and the rocky seacoast, only one-third of the land is habitable; therefore the Japanese tend to live compactly together and their lives voluntarily or involuntarily affect one another. Living in such a closely knit community, the necessity of an orderly organization or system of living became second nature to the people. From this arose their great love for well-organized festivals, ceremonies, and pageantry. The early Chinese could live wherever they liked in the vast area of China and were afflicted only by the terrible floods from the overflowing of the Yellow River in the north. From very ancient times the Chinese lived in the countryside in small peasant groups widely separated from one another. They seldom met other groups, owing to the lack of transportation and communication. Therefore they could not be easily gathered together for some movement or other. Later Confucianism tried to bind the people together through the blood relationship of a family unit. But the Chinese natural characteristics of being indifferent and detached gave rise to Taoism. With both Confucianism and Taoism already so deeply rooted in Chinese life, the Chinese received the Indian Buddhist religious faith for a while. Only Buddhist philosophy upheld Chinese scholars, but the Buddhist religious faith did not hold the mass of the Chinese people as firmly as it did the Japanese. Almost every Japanese can tell me who Kōbō and Nichiren are, but not all Chinese could relate something about our most celebrated T'ang monk, Hsüan Tsang, who spent seventeen years in India and translated a large number of Buddhist sutras from Sanskrit into Chinese. Hsüan Tsang has never been worshiped in China as a god; neither a temple nor a monument was erected there to commemorate his greatness.

Presently I walked into the front court of the Hakozaki Shrine, which had many healthy trees. I noticed a board with three kanji words "T'ang-Chuan-Ta," or "Pagoda of the Chinese boat." At the bottom of the board, two pieces of stone were placed together with a sign saying "Anchoring rock of the Mongol ship." At the right corner of the court, not far from the Mongol relics, stood a very old tree, called Ta-Nan, or Big Kusunoki, said to be over eight hundred years old. This tree could have been in this very corner during the Mongol invasion. This Hakozaki Shrine, known to be one of the most noted three Hachiman shrines in Japan, was established in the sixteenth century. The most archaic looking of the two-story gates of the shrine was erected in 1592–1595 without a single nail being used in its construction. I wanted to see other relics of the Mongol invasion, which were said to be inside the shrine, but I could not find anyone who could give the permission to see them.

Anchoring rock of the Mongol ship

After coming out of the Hakozaki Shrine, I composed the following little verse:

Not knowing the nature of water and living far
    away from rivers,
The fond-of-fighting Mongols came to invade
    Hakata.
Suddenly a typhoon wiped out the whole fleet,
The old Kusunoki tree in Hakozaki witnessed
    it.

未諳水性遠江涯
好勇元蒙侵博多
忽爾颱風遭覆没
筥宮證出古楠柯

One thing more interested me about the Mongol invasion. Kaza-miya, the wind god of Japan, was not originally regarded as important as many other gods and occupied a much lower position in the hierarchy. But after 1293 he was granted the supreme honor of ranking himself next to many major kami in recognition of his great service in having raised the typhoon in Hakata Bay which destroyed the armada of Kublai Khan! The Mongols were nomads who lived chiefly in the northern desert of China. They were not accustomed to rivers or the sea. That was why Kublai Khan failed in his invasion of Japan, though he had great success everywhere else.

Nichiren statue

X X I

Matsue and Izumo

IT WAS A long train journey from Hakata to Matsue, almost seven hours. But I hardly realized that the train had crossed through the Kammon Undersea Tunnel from the island of Kyushu to the western part of Honshu. My thoughts had been so intent on things concerning the Mongol invasion at Fukuoka that I did not notice how long the ride was. From the window I saw rice fields where many workers, chiefly women, were busy setting the young rice plants in regular rows in the earth.

From the station it was again a little distance to the Ichinujiya Hotel and I was well received by the proprietors, Mr. and Mrs. Kazuaki Kageyama, and their staff—all young women—who in a row all bowed to me. I have become used to this kind of bowing, which I reciprocate.

The name of Matsue in kanji, pronounced "Sung Chiang" in Chinese, is exactly the same as that of a district not far from Shanghai, where I had been years ago. The Ichinujiya Hotel was of recent construction in the modern style. A few other hotels of similar kind were grouped nearby. This area appeared to be a newly developed housing project of the city. There is a well-paved road with a low wall running beside the waters of Lake Shinji, which provides a lovely view of great expanse. After a substantial meal I went out for a walk along the lakeside, following the low wall, gazing at the unruffled surface of Lake Shinji. It is about thirty-two miles in circumference and looked good for boating. There was a small island with some pine trees growing on it and between the trees a tiny structure like a shrine could be detected. I read

Yome-ga-shima

that it is called Yome-ga-shima, or Island of a Bride. According to local legend, there was no island here originally, but one morning the island suddenly emerged above the lake surface bearing the drowned body of a young lady who was known to be lovely and pious but unhappily treated. The local people thought this to be a heavenly gift and dedicated the island to the goddess of eloquence and beauty, naming it the Island of Benten in similar sense as the one near Kamakura. They built a shrine on it, and buried the dead body there placing a number of rocks around it.

Moving on toward the left, I was interested in the many well-shaped pine trees along the pavement. They might have been the reason for calling the city Pine River, as the name Matsue in kanji means "Pine." There was a local Shinto shrine at the corner of the park in which stone lanterns stood by the pine trees. Again I turned left and crossed over a small bridge and found a good road which led me to the front of Matsue Castle. The castle grounds were well kept with flowers edging the grass lawn. I walked up to the top of the watchtower dungeon, which I was told was the only one of its kind in Japan. There I stood gazing at the entire city. I then noticed people rowing boats around the castle moat and soon learned that the nickname of this castle was Plover Castle, because it had various large and small gables in plover shape. It took five years to build under the order of Horio Yoshiharu, who was appointed the Lord of Izumo and Oki after he won the battle of Sekigahara in 1607. It has been repaired within recent years. Matsue was known as the military center of the most ancient province of Japan. There were a number of old samurai residences left in some parts of the city, one of which I learned was a one-story house with a big room and a gate lodge with a heavily barred lookout window from which someone could constantly watch passers-by. I did not know how to locate these houses, so I slowly strolled down the main street looking at the shops. In one I noticed some little objects made of well-polished agate of different colors, which is a special local product and I bought two of them.

To my surprise I saw an enormously long bridge lying ahead of me. It was called Obashi Bridge and many people were moving along it, on foot, bicycles, and in cars. The bridge reminded me of *The Great Bridge in Rain*, painted by Ando Hiroshige (1797–1858) ten years before the Meiji era. This painting or a wood-block print of it became well known to the Western world after van Gogh included it in the corner of one of his own oil paintings. I don't know if Hiroshige had actually based his work on the Obashi Bridge, but I took it to be so. Lafcadio Hearn described the sound of the pattering of geta over the Obashi—rapid, merry, musical, like the sound of an enormous dancing floor, and a dance it veritably was. No more geta are worn by the people walking over the Obashi now, but the sound of car wheels, of bicycles, and of soft shoes and the noise of the young women and girls chattering and giggling on their way home after office hours were still pleasing to the ears. Despite so much hustle and bustle on the bridge, I felt that walking on the 138-meter long bridge over the Kakaumi Lagoon with Lake Shinji and far beyond Mt. Sambe on one side and distant Mt. Daisen on the other was a splendid and most invigorating experience.

There is a popular folk song about this bridge called "Yasugibushi" and it has its particular legend—"Gensuke" and "Gensukebashira." Hearn described it as follows:

> When Horio Yoshiharu, the great general who became daimio of Izumo in the Keishu era, first undertook to put a bridge over the mouth of the river, the builders labored in vain, for there appeared to be no solid bottom for the pillars of the bridge to rest upon. Millions of great stones were cast into the river to no purpose, for the work constructed by day was swept away or swallowed up by night. Nevertheless, at last the bridge was built, but the pillars began to sink soon after it was finished. Then a flood carried half of it away, and as often as it was repaired so often it was wrecked. Then a human sacrifice was made to appease the spirit of the flood. A man was buried alive in the river bed below the place of the middle pillar, where the current is most treacherous, and thereafter the bridge remained immovable for three hundred years.
>
> This victim was one Gensuke, who had lived in the street Saikamachi, for it had been determined that the first man who should cross the bridge wearing *hakama* without a *machi* should be put under the bridge; and Gensuke sought to pass over not having a *machi* in his *hakama,* so they sacrificed him. Wherefore the midmost pillar of the bridge was for three hundred years called by his name— Gensukebashira. It is averred that upon moonless nights a ghostly fire flitted about that pillar—always in the dead watch hour between two and three; and the color of the light was red, though I am assured that in Japan, as in other lands, the fire of the dead is most often blue.

Hearn was indeed correct, for in China there is a traditional belief that the color of a ghost fire is blue.

Human sacrifice to appease some spirit of water or land had been a world-wide practice in the ancient days. Many examples could be cited to illustrate it. A similar sacrifice in connection with the building of the Great Wall of China sounds a little more humane than many other stories of this kind. It is said that the first Emperor of Ch'in, who united China into the first Chinese empire in the third century B.C. was afraid only of the Tatar nomads from the north. China's west being protected by the high Himalaya Mountains and her east and south by the sea, he decided to build the Great Wall along the north to prevent the northern nomads, the Tatars, from invading his territory. At first the many attempts of the laborers, though there were millions of them, failed to set up solid foundations for the walls, so a human sacrifice was suggested. As the Great Wall stretched for thousands of miles, ten thousand men would be needed for sacrifices. This worried many of the building commanders. They could not round up so many men for the sacrifice, for they needed many to do the work. Suddenly one of the commanders heard of a man whose family name was 萬 "Wan," which means "ten thousand" in Chinese and his given mane was 仁 "Jen," which means "benevolence" and also "man." When these two characters were put together they sounded like 萬人 "ten thousand men." So the commander got hold of this Wan Jen for the sacrifice. As a result the foundations of the Great Wall were then set up firmly till this day. To sacrifice one man in order to save 9999 lives is somewhat humane. My grandfather loved to tell this story to us when we were very young. His idea was that if there was a humane way out of an inhumane action one should try one's best to find it.

Thinking of these things, I now reached the south end of the bridge. Moving toward the right, I was now quite close to the Island of the Bridge along the Matsue Toll Road. However, it had become much darker and the tree trunks, branches, and the land mass of the island all mingled into a shape like a flowery boat. The day had melted into a luminous haze, violet, yellow, and even vermillion stretching over the great expanse of the lake far away to Mt. Sambe, which was now a rather drab dark green, its contour silhouetted against the broad expanse of the radiant sky. Unlike many sunsets I had seen at other places, there was not one single fragment of cloud in the sky. The mass of housetops were knit together into an edgeless purple carpet spread over the whole city of Matsue with the watchtower standing out like an obelisk of fire. Within the vast bright furnace I spotted the Ichinujiya Hotel, also lit up as though many sapphires were winking to me from the distance. I thought I ought to go back, but the rich light, so gorgeous yet so soft, made me catch my breath. On my way I remembered the words of the Russian avant-garde painter, Vasili Kandinski (1866–1944): "Color makes a more insidious attack on the emotion than form," which I endorse entirely.

Mrs. Hisa Kageyama and the young maid Miho greeted me at the desk with broad smiles. After supper, Mr. Kazuaki Kageyama extended his kindness and drove me to the house of his younger brother, who could understand some English. There I met the young man and his wife, and also Mrs. Kageyama's young sister. The brother promised to show me round Matsue the next day. Later lying on my bed, I could not help thinking how generous and helpful the proprietor of this Japanese hotel had been when he had so many other things to attend to.

The brother came with his car after breakfast. It was pouring outside, but rain did not seem to make any Japanese reluctant to move. Nor does it bother me, so we went first to Lafcadio Hearn's house, which is situated in the section near Old Otemae, in front of the castle by the moat. An elderly woman was there to look after the interior of the place, which was kept clean everywhere and most of the things were arranged just as when Hearn and his wife were living there. I looked at the little desk where Hearn used to sit and write his books and also at the number of different-shaped Japanese brushes and an inkstone which Hearn had used. He had married the daughter of an old samurai family and used his wife's surname when he became a naturalized Japanese, calling himself Yakumo Koizumi. The interesting part was that Hearn arrived at Matsue on August 30, 1890, married soon after and then taught English in the local high school for a year and half before he left for Tokyo. How quickly he made the decision to marry and settle in Japan! From what he wrote in "My first day in the Orient," he did not seem to know any Japanese before he left America for the Far East. I have not read any of Hearn's writings on Japanese politics and society, but I read a good many of his English translations of Japanese folk tales. I still have a few copies of his folk tale translations, published in 1892 by T. Hasegawa Company on a special kind of crepe paper and all are beautifully illustrated in color.

Once Mr. Sei Ito and I had a talk on early foreign writers on Japan. He told me that Hearn was born on Santa Maura, Greece, on June 27, 1850, of an Irish father and a Greek mother. His mother died when he was very young, yet he had an unusually strong love for her and longed for her all his young days. His father used to tell him that his mother was very small in size, very gentle in movement, and had a very kind heart. People used to say that Hearn tried hard to find someone like his mother but in vain; as soon as he got to Japan, he was immediately infatuated by the small lady whom he soon married. He seems to have had little connection with either Ireland or Greece after his arrival in Japan. It was an amazing achievement that he wrote so many volumes in the fourteen years he lived in Japan. Through his writing, he did a great service in introducing Japan to the Western world. He deserves to have his old home kept as a memorial to him, though he only stayed here for a year and a half. A Greek-type building, in which more of his personal belongings and manuscripts were displayed, was built nearby in 1933. I said to young Mr. Kageyama that I specially liked Hearn's living room in the old home with a small garden attached so he could have the fresh air and trees and plants to look at in the early morning when he woke up.

The rain was still falling heavily as we drove to see the Gosshoji Temple, the mausoleums of the Matsudairas. The first Matsudaira was the grandson of the powerful Tokugawa Iyeyasu, who had made the young boy the Lord of Izumo. Mr. Kageyama pointed out two things for me to see: one was a wooden bas-relief carving of a Buddhist deva king on the gate to the tomb of the sixth Lord of Matsudaira, and the other was a huge stone carving of a tortoise without the lower jaw and throat, for fear that it would otherwise wander about at night to swim in the lotus pond and eat the lotus. We next stopped to see the Kanden-an tea lodge and its beautiful garden, which was constructed in 1819 by Fumaiko, the seventh Lord of Matsudaira, who loved to stop here for a hot steam bath and for tea on his way home from hawking. We found nobody in the tea lodge and walked on the stepping stones to the edge of the garden, which commands a nice view of the fields and distant hills, all unfortunately hidden in the misty rain.

We took a long drive along the north side of Lake Shinji and through a wide, flat plain which was dotted by groups of pine trees, inside each of which a homestead was built. On one side only the pines were planted in a row and well trimmed to the same height to protect the house from the north wind. Mr. Kageyama told me that this was a typical style found only in Izumo. We came shortly to a sloping mountain with many trees, chiefly pines, growing all along its foot and up the slope—the famous Mt. Yakumo. Turning right I soon saw the golden outline of a building ahead with the mountain on one side. That was the Izumo Taisha Shrine, or Oyashiro, or Great Shrine of Izumo, which we had come to see. This is said to be the oldest Shinto shrine in Japan, but the present building was constructed in 1874 at the foot of Mt. Yakumo, which is called Peak of Eight Clouds. On the left was Tsuru, or Peak of Crane, and on the right Kame, or Peak of Tortoise. They were veiled with rain and seemed to be breathing steamy vapors upward with a mysterious hint of what lay within them. There was a small structure, squarish in shape, in the front of the main hall. The roofs of both structures were curved, unlike the roofs of other shrines I saw, which were in an inverted V with the roofs sloping straight down. The front wooden beams along the roofs were a plain yellow color. That was why they looked golden to me from the distance. There was a big bundle of straw bound together and rolled like a very thick yellow cord hanging under the eaves of the front structure, and this looked golden too. There were two long side wings, one on each side of the main building, making

Back buildings of Izumo Taisha

the whole structure look very big and wide, with an enormously spacious courtyard in the front and the mountains on almost three sides—a very impressive and imposing sight.

Mr. Kageyama then took me to see the sanctuary at the back, through the open lattice of the wooden corridors on the left side. This part looked very traditional and was built in 1744. It was probably because of the downpour that not many people were there. Though it was raining heavily, there was an unbelievable stillness. Presently a young lady, her long, jet-black hair hanging down over her white robe above a brilliant vermillion skirt, walked straight to the front of the smaller structure under the golden rope of straw. She—a priestess—was there to burn some incense and I thought the color scheme could not be better. Mr. Kageyama asked the young lady to show us the treasure house, where I was particularly interested in a few pieces of calligraphy. Then she was kind enough to hold her umbrella over us and escort us to our car. Mr. Kageyama asked to take a photograph of her and me in the rain. He thanked her with a deep bow and I followed suit. Mr. Kageyama told me that her white robe and vermillion skirt were the traditional dress for a Shinto priestess. I had seen similar dress in Ise and Nikko. This kind of dress is also worn by a priestess who watches the impetuous deity Susa-nowo-no-Mikoto with a monstrous eight-headed serpent in the Izumo *Kagura*, or Izumo Shinto dance, performed yearly at the Izumo Shrine.

The interesting part of the legend was that Susanowo-no-Mikoto, after killing Yamata-no-Orochi, a giant eight-headed serpent, to save the people from destruction, found in the monster's tail a sword named Murakumo, and gave it to his sister Amaterasu-Omikami. The mountains of Izumo were believed to have much iron ore and so there was a legend of early ironmaking in Izumo and a method for producing *Tatara* steel.

As a rule there would be no weddings taking place in Japan in the month of October each year, for the Japanese believe their marriages must be arranged by their local *kami,* and all gods came to Izumo Shrine for a big conference in October. A pair of long rectangular shrine buildings on the east and west sides of the main hall are believed to house the Shinto gods. October is thus called *Kannazuki* ("month without god") in all other parts of Japan, and *Kami-arizuki* ("month with gods") at Izumo. I was told that this belief has long been declining in Japan, particularly when a girl wants to marry an American or European who did not have the same belief and who could get married only in October. However, I could not help wondering how those small buildings on the east and west sides of the shrine's main hall could house up to 800,000 gods. Curiously enough I have found an exception when I spent some time in Kirishima of Kagoshima Prefecture as I mentioned before. Mrs. Tashiko Yano and her daughter Mikiko took me to see the Kirishima Jingu, or the Shinto shrine of Kirishima, at the foot of Mt. Takachiho. A young Shinto priest, the Reverend Tikamasa Kawakami, was so kind as to take us right inside the inner hall facing the shrine, a privilege which I had not had before in any other Shinto shrines. It was almost October and I asked if the god of Kirishima Jingu would go to attend the big conference at Izumo. The Rev. Mr. Kawakami answered no because the god at Kirishima was the god of all gods, who sent his servants to Izumo for the conference. He then told us that the Kirishima Jingu is dedicated to Ninigi-no-Mikoto, the divinity who came down to give Japan the imperial line on earth. According to the Shimazu belief, this is where the god came when he first descended to Japan. I then said that those young Japanese who wanted to get married in October would all flock to Kirishima and that the priest would be very busy for the whole month. The Rev. Mr. Kawakami laughed. However, it is said that the great Shrine of Izumo is erected in honor of the illustrious figure in early Japanese history named Okuni-Mushi-no-Mikoto, who was known to be fortunate in love and to have had a happy marriage. The Japanese make pilgrimages to Izumo Taisha all the year round, especially in February, May, and November when there are festivals.

On our way back to the plain, Mr. Kageyama wanted me to see the typical houses of the Izumo area and stopped at several of them. Indeed

Typical house of the Izumo area

he did his best to show me round Izumo. I could not find words and ways adequate to thank him for all his trouble and help.

The rain never seemed to end and I could not catch the ferryboat for a visit to the Island of the Bride. So I asked if there was a good Chinese restaurant, Peking style, in Matsue. The answer was yes, and Mrs. Hisa Kageyama and Miho went with me, but Miho had to go back to the hotel directly after we reached our destination. We were happily received by the manager. Mrs. Hisa Kageyama and I were shown to a room with tatami. We sat in the Japanese style and had four dishes. Before leaving the restaurant, I noticed the sign with a name Keijo Hanten. It was a Korean restaurant!

XXII

Sun Setting on Oki Island

MR. RIOZI KAWASAKI of Hankyu Express International Company telephoned me from Kyoto that he had made arrangements for me to visit Oki and that tickets for the trains and boats were being sent to me by express post. But I had not heard of Oki before and had no idea where it was nor what I would see there. Mr. Kazuaki Kageyama was good enough to suggest taking me to the boat. I appreciated his kindness. Next morning, Mr. Kageyama, his young chauffeur, and I left the hotel at ten o'clock. On arriving at Yonago, Mr. Kageyama got down to attend to some business in the city and told his chauffeur to motor me on. Though we could not converse, either in Japanese or English, I managed to learn that Yonago was a prosperous seaport, famous for its raw silk, tobacco, sake, and soy. After a half hour we reached Sakaiminato, where the driver took me to the boat office to confirm the ticket. He told me before he left that the boat would leave at 1:40 P.M. and arrive at Beppu, Oki, at 5:10 P.M. He was very kind and I thanked him warmly. I had more than an hour to kill, so I moved round the harbor leisurely. There was a long structure built along the edge of the shore in which were stacks of wooden boxes packed with fish, and many men and women in oilskin caps and long boots were busy sorting the fish from the boats that lay at anchor. The sea breeze was rather fishy and had blown me upstairs for a simple lunch in a small restaurant where the customers were all connected with the fishery industry.

I then found my place on the boat *Okiji Maru,* the departure of which was announced by beating a gong. The boat steamed close to the other side of the harbor and gradually came out to sea. It was a nice sensation to be on the wide expanse of water and breathing the sea air. I saw two black dots flying upward from a rock near the shore. They could have been cormorants.

After more than two hours on the high sea, a number of dark spots appeared on the sea in the distance, which turned out to be a big mound-like island covered with green trees. At first I thought it was only one island, but later the boat went through a wide passage between two big chains of islands, then headed toward the landing stage, where a large number of people were waiting. I took my two small handbags and followed the other passengers onto the shore. A young lady spotted me and, taking my bags, she told me to accompany her. She drove me to another landing stage where a much smaller steamer was anchored, and directed me to go aboard. I was followed by four young girls and two young boys. I was completely bewildered, for none of us could converse. I tried a few words in kanji, but they did not seem to make out what I was asking. One boy about eleven or twelve could say one or two English words, shouting, "Go," while moving his right hand round and round. He was directing the young man at the engine at the rear. All the girls were giggling and I just sat leaning against the bulwark and waited to see what would happen. Gradually the small steamer glided through a narrow passage which seemed to have been cut through two islands, and then came out on the open sea again. Many grotesquely shaped rocks stuck out of the sea and the steamer moved through the gaps between them turning one way and another. The young man steering the boat knew his route very well. Most of these oddly shaped rocks were black with many parts quite well rounded, which reminded me of the massive groups of lava that I saw near Hilo on the island of Hawaii after the 1959 eruption. Those were piled up on the land, but these volcanic rocks must have been even bigger than those when the nearby island erupted hundreds of thousands of years ago. The hot lava fell into the sea and gradually piled up so high as to appear above the sea surface.

The boy who knew a few words of English shouted, "Kuniga," which I took to mean we were at the scenic spot of Kuniga. The twilight was still quite bright, but a red hue seemed to spread over the sea. I remembered Wordsworth's lines:

> It is a beauteous evening, calm and free,
> The holy time is quiet as a nun
> Breathless with adoration; the broad sun
> Is sinking down in its tranquillity;
> The gentleness of heaven broods o'er the sea;
> Listen! the mighty Being is awake.

Indeed a mighty Being was still awake then.

I had forgotten my bewilderment of a moment ago and now I was dumfounded at the unusual scenery—a cliff like a skyscraper, with massive dark green mosses growing over parts of the enormous lava-built rocky hill. Suddenly the steamer made a turn to enter a cave under a steep cliff and moved in complete darkness. The young helmsman guided his boat skillfully and the steamer never touched the walls on either side. We moved slowly in the black cave and the steersman began to sing a popular local song. It sounded so beautiful inside the dark tunnel and seemed to drive away any feeling of fear or apprehension. For about twenty minutes we were inside the cave when a line of light appeared ahead and we soon emerged to move past a vast, bright red, sheer cliff. A young girl wrote two kanji words for me, "Chih Pi" in Chinese pronunciation, meaning "Red Cliff." This gave me an unusual sensation, for this brought me back to a place along the Yangtze River not far from my home town, which was called Chih Pi, and where a big battle was waged in the third century. The name of that place became known to almost every Chinese man of letters through two rhymed prose essays written by the Sung writer-poet, Su Tung-p'o (1036–1101). I had never expected to see another place with the same name.

The waves surrounding our steamer were not only glittering but were like red-hot sparkles now. Suddenly an enormous red ball seemed about to kiss the sea. I had not faced the setting sun so closely and on the same level before. As the steamer was small, I thought I was moving directly on the water surface, face to face with the sunset. Oh, so red and so hot it was, for the crimson light was floating all over the water surface as well as turning all those black ironlike lava rocks into red-hot ones as if the whole area became the burning furnace of an enormous steel mill. Our steamer was right in the center of the red-hot furnace. Though I felt somewhat hot, it was not really hot but just extraordinarily warm—one of the most unusual scenes that I have ever witnessed. Everyone in the boat looked reddish and we were all intoxicated by the unbelievable scene. Each of the four girls had their mouths wide open. So did the two boys. The young man at the rear began to sing again and his voice was not so high-pitched as it had been within the narrow tunnel, but the notes vibrated and trailed in the air and moved along the ripples of the sea, away from us.

Years ago I saw the sun rise high from the peak of Mt. Lu and also from the upper deck of the ocean liner *Queen Mary,* which I wrote about in my book *The Silent Traveller in New York,* attaching the following verse:

A mysterious whole united the vast emptiness,
The wholesome wind of heaven tosses and twitches
   my coat.
I watch the early sun rising from the ocean liner
And feel as if I were reading an unfamiliar book.

Now this unfamiliar book was written in Japanese and was still more strange to my eyes. So I wrote this verse to record it:

紅光漁面金烏墜
不似天邊旭出時
別有一般奇怪處
隱岐為醉我為癡

A red hue flies over the sea while the golden bird drops down,
It does not resemble the red sky at sunrise.
There is some strangeness somewhere,
Oki Islands are like a drunkard and I like a man who has lost his senses.

I usually tend to think of the morning sun as a charming young girl in a Ginza shop with well-rouged cheeks looking soft and gentle and rising up slowly in order to perform her duty for mankind. But now at Oki I saw her returning home with much sake, madly kissing the sea and soon completely wrapped in the bosom of the Japan Sea and disappearing into it.

It was not yet quite pitch dark when the steamer returned to the small landing stage where we had started. The young lady was there to receive me and drove me back to her home at Tsukamoto Ryokan, where it was arranged for me to stay. Her mother runs the inn and her father is in the local police force, and she herself drives their customers about. Her car must have been one of the very few on the island, for there seemed to be no others about. The short street had a number of shops on both sides, cleanly set up, and everybody smiled at the young driver, who must be very popular in the place. At the end of the street the car ran on a wide footpath with fields on both sides. To my great surprise I saw a farmer plowing his field with an ox. This animal was used in the olden days, but now most farmers use tractors.

Inside Tsukamoto Ryokan everything looked well kept and spotless. I was shown to a room with a hanging scroll of a painting of a red-crested crane in flight. A small lacquered stool was in the corner of a neatly laid tatami. Mrs. Tsukamoto came to greet me and later the young lady came in and told me her name was Shiko. I was given a towel and the direction to a Japanese-type bathtub in another room. After a good hot bath I felt fresh and relaxed as I put on the Japanese kimono provided by the ryokan. Mrs. Tsukamoto and her daughter brought in many small dishes in lacquer and porcelain containers. Shiko had changed her wool sweater and jeans for a blue-and-white kimono with a wide, brilliant red sash around her waist and looked more charming and attractive than ever. She has an easygoing manner, smiling gently at times. Though she has some modern ways, for she knows how to drive the car and other things, Shiko retains her Japanese traditions. As a rule I prefer to eat by myself as I did in many other Japanese ryokan. Shiko left the room slowly with a sweet smile. Mrs. Tsukamoto came and took all the dishes away without making the slightest sound in her movements. Shiko returned and sat by me as if she had a great deal to say to me. She must have learned who I was from Mr. Kawasaki and began to tell me about things by writing in kanji. Her kanji writing was well composed and her knowledge of kanji was far better than that of a number of young Japanese men whom I had met in Tokyo and Kyoto. She was twenty years old, had completed her high school studies, and was interested in modern machinery and reading novels. She also showed good taste in arranging a flower twig in a vase. She continued to write that she did not want to get married until she was twenty-three, but the reason she gave I could not make out. Later Mrs. Tsukamoto came to spread the bed on the tatami, and mother and daughter left the room murmuring a Japanese expression which I took to be "good night"; I returned a similar greeting. Resting on the bed in the dark while the wind whispered through the leaves of the trees in the courtyard, I lay awake trying to visualize all I had done since leaving Sakaiminato. All passed through my mind like a dream that I had never imagined in this old world place

I was getting into bed in the ryokan room

and I felt rather like the fisherman in the story written by a great Chinese poet, T'ao Tüan-ming in the fourth century and translated by the late Professor Herbert Giles.

Toward the close of the fourth century A.D. a certain fisherman of Wu-ling, who had followed one of the river branches without taking note whither he was going, came suddenly upon a grove of peach trees in full bloom, extending some distance on each bank, with not a tree of any other kind in sight. The beauty of the scene and the exquisite perfume of the flowers filled the heart of the fisherman with surprise, as he proceeded onward, anxious to reach the limit of this lovely grove. He found that the peach trees ended where the water began, at the foot of a hill; and there he espied what seemed to be a cave with light issuing from it. So he made fast his boat and crept in through a narrow entrance, which shortly ushered him into a new world of level country, of fine houses, of rich fields, of fine pools, and of a luxuriance of mulberry and bamboo. Highways of traffic ran north and south; sounds of crowing cocks and barking dogs were heard around; the dress of the people who passed along or went to work in the fields was of a strange cut; while young and old alike appeared to be contented and happy.

One of the inhabitants, catching sight of the fisherman, was greatly astonished; but, after learning whence he came, insisted on carrying him home, and killed a chicken and placed some wine before him. Before long, all the people of the place had turned out to see the visitor, and they informed him that their ancestors had sought refuge here, with their wives and families, from the troubled times of the house of Ch'in, adding that they had thus become finally cut off from the rest of the human race. They then inquired about the politics of the day, ignorant of the establishment of the Han dynasty, and of course of the later dynasties which had succeeded it. And when the fisherman told them the story, they grieved over the vicissitudes of human affairs.

Each in turn invited the fisherman to his home and entertained him hospitably, until at length the latter prepared to take his leave. "It will not be worthwhile to talk about what you have seen to the outside world," said the people of the place to the fisherman, as he bade them farewell and returned to his boat, making mental notes of his route as he proceeded on his homeward voyage.

When he reached home, he at once went and reported what he had seen to the governor of the district, and the governor sent off men with him to seek this unknown region. But he was never able to find it again. Subsequently, another desperate attempt was made by a famous adventurer to pierce the mystery; but he also failed, and died soon afterward of chagrin, from which time forth no further attempts were made.

The place that the fisherman unexpectedly found has long been considered a Chinese utopia. Most Chinese have longed to be that fisherman and find a similar place. What an unexpected feeling I had when I came to see Oki! Although I am no fisherman, nor does Oki resemble the country that the fisherman discovered, I had a feeling that the fisherman and the world he saw could exist somewhere outside China. I therefore thought of prolonging my stay in order to find out more about this place. I must have soon fallen soundly asleep.

The sunshine was pouring into my room when Shiko came in with breakfast. While eating, I discussed with her my idea of a longer stay. I could not explain the reason that occurred to me the previous night, nor could she understand what I was asking her for. But as she had been well trained in the business and as she possessed a logical mind, she went to work systematically on the plan she had devised. After breakfast she packed the bags and took me out for a walk. Her father was in the hall telephoning; she introduced me to him and we exchanged greetings with a deep bow. Then her mother came to see us at the door and I took a few photographs of them. First we walked down to the little beach, only a short distance from the house, and I saw a number of fisher-women busy putting seaweed on bamboo mats for drying. They arranged them in a neat pattern. Later Shiko and I drove through the street and she was again greeted by the people we met on the way. We next stopped by a large pine tree and Shiko led me up a number of steps to a small shrine with a stone inscribed with six kanji characters meaning "Kuroki-gosho ishi." Shiko asked me for a piece of paper and then wrote "Emperor Go-Daigo" in kanji, indicating with some gestures that the emperor had spent some time here. This reminded me that I had read a story called "The Exile of Go-Daigo," translated from a Japanese book *Masukagami* by Donald Keene in his *Anthology of Japanese Literature*. While we were standing in front of the little shrine I could not help imagining how the place looked when the exiled emperor came to this very spot. He would still have a large retinue with him filling the whole space. The inhabitants of the island might have been allowed to come and see the emperor, the direct descendant of the Sun Goddess and a god himself whom nobody could see in the capital, then Kyoto. Before Go-Daigo came here, another emperor, Go-Toba, was also exiled here and died. In the translated story, Oki was described as a miserable place to which the emperor Go-Daigo dreaded to come.

However, times have changed and Oki must have changed a great deal too. There was a wooden bench a little way down from the shrine. I asked Shiko to sit down for a rest. Facing us through an opening in the trees was the bay, enclosed by the other islands as if it was a big pond with an unruffled surface. The bright sun shining over the water had turned it into a sheet of silver while the trees stood still with no wind to stir them. It was a beautiful morning and how tranquil was the air in that spot where Shiko and I were! Soon Shiko stood up and pointed toward the bay as if saying, "There comes your boat!" The same type of boat as the *Okiji Maru* entered the opening between the headlands. From a long distance and high up on the hill I could see the boat moving slowly as if she did not want to stir the water at all with her propellers. After having watched the boat approach, Shiko told me to follow her down to the car and she drove to the landing stage where I had come the previous afternoon. Just as she parked the car, two young men walked over to greet her. She introduced the taller of the two to me saying, "My boy friend" in a most happy voice. Shiko had not said a word of English to me before and she must have kept this to the last moment on purpose. It seems that most young Japanese people nowadays know some popular English or American expressions whether they have learned the language or not. The two young men took my bags on board and found a place for me. Leaning on the railing, I saw Shiko busily giving rolls of colored streamers to the two young men, who began to throw them toward me while holding one end as the boat began to move. Shiko and her two friends laughed happily while waving their hands. I shouted to them, "I'll come back!" No matter whether they heard and understood it or not, I was very much touched by this sendoff.

The boat was soon at sea with no land in sight. My mind turned back to the exiled emperor Go-Daigo, who with several court ladies and two men, Yukifusa and Tadaaki, in twenty-four large, and innumerable small, vessels were rowed to Oki Island. Such a large number of boats when spread out over the water must have covered a wide area of the sea. With so many people with him, the place could never have been very quiet and secluded. Yet the emperor Go-Daigo was unhappy, for his palace life had been so different. It is known that Go-Daigo was a very intelligent, ambitious, and learned person who wrote many verses during his captive days at Rekuhara and must have written many more while he was on Oki Island. It is a pity that they are not known. I think sending an emperor into exile must have happened in Japan only in a few cases. As Japan's emperors were gods, how could the shogun send them into exile? Chinese history contains no such record, though a number of emperors did die in captivity under the rule of a new emperor of a succeeding dynasty.

Though my stay on Okishima was very brief, the way of life I experienced and the people I met were not much different from those on the three main islands, Honshu, Kyushu, and Shikoku. How homogeneously and evenly has the Japanese civilization spread to every corner of their lands. The British Isles have the English, Irish, Scottish, and Welsh, while Italy's north is not the same as the south. Scandinavia consists of four different countries, while China has her north as well as her south. Though the smaller size of Japan as a whole may account for the homogeneity of her civilization, the thoroughness of conducting mass education in the Meiji era, I think, could be the real factor in achieving such homogeneity. However, while I was on Okishima I saw no pachinko shop, no movie house, and hardly any public bar. Everybody seemed perfectly happy without those things. But the central government is now creating a national park on Okishima. Will it be the same when I go again for another visit?

Kuroki-gosho ishi

XXIII

Tottori's Sand Dune and Kurashiki's Art Treasures

AFTER MY UNUSUAL experience on Oki Island I caught the JNR train from Sakaiminato to Tottori. There was a heavy mist covering the April morning sky. The young green rice plants stood out clearly in the terraced fields, indicating that they had recently been planted. Though Japanese farmers have long used tractors to plow their fields they still plant the small bundles of young rice by hand. The Japanese countryside was an almost interminable succession of tranquil beauty.

When the train reached Tottori station, it began to rain. Mr. Taneo Kotani, owner and manager of the Hotel Kozeniya, received me with a smile. He knew a few words of English and we could also communicate in kanji writing. Kozeniya is a Japanese hotel but has a Western look externally. The main entrance to the grounds reminded me of the entrance to an English mansion, though the driveway was only a short one. Not far inside was a Japanese garden surrounded by some trees and a blossoming cherry and two or three beautifully shaped pines shading a small teahouse. Beside this was a pond with goldfish swimming in it. A maid came to take my bags and showed me to my room, which was arranged entirely in Japanese fashion—nicely spread tatami, a low table, cushions, and a scroll painting hanging on the wall. Tea with cakes which were a local speciality was brought, followed by several small dishes of food for dinner. Afterward Mr. Kotani came in for a talk and slowly but clearly he explained that Tottori was once an old and quiet castle town in San-in District, but it suffered great earthquakes in 1943 and again in 1952, which almost destroyed all the busy quarters of the city. However, the local people determined to rebuild the city, and after years of hard work it had now become the center of Tottori Prefecture. The old site of the castle was converted into a public garden. The Tottori University, which has three departments, liberal arts, medicine, and agriculture, is situated on the western side of the city, while on the southern side the Tottori Spa with its hot spring flowing all day long is the chief attraction for many. The city is noted for a particularly fine species of pear known as nijisseiki nashi, which is brought in from the countryside for sale in the autumn. In winter and early spring local fishermen would catch many crabs of a kind especially found in this area called matsuba gani and boil and sell them in the streets. These matsuba gani were caught for the first time in the Genroku era (1688–1704) by a fisherman of the Tanjiri fishing port—a small village. Now the Tottori Prefecture catches about twenty-four hundred tons of them each year. The principal products of the city are lumber, woodenware, paper, raw silk, and articles of coral. Tottori paper is a speciality known as inshu-shi. There are also four local kilns: Ushinotoyaki, Inkyusanyaki, Kazu-wayaki, and Hashojiyaki. Tottori also boasts the largest sand dune in Japan, a beautiful lake called The Silent Lake, and Kakuto Beach.

When I awoke the next morning, a high wind was blowing and sudden showers dashed against the trees outside my windows. Mr. Kotani already had tickets for me to do some sightseeing. Disregarding the rain, I went out after breakfast and was surprised to see the bus station packed with people with a similar object, but not one Western face was to be seen. Gradually one bus left after another; I found a place in one bound for the famous sand dune. I had no idea what of special interest I would see there; after all, I had seen many sand dunes in America around Provincetown on Cape Cod, Massachusetts. After about half an hour the bus stopped and I followed the crowd past some gift shops and restaurants, up a footpath to an opening between two bushes. Here everyone stopped to change their shoes for long rubber boots, for which a small sum was paid. A woman was there to supervise the change; I had never encountered this specialized profession before! The rain had now turned to a drizzle. Coming through the opening, we found ourselves walking on fine loose sand, and I soon realized the necessity of our long rubber boots. There was nothing to see on all sides but an enormous stretch of sand—an unbelievably colossal dune which is said to extend for sixteen kilometers from east to west and two kilometers from north to south. If all the sand dunes I saw at Provincetown were put together, they would not be able to match this grand sand dune

An unbelievably colossal dune

of Tottori. Many people had climbed to the top; their bodies seemed to have diminished to the size of African ants. There were two old-fashioned horse-drawn wooden carts, each of which would carry about ten people. They were making short trips down to the beach and back. A printed notice described this sand dune as being the rarest of its kind in the whole world. I wondered if any geologist had an explanation for the unique formation of this single huge dune on this short strip of the coast at Tottori. Some unusual designs such as suribachi ("conical piles"), saren ("rattan blind"), and colorful patterns of fumon ("wind ripples") formed on the sand by the wind could be observed here and there. Apart from these, there were masses of footprints, one on top of another, all along the sand in front of the dune and some on the way to the top of it. I could not help admiring the Japanese love for something unusual and new. So many had come to see this enormous sand dune in spite of the rain. Even the woman who was merely hiring out the rubber boots for a few hours was thriving; she must have been standing by the opening day after day. The only strange object there was a camel tied to a post on the sand for anybody who cared to have a photograph taken with it. Many did and the man who owned the camel was also doing a good business. It was strange to see a camel on Japanese soil.

Afterward our bus took us to see the so-called Silent Lake, "Koyama Ike" in Japanese. It lies on the western side of the city and is about sixteen kilometers in circumference and three meters deep and has seven small islands. Where our bus stopped there was a modern sculpture of a nude girl posed on a big rock resembling the Mermaid in Copenhagen. The rain came down heavily again. Most of the surroundings were covered in mists and clouds and I could see very little except the nearest objects. Afterward I found a taxi to take me to Kakuto Beach, known as the Beach of the White Rabbit. This white rabbit is known from one of the popular Japanese folk stories. He had wanted to cross from Okinoshima to Cape Keta. In order to do so he had a contest with crocodiles to see which were the more numerous, the crocodiles of the sea or the hares of the land. He asked the crocodiles to line up to be counted. All the crocodiles then formed a long line, stretching from the island Oki to Cape Keta. Then the hare quickly ran over those horny bodies and reached his destination. Afterward he laughed at the crocodiles, saying that they were very foolish to form the line and let him achieve his purpose. It was said that the crocodiles then combined together to scratch off all the fur from the hare's body and caused him to suffer terribly. I heard this story while on Oki Island, but there have never been any crocodiles in Japan on sea or on land. So at Tottori this legend was told about a troop of sharks instead of crocodiles. Japanese eat sharks, or *same*, in a preparation of a kind of fish sausage called *kamaboko* with shark flesh in it. The Japanese also use same, *kujira* (whale), *ebi* (lobster), and various shellfish meats to make sashimi. But the Chinese regard dried shark fins as a delicacy for a special soup. The best dried shark fins which the Chinese use in cooking are generally imported from Japan.

When I returned to tell Mr. Kotani that I had not been able to see much round Silent Lake on account of the rain, he told me a legend about it. There used to be, he said, a rich man named Koyama Choja, who lived in that area hundreds of years ago. One day his peasants could not finish their rice planting for the day as he wanted. He felt very disappointed, so he lifted up his golden fan to pray to the setting sun, "Go back once more, please!" Indeed, his prayer was answered and the sun rose again till the rice planting was completely finished. But, to his astonishment all his rice fields had become this silent lake when he woke up next morning. That is why it was called Koyama Ike. It was an interesting legend. But I wonder why the sun after helping Koyama's peasants to finish the rice planting should have punished him by sinking his land into a lake.

Afterward we talked about the Tottori hot springs, which Mr. Kotani regarded as an important attraction. I told him the story I had heard about the origin of the Yoshioka Spa in Tottori. In the tenth century there was a rich landowner named Ashioka who had one daughter. Unfortunately this girl contracted a boil which was infectious and spread all over her body. No physician could do anything for her, so her parents offered prayers at the Shrine of Yakushi (Bhechadjaguru) on Mt. Shobu (Mt. Iris). Then both Mr. and Mrs. Ashioka had the same dream, that they should tell their daughter to take baths in the hot springs under the willow tree in their own compound to get rid of the boils. The young girl did so and was cured. Mr. Kotani laughed with approval.

But he did not know about two shellfish which have become deities at Oe-machi in the Tottori Prefecture. An Oe Shrine was erected there in honor of these two shellfish. It was said that in the early mythological days, the god of harvest and happiness, Okuninushi-no-Mikoto, was a kindhearted and upright man, who had an elder brother, Yasaogi, cruel and irritable by nature. A neighboring beauty named Yakami-Hime was Yasaogi's hope for marriage, but she chose his young brother Okuninushi instead. This angered Yasaogi terribly and he decided to do away with his young brother. One day he heated a huge rock red-hot and hid it in the long grass, then lied to his brother, telling him that there was a big brown boar in the grass and urged him to go and catch it quickly. The latter did so in haste and got his body badly burnt all over. Their mother was in despair for Okuninushi's life and went up to heaven to ask help from the god Kammusubi-no-Kami. The god immediately dispatched two female physicians, Umuki-Hime and Kisagai-Hime, to give Okuninushi treatment. Kisagai-Hime crumpled a shell into a fine powder while Umuki-Hime got some liquid from a shell to mix it into a paste and applied this mixture to the burn. The treatment was most successful and the two female physicians were given shrines for their great service in preserving Okuninushi from death. Umuki was a clam and Kisagai an ark shell. It interests me that shellfish are regarded as feminine in gender in heaven too!

Mr. Kotani remarked that there are so many legends in Japan that one would be unable to know them all. Unfortunately most of the young Japanese do not care to learn them and they will soon be forgotten. I said that this was the modern tendency everywhere; China had as many legends as Japan, but very few modern Chinese know them.

A rainy day in Tottori was compensated for by a sunny one in Kurashiki. After breakfast the young man at the desk of the Kurashiki Kokusai Hotel showed me a local map and explained in English that most of the things visitors came to see in this city were all near the hotel. I asked if I could see something interesting outside the city while the sun shone so brightly in the morning, for I could make the local rounds in the afternoon. So he suggested Washuzan Hill and directed me to take a bus there. The route was very picturesque and the soil of the country looked very fertile, for every field was filled with young shoots of rice and other crops. *Kurashiki* in kanji means "The Seat of Granaries" from the abundant harvests from the area during the Edo era. According to the local guide, in ancient times the present-day Kurashiki was covered by the broad expanse of the sea. It was the Achi-no-Omi family from ancient China that brought the area under cultivation and gave the name Achi

View from Washuzan Hill

MONKEYS OF BEPPU

NAGASAKI HARBOR

to the bay that developed there. Gradually, as the water receded and
more land was reclaimed, the village of Masu developed in the period of
Manju (1024–1027). Here cultivation went on apace and various types
of crops gave abundant harvests. I was interested in the unexpected connection of my home country with this city. Unfortunately the local guide
did not say when the land first emerged from the sea and when and how
the Chinese family Achi-no-Omi came to this part of Japan. By the
sound of the first syllables, *Achi,* the family could have come from south
China. It was a pity that this family did not leave any written record.
They were probably illiterate like many of the Cantonese Chinese who
left China to scatter themselves all round the islands of Southeast Asia
and North America, and nearly every corner of the globe. Simply
because they were not educated people they never had any political
designs to colonize the land on which they came to live and settle down.
They all hoped to go back home one day.

The bus made two short stops at two country towns but after about
two hours my destination was reached. Washuzan Hill is a promontory
jutting into the Inland Sea, rising to about 440 feet above sea level. Like
many others I started to walk steadily up to the high point of the hill
and was surprised at the perfect tranquillity of the bay and the number
of islands, big and small, far and near, lying on the deep blue sea. There
was such an ethereal sunny haze over all of them, as if they were not
built by, nor for, men. Every segment offered a good composition for a
picture.

A large group of happily chattering school girls and boys, led by their

Students wearing the same kind of bright yellow caps

teachers, walked down the slope and then climbed another promontory. I did not follow them at once, for I was interested in watching them, all wearing the same kind of bright yellow caps, moving along like a long golden Chinese dragon lantern show, wriggling upward. At the foot of the promontory was a stone monument with three big kanji words, "Chung-hsiu-feng" in Chinese pronunciation meaning "Peak of Auspicious Beauty," said to have been written by the noted Japanese journalist, Soho Tokutomi (1863–1957) after his visit to Washuzan Hill in October, 1931. He was the elder brother of the writer and historian Roka Tokutomi (1868–1927). The two kanji words "Chung-hsiu" could have been taken from a well-known line of a Chinese poem "Ts'ao wu chung ling hsiu," or "The creator bestows the auspicious beauty on the land." Soho Tokutomi must have known Chinese poetry well and the two words for this spot on Washuzan Hill were most appropriate. I reached the top and stood together with a few young students among several jutting rocks, gazing far and wide. A good many islands, the nearer ones darker while the farther ones were fainter, looked like a school of whales gliding gracefully and slowly over the sea surface. Nay, those islands were not like whales, for the colors of their bodies were changing from one moment to another. Some thin vapor was moving fast over the sea surface. There was a warmth in the air too, for Kurashiki lies in the south and has a milder climate than Tottori. Mr. Taneo Kotani had told me that in the Stone Age men lived around Washuzan Hill, and three ancient tombs were found between the summit of the hill and the monument of "Chung-hsiu-feng." I tried to locate the tombs from the top but there was no trace of them.

Suddenly another loud cheerful noise was blown up from below and I saw a long chain of boys and girls, about five to seven years of age, led by their teachers, climbing up step by step and giggling all the way. We had to make room for them. I could not help thinking that Japan has devised a good way to teach youngsters geography and history without relying on textbooks. But these trips for the youngsters all over the whole country take a great deal of planning and organizing, as well as controlling and guiding.

I later managed to get myself near the shore and to have a look at the famous Elephant Rock by the side of Mukuchi Island. From the distance this enormous piece of white rock is shaped like an elephant about to drink water from the sea. An interesting creation of nature!

Later that afternoon I strolled round the right side of the hotel to the Ohara Art Museum. I was startled to find the building in the style of a Greek temple in the heart of Japan. There were about one hundred exhibits altogether and I took my time looking at them one by one, without being pushed and rushed. I was surprised to find El Greco's *The Annun-*

Ohara Art Museum

ciation here, for I thought that by the end of the nineteenth century no works of the great European masters could have left Europe or America for other lands. The bulk of the collection was composed of paintings by the impressionists and postimpressionists—Pissarro, Monet, Sisley, Degas, Cezanne, Renoir, Toulouse-Lautrec, van Gogh, Gauguin, Vuillard, Matisse, Picasso, Braque, Derain, Utrillo, Rouault, Chagall, Rodin, and so on. All these paintings demonstrate the taste of the collector, Magosaburo Ohara (1880–1943), a wealthy Kurashiki businessman, who must have gone to Paris just at the time when the impressionists' and postimpressionists' works were being feverishly collected. It was not only necessary to have money in the race with the Europeans and Americans, it required great courage and good taste as well. It was through the advice of a good artist-friend of his own country that Magosaburo Ohara made two trips to Paris for his collection. In celebrating the thirtieth anniversary in 1961, an addition was built to house modern Japanese paintings as well as many antiques from Egypt, Persia, and Turkey.

Afterward I went to look at the pottery, woodenware, textiles, and particularly the bambooware in the Kurashiki Folkcraft Museum and also in the Kurashiki Archeological Museum, the archeological relics, particularly human bones, discovered mainly in the Kibi Plateau. In the same place there were a number of archeological objects from ancient China, two of which interested me particularly. One was a pair of Han doors, bas-reliefs of five birds on one—three standing and two flying—and on the other a hare. The most unusual piece was a pottery figurine of a foreign face in a three-color glaze, dated as Northern Wei of the third century A.D. I said "unusual" because I had not seen anything like it before. So I made an inquiry and got an answer from Mr. Tadahiko Makabe, vice-director of the Kurashiki Archeological Museum, who said, "Its size is sixty centimeters in height and its material is colored pottery, not wood. I regret that I cannot tell you when and where it was discovered in China. Besides, color-glazed pottery begins in later Han in China." My doubt over the piece was due to its color, which was not even or glossy like color-glazed pottery. So I sent a postcard of it to find out the opinion of my good friend, Dr. Laurence Sickman, director of Nelson Art Gallery and Atkins Museum of Fine Arts in Kansas City, for he is an expert on Chinese art. The following was his reply:

> Regarding the postal card of the tomb figure you sent me, I must assume the colors are somewhat off, as both the shades of yellow and green are not quite right. In any case there can be no question of it being Northern Wei as they claim, but rather a figure from the full T'ang period, say first half of the eighth century when three-colored glaze would be in perfect order.
>
> Within my knowledge there are no glazed tomb figurines of the Northern Wei period, the earliest possible date for such would be Northern Ch'i or Sui.

Ancient China's figurine

The cloud over my head about this particular piece was then dispersed. It was interesting for me to encounter this piece in Kurashiki, not in China nor in any other big museum in Europe or America.

The Ohara Art Museum and the two museums are situated very close to one another. What amazed me was that not a single porter or guard was to be seen in the rooms of the three collections, unlike anywhere else I have been. The directors of Kurashiki museums show great trust in their visitors. In front of these three museums runs the Kurashiki River with willow trees swaying gently on both stone banks with two small stone bridges across it. There are a number of old houses, well kept and apparently in a typical style of the city with black-and-white checkered walls, somewhat like a corner of Soochow or Hangchow which I knew in the 1920s and '30s. A very quaint city is Kurashiki but at the same time it has become one of the newly risen industrial cities of Japan. One of its principal products is cotton yarn and the Oharas' is one of the richest Kurashiki spinning mills. Magosaburo Ohara not only brought the modern rayon industry to Kurashiki, but also introduced Kurashiki to the world's eyes through his collection of Western art. He must have influenced the Japanese modern art movement greatly. This is something else that Japan has done better than China. China has her wealthy industrialists but none of them has picked up new and modern ideas with the intention of improvement and progress. Besides, wealthy Chinese industrialists seldom possess any aesthetic sense for the great art that China produced in the past, let alone a taste for Western art. It has always made me feel sad after a good round of an art gallery or museum in Europe, America, or Japan, big or small, where I could see so many good Chinese art objects among all the other native masterpieces, to think that not a single, small piece of European, American, or Japanese art is to be found anywhere in China. There may be excuses for us to make, simply because no great Western art objects are available for China to collect at the present age, or they are usually much too expensive to buy. However, I have known many of my fellow countrymen to feel uncomfortable when other people show no interest or appreciation for Chinese art, or even things Chinese, but none of them seem to ask themselves if they are able to appreciate things not Chinese. I still cannot understand why we Chinese must be so obstinately Chinese. This is definitely not included in Confucius's teachings!

High school students picnicking on the top of a hill

XXIV

Korakuen Garden of Okayama and the White Egret Castle

MY REASON for coming from Kurashiki to spend a day in Okayama was to complete my visits to the three famous Japanese gardens—this one called Korakuen, in the old Bizen city. A bus took me almost to the entrance of the garden. It was a fine day of May. Many people were already on the footpaths and a few young women wore brightly colored kimonos. A pine grove grew by the southern tip of the big pond called Sowa-no-Ike, which has three little islets in it, one of which stands by itself and the other two are joined by a small wooden bridge. Standing where I was by the pine grove, I could see Okayama Castle beyond. On the northern tip of the pond stood two small arborlike structures forming a pleasant scene with their reflections in the clear water. Following others, I strolled round and moving left I soon reached the spots marked tea plantation on the left and rice field on the right. Later I came to

A small old cypress tree

another pond called Ayam, or Iris, Pond and found a good many irises in bloom. In a wooden cage with iron bars was a Manchurian red-crested crane, a gift to the city in 1955 from Kuo Mo-jo of China, who was said to have studied in Okayama forty years before.

Presently I was in a cherry grove, but there were not many blossoms left. A few petals were still drifting in the air. The smiling red azaleas displayed their brilliance in the bright sun. I noticed a small old cypress tree whose trunk was twisted and whose branches were bent over the grass in most artistic shapes, and I soon made a rough sketch. There was yet another little pond called Kako-no-Ike, through which a small stream was flowing steadily. All three of the artificial ponds have fresh, lively water from the constantly flowing stream which joins them all. Standing nearby was a teahouse, and I followed others in for a look.

The Korakuen Garden was built in 1786 by Lord Ikeda, the son-in-law of the first powerful Tokugawa shogun, Iyeyasu. In those feudal days, it is said, the samurai and their ladies used to come here for tea or for poetry parties, and they would throw their poems into the stream to let them float down to the intended readers.

I then entered Okayama Castle for a look. From its highest tower I could see many people rowing on the river Ashai. Unlike most European castles, Japanese castles do not seem to have provision for defense. I also wondered why the Chinese had never built such castles for defense, though the city walls became dependable in their stead.

The next day I arrived in Himeji. The sun was shining brightly and the air was balmy. I thought of spending a whole day in this city, so I

Enkyoji on Mt. Shosha

asked the person at the desk of the hotel what I could see nearby in the suburb. A trip up Mt. Shosha was suggested, for there is an ancient Buddhist temple, Enkyoji, on the summit. It was founded in A.D. 988 by Priest Shoku (910–1007) and is known as one of the thirty-three most holy temples of the Kansai District. It is seven and a half miles away from the Himeji station and I took a taxi to the ropeway. Nobody was there to give me directions so I went up to the observation roof for a look around. To my surprise I saw on my right a most un-Japanese construction of the Syaka's relic of the Nagoyama Cemetery standing conspicuously in the distance on the top of a vast promontory in the middle of an open flat ground with the city houses far, far away behind it. It was a big Indian stupa construction with four small ones on its four sides and it is said to be the gift of the late Indian premier Mr. Nehru. It did not seem to fit in the Japanese landscape and struck me as unusual. I then turned my eyes to the left and lo! a well-known Chinese literary term "yun hai," or Cloud-sea, stretched far away with mountain ranges one after another in the clouds. Just then a young girl in uniform called me to board the ropeway carriage which had just come down. At the end of the ropeway, a good footpath was cut out along the mountain slope and all walked in the same direction. Presently we approached the Nio-mon gate built in plain wood. The look of this gate indicated its antiquity. Farther along the footpath, a big two-story building came in sight. A number of pink cherry trees in full bloom led my way up there. The building was neither painted nor lacquered, so the plain wood texture shone in the sun like yellow gold. The upper story of the main hall of the temple was burned out by fire in 1921 and rebuilt in 1933, the lower part was supported on poles sunk into the hillside. The view from the balcony was the most imposing imaginable. What a peaceful, dreamlike place! Then I went down to see the three famous halls, which are Daikodo Hall, Jikodo Hall, and Jokyodo Hall. All looked quite new although built hundreds of years ago. The great Lecture Hall, rebuilt in 1322, has very graceful roofs and is exquisite in structure as a whole and is preserved as an Important Cultural Property. I entered the Meditation Hall, rebuilt in 1348, and looked at the few Buddhist statues— Sakyamuni, Manjusri, Samantabhadra, and so on—all Important Cultural Properties. In the back corridor were a series of paintings on silk hanging in glass cases. This series looked to have been painted by later Japanese artists after the style of the five hundred arhat paintings by the Sung masters, Li T'ing-kuei and Chou Chi-ch'ang, in the Daitokuji at Kyoto, but the colors were too bright and fresh, and the brush strokes rather weak at places. Though I had been walking about the place for a good while, I met no priest. Yet the buildings were kept spotless. The stillness of the air was enhanced by the aged but healthy tall trees which encircled the antique hues of the temple buildings, particularly the inner temples—Kaisando, Gohodo, Gohodo-Haiden, Kongodo, the Bell Tower, and Juryo-In. This most unexpected ancient world is very much like it was a thousand years ago. On my way back to the hotel my mind was constantly revisualizing what I saw up on Mt. Shosha. Two little poems took shape at the same time:

Climbing up by the ropeway to Mt. Shosha

Myriads of ravines and hills inhabit the sea of clouds
I sped up Mt. Shosha into a new clear sky.
Here and there on the mountain path came the cool breeze,
At leisure I walked silently by the tall pines.

Visiting Enkyoji Monastery

On the summit of Mt. Shosha is the Enkyoji Monastery,
Those thousand-year-old trees seem to touch the sky.
Had there not been a ropeway to take me half way,
How could I have visited this ancient monastery?

Next morning I saw Himeji Castle from the window of the Himeji Shin-Osaka Hotel. Directly after breakfast I took myself to the main gate, Hishi-no-Mon, and found the grounds of the castle were enclosed by a low wall, of which Professor Alexander Soper says: "a wall with corner pavilions suggests comparisons with the city fortifications of China; they are much lower but are built more substantially in their lower courses, of stone instead of brick." No other Japanese castles that I have seen have this kind of lower wall. Within the enclosing walls I learned that there were thirty-eight buildings, twenty-one gates, and a number of footpaths winding through tall trees of all kinds. I followed other visitors up to the top floor of the castle, called Tenshoku. This castle was originally built by Akamatsu Sadanori in the fourteenth century, by order of Prince Morinaga Shinno. Some hundreds of years afterward Lord Ikeda was appointed by his father-in-law Tokugawa Iyeyasu to be stationed in Himeji and he built the citadel, including the five-story main tower on Himeyama Hill. The construction took nine years to finish and a total of fifty thousand people worked on it. The next feudal lord, Tadamasa Honda, added a number of castle gates and turrets to this wonderful construction. One of the most famous and interesting additional structures is what is called Nishinomaru Kesho-Yagura, or the western keep cosmetic turret, which was the beautiful living quarters intended for his son's wife, Senhime, granddaughter of Tokugawa Iyeyasu, who was admired as the fairest lady in the Tokugawa period. There were many relics of the past like armor, warrior swords, helmets, and many other objects displayed in various glass cases. When I reached the castle grounds again, a short verse came into my head:

How many changes of the human affairs during the past thousand years;
Yet the cherry blossoms still smile in the fine springtime.
While I move around to read the history in Tenshukaku,
The same clouds and sky are above the Castle of White Egret!

The castle is called Rojo, or Hakurojo (Egret Castle), from its white-plastered walls.

On the ground floor of the main structure there is a good-sized model of the whole castle with its many buildings and gates clearly indicated. But many other buildings were not opened to the public. I then left the crowds and strolled round the castle grounds aimlessly. I saw an old well with a sign and story in English describing the legend of the Well of Okiku—a young maid who was wronged and who drowned herself here.

I also heard a story about Lord Sakai of Himeji. He and his spaniel had been fast friends for some time and they would go everywhere together. In 1781 when Lord Sakai was called upon to act as the shogunal messenger from Edo to the capital, Kyoto, he thought he could not very well take his spaniel with him on this important mission, so he

An elderly man making a
dragon out of sugar taffy

decided to leave it at his Edo residence. But the dog could not see the
reason why he had to be left at home, so he trotted along with great
determination, no matter how harshly Lord Sakai ordered him back.
After going a good way Lord Sakai picked up the dog and thought of
sending it home from Shinagawa, but it was useless; the dog trotted all
the way to Kyoto. Afterward the emperor Kokaku heard of the dog's
fidelity and bestowed on it the fifth court rank. It is a nice story. I
thought there might be a memorial stone to this official dog in the castle
grounds but I could not find one.

To my surprise I found an inner moat within the castle walls, unlike
all the external moats round other castles. Two white swans were gliding
gently by and added a new color to the surrounding scene. On my way
out of the Hishi-no-Mon I saw a group of young boys and girls standing
around an elderly man, who had a small stall close by the castle wall
and who was fashioning on a bamboo stick a miniature green dragon out
of sugar taffy, which he was using like modeling clay. He had already
made a white crane and a Kabuki actor. The small green dragon he was
making to order for a young boy. This reminded me of my boyhood
days in my home town, where these peddlers used to come around. I
have never seen anything like this in Europe or America. This type of
peddler's way of living could not fit in the modern machine age.

Outside the castle grounds I came to a special corner with a view of
the whole castle in the distance and a big rhododendron bush in the foreground; in between stood a carved stone, thirteen-story, square-shaped
pagoda. I thought this would be a good composition for a painting.

On leaving Himeji I suddenly remembered that I should have made
an effort to taste the beef in this city because Kobe beef has become so

Outside the Himeji Castle grounds

famous since the Second World War. In New York there is a restaurant specializing in Kobe beefsteak, said to be directly flown over from Kobe. But Dr. J. J. Space, a Belgian Catholic priest and editor of a Catholic publication in Japan for many years, told me a common saying in Himeji, "Tajima no ushi, Kobe no niku," which means that Kobe beef is from Tajima cows! Apparently Tajima people of Himeji felt it unjust that Kobe should have become so famous for the beef not produced there. Therefore I should have tried the beef in Himeji, but I did not. A great pity!

XXV

Takarazuka Girls

I WENT TO Kobe by train from Himeji, on my way to Takarazuka. All along the journey I saw many village houses which had long strips of paper or cloth in the shape of fish, particularly carp in red or black on white backgrounds, and blowing in the wind from the tops of poles. They indicate a typical Boys Festival Day, called Tango-no-Sekku, which takes place on the fifth day of May. According to the Chinese lunar calendar, the fifth day of the fifth month would be the Chinese Dragon Boat Race Festival—a day established by the king of Ch'u State in the fourth century B.C. to commemorate the first known Chinese poet Chu Yüan, who committed suicide by drowning himself in the river Mi-lo. As the poet was regarded as the greatest patriot in the kingdom, the king ordered all the boats to rush out to find him, dead or alive, but the search was in vain. So the king decreed that the day on which the poet drowned should be kept always as a memorial day for him. All the boats hastening along the river toward the same spot appropriately suggested a boat race for the festival and the boats were all made in the form of dragons. This Dragon Boat Race Festival has been carried on in all cities in China for the past two thousand years or more, and even in Annam and Burma in early days, though not many people are aware of its origin. I don't know if any other country on earth has ever commemorated the death of its poets for so long a time.

The Japanese Boys Festival bears traces of the feudal days of Japan, for it implies the encouragement of young boys to be manly, brave, and ambitious. The symbol of the carp has a Chinese origin, for the carp has been an important object in Chinese eyes since time immemorial. The whole world knows of Confucius but very few know that he had a son named Carp. It is said that when Confucius's wife was about to give birth to this son, a friend brought in a pair of carp as a present. So Confucius named his boy Carp, which became associated with the idea of blessing, luck, and happy occasion. The earliest Chinese civilization started along the northern part of the valley of the Yellow River—one of the two great rivers of China—and the best fish produced in the Yellow River is the carp, a most edible and useful food. Confucius lived near the mouth of the river, so the present he received from his friend naturally was carp. This carp is considered the best of its kind and the Chinese living in central China along the Yangtze River valley all sought carp from the Yellow River for their New Year Festival preparations. I remember as a boy of eight or nine seeing a few big Yellow River carp bought which weighed nearly a hundred pounds each. There are many good stories about carp being so strong and brave as to be able to jump the river rapids like salmon. One story tells of a big carp that leaped over a voluminous rapid and turned into a dragon. This story indicates advancement from a mere fish into the most highly revered dragon, and the Chinese use this as a symbol for anyone who passes the most difficult civil service examination and goes on to hold a high office; he is like the carp that jumped over the rapid and became a dragon. I doubt if the English word *dragon* is the exact equivalent to the Chinese *lung*. Unlike the dragon in the West that had to be killed by St. George, the Chinese dragon is a friendly and beneficent creature symbolizing the personality of the Chinese emperor.

The Japanese do not think of the dragon in the Chinese manner, for it has never been used as a majestic emblem for the imperial household designs or decorations, but they take the carp as an emblem for the great future to be hoped for a young boy, and that is why carp made of paper or cloth fly from the flag poles on the Boys Day Festival. I was told that on this day a ceremony takes place in which the boys of each family bow reverently before the family heirlooms of their warrior ancestors—their armor, their helmets, their swords, and many other things which would be displayed in the best room of the house. If a family did not possess these trophies, they would have bought some dolls in the costumes of former feudal generals, samurai, and so on. This festival is also called Shobu-no-Sekku in Japanese, or Iris Festival, for the long, narrow leaf of the iris is somewhat like a sword blade, and on this day the boys have a hot bath with iris leaves boiled in the water to instill in them a samurai or warrior spirit.

In 1968, a good friend of mine, Mrs. Nobuko Morris, gave the boys of Tokyo a most unusual celebration for their Boys Day Festival. She is the most talented, capable young lady of Japanese birth that I have ever known. Having been a representative of Toho International, Inc. in New York, she organized a group of thirty-seven actors, actresses, technicians, a director, a choreographer, a lighting designer from London, with fifteen New York children from seven to thirteen together with their mothers, to perform the famous musical play *Oliver* on a Tokyo stage. The show went on for eleven weeks with great success, costing altogether about a million dollars. I could not help but admire Nobuko's great ability in putting on that production. I have already mentioned that the Japanese are good organizers and Nobuko is an outstanding example.

When I told Nobuko that I would be going to see a Takarazuka show, she told me it was entirely one man's genius that created this great international center of entertainment in the previously unnoticed old small town of Takarazuka, which has now become world famous. Dr. Ichizo Kobayashi, a founder of the Hankyu Railway, conceived the idea of popularizing the Takarazuka Spa when his railway line would link it to Osaka and Kobe. After making Takarazuka easily accessible by rail, a new Takarazuka Spa was to be built and completed by the spring of 1911. In order to attract people to the new spa, an all-girl singing and dancing troupe was organized, starting with only sixteen girls, in 1913. Dr. Kobayashi actually wrote one of the earliest revues using the pen name Hata Ikeda. He was really a genius, not only with a modern technological mind but also with an interest in art, music, drama, and literature, all of which he practiced himself. He also had a driving energy to push through all his aims regardless of difficulties. He established a school to train the girls and also sent them to study in France, England, Spain, and America under noted masters. During the past fifty years with continued effort for improvement the Takarazuka Opera Company has grown from the original sixteen girls to more than four hundred, with a staff of writers, composers, choreographers, and designers in residence. The Takarazuka troupe has made several trips abroad, touring Italy, Germany, Poland, and America. I asked Nobuko why all girls? She smiled and said, "Girls can do everything just as well as any man. In the old Japan, Kabuki plays used to have an actor impersonating a woman and they still stick to that rule. In the same way the Takarazuka Company has actresses impersonating men and they still stick to the rule as they started."

With Nobuko's words in mind, I made a special arrangement to stop at Takarazuka on the way from Kobe to Osaka. From Kobe station I caught a train to Sannomiya and then to Nishinomiya, where I changed to a local train for Takarazuka. Nearly everyone on this train was bound for the same destination. After leaving the station we walked down the main street of the city. In the center of this road was piled a long mound of earth and it was lined with many pink cherry trees in full bloom. A throng followed us and the theater soon became much too full, but everyone had his ticket booked long in advance. I was told that the theater could seat four thousand, but I noticed very few European or American faces. Masses of small boughs ornamented with cherry blossoms made of pink paper decorated every corner of the building and stage.

There was a moment of complete silence when the curtains started to

Takarazuka's *Otemoyan*

be slowly drawn. The first show was a musical comedy, *Otemoyan*, specially written for the year. The players dressed in all types of Japanese costumes—some samurai, some city dwellers, some countryfolk, and some farmers—though all men were impersonated by girls. The story related to the Japan of 1867 when the prestige of the Tokugawa shogunate began to decline. Many bands of samurai engaged in evil activities to overthrow those in power while foreign fleets moved in to force Japan to end her isolation policy by opening her door to trade. The daughter of a Kumamoto farmer, Otemoyan, had to sell vegetables round the neighboring villages to get money to feed her eleven brothers and sisters. One day she encountered an evil-intentioned samurai and just at a critical moment a young man named Shintaro came to her rescue. Shintaro, a good-looking youth, the son of a wealthy local merchant, had studied Western medicine at Nagasaki, was influenced by Western ideas, and had become involved in the samurai movement to pull down the shogunate. Somehow, he had upset a plot made by a band of samurai. It was now Otemoyan's turn to rescue Shintaro by hiding him in her house for the night. So they were secretly united by the bond of love and promised each other to dance on the night of the Sentoro Festival, a traditional occasion for rendezvous among lovers. They did dance that night, but

Otemoyan soon realized that Shintaro already had a fiancée named Oyu and that she could not marry him, for she was a mere farmer's daughter. Just at that time the antishogunate movement became very active and many groups of samurai were hurrying to Kyoto. Shintaro was among the samurai on the move. Otemoyan saw him in the crowd and called out "Shintaro-san" many times, but her voice could not reach his ears for the volcanic explosion of Mt. Aso drowned every other sound at that moment. Shintaro never came back to her. It was a sad story with a typically Japanese background, but the many dances and songs with the Western orchestra playing throughout dispersed any sad feeling. A completely different setting and diversion from the traditional No and Kabuki plays—a twentieth-century Japanese work.

The second show, called *The World is One*, was a grand revue. The meaning of the show was obvious from the title, illustrating one nation after another—China, India, Switzerland, England, France, Spain, Africa, America—and then the finale. The costumes for each act were lavish and gorgeous, except those for China and Africa. The costume designer recognized the change of time and purposely did not follow the Russian ballet designer, Leon Bakst, who, to annoy modern Chinese, always made the Chinese wear long fingernails and whiskers so long that they could be wrapped up on the top of the head. The African dress could hardly leave part of the wearer's body naked. The leading player, Shibuki Maho, acted exactly like a man, a tenor with a very loud voice. Her hair was either dyed a brilliant brunette or she was wearing a wig, and her large eyes, which seemed unusual for a Japanese girl, commanded the audience's attention. Many of the girls in the part of the scene for Switzerland, England, France, Spain, and America wore blonde or brunette wigs, dancing and singing in the Western manner with the Western orchestra playing Western music. While sitting in the audience, I felt I was back in Europe or America.

I don't know if the creation of the Takarazuka troupe was a sort of retaliation or purposely a counterpart to the all-male Kabuki. But both have their troubles. A well-experienced Kabuki actor, grown old through years of acting, could not help the illusion of a play with his stage impersonation of a young female, and a well-experienced Takarazuka girl, grown up through a few years of acting, could give the producer a great headache if she wanted to leave the company to marry.

XXVI

The Enormous Rocks of Osaka

BEFORE I WENT to see Japan I read a few English translations of
modern Japanese novels, one of which was *Thirst for Love* by Yukio
Mishima, translated by Alfred H. Marks. In the first pages I found the
following passage:

> For Etsuko—born and brought up in Tokyo—Osaka held inexplic-
> able terrors. City of merchant princes, hoboes, industrialists, stock-
> brokers, whores, opium pushers, white-collar workers, punks, bankers,
> provincial officials, aldermen, Gidayu reciters, kept women, penny-
> pinching wives, newspaper reporters, music hall entertainers, bar
> girls, shoe shine boys—it was not really this that Etsuko feared.
> Might it have been nothing but life itself? Life—this limitless, com-
> plex sea, filled with assorted flotsam, brimming with capricious,
> violent, and yet eternal transparent blues and greens.

I thought Tokyo would be similar to New York, London, or Paris, which
are all big cities and anything could happen in any one of them. But this
lady, Etsuko, born and brought up in Tokyo, even dreaded to be in
Osaka; then what sort of a city could Osaka be? So I did not mind if I
missed seeing Osaka on my trip.

Curiously enough, despite what I felt about it beforehand, I paid
Osaka three visits on my four trips to Japan. The night I arrived at
Osaka from Takarazuka for the first time it was raining and the wet
streets with streetcars still running in the center reminded me much of
what I remember of Shanghai in the 1920s. I came to Osaka not to see
those people that Etsuko dreaded, but the historic past of the city. The
next morning turned out to be very fine. I walked from the hotel to
Temmangu Shrine, which I entered for a look and realized that it was
dedicated to Sugawara-no-Michizane, god of literature and calligraphy. I
then proceeded to go over the Temmabashi, a stone bridge, to the
ground around Osaka Castle. Past the park gateway a wide waterway
came into sight, which could be the outer moat of the castle. Inside the
entrance of the main gate to the castle, two large cherry trees were in
full bloom with pink blossoms. An enormous rock as the foundation for
a mound directly facing the entrance was most conspicuous. It is said that

The enormous rock of Osaka Castle

when Toyotomi Hideyoshi started to build this castle in 1586 he wanted it to be built with granite stones, larger and different from any other castle already in existence in Japan. So he made requests for material to all his generals, who vied with one another to supply the largest rocks possible. One of the two immense stones inside the entrance was called Higo-ishi. It was furnished by General Kiyomasa Kato (1562–1611) from Shodo Island, and measured 5.9 meters in height, 14.5 meters in length, and 82 square meters in area. How did General Kato manage to move it from Shodo Island to Osaka some four hundred years ago? The Italian Jesuit missionary Frois, in his report to the Vatican in 1586, wrote:

> Sixty thousand laborers are working. They are now digging the moat around the castle. I do not know from where all the rocks are coming, for there are no huge rocks in the immediate vicinity of Osaka. Yet, from the Osaka Church, which is my present residence, I can see the river Yodo filled every day with hundreds and thousands of vessels full of rocks.

Evidently only a most powerful person like Hideyoshi could command so many laborers to work and to transport all the rocks to build his castle. On the other hand, the above report shows that the Jesuit missionaries had little contact with the authorities at the time, for Frois could not even make an inquiry about where the rocks came from.

I read an article entitled "Art and Strategy and Its Master, The Monkey, Hideyoshi and the Momoyama period" in the magazine *The*

East, published in Tokyo, and was surprised to find the writer of this article calling the most important figure in Japanese history The Monkey. It could be because Toyotomi Hideyoshi was born in a lowly foot soldier's family and that he was small, with a thin face containing a pair of sunken eyes, but very quick in movement: so he was nicknamed Kozaru since boyhood. He did not mind being called this and in fact most of his intimate friends and his superiors called him so affectionately. Though from a very low origin, he was ambitious and at fifteen he left home for the east in search of a powerful master to serve. Three years later he returned to serve Oda Nobunaga, the lord of Owari of his own province. Gradually he rose higher and higher, for he was an excellent strategist. By 1582 he and Tokugawa Iyeyasu had become the two most powerful men in Japan. Through clever political intrigues Hideyoshi was eventually in 1585 officially appointed *Kwampaku*, a position equal to prime minister, and Tokugawa Iyeyasu became the vice premier. He became the unifier of feudal Japan and built the castle for security. With the introduction of firearms, Hideyoshi took no chances; he did not want the crumbly plaster for his castle, so he used immense granite blocks. The writer of the article continued to describe Hideyoshi:

> To improve his manners and broaden his sense of culture, Hideyoshi began in 1575 to study No, poetry, and chanoyu. He developed a great love for No dances and progressed to the point where he was able to perform several dances himself in 1593.
>
> When at the pinnacle of his power, to prove to himself and others that he had overcome his peasant coarseness and acquired culture,

Toyotomi Hideyoshi

Hideyoshi held a series of *chakai* ("tea ceremonies") to which only daimio ("feudal lords"), wealthy merchants, and other nobles were invited. His most famous chakai were held at Daitokuji Temple in 1585 and at Kitano Shrine in 1587. At his tea receptions he sometimes served the tea himself. For these receptions, Hideyoshi built gorgeous tearooms gilded with gold—quite contrary to the teachings of Sen-no-Rikyu on chanoyu. Sen-no-Rikyu believed that the smaller and the poorer the room was in which the tea was served, the more fully the true spirit of chanoyu was attained. Hideyoshi believed that the more gorgeous the setting in which he served the tea, the more effectively chanoyu expressed his person and power. He also took great pride in displaying on these occasions his unique collection of precious tea bowls and utensils.

At the age of sixty-two, The Monkey died of tuberculosis. This is his swan song:

> How fleet has been my life.
> I was but a dewdrop that fell in early morn,
> Only to be dried up all too soon by the sun.
> All the glories of Naniwa [Osaka]
> Turned out to be but a dream.

This writer had great skill in bringing out the true character of Hideyoshi. He was of humble origin, blessed with cleverness and even craftiness, but I think it was an innate greatness in him that brought him to so high a place in Japanese history. Unfortunately he was not clever enough to foresee trouble from the second most powerful man in Japan, who besieged Osaka Castle after Hideyoshi's death and killed his son and wife in 1615. In 1868 most of the superstructure of the castle was destroyed when it was set on fire by the Tokugawa troops before they made their retreat on the approach of the Meiji army. The present castle is a concrete replica rebuilt in 1931.

Before I went up to the castle itself I took a walk round the grounds for a while and I was wondering how the cult of chanoyu in Japan would have developed if Hideyoshi had not taken a great personal interest in it. Later on, chanoyu associated itself with the spread of Zen Buddhism in Japan, though I do not know how these two came together. Tea is universally known as a beverage that originated in China some time in the first century B.C., if not earlier. In old Chinese books there is mention that Yang Hsiung (35 B.C.–A.D. 18) used tea as a drink. By the eighth century A.D. a Chinese scholar, Lu Yü (A.D. 740–804) wrote *Cha Ching,* or *The Tea Classic,* and many beautiful Chinese porcelain bowls and cups were manufactured for drinking tea. The Sung poet Su Tung-p'o mentioned that people in his province, Szechwan, drank tea with salt, the Mongolians with mare's milk, and the Tibetans with fried rice flour. Of course, the English drink tea with milk and sugar. Unlike the Japanese with their chanoyu, the English have a definite time for tea and love to give tea parties.

I then paid the admission fee to go up to the castle. On the first floor there were models of the castle and relics of armor used in the many campaigns before the Tokugawa period. I was interested to see the portraits of four famous Osakan mathematicians; the most well-known one was Murai Kyurin (1755–1817), whose teacher was Saka Nasanobu (about 1730). The other three were Takeda Shingen (?–1846), mathematician born in Osaka, Asada Goryu (1734–1799), an astronomer, and Hazama Shigetomi (1755–1816), an astronomer and a successful merchant in Osaka. It is interesting to note that the Japanese honored their mathematicians since the early eighteenth century. This kind of high respect has been followed on to the present day. Every two or three years the emperor of Japan would award a culture medal to their distinguished scientists, inventors, writers, poets, and novelists. Many of her Nobel Prize winners have received these culture medals.

On the third floor were a series of pictures depicting the story of Hideyoshi's life first as a young boy, then as a samurai, and finally as prime minister, with one picture to show the enormous rock on a cart being dragged along the road to the castle grounds by many laborers. Another picture showed how Hideyoshi received Chinese envoys who had to prostrate themselves in front of him.

I was also interested in seeing the special exhibition—The Beauty of Momoyama Period—the painted life of common people, consisting of twenty-five large screen paintings. The decorative value in Japanese art was most evident in each exhibit. A six-fold screen, owned by Koenji Temple of Kyoto, detained me longer than the rest. I have never seen Japanese folding fans painted and symmetrically arranged.

On the top floor I found I could read quite a number of kanji words in the description of the history of Japan in Hideyoshi's days, for they were even composed in the Chinese manner. From the top windows a magnificent panoramic view came in sight when I moved round the four sides. It quite tantalized me with the brilliant sun careening through so beautiful a sky and white, fleecy clouds driven vigorously along by a strong breeze—now veiling and now exposing the dazzling luminary above and the green patches of trees and white clusters of cherries and the distant hills far down below. I wonder if Hideyoshi had climbed to the top of his castle from time to time, saying that this was what he expected Osaka to be! Indeed, Hideyoshi was a great soldier-hero in his time and will remain so to future generations. After I came down, I had another walk round the castle grounds for a good look at the blossoming cherries and also the fresh pines. I then composed the following little poem on my way out of the castle after another look at the enormous rock flooring:

The enormous rock still shines itself in the set-
ting sun,
The famous castle, Osaka, had her ancient glory.
Where is the mighty Hideyoshi now?
The green pines have never grown old and the
cherries renew their blossoms again.

巨石依然映彩霞
名城大阪舊豪華
聖云秀吉今何在
不老蒼松櫻又花

I later spent an hour going round the exhibits in the Osaka City
Museum, which is situated within the castle grounds. One exhibit interested me and alarmed me at the same time. It was a written edict of the
Chinese emperor Wan Li of Ming Dynasty in 1595 enfiefing Toyotomi
Hideyoshi to be the king of Japan. It indicates how haughty the Chinese
could be with her neighbors. At the same time it exposes the unpardon-
able ignorance of the Chinese ministers of those days, who knew nothing
about Japan and did not even try to find out before they wrote the edict
for the emperor. It is a hidden fact that the Chinese have not shown any
interest in trying to know others.

A year later, my visit to Osaka was from Koyasan on a warm August
day. After having spent three days up on Koyasan I caught the bus outside Rengejoin for the train to Osaka. The late morning air was quite
fresh and clear high up on the mountain. I could see everything from the
train window while descending the hill, unlike my journey up in the
dark. The way down was most picturesque, one superb panorama succeeding another with massive growth of tall trees covering all the hills
and ravines. I still could not understand how the great Kōbō Daishi
managed to climb up Koyasan on foot in the days of no railroad cable
cars. Some shafts of the sun's rays managed to penetrate through the
trees to shine on the lower trees with a mysteriously soft look—never
more beautiful and pleasant!

A friend of mine, Mr. Fu-kang Chu, who represented an American
firm and was supervising the construction of a ship in Namura Shipyard,
came to meet me at Namba station with his car. He suggested showing
me the building of the ship in his charge. The idea sounded a little
strange to me, for I am no student of mechanical engineering. However,
I did not want to reject his good intention and went with him. On our
way Chu told the driver to show me how big Osaka was and the car
went to the historical center, the entertainment center, the shopping

center, and lastly the industrial center. Indeed, Osaka is a big city and
the greatest industrial and commercial city of Japan. Chu told me that
Osaka used to be called the Venice of the Orient with her numerous
canals and riverlets and more than a thousand bridges. But all the canals
and rivers of Osaka have long disappeared, for they had been filled in to
create more land for the city's expansion hundreds of years ago. This
was evidence of how man's will could alter the face of the earth.

When we reached Chu's office, his Japanese secretary greeted me with
tea and also a watermelon freshly brought from a famous melon-
growing area. Afterward Chu gave me a steel helmet to wear while he
was adjusting his own and said that this was a necessity in case my head
struck one of the iron or steel bars of the steel structure. At first we
climbed over one steel stair after another and met a number of workers
with blackened faces and hands. Then we were standing on the wide
steel deck of the half-built ship and watching an enormous steel crane
moving a vast sheet of thick metal from outside to drop it into the center
of the construction. All the things I saw there seemed to be a dream, for
I could never have imagined myself in such a steel environment. The
moving of such a wide sheet of steel, which looked so heavy, could
never have been achieved by the mere hands of man. Yet man's brain
had invented the scientific methods to accomplish the task. Men still had
to be there to work the enormous crane though. How glad Hideyoshi's
sixty thousand laborers would have been if they had had the enormous
crane to move the immense rocks to the castle grounds. Chu took me
around every part of the half-built ship, part after part, with explana-
tions all the way, though I could not follow the technical terms at all.
For a layman like me to witness a gigantic construction which could
carry thousands of people and an immense amount of cargo on the sea
is an extraordinary experience. This was the first time in my life that I
saw such an undertaking.

Later on, we climbed another steel stair to reach the upper deck,
facing Osaka Harbor. I could see that the spacious and very deep natural port could accommodate many ships, even large ocean liners. A
newly completed ship in the adjoining shipbuilding yard was about to
be launched. Many ships were lined up together on both sides of the
harbor. There were seven shipbuilding companies and Chu was working
for one of the three biggest in the area. It is just hard to believe that
Japan, with so little natural resources of her own, could have jumped up
to become a leading shipbuilding country, relying on raw materials from
abroad. I cannot help but admire the Japanese people who are always
trying to make the best use of their ability and talent.

On my way to the hotel my mind was full of what I had seen in the
shipyard and I tried to visualize the days when Kōbō Daishi travelled
to China in the ninth century. It was recorded that in the year 804 of

Euryaku 23, four Japanese government ships set their sails for China from Tamanoura in Kyushu. Kōbō boarded one, and Saicho for T'ien-t'ai another. No sooner had the four ships sailed from the Japanese shore than they were separated by a terrible storm. Kōbō Daishi's ship reached a port in Fukien Province of south China after a month, while Saicho arrived at Ning-po of Chekiang Province after two months. It was known that in those days Japanese shipbuilding was far inferior to that of Korea and China and the art of navigation so poor that the so-called navigators then knew very little about taking advantage of a seasonable wind. Therefore very few ships sailed to China in those days without encountering many dangers and even shipwreck. The ninth century was also a time when Japan maintained close contact with China and the Japanese government sent envoys there from time to time. Each time a decision was reached to send envoys to China, a great commotion and disquiet would immediately assail the lower-ranked Japanese government officials, for they dreaded being chosen to go to China in view of the dangerous voyage on the sea. Some tragic and even comical stories about the selection of such envoys were recounted. Some received punishment for evading the appointment and some even became mentally ill from fright before they embarked on the ship. It is human nature to be unwilling to risk one's life on an obviously dangerous voyage. But who would shrink from being sent abroad as an envoy from Japan nowadays? Everyone would rush for the appointment without any hesitation. The change has been entirely brought about by the resourceful and energetic ability of the Japanese people! Of course, it was the great Meiji era that initiated the change.

I read that when Hasekura Tsunenage (1571–1622) was ordered by Masamune Date to proceed to foreign countries on a tour of investigation, a small deep-sea craft, modeled after an English ship which had been wrecked off the coast of Uraga, was built for the purpose and named the *Date Maru*. This was the first Japanese-manned craft to cross the Pacific. Hasekura set sail in September, 1613, with a ship's company of 150. The *Date Maru* touched first at Luzon and then sailed across to Acapulco, which was reached on January 25, 1614. Then the party spent many years travelling around South America. Eventually Hasekura returned to Japan from Mexico in August, 1620, having spent seven years on his mission. The *Date Maru* must have been the first well-built Japanese ship which could sail on the seas for seven years. Something later came to my mind about William Adams (c. 1564–1620), whose tomb I visited at Tsukayama Park. It is described as follows:

William Adams was born at Gillingham in Kent, England. At the age of twelve he entered a Limehouse shipyard in London, and there studied shipbuilding for thirteen years. During the following ten years he lived as a skipper and navigator on the sea, at the same time operating his own trade house. In June of 1598 he joined a Netherlands trading company and set sail for the East as the chief pilot of a merchant fleet. The voyage was ill-fated and in the course of time the fleet met a severe storm in the Atlantic Ocean and was later forced into the Pacific. Adams's ship, the only one to cross the Pacific, finally drifted off the shores of Bungo (Oita Prefecture) in Kyushu, on April 19, 1600, twenty-three months after leaving the Netherlands. Out of the crew of 110 only eighteen had survived. After reaching Japan, Adams was more fortunate. Tokugawa Iyeyasu (1542–1616), first Tokugawa shogun, recognized his extraordinary ability and took him into his own service. Adams taught Western gunnery, shipbuilding, mathematics, navigation, and other technical Western subjects. He later took a Japanese wife and adopted the Japanese name Miura Anjin, after the Miura district of the Miura Peninsula where Iyeyasu had given him a grant of land producing annually 250 Koku (about 1,275 bushels) of rice. However, he had his residence in Edo (Tokyo) at a place called Anjin-cho in Chuoku, now a part of Muro-machi. He died at the age of fifty-six at Hirado near Nagasaki on May 16, 1620.

This account interested me because it tells how Tokugawa Iyeyasu was quick to make use of Adams's knowledge and ability for the benefit of Japan, though he was known to be the first Tokugawa to prohibit foreigners from entering Japan, which resulted in Japan's isolation for two hundred years. Many writers have described Tokugawa Iyeyasu as merely a military man, but his foresight in making use of Adams's knowledge and experience exceeded that of a mere military man.

Apart from the shipbuilding industry and other commercial enterprises, Osaka has a great name for the No dances, which Hideyoshi learned, the Kabuki plays, with a history of having reached its peak of popularity in Osaka in the late seventeenth century, and above all as the birthplace of the Bunraku puppet shows. It was in Tokyo that I met my friend and former colleague, Miss Fumio Fujikawa, who told me that she knew the chief performer of Bunraku which was running in Osaka at the moment. She immediately wrote to tell her friend that I would be coming to Osaka to see his performance and also to see him. Unfortunately I got to Osaka on the last day of the performances and was unable to see Miss Fujikawa's friend. However, I had seen a Bunraku performance in New York a few years before. A puppet show has always had a great attraction for me ever since my childhood days. When the New York papers announced the Bunraku puppet show, I wondered whether it would be similar to the Parisian marionettes, and I went to see it straightway. At first I was surprised to see no small wooden stage for the puppets but three persons all dressed in black standing on a platform behind a low railing. Next a puppet, a little less than half life-size, supported by a person in black, gradually moved to the center of the railing of the platform. Then the puppet began to act as well as talk. Its voice came from another person who sat at the corner of the stage with two musicians, one playing a samisen. Later one or two other puppets came to join the first one as if they were acting together. While my eyes were focused on the action of the puppets I saw nothing of the operators, who became nonexistent. Afterward a lady puppet in a beautifully embroidered silk kimono appeared in the center with her head downcast as if in great grief. Each movement of her hand or body indicated the unbearable sorrow she was suffering; then she began to dance in very quick movements as if she was trying to expose all she had in her mind. She looked like a real person on the stage. This was a most skillful performance. The inventor of the Bunraku puppets must be regarded among the greatest artists in the history of the performing art. Professor Donald Keene has written a book on Bunraku—*The Art of the Japanese Puppet Theater* with an introduction by Tanizaki Juni-chiro, who wrote:

> The Peking opera is not meant to be seen but to be heard. . . . The Bunraku is not meant to be heard but to be seen. . . . Why the movements of the Bunraku puppets at times suggest those of living persons is that these puppets, unlike marionettes—whose hips and shoulders are apt to change in mid-air—remain in the firm grip of the three operators while they move their hands, arms and legs and (in certain cases) even their wrists, joints of the fingers, and eyelids. . . . In retrospect one can usually remember only the puppets; in most cases it is all but impossible to recollect anything whatever about the appearance of the operators.

That is the great part of this art—to be able to reduce the importance of the operators to nothing on the stage. It is said that the tradition of puppetry on the island of Awaji is among the oldest in Japan, dating back to the late sixteenth century. Under the influence of the Osaka Bunraku the three-man puppet was soon adopted.

While there was still light in Osaka I took a taxi to see the Shitennoji Temple because it was founded in A.D. 593 by Prince Shotoku (573–621), who was the founder of the Horyuji Temple in Nara. Unfortunately Shitennoji suffered several big fires and nothing of the old parts remained except one gate, the Nakanomon. I also had a look at the stone torii at the front entrance, which is said to be the oldest torii in Japan, for it was erected in 1294. This is the only torii made of stone that I saw; the rest are made of wood and cement.

At dusk Fu-kang Chu rang me up to invite me out to dinner. I suggested to him to come to my hotel for a Chinese meal at the hall of

Chinese Viking "Hakurakuten" (or Po Chü-i in Chinese, a great T'ang poet), for I had found the food here really good. So we had a good talk and tasted almost every Chinese dish possible. Chu insisted on my having a taste of the special Osaka sushi before I left. This is crawfish and rice packed in a box and was invented for the Osaka Kabuki viewers to have meals while viewing plays, as a century or two ago, the program continued from early morning to dusk. After that, Chu took me to see a floor show in one of the biggest nightclubs in Osaka. I did not feel keen to go for I thought it could not be much different from those in Paris or New York, and besides I could not dance. However, Chu is an unmarried young person and very fond of Western-style dancing. So I went with him for a good ending of the day.

As I was in Japan for my fourth trip while Expo '70 was still on I made a good round of Kyushu and Yamaguchi Prefecture and went to spend a night in Osaka before I caught my plane back. Expo '70 had made a startling advertisement to show people what the future world could be. But I did not get any feeling for the future world there, for most of the pavilions displayed the world of the past and of the present. A very few cases tended to point to some future development from the present. Though every country which participated had its best brain design an outstanding structure to represent it, yet architecturally speaking the whole ground looked like toys cramped together in a child's playroom. I think this Expo indicated that all the top architects of the world have reached their limitation in creation externally, for they could not give a new form or shape beyond that of a cone, a square or rectangular box, or even a ball or a series of balls. However, I have never seen such an enormous number of people gathered together peacefully on a comparatively small piece of land. Neither the New York World's Fair nor any other one had that. The Japanese themselves contributed much to its success. Most visitors from other lands came not with the sole purpose of seeing the Expo but combined this pleasure with seeing the exotic land. Each pavilion took two hours or so to get in so I did not see many in my two quick visits. On the afternoon of August 31 an unbelievable torrential rain poured down, for a typhoon was just passing by the outskirts of Osaka. I was fortunate to have just entered a shelter. But many Japanese stood upright to have a forceful shower bath with their clothes on. An admirable act of an indomitable people!

Two girls consulting a fortuneteller

XXVII

Former Whaling Shore of Kii-Katsuura

WHEN I reached Nagoya station to catch my train for Kii-Katsuura, I found the platform densely packed with people. I heard that nearly two-thirds of the population of Japan would be on the move in summertime. It was the second of August and that report seemed to be true. Apart from many groups of school children in their uniforms, most people seemed to belong to one organization or another and some of them brought their children with them. Many of them were holding long rods or sticks, and a number of older men were dressed in short tunics with a belt round the waist and the lower ends of their trousers tied— they were going mountain climbing. Little noise was heard, unlike the stations of Paris or London during the holiday season. It was very clean inside the carriage of the train and two young girls came to serve each passenger a hot towel, a most civilized item for any kind of travelling. Nobody was inclined to talk, not even the youngsters. When the train reached Kameyama it turned in a new direction. I now saw many large patches of tall lotus leaves growing together with a good many pink flowers opening as if bursting into happy laughter at the bright sun. There were also some patches of taro, which looked similar to lotus, only they had no pink flowers. After another hour a sign of Matsusaka came in sight and the city here seemed to be full of factories. I saw many houses with thatched roofs after passing Taki station. After Sana station, the train went through a long tunnel cut through the mountains. We were now moving along a wide plain surrounded on all sides by high mountains. Though the sun was shining brightly the scenery, with its masses of luxuriant green passing by all the time, made me feel cool.

Before the train reached Owase, which is the center of a big Japanese petroleum industry, I saw many tiger lilies blooming on the mountain slopes and among the rocks. There were a good many scarecrows in the fields along the way and it seemed that the Japanese crows had a special love for this area. Eventually the industrial city of Shingu came in sight. My friend Lee Chia, Chief of China's News Agency in Tokyo, made a historical study of the Ch'in period (221 B.C.–206 B.C.) and described how the first emperor of Ch'in, who had the Great Wall of China built, once sent an official, Hsü Fu, and five hundred young boys and girls, eastward across the China Sea in search of the magic island of Peng-lai. Hsü Fu and his followers landed in Japan at this very place. Lee told me that the city of Shingu has built a temple to commemorate Hsü Fu's journey. So it seems that Japan and China had been related since the third century B.C. I took a taxi to find the Hsü Fu temple but nobody knew where it was. Since no more time was available, I returned to join another train for Kii-Katsuura.

Katsuraso Inn, where I was to stay, was not near the station of Kii-Katsuura. The taxi driver put me down by a landing stage where a small steamer would take me where I wanted to go. This was new to me and I could not find anyone around the place who could understand me either in English or Chinese. After having found two wrong steamers which were bound for two other large hotels, a third one came for me with the name of the inn on the bow. It took a quarter of an hour to cross the smooth harbor to the opposite landing stage. A man from the inn was waiting to lead me and two other visitors through a rocky tunnel to a very modern building, inside which every part—the main lobby, the grand banquet hall, the entertainment hall, guest rooms, and so on—were all similar to those in any luxurious hotel in a big American city. But no big American city hotel has any hot spring or cavernous hot spring attached. The whole inn, from its external and internal arrangement, gives no indication of being a Japanese establishment, but it is secluded with its back against three large rocky hills and its front facing an expansive sea dotted with a number of islands. The main lobby is very spacious with big glass windows facing the sea. I saw many people climbing the rocks along the shore, which were battered with the sea's white foam with water splashing all around. An interesting sight for the eyes and a delightful sound for the ears!

After lunch I asked the receptionist about taking a cruise round Katsuura Bay. I was soon led through the rocky tunnel again to join the cruising boat which had come from one of the other two big hotels. There is no communication between these three hotels in the harbor except by boat. We were soon moving around the harbor, which was very calm, for it is virtually landlocked by an island called Nakanoshima lying at its mouth. Both inns of Koshinoyu and Katsuraso were built at the foot of this island. There are a number of small pine-clad islets within the harbor, similar to those in Matsushima and therefore they were called Kii-no-Matsushima, or the Matsushima of Kii. The boat moved past many of the islets and a longish one had the shape of a camel lying down on the water instead of on the desert, with a well formed camel's head and a hump. Later we reached a large island with a big arch, which the boat went through; one of the passengers on the boat gave a terrific shout in order to enjoy its echo from the rocky walls, and this was followed by a big laugh from the others. The cliff at Noro-shiyama was pointed out; so were the few small islets in Nachi Bay. The water seemed much rougher than the calm inside of the harbor. On our way back someone noticed a few naked persons bathing on the roof bath of Koshinoyu Inn and spoke loudly to his companions with much chuck-ling. I thought the Japanese were used to seeing people naked in the public bath and was a little surprised at their showing special interest at the unexpected sight.

Katsuura Bay is too small to become a big business center, though it is said to be very deep and that large steamers could anchor close to the shore. Not much activity can be seen on the water except for the small steamers that take guests to the three different hotels and the cruising boat. Presently dusk had come to reign over the entire scene and every island soon changed into its evening gown of black silk. I returned by walking through the rocky tunnel. It was still twilight. I found my way to the seashore through a basement door. Before I walked through I had to change my slippers for a pair of wooden clogs. This was the first time that I tried to walk in clogs and I had much difficulty in moving step by step, particularly on large pebbles, for my big toe was obstinate and kept coming out of the cord ring. The shore was full of stones which stretched as far as the big rocks standing in the water. Though my body was swaying unsteadily, I managed to climb on a small rock to watch the sea battering it incessantly. The white foam jumped high up like flying pearls. The waves lapped the shore where young reeds tried hard like me to stand against the advancing water. I thought of man's life resembling

Back of Katsuraso Inn

IZUMO TAISHA NEAR MATSUE

THE SCENIC SPOT OF KUNIGA, OKI ISLAND

that of the reeds. The lines written by Walt Whitman came to mind:

Last of ebb, and daylight waning,
Scented sea-cool landward making, smell of sedge and salt incoming
With many a half-caught voice sent up from the eddies,
Many a muffled confession—many a sob and whisper's word,
As of speakers far and hid.

Walking on the wooden clogs for the first time had tired me out. Before evening I went to have a bath in the famous and popular Soto-noyu hot spring surrounded by rocky walls and felt wonderfully refreshed and as though completely changed into a new person. After dinner an unusual silence seemed to reign over the place, unlike my experience in other Japanese cities. About midnight I suddenly became wide awake when the strong wind battered on the window with a noisy chorusing and the intermittent sounds of the voluminous waves down below. A verse soon took shape in my mind:

Facing the great sea with my back to the high
  cliffs,
I come to this utopia full of uplifting feeling.
What has waked me from my dream in this silent
  night?
The rushing waves I hear up in the Katsuraso
  Inn!

I could not go to sleep again. Thinking of what I had seen during the day, I remembered reading that Shingu-Katsuura was an ancient Japanese whaling area. Mr. Saburo Egami of Tokyo Tourist Information Center told me that whales still occasionally appear off the Katsuura shore. However, the number of whales is much smaller than in past times. Today, in Taiji, he said there is only one boat (eight tons) owned by the town hall and it catches an average of more than one hundred blackfish a year. He also extended his help by quoting the following information for me from "Japanese Whaling Industry":

Although the history of whaling in Japan dates back more than a thousand years, it was not until the early seventeenth century that whaling was established as an enterprise.
Taiji Town of Wakayama Prefecture was the birthplace of com-

mercial whaling. The descendants of the war-defeated feudal lord Wada, who emigrated and settled in the town, began whaling for a livelihood. Through devices and improvements of the whaling method through the generations, the Wada family completed a commercial type of whaling which was later employed widely in Japan. . . .

The whales were most utilized for human food. The blubber, cartilage, and various viscera were eaten as well as the flesh. Whale oil was mainly used for lighting, but it was also used as an insecticide for rice plants. Bone and deteriorated meat were made into fertilizer. . . .

After the Meiji Restoration of 1867, the local whaling industries declined because they had lost their feudal lords who had been the supporters of the industry. In addition to these circumstances, a catastrophe which took place in Taiji, Kii-Katsuura, a whaling town mentioned as the birthplace of the Japanese whaling industry, almost ended traditional whaling in Japan.

On December 24, 1878, the people of the town, who were almost at the verge of bankruptcy on account of the poor catch in that year, found a whale for which they had been longing badly. The whale was a female accompanied by calves.

Although it was forbidden by traditional custom to hunt such a whale, the distressed whalers, who could not observe the taboo, began the chase. With a sudden storm all boats were sunk and more than a hundred men were lost in the sea.

Nachi Waterfall

I was amazed to learn that such a long tradition could have come to an end because something had been done against the tradition itself. This seemed to be so. Mr. Saburo Egami continued that whaling is still carried on. Among the twenty-one whaling countries of the world, Japan ranks third in the total catch, being surpassed only by Norway and the British Commonwealth. The whaling grounds for Japanese whalers are now in the Antarctic, northern Pacific, and the waters around the homeland. I suppose the waters outside Katsuura Bay are still included.

Next morning a taxi took me to see the Nachi Waterfall. Nice scenery surrounded me the whole way up Mt. Nachi. Many visitors were already there and I walked up the hundreds of steps to the observation platform directly facing the magnificent waterfall. A wooden structure was built there and many Japanese were burning incense and folding their hands together with a deep bow to worship the enormous waterfall. I did not know that the waterfall is a god to be worshiped by the Japanese. We Chinese are only fond of gazing at waterfalls. Nachi Waterfall, of some 430 feet, is said to be the highest waterfall in Japan. But I found it even more impressive when I climbed up another five hundred steps to go round the Kumano-Nachi Shrine. It reminded me of the poem written by the great T'ang poet Li Po on seeing the lovely waterfall on Mt. Lu, at the foot of which I was born:

The sun shines on the incense-burning peak; purple smoke rises;
From the distance I see the waterfall hanging like
a long stream.
Flying straight down over three thousand feet,
I wonder if it is the Silver River falling from
heaven!

日照香爐生紫煙
遙看瀑布挂長川
飛流直下三千尺
疑是銀河落九天

The Chinese Silver River is the West's Milky Way. I have seen a good
many waterfalls in Japan and Nachi Waterfall impressed me most. Perhaps it induced a nostalgic feeling in me. Up Mt. Lu in my native city I
used to climb on the rocks to get close to a fall, but a good-sized waterfall should be gazed at from a distance. I remember seeing a reproduction of the famous hanging scroll of the Nachi Waterfall painted in the
Kamakura period by an unknown artist. It is in the Nezu Museum in
Tokyo. There is a legend which identifies Mt. Nachi with Potolaka
Mountain of India for good reasons. It is said that during the time of
Emperor Keiko (71–130) an "Indian" or "Tenjiku" priest Ragyo
Sennin recovered an eight-inch statuette of Kwannon from the bottom of
the Nachi Waterfall.

Before I left Kumano-Nachi Shrine I saw a crowd around a Japanese
painter in monk's robe and moved near to watch him paint a curled-up
serpent in one continuous movement of his brush. He seemed to have
worked out a special technique for his subject matter and made his hand
like a printing machine, for he could repeat the same picture over and
over again without the slightest variation from the first one. An attractive performance to watch.

Painting a curled-up serpent

Down below Mt. Nachi I saw a number of ink slabs, large and small,
arranged together for sale in a gift shop and I went in to buy one, for
the stone was said to come from the local black rocks of Mt. Nachi. A
Japanese man who was in the shop at the same time told me that the ink
slab is very famous, but the local black rocks had long been exhausted
by continual cutting over the centuries. What they sold now had been
imported. I replied with a smile that there were similar practices in
China.

XXVIII

One of the Three Wonders of the World

MY GOOD FRIEND and colleague Professor Yoshito Hakeda was spending his sabbatical leave in his own country, Japan. Before he left New York, he told me that he would be staying for a few months at his Buddhist College on Koyasan and that I should go and see him there if I found myself in Japan. Two days after my arrival in Tokyo, I met him and Mrs. Hakeda and their son Yuji, who had delayed their departure from the city in order to see me. I was much touched by their kindness and we then made an arrangement for my visit to Koyasan. It is not only that a promise should be kept; I very much wanted to see the great Buddhist center in Japan, where the famous Japanese Buddhist priest Kōbō Daishi had spent many years and established his sect of the Shingon doctrine of Buddhism. This great Buddhist center receives more than a million pilgrims annually and was not to be missed by me in any case.

I caught a train from Katsuura for Shirahama on a fine August day. Upon arriving at the station, I saw more people on the platform than at Katsuura. The stationmaster, who could speak English, came to persuade me to find a seat in the second class, for the first-class compartment was full. He wrote on my ticket to indicate that something should be refunded at the next stop. This action astonished me greatly, not only for the unusual courtesy from the stationmaster, but also his suggestion that I should collect the difference in the tickets. I had not had this experience in all my travels before. After reaching Hashimoto, I changed for a local train for Gokurakubashi. The sun had long set behind the high mountains, but even in the twilight I could tell that we were now moving up a rather high steep slope. There was hardly a breathing space between the stepping out of the day and the stepping in of night. There floated a subtle spell in the dusk; myriad beauties glowed over the endless mountain ranges while the treetops nearby vibrated slightly. I had never been up a high mountain at this time of the day.

In pitch darkness the train stopped at Gokurakubashi. I followed many people into a cable car which was lit up. The longer the suspense in reaching my destination, the more magical the slow, gradual ascent of the car became to me. Nothing could be seen outside and I did not know what kind of place I had come to. When I got out of the car, someone asked me where I wished to go. He then gave me a small piece of paper with a pen mark for the second bus for Rengejoin. After ten minutes more of suspense, I emerged from the bus and stood in the darkness without any knowledge of where I was, yet I felt this was a place full of sound and fragrance. Someone was calling me by name. There was Professor Hakeda, who said that he had come out to look for me on and off for the whole day. No words could express my feeling of gratitude at that moment and the joy of hearing his voice was beyond description. Yoshito knew that I would be coming that day, but I had had no opportunity to tell him the time of my arrival.

Yoshito led me through several gates and many corridors. till eventually I could put down my two little handbags in a good-sized room with a nicely spread tatami and a sliding door. Yoshito informed me that the organization in the temple was unlike any Japanese inn or hotel and that most things took place in a communal manner. Apparently there were about fifty temples, each of which provides a number of rooms for visitors to spend the night or nights while on Koyasan. Necessary arrangements for food are made beforehand. People come to visit this Buddhist center almost every day of the year but particularly in the summer. There were also special arrangements for large groups of school children to stay for a number of days during the summer vacation; the youngsters not only come to enjoy a new place but to learn the history, to get acquainted with Buddhist temple life, and to attend morning and evening services. On our way in, we passed a big room where about two hundred young students were about to have their evening meal and Yoshito's son Yuji was there helping to distribute food. Each had his own implements and bedding and looked after himself. They are under strict discipline and how well behaved they seemed to be when I passed by. While they were eating no noise could be heard and when they finished, each cleaned his own utensils and put them away. I had not imagined that when two hundred youngsters gathered together in a room quiet could be enforced. This gathering would not have been possible in China anyway. Though the famous Chinese monasteries would have one or two rooms provided for visitors, no woman would be allowed to come except at those Buddhist centers specially run by nuns. Besides, most of the important Chinese monasteries are situated on high mountains, no modern transportation was provided for easy access, and there would hardly be more than one or two visitors in a whole year. This showed me at once one of the great differences between Chinese and Japanese Buddhism: Chinese Buddhism keeps itself apart from the mass of the people while Japanese Buddhism tries to get as close to the people as possible. This is why Buddhism is a national religion in Japan but not in China. I then said to Yoshito that though I had been on Koya-san for only one or two hours it had taught me a lesson that a religion is for the mass of the people, not for itself. Neither Buddhism nor Taoism have reached their goal as a religion in China. Confucianism is not a religion in the strict sense of the word and it does not extend beyond the limits of individual families.

When I had finished my evening meal, the wife of the bishop of the temple, who took charge of all arrangements, asked her son to drive the five of us, including the three Hakedas, to see the Bon dance in the big square of the Buddhist center. Though it was about nine o'clock at night and completely dark all around, the square was lit up with many lanterns, and many women and men were dancing on a wooden structure in the center. Most of the dancers were in white-and-blue patterned cotton kimonos and a few were in modern Western suits. I have seen a similar dance (*Bon Odori* in Japanese) on Sado Island and other places. It seemed to be a kind of dance that every Japanese, old and young, could dance. There is no limit to the number of dancers, and anyone could join in at any time. It seems to be very similar to the New England square dance. Actually the Bon dance has a religious origin from the Indian *Ullambana*, which was brought to China and then to Japan. It is interesting that a highly religious service eventually turned into an occason for common rejoicing in Japan.

Despite the music played for the dance, the surroundings seemed wonderfully quiet. On our way back I noticed a short street with shops, chiefly gift shops, and eating places on both sides. Many people, some of whom were staying at other temples and had changed into kimonos, were strolling about and buying things as well. Yoshito gave me some information about Koyasan, saying that Mt. Koya is 2,858 feet high, situated on a big flat tableland right on the top of the mountain with eight high peaks surrounding it. Nobody had ever been up there until it was discovered by Kōbō Daishi about 816. The real name of Kōbō Daishi (774–835) was Priest Kukai, Kōbō Daishi being the posthumous title given him by the emperor Daigo in 921—meaning "Law-spreading great teacher." When he was thirty years old Kukai ventured the hazardous journey to China and studied there for two years. While residing at Hsining Temple in north China he visited many Buddhist teachers until he finally met Master Hui-kuo (746–806), the Patriarch of the Esoteric Buddhism in China, who lived at the East Pagoda Hall of the Green Dragon Temple. Master Hui-kuo was the highest authority of the sect at the time; he had learned the dharma of the Esoteric tradition from the famous master Pu-k'ung, or Amoghavajra (705–774). The Buddhist

School was transmitted to China in 716 when an Indian master Subha-karasinha (637–735) came to China at the invitation of Emperor Hsüan Tsung. After his return, Kōbō Daishi decided to establish the new sect of Esoteric Buddhism, which he had learned about in China, and he travelled everywhere in Japan in order to find a good place for his teaching center. A legend says that he once had a dream of preaching Esoteric Buddhism in a land shaped like a lotus with eight petals surrounding him. So he went everywhere in search of this land and eventually found the flat tableland on the top of this mountain, which he named Mt. Koya, meaning "Mountain high and wild." It also says that when he found the mountain, two dogs, one white and the other black, soon appeared and guided him all the way. They were the mountain gods, who had transformed themselves into dogs. The building of this precinct covering twenty-four square miles enjoyed great support from the imperial family. It must have been a great undertaking some twelve hundred years ago. Gradually it grew till there were 990 temples altogether. In 1887 the whole precinct suffered the last of a succession of fires, and many temples were destroyed. However, 123 temples still remain to the present day.

On our return we all sat in my room. Mrs. Hakeda told me to listen carefully for soon there would be an imitation of a bird singing. A few minutes later, three notes sounded and were continued intermittently for a good while. This apparently was the sound of a bird which used to be heard at night on Koyasan, but the bird had now disappeared, so these sounds were made to imitate its singing at night. Yoshito joined in to tell me that this bird was named San Pao in Chinese, or Three Precious Treasures—the Buddha, the dharma, and the Buddhist community. Dr. Yoshimaro Yamashina, the great Japanese ornithologist and author of *Birds in Japan*, wrote me:

> This species of bird is the Japanese Scops Owl, *otus scops japonicus*, and it also has been known in Japan by the name of Konoha-zuku.
>
> The singing of this bird is distinctive in three syllables, sounding something like Bup-Po-So, according to the way of hearing to someone who listens to it. The literary meaning of Bup ("Buddha") Po ("teaching") So ("monk") is Buddhist priest, as you see, so that the name of San ("three") Bo ("Precious") Cho ("bird")—Sanbo-cho became the general usage since a long past.
>
> The Konoha-zuku can be found in mountainous regions where big trees grow thick, not only in Koyasan but all over Japan. However, this bird has noticeably decreased lately since the forest of large trees has been greatly reduced in recent years after the ending of the World War.

Kobo Daishi once wrote this poem about the bird:

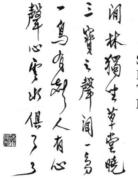

Sitting alone in the hut at dawn in the quiet forest
I hear a bird singing with the sound of Bup-Po-So.
The bird has a song while man has mind;
Bird song, human mind, cloud and water all mingle
    into oneness.

The imitative sound of the bird's song indeed enhanced the silence outside of my room. Everything became crystally clear in my head. Afterward I lay on the bed thinking that I had just plunged into the remote
labyrinth of a high mountain and regained peace of mind and calmness
of heart. Some incense fragrance penetrated the room, swirling over my
head to lead me to the sweetest paradise for seven or eight hours.

The next morning Yoshito came to take me to visit the head of Rengejoin, Bishop Ryushun Soeda, who is a noted calligrapher. We
exchanged views on a number of famous Chinese calligraphers, such as
Yen Chen-ching, Chu Sui-liang, Liu Kung-chüan, Ou-yang Hsün, Su
Tung-p'o, and Huang Ting-chien. I mentioned that Huang Ting-chien
was born in the same province as I, Kiangsi, though there were more
than nine hundred years between us. In his studio Bishop Soeda showed
me a set of stone rubbings of Wang Wei's rhymed prose on a white
cockatoo, written by Han Yü, the greatest Confucian scholar of the
T'ang period, who wrote a famous essay against Buddhism. This surprised me, for Han Yü was not known as a calligrapher and the rubbing
was not known to me when I was in China. The bishop has a rich collection of well-reproduced sample books of Chinese calligraphy. As he is
a keen practitioner of calligraphy, Bishop Soeda became a connoisseur of
brushes and inks. He frequently purchased brushes from China and he
has an especially good inkstone made from the stone of Tuan-hsi in
Anhui Province of China. Tuan-hsi inkstones have been esteemed by
calligraphers ever since the T'ang period. I told him that before coming
to Koyasan I had been to see the Nachi Waterfall and bought a Nachi
inkstone. He admitted that it was a good inkstone but not as good as the
Tuan-hsi ones. He also told me about a Mr. Hu Chin, born in Manchuria, who had studied Shingon Buddhism under him and had a Buddhist
name Tsung-chin. He was also a calligrapher and poet. He went back to
Peking, re-establishing Shingon in China, but the bishop had not heard

from him for many years. I was the second Chinese, he said, to have come from China to exchange views on calligraphy with him. A most enjoyable morning, for I had not met anyone who knew so much about Chinese calligraphy before.

Young Soeda then drove Yoshito and me to Okunoin, the mausoleum of Kōbō Daishi. A big crowd was already packed into the corridor, in the center of which stood a large metal incense burner with much smoke spiraling upward, while many stood with bowed heads in deep prayer before a row of lighted candles. A young Japanese guide explained in a loud voice about everything there, but I could not follow his words. It is still believed by many that Kōbō Daishi entered the vault of his necropolis when he intuitively knew the time had come for him to leave the physical world and sat in a meditative position while still alive. Afterward a statue was made of him in that sitting posture in the vault. On March 21 each year a special ceremony takes place and the chief bishop of Koyasan goes down into the vault to change the Master's clothes. Some said that the lower edge of the old dress was often frayed and spotted with mud, which meant that the Master would still walk to various distant villages as he did in his lifetime. A depository in octagonal shape was erected nearby for the bones of the poor people who could not afford proper burial, and also for the bones of those who wished to be near the Master. A long bench was built along the back wall of the main hall, every inch of which was occupied by those who were enjoying a little rest. Unexpectedly a young man came to ask me to take a photograph of him and his companions with his camera. Obviously he took me to be a fellow countryman. I did take the photograph for him without saying a word. Yoshito and I had a good laugh afterward!

We then entered the Hall of a Thousand Lanterns, each of which was spotlessly cleaned and lighted. All the lanterns were gilded and they seemed to brighten up the rather dark hall. Every one was donated by an ardent follower of Shingon Buddhism. In the center of the hall near the shrine was an ancient-looking lantern, which was said to have been lit up by Kōbō Daishi himself and had been burning continuously for over eleven hundred years. It is said that in the early days the flame was maintained by the use of heavy vegetable oil. Several lanterns are kept in reserve so that if there was any failure in the ancient lantern, the flame could be immediately transferred to another. Every priest of the various temples on Koyasan was assigned this religious duty to keep the flame burning forever.

Just before crossing a small bridge after leaving the mausoleum, I was told that this bridge would collapse and prevent anyone passing over it if he or she did not possess a perfectly clean heart. It was said that Toyotomi Hideyoshi came to see Koyasan after his Korean expedition and secretly visited the bridge alone at night in order to test his eligibility. The next morning he made a state entry. After we had left the bridge far behind, we began to walk along a paved road with Japanese cedars and pines lining both sides. The lofty dark brown trunks of the cedars were very impressive and some of them had grown so thick that it would take seven or eight people with outstretched arms to surround them. In between the big cedar trunks were burial grounds with stone tablets of various sizes and in the different shapes of Indian stupas with five Sanskrit words engraved on each section. At intervals the long shafts of sun rays falling through the tall treetops in slanting lines were bright. Yoshito pointed out to me a number of interesting tombs. After passing by the family burial grounds of the Toyotomis we came to an enclosed ground with a number of tombs commemorating the dead killed in Hideyoshi's Korean expedition, not only those of Japanese birth but also the Koreans who had been the enemies and had died in the wars. These commemorative tombs were said to have been built by Hideyoshi's son Hidetsugu, who disagreed with his father's conduct and later committed suicide on Koyasan. Hidetsugu's having opposed his father's unreasonable use of power to conquer Korea was an unusual happening in Japanese history, for obedience and loyalty are two important virtues in the Japanese people. Though a failure, Hidetsugu's effort should be made known to the world. Not far from these tombs was a new tomb with five kanji words "Fubo Onji hi" in Japanese meaning "parents' kindnesses are great," erected by a Japanese who opposed Japan's part in the Second World War and was put in prison but later released after the war ended. So he erected this monument in remembrance of his parents' love for him. Close to this monument was an old stone on which was engraved a line of Basho's writing "Hearing a pheasant crying I think of my parents." The whole cemetery extended for two miles and was a very impressive one. Yoshito told me that Bishop Soeda thought this should be regarded as one of the three great wonders of the world, the other two being the pyramids of Egypt and the Great Wall of China.

Before reaching the Ichi-no-bashi, or First Bridge, from the entrance, there stood a replica of the famous stele of the Nestorian monument at Sian, China. It was erected here in 1911 by Mrs. C. A. Bordon, an Irish lady who was once a lady in waiting to Queen Victoria. A nice spot for it but how strange to have a Nestorian Christian monument standing in a Buddhist burial ground. Nestorian Christianity had been brought to China by Sogdian caravaneers who settled in Ch'ang-an (Sian), where they founded a trade colony governed by an Irano-Syriac clergy. (A church was built in this city in 638, and a Syro-Chinese stele of "Sianfu," inscribed in 781.) There was a rumor that Kōbō Daishi's own teaching had been somewhat influenced by Christianity; thus perhaps

The walking attitude
of a bronze statue

the reason for the Nestorian monument being erected on Koyasan.

Yoshito then took me to see the garden of Ekoin and also to make a round of the walls inside Karukayado, where hung a series of paintings depicting how a woman devotee enters into Buddhism from the start to the end. Coming out of the Karukayado Temple, we were on the narrow street which I saw the night before. There was more activity than ever on this bright sunny morning. Apart from one or two motorcars, there was an old-fashioned wooden cart drawn by a horse plodding on and on, producing an unusual yet familiar sound of its hoofs on the ground. A typical sight on Koyasan. While we were having a quick lunch, Yoshito told me that the population on Koyasan was a little more than seven thousand in 1950 and had now increased to nine thousand. During the summer season the number would be increased by visitors. For example, Rengejoin, where we were staying, could house three hundred students alone. Modern means of transport have made Koyasan very easily accessible. In other words, the Japanese Buddhist sects have mingled with the masses. Many of the emperors and noblemen of the past retired into the priesthood at the end of their lives. This has never been so in China's history. Apart from Emperor Wu Ti of Liang dynasty (reigned 502–547), who avowed himself an ardent Buddhist, no other royal head has attached himself to any famous monastery in China.

We planned to see Koyasan University, where Yoshito spent four years as a monk-student before going on to finish his Ph.D. studies at Yale University. On our way we met Bishop Zenko Kusanagi, head of Sanboin and bishop over all the bishops of all the temples on Koyasan, who is in charge of the entire system of Koyasan and whose authority is similar to a mayor of a big town. His silk robe indicated his rank and authority. He wore an additional robe of purple with the emblem of a chrysanthemum, over the usual gray black robe. He has a round, full face with a half smile. Yoshito had studied under him for a good while, so they conversed in front of his temple Sanboin, which means "Temple of Three Treasures." I was introduced to Bishop Kusanagi and made a deep bow to him before we left for our destination. Koyasan University is a long-standing institution and has many students. It not only trains the divinity students in the old Japanese scriptures but also conducts courses in English, French, and German—a very modern, up-to-date institution. No Chinese monastery has ever thought of running a school to spread the teaching of Buddhism. But Yoshito, having acquired a knowledge of English there, was able to go to Yale University after graduating from Koyasan University. The campus is not big but compact and has the spiritual atmosphere of all the temples surrounding it. Yoshito showed the place to me with indescribable pride.

Upon entering the main hall, Kongobuji, Yoshito asked if there were any like it in China. My mind immediately turned to a similar arrangement of the main hall of Ching-tzu Szu at Hangchow by the West Lake in Chekiang Province. But there were more elaborate structures and gilded ornaments in Kongobuji than in Ching-tzu Szu. All the gilded lanterns were lit and the smoke from the spiraling incense filled the space. Many visitors were burning incense as an offering. I was told that Kongobuji was specially built by the powerful Hideyoshi in memory of his mother, but it has been rebuilt once after a great fire. The famous original Fusuma panels painted by Kano Tanyu were saved from the fire and they were still on the wall in a room past the main altar. We also had a look at the wall painting of a big rugged pine tree in snow. It is in this room that Hideyoshi's son committed suicide. A number of other rooms which joined this one also had good panel paintings, for it was a traditional decoration during the Tokugawa period. Later we went to see the enormous kitchen with its open fireplace and a big chimney, very rare in Japan. There was a small shrine built above the kitchen wall to house the kitchen god. This is the only place that a kitchen god exists in Japan to my knowledge. Most old Chinese houses have a kitchen god, believed to keep a close watch over the financial situation of the family and to make a report to the Heavenly Palace near the end of every year.

Yoshito then led me into a big reception room where tea was served with two small pieces of Koyasan cake and a printed picture of Kobo Daishi given to every visitor to Kongobuji. The cakes were made in the shape of the chrysanthemum, the royal emblem, on one side and a maple leaf, the emblem of the Koyasan monastery, on the other. Several ladies were busy serving, and the people streaming in seemed endless. What a business for a Buddhist monastery to be able to cater for so many day after day!

Crossing the square where we saw the Bon dance the night before, we came to Reihokan, the Treasure House of Koyasan. Yoshito asked for the director, whom he knew very well and who soon came out to receive us with happy greetings. Dr. Chikyo Yamamoto, an expert on Indian art, took us around the museum. I was very interested to see the famous silk painting of *Parinirvana*, dated 1086, of the Heian period. I have been familiar with a reproduction of it for many years. I was also interested to see the original painting of Sakyamuni Buddha by an anonymous Sung artist—a good example. We then went over several other paintings and one of them, after a discussion, was realized to have been painted by a Korean artist instead of a Chinese. This museum has several thousand treasures, but only a fraction of them could be shown in the limited space. Many fine Japanese carved-wood Buddhist statues such as *Vairocana*, Peacock King, were all preserved on Koyasan. Kobo Daishi brought back a number of Buddhist portraits of Shingon patriarchs by Li Chen and other Chinese artists, one of which represents the Indian monk Amoghavajra and is now in the treasure collection of Toji Temple in Kyoto. Kobo Daishi's own writing, *Goshoraimokuroku*, has a message that "the reverend Divine [the Chinese master from whom he received instruction] informed me that the secrets of the doctrines of the Shingon sect could not be conveyed without the aid of pictorial representations. Thereupon I brought home with me sixteen artists, including Li Chen, and had them draw different sacred figures." But Yoshito doubted that Kobo Daishi would be able to bring back many Chinese artists, for he was not well provided for when he went to China at thirty years of age. The passage could be read differently. However,

The pillow box of three folded pieces

the well-known pillow box of three folded pieces, each containing a carved wood Buddhist statue of T'ang work, which Kobo Daishi brought back from China, is now housed in the Kongobuji of Koyasan. This might have started the Japanese fashion for keeping small Buddhist lacquer shrines in private homes. Dr. Yamamoto also showed us the recent large publication on Koyasan treasures—a thick book with many colored reproductions. I particularly like the piece of calligraphy in Kobo

Daishi's own hand on the mendicant which he wrote before he went to China—a beautiful essay in the Chinese classic style by an ardent follower of the T'ang style of calligraphy.

From Reihokan to Daito, or Great Pagoda, took no time. The building close to the Great Pagoda is called Kondo and has an elegant roof.

We were now near the main entrance of the whole establishment, Daimon, or Great Gate, with two stories, an immense, impressive structure. A wooden railing runs around the top floor.

As the whole precinct of Koyasan covers twenty-four square miles with 123 temples, it would take some days to go around to every part, but Yoshito managed to show me all the important centers in one day. Without his help and direction I could not have seen so much during my short stay on Koyasan. Before we reached the Daimon we saw a big bronze statue on a high stone base of Kōbō Daishi in a walking posture, holding a long staff as if he were making for the north. The big wooden seated image of him, carved in the Kamakura period, was more commonly seen in reproduction. The walking attitude of this bronze statue indicated that he was very fond of travelling on foot. He seems to have visited every place in Japan, except Hokkaido. Legends tell that he even performed many miracles and there are strange legends and anecdotes about him. For instance he could strike fresh water out of dry land for people to drink, and if he left his bamboo staff on the ground, it would gradually sprout into a big bamboo tree with branches growing downward. It was said at one place where his bamboo staff lay it sprouted into a big bamboo forest. Most of the temples built in the ninth or tenth century were associated with him. But the precinct on Koyasan was entirely his creation. During my short stay I felt his presence almost everywhere and every minute. Before the construction of the railroad and later the cable car and the motor road up to Koyasan, the walk up the thickly wooded forest more than twenty-eight hundred feet high must have been an impossible task for any common man. And not only did Kobo Daishi walk up through the thickly wooded forest, he also managed to foresee the future development of the flat tableland he had found and made a big plan for the buildings. Was he not a superman to have been able to do these things? Apart from being a writer in good Chinese style, a calligrapher, a poet, and also a painter and sculptor, he was also known as an inventor of the Japanese kana writing. He was, too, the inventor of Koya-tofu, a special kind of soybean curd for food! Once he was walking back to the monastery on Koyasan and saw a man about to eat a baked fish on the roadside. He asked if the man would sell him the baked fish and the latter agreed. After settling the amount, Kobo Daishi threw the fish into a stream beside the road and the fish immediately became alive, swam away, and disappeared. The modern

Japanese *seimeigaku*—a special science of names—is said to have been derived from the same science of names which Kōbō Daishi brought back from China. Seimeigaku in Japan has been a unique science whereby practitioners could tell fortunes by one's name, cure illness, save one from financial disasters by changing one's name, or guarantee newly born babies their future wealth and prosperity by suggesting lucky names to give them. I don't know that China has ever had Seimeigaku.

Kōbō Daishi only lived to the age of sixty-one. The first twenty years of his life he had to study. We don't know what he did during the third ten years before he went to China at thirty. He did most of the things after his return to Japan. It was only for thirty-one years that he was really hard at work. How could he have accomplished so much within only thirty-one years? It is said that Kōbō Daishi was the one really responsible for reforming the Buddhism of his time, which was so closely involved in the aristocratic atmosphere of the Heian period, and for bringing it to the people at large. In other words, Kōbō Daishi was the one to have acted as the Buddhist leader of a Japanese state religion side by side with Shintoism. It is no wonder that the Japanese chant "Namu Daishi Henjo Kongo" instead of "Namu Amidabutsu." He was not an ordinary Buddhist monk but a Japanese Buddha!

A horse cart on Koyasan

XXIX

Monk-Painter Sesshu and Ama-no-hashidate

AFTER LEAVING Toyokoko the local train took me to Ama-no-hashidate late in the afternoon. Someone from the Monjuso Inn was waiting to take me there by car, which wound its way up Monju Hill (Manjushri in Sanskrit) and stopped in front of a fine ancient Japanese building. My room had a wide window which commanded a most extensive view far down below, stretching over the Bay of Miyazu on the right. I also noticed some bright water behind a large group of trees on the left. The sun was already setting, though it was not yet dark. On the water of the bay there were a number of red strips like many red carp swimming in one direction in a glass bowl; lifting up my eyes toward the sky, I realized that they were the reflection of the red clouds from the setting sun. To the farthest left a good many lights could be seen as if they were winking at me. There must have been a rather strong wind blowing the tree branches over the lights now and then. The maid soon brought in supper and invited me to leave the window to come and eat.

After a substantial meal I had a walk round the inn and in a small guest hall I noticed a number of photographs hanging on the walls indicating that they were taken during the three royal visits when Emperor Hirohito and the empress had stayed in this inn. The whole inn breathed the fragrance of Japanese antiquity. I felt content and soon fell sound asleep.

About five o'clock the next morning I woke up and saw a bright reddish hue creeping through the window. I jumped up from the tatami and, resting my hands on the window sill, stared hard into the far distant hills that enclosed the Bay of Miyazu, but early mist had shrouded them. The whole expanse, including the group of trees near the shore, was tinted red. Later the bright red rays penetrated through the trees as if trying to separate them while the great ball of fire gradually rose and then changed into a ball of transparent crystal which my eyes dared not face directly. I held my breath in great wonderment and excitement.

After breakfast the lady manager already had a car waiting to take me down the hill. She told me that I could telephone to ask for a car to fetch me when I wanted to come back and also advised the driver to show me to the ferryboat for Mt. Nariai. While the boat was approaching a red wooden bridge on the left, which swung up to make way for the boat to pass through, I realized that the boat was from Iwataki Lagoon on the opposite side of Miyazu Bay. This little red bridge joined the long, narrow stretch of land known as Ama-no-hashidate, or Floating Bridge of Heaven, with the southern shore. This is one of the three great scenic spots in Japan. Our boat was moving past the whole length of the Floating Bridge of Heaven, which is a two-mile-long narrow spit of sand of almost even width, about fifty-eight meters. The trees growing along the whole length of it are pines. The legend says that the two creators, Izanagi and Izanami, stood on Ama-no-hashidate and with their jeweled spears stirred up the sea water to form the land of Japan. So here was the place where Japan first came into being.

On arriving at the northern shore, I followed the rest of the passengers to walk through a small town where a number of gift and souvenir shops displayed their goods and the shopkeepers all welcomed us with broad smiles. None of us stopped but went up on the Ejiri cable car to a place called Kasamatsu Park, where there were food and gift shops. In front of the shops were a few stone benches and many people stood with their backs to the scene and bent over to view it upside-down between their legs. Such was the local custom, for someone suggested that the scene would look better that way. I half-closed my eyes and the Floating Bridge of Heaven seemed to be really floating in midair.

Next a bus took me and many others to the entrance to the old Buddhist Nariaiji Temple on the top of Mt. Nariai. There was a long flight of stone steps going up. Before climbing them, I looked at a stone monument with two kanji characters "hsia ma" in Chinese pronunciation, which means "getting off the horse." In the old days visitors must have come there on horseback and I suppose people can still go round the southern shore of the Aso-umi Lagoon to ride up there. At the top of the steps on the right stood a beautiful bell tower, full of antique feeling. The temple dated back to the ninth century and belonged to the Shingon sect of Koyasan. It bore no sign of having been repaired or rebuilt. This was almost the only temple that I saw in Japan that had not suffered any fire damage. Inside the main hall hung an oil portrait of a monk, which looked a little out of place; on the other side there was an ancient-looking painting by a Japanese artist. In the front and on all sides of the temple were many tall, rugged pine trees with their crooked branches. Standing outside of the main hall of the temple, I could see a panorama down below, though parts of Ama-no-hashidate were hidden in trees. It became small like a tiny green snake wriggling on the Bay of Miyazu.

Presently we came down on the cable car to the shore town. In one of the gift shops, I noticed, hanging in rows, many of the big globefish

A beautiful bell tower

with their bellies blown up to a ball-like shape with many spines sticking out of the surface all round. They were dried and sold as lanterns. The globefish contains a poisonous gland, yet its flesh is generally regarded as a great delicacy. In the Yangtze River, where my native city was situated, there was a small type of globefish and it was good for eating, provided the cook knew how to take out its poisonous part before cooking.

The return journey on the ferryboat gave me another good look at the Floating Bridge of Heaven. On reaching the southern shore I went in the Chionji Temple for a look and then strolled down the short street but no pachinko shops came in sight. Most people came here for the scenery. The pine-lined Floating Bridge of Heaven intrigued me, so I went to walk through it. I stood with the crowd waiting for the little red bridge to turn into its proper position and then crossed over it. A large number of people were lying on the sand or bathing in the water on the bay side of Miyazu. A tall, slender stone monument was erected nearby, on which were nine kanji characters meaning "old spot where Iwami Jutaro took his revenge." Mr. Makoto Yamazaki told me that Iwami Jutaro, an expert swordsman, chased three samurai warlords—Hirose Gunzo, Naruo Gunzo, and Okawa Hachizaeman—as far as Miyazu to avenge his father's death. There was a good footpath along the center of the sand spit. Many interestingly shaped old pine trees were growing on both sides, all along the way with no other kinds of trees in sight. I always like to paint pine trees and Ama-no-hashidate provided me with plenty to study.

While I strolled slowly on and on, a young man came to ask me to take a photo of him with his camera. At first he must have taken me for a Japanese, for he spoke to me in Japanese. Hearing my answer in English he switched to English too, though he hesitated over a word or two at times. We then walked together to the north end, for he was exploring like me. He seemed to have questions to ask me, so we talked while walking along. We had not realized that it took almost an hour to reach the other end, though we stopped to gaze at the pines and other scenes intermittently. I pointed out some interesting pines here and there to admire. The Japanese soil appeared to be particularly agreeable to pines and the special Japanese red pine, called *Pinus densiflora*, was indigenous to the land. I then learned that the young man, Katsumi Yamano, was a student at Oita University, majoring in economics and, after graduation the next summer, he hoped to be working in the Matsushita Electric Company. His hobbies were climbing and hiking, and he had been up Mt. Fuji, the Japanese Alps, and in Hokkaido. He made all the journeys on foot; he was going to Kyoto from Ama-no-hashidate in an hour or two, and I told him that I would be going to Hokkaido in two weeks' time. His face broke into a happy smile for he loved Hokkaido, where he had met a young lady whom he hoped to marry. He showed me a photograph of her. Nothing could make any young fellow happier than a remark on the good looks of the lady he loved! I then suggested taking a smiling photo of him to send to his love and he jumped at the idea, instantly standing before a group of pines laughing merrily. A very happy moment for him and me too.

I had been travelling in Japan for over a month without talking much, but that afternoon I seemed to have done quite a good deal of it. Mr. Yamano showed great interest in international affairs and had heard of the student strikes at Columbia University a few months earlier as well as those in Paris and Tokyo. I was surprised at his question about the coming election of the next American president and his knowledge of the possible candidates. A few minutes later he mentioned the forthcoming anniversary of the dropping of the first atom bombs on Hiroshima and Nagasaki, adding that no Japanese would ever forget this day. This set me back a little, and I asked him what he meant by "never forget." I said that this implied two kinds of feelings; one suggested a most unforgettable day, the day of the most tragic event that ever happened in human history, and the other an everlasting hatred for what had happened to the Japanese people. I hope that he did not experience solely the second kind of feeling. I continued to expound that we modern men should have a much broader point of view of the past happenings, for our knowledge has increased with time. The wrongs which happened in the past should not be brooded over by those living in later ages, for then there would never be any peace. Mr. Yamano nodded in agreement, but he remarked that peace would take a long time to come anyway. We both laughed and then stopped to have a cold drink together. Mr. Yamano kindly offered his help to ring the inn for a car to fetch me back before he went on his way to Kyoto. A pleasant encounter!

As I was high up on Monju Hill, no sounds from the shore of the sand spit could be heard. There was an enchanted stillness in the impressive sight from the window. My mind suddenly went back to a good reproduction of an ink painting of Ama-no-hashidate by the noted Japanese artist-monk, Sesshu, in the collection of Mr. Yamanouchi Tokyoege, Tokyo. I tried to locate where Sesshu would have stood to work on his composition. He would have done the painting about 1482 when he was over sixty years of age, as most of his work was done after sixty. Though there was no signature or date on the picture, it was unmistakably his work from the names of the Buddhist temples he wrote on the painting. With those names on the work, it could be only an original sketch for a later finished work. I doubt if in those days there was any building on the site of the present Monjuso Inn. He could not have had the view of the whole scene from where I was looking at it. The long, narrow sand spit of the Floating Bridge of Heaven was lying in the foreground in an impressive position while the buildings of Nariaiji on Mt. Nariai were visible. But the entire background of hills was unclear, as they were far away in the evening mist. Sesshu must have walked around the place from the top of Mt. Nariai down to the small town at the bottom and carefully took down the name of each place he visited. He then put down the names on the sketch to remind himself later. While he was working out his sketch, those temples he visited came to his mind vividly, and unconsciously he put greater emphasis on them and Mt. Nariai in his work rather than on the long, narrow sand spit. Though Sesshu made this sketch almost five hundred years ago, the positions of the Floating Bridge of Heaven and Mt. Nariai could not have been much different from where they are today, except the lower part of Monju Hill has an established town which Sesshu's work did not suggest. If the title of the work was Ama-no-hashidate, the emphasis should be centered on the long, narrow sand spit, but Sesshu's Floating Bridge of Heaven looked rather short for a two-mile-long sand bar. He did not try to exaggerate the length of the pine-studded sand spit but added a good deal of height to Mt. Nariai, which overwhelmed its foreground. In Sesshu's day, the little red wooden bridge which joined Ama-no-hashidate to the southern shore of the little town could not have been built. But Sesshu left the gap too wide for a small red wooden bridge. It is difficult indeed to locate from where Sesshu saw his view of the scenic Ama-no-hashidate. This is not meant to be a criticism but a suggestion for a discussion of his way of composition, for in fact I have much admiration for Sesshu as one of the great painters in the history of Japanese pictorial art. Japanese publications on his works comprise more than fifty volumes. One of the most reproduced and talked about of his works is the longest piece known as *The Larger Landscape Scroll,* painted in ink with slight color on paper, 40 by 1807 centimeters, in the collection of Mr. Mori Motomichi, of Yamaguchi. It shows distinctly Sesshu's taste and training in the Chinese Ma Yüan and Hsia Kuei school of the Southern Sung dynasty (1127–1279), simply called the Ma-Hsia school. This long scroll is impressive enough for its great length. When going over it part by part I found every brush stroke, even every dot, expertly executed all the way through. Not one gave an appearance of fatigue or carelessness. He signed the scroll saying that he painted it when he was sixty-seven years of age. At that age he seemed to be full of vigor, energetic as well as meticulous in executing such a long scroll for many days or even months. Sesshu's treatment of keeping each stroke apart from every other, like the mei trees and bamboos in the first portion of his long scroll, may actually have set up a typical style for the Japanese ink painting of later periods. It is known that the influence of his art in Japan was very great and he had many followers in many periods, not only those of the Unkoku, Hasegawa, and Kano schools, who were manifest votaries of his painting, but of nearly all other schools who made it an indispensable course of their training to study him.

Sesshu's art covered a wide range of subjects—landscapes, flowers and birds, and figures. They were chiefly done in the Chinese manner of the Sung masters; even his figures were all Chinese. Most of his landscape paintings were of lofty rocky mountains, rugged and angular, as he would have seen in his year in China. But there are many interesting rocky, precipitous coastlines along Japan and Sesshu did not seem to try his hand on them. I wonder why he had only painted one Japanese scene such as Ama-no-hashidate.

It is obvious that Sesshu was much interested in the brush technique of the Chinese Ma-Hsia school. He had sometimes adopted another brush technique as shown in his small landscape scrolls. His artistic insight with the help of his great ability in manipulating his brush led to the use of the much-economized brush stroke technique of the Sung artists Yü-chien and Liang K'ai for his creation of the well-known Haboku-Sansui ("splashed ink landscape"). This is Sesshu's and Sesshu's alone. His greatness and ability enabled him to make use of his brush on many types of subjects. His Haboku-Sansui is now regarded as the best type of Zen painting. Unfortunately Sesshu did not create many of them.

Another interesting point is that although Sesshu painted all his life and adopted almost all of the Chinese forms for his works, such as the hanging scroll, the long hand scroll, and even several round-shaped or square-shaped silk fans for albums, he never painted one folding fan. The early Chinese fans were either square, hexagonal, or circular shapes of tightly stretched silk on a bamboo or thin wood frame, on which some paintings were done by well-known hands. It was not until after 1420 when a Korean court lady paid a visit to the Chinese empress in Peking holding a Japanese folding fan, that the emperor Ch'eng Tsu of Yung Lo reign took a great interest in it and told his minister to have it copied and manufactured for common use. When Sesshu spent his year in China from 1468 to 1469, the folding fan had not yet become popular, so there was no example to give Sesshu the idea to try his hand. But one or two decades later folding fans must have been extremely popular and almost everybody used them. They were not only used for the practical function of cooling oneself, but gradually many fans were adorned with interesting calligraphy and paintings by well-known artists. Almost every well-known artist in the Ming dynasty and afterward painted folding fans, such as Shen Chou (1427–1502), T'ang Yin (1470–1523), Wen Cheng-ming (1470-1559), and Ch'iu Ying (1501–1552). It is said that people carried the folding fans not only in summer but at almost any time of the year, for it had become a conversation piece. When two or more people met, if they did not know each other too well, they would ask to look at each other's fans. From the calligraphy or painting on the fans the onlookers would understand or imagine what types of friends the owners might have. I mention this in order to let people know that China did take something from Japan, contrary to the general belief that the Japanese have taken everything from China.

It was now time for dinner and the maid brought in the food with two small dishes of fish. I jokingly asked why the cook did not give me sardines, *iwashi* in Japanese, one of the very few words I had learned. She understood what I meant and laughed but with her nose and eyebrows drawn together, and shaking her head. I guessed her to mean "very cheap fish." But I tried to explain to her that I heard sardines from Ama-no-hashidate Bay were considered better and tastier than sardines caught in any other bay of Japan. I even told her that Ama-no-hashidate sardines were called kintaro iwashi. She was still laughing, but did not know what I was talking about and soon left the room. Perhaps she came from another part of Japan and never heard the story about kintaro iwashi. It was said that the Lord of Tamba, Fujiwara Yasumasa, came to spend a day with his friends boating on Ama-no-hashidate Bay and unexpectedly his favorite treasure, a gold box, dropped into the water. He immediately called all his retainers to find the gold box, who in turn summoned all the local fishermen to do the job. The fishermen did not find the gold box but caught a large quantity of sardines, which happened to be plentiful at the time. The Lord of Tamba became very angry, but the fishermen replied that he should feel satisfied to have caught so many tasty sardines which could be equal in value to that of the gold box. Since then Ama-no-hashidate sardines were known as kintaro iwashi.

As sardines breed abundantly in the Japanese sea all around the four Japanese islands, they were very cheap and common and the Japanese people became tired of eating them, so they were canned to be sold abroad everywhere in the world. I also heard that Lady Murasaki, author of *The Tale of Genji*, was very fond of eating sardines. But the sardines produced a strong smell when they were grilled. As soon as her husband smelled the sardines, he would give her a noisy rebuke for liking so cheap and common a fish. As Kyoto is not far from Ama-no-hashidate, some of the sardines which Lady Murasaki ate could have been kintaro iwashi. Japanese people still eat them at times. They have created a good excuse for the smell of the sardines, by making it a charm to drive away the devils from the house. Human beings are very clever at inventing reasons! I still feel something is missing, not having eaten any Ama-no-hashidate sardines while staying in the place.

I woke up early the next morning and like the previous day, every-where was tinted with a glowing red hue, while the sun was just about to emerge far away on the horizon of Miyazu Bay. I held my breath watching the day become brighter and brighter until the sun's rays shot into my eyes. I soon composed the following verse:

此心入仙郷　宇宙何曠潤　初日已高還　宿霧漸消散　一鳥入蒼茫　漁舟三五黙　倒影白浪翻　天橋半空言　遠近着紅裳　極目雲天外　日上宮津灣　晨興玄妙庵

Watching the sunrise on the upper floor of Monjuso inn

Morning wakes on Monju inn,
Sun rises above Miyazu Bay.
My sight goes beyond the cloudy sky,
Far and near are glowing red.
The Heavenly Bridge suspends in midair,
Reflected in the water amid the white foam.
Three or more fishing boats are here and there,
A bird flies into infinity.
The remaining mists are gradually dispersing,
The early sun is already high up.
How expansive the universe is!
My heart enters fairy land.

XXX

The Basalt Caves near Kinosaki

ON MY ARRIVAL at Kinosaki from Osaka I noticed someone with the name Mandaraya Inn on a flag, and he had come to take me there. A beautiful entrance with several green pines and small piles of rocks outside the inn gave me a graceful Japanese welcome. The whole atmosphere inside the inn was traditionally Japanese. No midday meal was provided, so I went out and found a small eating place that sold Chinese noodles and dumplings and some other Chinese dishes. After the meal I walked to the left of the inn toward some hilly ground. A small red bridge across a stream looked inviting and I stepped over to find it led to an enclosure where stood a small antique-looking shrine. On the right of the shrine, past a small stone pagoda and a statue of Mokuren, was a wide flight of stone steps, almost concealed by the thick leaves of tall trees on both sides. It gave a most mysterious impression and I wanted to find how far up it led. Step by step I went up quite a distance and felt hot and sweaty, for it was a sunny August day. I stopped to look at some of the old trees with enormous and rugged trunks. They were very paintable and I made rough sketches for future use. An inscription on a stone told me that the steps led to the Hot Spring Temple, which had been founded by the Buddhist priest Togi, who was the first to discover a hot spring in this area. When I came down to the ground level I found a way where a cable car would take me up the mountain called Mt. Kanmabe. I did not get out at the halfway stop to visit the Hot Spring Temple but continued to the summit. The views all round from such a high place were splendid and picturesque, for I could see mountain range after range as far as the Sea of Japan, where the deep blue river Maruyama flowed into it. The air was clear and soft, though the sunny haze veiled the distant range. What charm, what poetry, what beauty of color and composition! The clamor of some birds, startled at my approach, even enhanced the peace of this lovely setting. I was the only visitor there at the time. A number of curiously twisted pine trees with their outstretched branches vibrating gently in the breeze interested me very much.

I descended the mountain and returned along the same road and, passing the entrance to my inn, continued on toward the center of the city. There were few people about and most of the shopkeepers looked quite at ease. I turned right after crossing a stone bridge. At this corner stood a handsome old-type house with an entrance gate and a courtyard of fine trees. From the name Goshoyu I could tell this must be one of the six famous bath houses managed by the town council. I was told that long ago a crane with wounded legs came to Kinosaki and after standing in the hot water for some time day after day its legs were completely healed and it flew away and was seen no more. That was during the reign of Emperor Jomei in the seventh century. Since then the local council opened this bath and named it Ko-no-yu, or Crane Bath. The hot spring here is clear, colorless, and salty, good for curing gout and anemia, as well as some intestinal troubles. It has been most popular in Japan till the present day and many noted Japanese personalities have come to Kinosaki for the baths.

The Maruyama River ran through the center of the town between high stone banks, along which were planted a long row of weeping willows. Their young green tassel-like branches were now swaying gently in the breeze. Occasionally cars and bicycles went by but they did not disturb the quiet for long. There was such an easy air about the place and I felt no urge to quicken my steps. I strolled over to lean on the low wall beside the river and watched the clear flowing water. At times the reflections in the water of the swaying willows, together with the stone banks

Weeping willows on both sides of Maruyama River

and the houses on them, reminded me of the Chinese city of Soochow near Shanghai, not only because the banks of Chinese rivers and lakes are always planted with weeping willows, but the one-story houses and shops were quite similar. In my younger days I saw many women and girls in Soochow washing clothes by the river banks, but none could be seen in Kinosaki. Suddenly five young men in their summer white-and-blue-checked kimonos appeared on the other side of the low wall directly opposite me. They chattered loudly and laughed together as though they saw something interesting about the river.

While I was still looking at the river a pair of swallows darted down through the swaying willow tassels right to the water surface and then darted up again. These movements were repeated and the birds flew so swiftly as if flashing. I had not seen swallows for many, many years, since I left China to live in the big cities of Europe and America. I was so thrilled at seeing these swallows that two lines of a well-known T'ang poem came into my mind:

The what-can-I-do-with-them flowers have fallen,
The as-if-we-have-met-before swallows have
   returned.

The expression "as-if-we-have-met-before" seemed to be most appropriate for me at the time. I did not see any difference between the Chinese and Japanese swallows. Swallows came to the Chinese houses, in the country and in the cities, in order to build their nests. Those two lines convey the feelings of a lovesick person on an enervating spring day. It is warm and flower petals fly about, but the beloved one is not there to whisper to. The swallows, which have just returned, darting hither and thither busily build new nests; and they do it always in pairs. To the Chinese they symbolize love and happiness, because they always fly two together.

However, the Japanese are not so sentimental toward swallows; at any rate not the people of the Kumano District. When I was visiting the Nachi Waterfall, I walked round the Kumano-Nachi Shrine and some-one talked about the local belief that the ancestors of the swallows and sparrows used to be sisters. One day a swallow and a sparrow were play-ing together happily, far from home. Suddenly came news of their par-ents being seriously ill and both of them decided to go home to see them. But the swallow took time to make her toilet and adjust her feathers; when she got home her parents were already dead. The sparrow did not bother to beautify herself and went home straightway to see her dying parents; being so filial, the sparrow was blessed by heaven so that she always had plenty to eat, though remaining ugly. Since the swallow was vain, though she retained her beauty, she was punished by having to seek food everywhere, even eating mud. I was told that most of the children still believe this story, which has in it the moral implication to be filial.

Unexpectedly the five young men in kimonos who were leaning on the opposite wall broke into even louder laughter which woke me up from my thoughts. I left the river wall as they did. Upon reaching the end of the street, I followed the stream, which turned right to join the main body of the Maruyama River. I noticed three fishermen with long bamboo poles by the turning point. I strolled on along the bank toward the sea. A few housewives were busying themselves hanging their wash on poles for airing at the back of their houses. I reached a long bridge which stretched across the river to a grassy island, which must have had another bridge or road to join it to the mainland. All along the wooden railing of the bridge, many people stretched out their bamboo rods, fishing. Most of them wore white shirts and they could have been office workers. A combination of relaxation and pleasure together!

Though the opening to the sea was in sight, it was yet a good distance away, so I returned through a side lane to the center of the city. I agree with Shiga Naoya, who wrote the novel *Kinosaki Nite,* that there are many good places for walking in Kinosaki.

The next morning a taxi came to take me away. The driver drove all along the bank of the Maruyama River for a good distance where I had walked the previous day. The car was stopped near a boat landing where a number of people were already seated in the boat. After I had taken a seat in the bow the ferryboat started moving slowly. The width of the river at this crossing was considerable and it took about fifteen minutes to reach the other side. Walking up some stone steps, we found ourselves in front of a rocky cave of very unusual appearance, both externally and internally. It was composed of rocky formations in regular octagonal, heptagonal, hexagonal, and pentagonal shapes, as if some heavenly beings had put them together. The ceiling at the entrance to the cave was like a Japanese folding fan, huge and many-folded. The rocks that supported the cave were small and irregular. They were well divided and piled up into many perpendicular pillars of similar angles as if built of man-made bricks. Each of the pillars looked like the design on the back of a tortoise. That is why the cave was named Gembudo, or Hsüan-wu-tung in Chinese, by the Japanese Confucian scholar Shiba-

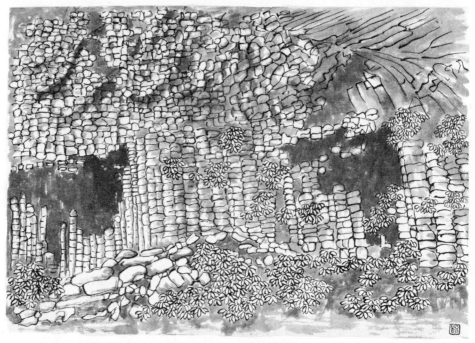

Gembudo

no-Ritsuzan when he visited this spot in 1807. He claimed it was "the strange wonder under the heaven." Hsüan-wu is an ancient Chinese name for the tortoise. Later I noticed another cave named Chu-chüeh-tung in Chinese, or Redbird cave, on the right and I went to have a look. It was similar to Gembudo but smaller, less spectacular in arrangement. I also found the third one named Ch'ing-lung-tung in Chinese, or Blue dragon cave, which was less striking still. By the side of Blue dragon cave was a small board with the name Pai-hu-tung, or White tiger cave, which did not look like a cave at all. These four names chosen by Shiba-no-Ritsuzan indicated that his Chinese studies were profound, for these four terms came from the ancient belief about the deities of the four parts of the compass: Hsüan-wu represented the north, Chu-chüeh the south, Ch'ing-lung the east, and Pai-hu the west. These four animals—the black tortoise, the red bird, the blue dragon, and the white tiger—often appeared on the designs on the back of Chinese Han mirrors.

I was told by Mr. Mitsugu Sakihara, who kindly looked up a reference for me, that the Gembudo was formed about ten thousand years ago when the magma basalt erupted in this area. In accordance with the nature of the magma basalt and the form it took in erupting, numerous central lines of congelation were created, which attracted the magma and formed the nearly hexagonal pillarlike joints. When the magma erupted and congealed on the surface, numerous kinds of gaseous matter, which had until then been contained within the magma, escaped rapidly, causing many caves to be formed as a result. The main cave Gembudo is about seventy-eight to over one hundred feet deep, and the hundreds of basalt pillars which filled it, many jet black in color, gave it an appearance not only of an enormous folding fan but also of a colossal beehive.

On the way down to the ferryboat a number of young boys and girls rushed down the steps ahead of me chattering happily. It was still very sunny and bright but not too hot owing to a gentle breeze sweeping over the river surface. The hills on our left stood there as blue as ever, and the trees and grass were green and fresh looking. They all seemed to stand upright and in great silence, watching us come and go. The breeze was so gentle it was not even able to disturb a single leaf on the trees. The following verse took shape in my mind:

The creator displays his miraculous skill every-
    where,
Those angular rocks of Gembudo reveal a magnifi-
    cent cave.
I have a word to add to the Heavenly Questions,
"Which God on what day has piled them up to-
    gether?"

The expression "T'ien Wen," or Heavenly Questions, in the third line refers to a famous Chinese anthology written in the fourth century B.C. It consists of hundreds of questions from which "we are able to gain a comprehensive picture of the world and its history as seen through the eyes of a Chinese poet living in about the fourth century B.C." This anthology has been well translated by Professor David Hawkes of Oxford University; the first few questions from his translations are as follows:

Who was there to pass down the story of the beginning of things in the remote past?

What means are there to examine what it was like before heaven above and earth below had taken shape?

How is it possible to probe into that age when the light and darkness were still undivided?

.   .   .   .

How do they originate things, and how change them?

Who planned and measured out the round shape and nine old gates of heaven?

Whose work was this, and who first made it?

The question I added was "Who had created the Gembudo Cave and when?"

XXXI

Cormorant Fishing in Gifu

THE OBJECT of my trip from Kyoto to Gifu was to see the cormorant fishing. I had had no idea that the city of Gifu was an immense commercial center as busy and noisy as Osaka or Nagoya until the taxi began to take me through one wide street after another. Cormorant fishing was one of the many sights that I loved to watch in China in my younger days. But I have been living outside of China for the past thirty odd years and no fishing of this kind could be witnessed in Europe or America. When I heard about cormorant fishing in Japan, my enthusiastic fancy was immediately aroused as well as a nostalgic longing to see it again. However, going through the modernized streets of the up-to-date Japanese city I soon became doubtful, for I remembered seeing cormorant fishing only in a secluded river or lake in China. Eventually the taxi passed over a long concrete bridge with a large crowd bathing and paddling down below and then set me down in front of the modernized Gifu Grand Hotel.

After lunch I went up to the roof of the hotel for the extensive view over a wide strip of the Nagara River and the grandeur of the mountain scenery on the opposite side, with Gifu Castle perched on Mt. Kinka. The air, though not cool, was invigorating. The clerk at the desk told me that cormorant fishing would take place right in front of the Grand Hotel starting at seven o'clock in the evening. There would be a boat to take me on the river, and I should board it one hour before. I did not know what to think but just waited for it. The sun was still very high in the sky and I went out for a walk along the river. Near the Nagara Bridge, hundreds of people were paddling and bathing along the shore. On both sides of the bridge and both banks of the river were many magnificent hotels and inns, twenty-three altogether. I learned that all these could house more than two thousand people and nearly every guest came here to see the cormorant fishing. This made me gasp, for I would never have imagined so many people would come here for such a sight.

The sun was beginning to set and the crowds who were bathing in the river disappeared. In the middle of the river a few canopied boats were moving slowly one after another as if they were chained together. The river was apparently not very deep, for the boats were moved by long poles. The boats, called *yakata-bune*, resembled the pleasure boats on the Ching-huai River in Nanking and those on the West Lake of Hangchow. The roofs of all the boats were of a grayish red color. Some of the first yakata-bunes anchored a little way up the river and the late-comers joined together to form an almost solid line in the middle of the river. Each boat carried a full load of sightseers.

It was quite dark when I followed some others aboard a boat moored very close to the river bank directly below the Grand Hotel. I found a seat on the side of the boat and saw all the other boats were lit up with hanging lanterns. Many more boats were finding their way by following the movements of the rows and rows of lanterns reflected in the water. Our boat joined them and moved further upstream when big drops of rain began to fall forcefully. The boatmen waded into the river to loosen the side curtains for our protection. They then jumped aboard and began to pole the boat along. There was an unusual noise in the air above the water, for both sides of the river were simply packed with boats and the boatmen were talking incessantly. Our boat managed to squeeze in between two others. Suddenly one of them let off a rotating firework with its sparks shooting all around, causing a roar of laughter from all nearby. Many other fireworks seemed not content just to whirl around by the boat side but shot into the air like shooting stars. A boat with two women selling fireworks came around again and again. Presently a bigger boat appeared, brilliantly lit with lanterns and carrying a number of women dancers dancing feverishly inside while four boatmen poled in the bow, making the boat swing around. This added another gay note to the whole scene and many more fireworks were let off which spun and crisscrossed on both sides amid much laughter and shouting. I never connected so much merrymaking with cormorant fishing before. Did all these displays of mirth encourage more fish to gather together and to float near the water surface to share in the merriment?

All of a sudden an even bigger commotion stirred the river surface and all the boats including ours started rocking violently. We were all dazzled by a number of enormous torches, hanging above the bows of several larger boats. The cormorant fishing had begun for all of us to see. The bright torches lit up the area around those fishing boats a distance away, farther than our eyes could discern. Here and there some black objects were moving up and down on the water with strings attached. I could hardly see a cormorant actually bring up a fish to the men on the boat. They must have caught a number, for the men were bending and stretching like puppets. Many boats were moving along with the fishing boats and our boatman stood right in the center of the river hesitating whether he should move by with the others or not. The

The cormorant fishing had begun

seven cormorant-fishing boats came down from upstream and made a turn before they reached Nagara Bridge. The rain, though still falling intermittently, did not seem to interrupt the performance. Gradually the seven brilliant torches became dim and then extinguished; so the whole show came to an end. The performance lasted about an hour or a little less.

While walking back to the hotel, a California couple asked me if I saw any fish being caught and what I thought of the whole event. My answer was negative, for it was not easy to see under the blazing light of the torches. I again said that my memory of cormorant fishing in China was not like this. They burst out laughing at hearing that even cormorant fishing in Japan had come from China. "This needn't be taken as a joke," I remonstrated. "Just think how many things America has taken over from England and Europe." Both Japan and China started to use cormorants as an easy means to catch fish in the early days. Which country first employed this method there is no record to tell. But fishing with cormorants has long been a common practice in China, for the country is full of lakes and rivers. The cormorant was found to be a

A hand-scroll of cormorant fishing by Hsia Kuei (fl. c. 1190–1230)

swift bird with very sharp eyes, which can see under water; whenever it dived in, it was sure to catch a fish in its beak. So the early Chinese fishermen put a small ring round its long neck to let it swallow small fish but trained it to release the big fish to the master. I remember once seeing a cormorant-fishing boat in Soochow when two cormorants were carrying a large fish to the boatmen, for they had found it was too heavy for one to move. Cormorant fishing is a favorite subject for Chinese artists and there is a well-known scroll of cormorant fishing by Hsia Kuei (flourished c. 1190–1230) in the collection of the National Palace Museum.

The Japanese cormorant fishing which I had just witnessed on the Nagara River is a very well-organized affair. It is beyond my comprehension that so many fine hotels should have been built along the Nagara River simply for sightseers of cormorant fishing. Usually any fish would run away when a human shadow was cast on the water. Ayu must be a fish that loves crowds and noise. I understand that the cormorant-fishing season runs only from May 11 to October 15 each year. What kind of business would all these hotels have during the off-season? Though I may be wrong, I am inclined to regard Japanese cormorant fishing as a big show business, not concerned with how much the birds could catch in an hour or two. The Japanese genius and ability for organization that created and ran such a large scale business with such success is simply admirable. The California couple agreed with me that those seven fishing boats could not have caught many fish in the hour and that the fishermen could not live on what they caught.

Lying on my bed, I read about cormorant fishing in the ancient Chronicle of Japan, how during the Enki era in 907 seventeen fishermen started the custom of presenting ayu, a kind of freshwater trout, to the emperor annually. The fish were caught with the aid of cormorants. Later the emperor pronounced that the ayu caught from Nagara River were the best among all the rivers of Japan. Thus, protected by the shoguns in each era, the cormorant fishing on the Nagara River has been continued to this day. It is said that Japanese ayu eggs are generally hatched in clear streams in the autumn and the little fish then travel down the river to the sea, living on animal plankton at the bottom of the ocean. In the early spring they swim upward to the shore and later move up to the river about May. By this time their diet changes to diaton, or rock mosses. If they live most of the early stages from very young till fully grown in the sea, they should be called sea trout; but *ayu* means "freshwater trout." It is interesting to know that most ayu mothers, having laid their eggs in September, go down to the river and die soon afterward. This is evidently why cormorant fishing in Japan generally takes place from May to October. Besides its good taste, the ayu is regarded in Japan as a lucky fish and it is always used for the New Year Festival and on other auspicious occasions. There was one great tradition in Japan about the ayu. When the first emperor Jimmu was having difficulty in pacifying the ancient tribe, Ukashi in Yamato, he desired to know if he would be victorious in his campaign. So he ordered an earthen jar full of wine to be put into a river, to act as a kind of divination and, if all the ayu should become drunk and float up to the surface, he would win over the tribe. Numerous ayu, large and small, floated to the surface of the river, and he soon had all the country under his control. Since then the Japanese have employed the design of a wine jar and floating ayu on the Banner of Banzai, which is used at the enthronement ceremony of a new emperor. The 1940 commemoration postal stamp issued to honor the celebration of the 2,600th anniversary of the founding of the Japanese nation had this design from the Banner of Banzai.

What has interested me most was the following poem written by Norigaga Motoori, a famous Japanese classical scholar of the sixteenth century:

> Nowhere but in Nagara can we see
> That antique sight of cormorant fishing,
> So picturesque and impressive,
> Bonfires reflected in the water rushing.

Basho was also known to have written the following lines:

The cormorant fishing of the Nagara River in Gifu is very popular all

over the country. True to its name, that exciting event is quite beyond
my description. I can't help feeling awfully sorry to part and heartily
wish to let my acquaintances take a look at the sight:

> After the brighest sight
> Of the cormorant fishing,
> There remains a loneliness alone,
> The gaiety diminishing.

The above poems by different poets indicate that cormorant fishing had
long been a sightseeing affair for the Japanese. It gave an insight of
Basho as a poet who would come, too, to see the interesting sight and
afterward feel lonely. His poem shows that Basho was a man who loved
company. Once I had a talk with Professor Burton Watson about
Basho's character. Burton said that many of Basho's poems expressed a
feeling similar to that of the Chinese Taoist poets in their great love of
nature. But I remarked that Basho could not have become a real
Chinese Taoist hermit, for he could not be entirely by himself. He even
had companions in his "The Narrow Road to the Deep North." Burton
agreed that very few Japanese could live by themselves.

Regarding the cormorant fishing, I once had to laugh at a remark
made by a young Japanese guide who was showing a group of twenty or
thirty Americans and Europeans around the Hall of the Great Buddha
in Todaiji Temple in Kyoto. A few of the American women were less
interested in what they were seeing than in what they could find out
from the young Japanese about the Japanese way of life. One middle-
aged lady asked if he had any household problems and the young guide
shouted in a loud voice in English that "we young Japanese men do not
want to become cormorants who have to give up every fish they catch."
Obviously none of the people in the group except me knew anything
about the cormorants. How could they visualize what a cormorant
would have to do in the fishing season in Gifu. The guide's reply meant
that a Japanese husband had to give up all his earnings to his wife!

XXXII

Takayama's Festival and Kanazawa's Lotus

A JAPANESE FRIEND thought I had come to see Takayama at the wrong time and suggested that I should have gone there to see the festival. My answer was that I did not live in Japan the whole year round. Every city in Japan holds one kind of festival or another, enough to fill the entire 365 days of the year. Most people love pageantry but the Japanese seem to love pageantry more than all. The Takayama Festival is said to be second only to the one in Kyoto; I have read somewhere a description by an Australian correspondent, Mr. Michael Conners, of the Takayama Festival, in which he writes:

> The gorgeous ceremonial floats, pulled slowly through the streets by men in feudal costumes, looked like a treasure caravan of some fabulous kingdom. Their rich gold mountings gleamed. Elaborate carvings formed splendid panels. Rare scroll paintings hung in front. Scarlet curtains screened the inside. Silken tassels swung back and forth. And the miniature shrine roof on four posts above the top of each showed that the blessing of the gods went with them. As they reached the open square before the gate of the old administrative center, you almost expected to see the curtains on the most gorgeous float of all, the one called Kinrintai, open and some potentate step down, bearing precious gifts. For these floats are no flimsy and temporary stage props but masterpieces created centuries ago. And with them the old mountain castle city of Takayama in the Japanese Alps of central Honshu relives the past every year in the Takayama Matsuri (festival). One of the grandest festivals in all Japan.

This vivid description almost made me imagine I was watching the procession. The journey from Gifu to Takayama took nearly three hours and I enjoyed the mountainous scenery as the train climbed gradually up. Villages, cities, and towns followed one another in an almost uninterrupted line. It was not a bright day for August and it began to rain heavily as I came out of the station. The taxi driver took me by a meandering route through narrow streets, along a river, and then up a hilly road for a good stretch, and finally put me down in the front of the Takayama Kanko Hotel. It was recently built in modern architecture and none of the staff seemed able to speak anything but Japanese. Soon many small dishes were spread before me and after lunch, I decided to venture out. A taxi was called to take me down to see the city. The rain was now only a drizzle. I first had a look at the open square of the old administrative center and then entered the Hachiman Shrine to see the carvings on the festival floats. The mythical winged animal at one end of the Sanboso float interested me, for its head looked like a carved Chinese dragon's head and its tail like a phoenix's. And the two children feeding a pair of cranes in one of the panels of the Kinrintai float by the Takayama sculptor Yoroku Taniguchi were like two Chinese boys in Chinese dress with their hair arranged in the Chinese manner.

Afterward I asked the taxi man to take me to the city's outskirts to see the Joganji Temple, for its origin is one of the strangest of any Buddhist temple. The present one was rebuilt on the site of an old delapidated Joganji Temple, not by the feudal daimio, nor by local wealthy merchants, nor by ardent Buddhist believers, but by a special group of women. It was said that in the late seventeenth century the chief priest of the original temple fell madly in love with a beautiful and gifted young woman of the city's "Flower and Willow area," as the Chinese would say. He spent all he had on her as well as the money contributed to the temple, so that both his fortune and the temple's were ruined. But the lady beloved by the disreputable priest had many good friends in the same quarter who felt sorry for the unfortunate couple in their plight; so they collected money among themselves to rebuild the Joganji Temple, and that is the building which is flourishing today. A most extraordinary event which one could hardly imagine happening in Japan and certainly not in China. In China a Buddhist priest or monk (or nun) is called Ch'u-chia-jen, or person who went out of home. In other words, he or she is a person no longer belonging to a family and has no family life. The Chinese term "Ch'u-chia" is a transliteration of the Indian Sanskrit "Pravraj." According to Buddhist five *sila*, or five commandments, one is not to commit adultery. It has never been possible for Chinese monks even to have an innocent conversation with a woman, nor for a Chinese woman, unaccompanied, to enter a Buddhist temple. If a Chinese monk were openly known to have a lover in the city, it would be a terrible scandal particularly in the eyes of many Confucian moralists, who would lodge the strongest protest against him to the local authority. Most of the Chinese monasteries and temples were built by orders of the emperors or from wealthy donors in the olden days but very few new ones have been built in the past hundred years or so. There is no record of a Chinese Buddhist temple being built with the money collected specially from the ladies of love.

The taxi driver next took me to see the Hida Folk Customs Museum, which displays many local historical documents as well as crafts produced locally. The old-type wooden house along the street was very interesting to look at, for it was well polished and well kept. Then we went to see a typical old farmhouse brought over to the city from a

The old-type wooden houses not far from Hida Folk Customs Museum

nearby village with thatched roof and three floors with a tiny window up in the attic, somewhat similar to an old English cottage in Devonshire and Wiltshire. Quite close to the old farmhouse were a number of shops selling gifts and local products, a type of carved wood mask, which I saw used in some Kabuki or No plays. A young man was working with a piece of wood and a chisel carving one while we watched.

Later we went through some narrow streets with beautiful wooden houses on both sides. Japan is very rich in timber and perhaps Takayama is better supplied than many other cities, for it is set in heavily wooded mountainous country. The local people make extensive use of

A young man carving a piece of wood

their wood for building houses and for carving. My attention was drawn to a red-painted bridge, over which the gorgeously decorated floats of the grand festival passed each year.

The sun never showed its face for even a moment, so there was no sunset visible. On our way back the driver drove me along the narrow road beside the river Wayi. As the car climbed the hill the surrounding scenery was even more enchanting than before, for the mist had thickened and many electric lights now winked and glittered continuously. At the hotel, the food brought to my room by two young girls included a very tasty speciality of a small mountain trout from the Kombo Trout Farm.

Immediately after the girls had taken the dishes away, the proprietor of the hotel came in and greeted me warmly with a few words in a northern dialect of Chinese. He told me that he had been in China for a year. He then told the girls to give me a special bow; they were his daughters, both of whom were in high school, and the elder almost ready for graduation. I appreciated this special act of his. He then brought out a small woodcarving as a personal gift to me and managed to make me understand that Takayama was very famous for woodcarving and that many famous sculptors had worked here. He wrote down the name "Enku," as that of the best carver in Takayama, who had left many of his works in the city.

After my host left my thoughts returned to the mask carvers in the old farmhouse quarter. I cannot help sticking to my own theory that the difference in art creations from one country to another is not in beauty or artistic value but in the techniques and mediums used. Japan is the most wooded country that I have ever found in all my travels; many kinds of trees seem to grow on the Japanese soil so easily and healthily, and the Japanese have made full use of wood in every way. They have a special technique in building houses and many fine wooden temples have stood for hundreds of years; they excel in carving many subjects, particularly Buddhist statues and likenesses of famous monks, as well as masks, and of course wood-block printings. From the abundant wood supply they have developed an ever-expanding industry in lacquer and paper products. They possess nature's gift of wood and pour out their energy to make the best use of it. Japan has comparatively few natural resources and has to rely on imports of iron and many other raw materials for shipbuilding and heavy industries. That is a modern development, but the artistic creations from their own wood is centuries old and can be regarded as one of the kernels of Japanese culture. Abundance and the cheapness of wood helped many unknown artists to eventual fame. In studying Japanese art, wood should be noted as their best medium.

I simply cannot forget Kanazawa, for within five hours I caught two wrong trains from Takayama to get there. One could miss one's train by arriving at the station one or two minutes late, but this was not my case. I simply got on the wrong train not once but twice. There is no excuse I can make, but I comfort myself with the bittersweet memory of this incident.

After a good night's sleep in the Miyako Hotel, I took a taxi to have a look at the grounds of the old Kanazawa Castle. This castle had suffered many vicissitudes and was entirely destroyed by fire in 1881. Only the castle grounds were left.

I then found my way to Kenrokuen Park, one of the three most famous gardens in Japan. The most startling sight that first caught my eye was the mass of purple irises in bloom with their green swordlike leaves, planted all along the running stream up to where an aged pine tree with its wide branches stretched all around like a natural bower. This aged tree was grown from a tiny seed brought from Karasaki on the shore of Lake Biwa near Kyoto. The irises were so well arranged they looked almost like those on the screen painting by Ogata Korin (1658–1716) in Nezu Art Gallery. I cannot help feeling that Ogata Korin must have come from time to time to contemplate the irises in Kenrokuen. Ogata devised his color scheme of the swordlike leaves in emerald green and the deep purple flowers against the golden background—a very pleasing pattern. Japan had long adopted the Chinese written language as a part of its own and it was unavoidable that they would use a similar type of brush and paper. But the way of writing and painting depends on the individual artistic insight. Screens are an important item of furniture in any Japanese house. Though the Chinese use screens too, they are usually large and tall for the main hall only, not for every room. As the Japanese use screens in many rooms of their houses, they naturally developed a new type of artistic trend for its decorative value. Therefore screen painting becomes an interesting kind of art in Japan and should be included in any study of Japanese art. The good decorative quality, brought out by the great sense of Japanese artists and craftsmen for well-proportioned composition, is the best achievement of Japanese art in general. The early Chinese Sung masters of bird and flower paintings aimed at being naturalistic to bring out the living quality of the subjects painted; the Japanese masters of bird and flower subjects also aimed at being naturalistic but emphasized their decorative quality. To invest a subject with living quality means that it cannot be set in patterns. This may be considered as one of the differences between Chinese and Japanese paintings. With this innate decorative sense the Japanese naturally established their way of living in a sort of pattern, having a decorative value of its own.

The Kenrokuen Park was constructed on the old site of the Marquis Maeda's mansion and it was reconstructed in the Kanei era (1624–1643) by the daimio of the time. The name Kenroku indicates that the garden has six prominent features: (1) vastness, for it covers an area of twenty-two acres; (2) solemnity; (3) careful arrangement; (4) venerability; (5) coolness induced by running water; and (6) charm of scenery. It has three artificial hills and two ponds— Kasumi-ga-ike and Kisago-ike. The water from the latter descends in a waterfall, and on the opposite side is a little arbor called the Yugao-tei, said to have been designed by Kobori Enshu (1579–1637), a famous master of tea ceremony and of garden design in his time. I saw a gardener punting a small boat with a long pole through the few willows along the bank. The reflection of all surroundings in the water was tantalizing. The celebrated stone lantern known as Kotoji-no-toro was also reflected as clearly as I saw it on the bank. In the garden there is a tree called Kikuzakura, or chrysanthemum tree, actually a cherry, so named because its flowers have two or three petals together like a chrysanthemum flower. But I could not find it, perhaps because it was past its blossoming season.

After having walked over to the celebrated stone lantern, I came upon a large group of people gazing at the conspicuous bronze statue of Prince Yamato-takeru (82–113). It was said that when this prince was full grown, his stature reached ten feet and his body was stout and his limbs of immense size. He could have dispersed the misconception about all Japanese being small in body.

I now strolled back to the interesting arbor, in which there was a light behind the paper-covered lattice window, which looked unusual for a garden scene. A snow white swan came gliding by on the water. A little distance away a number of tall pine trees seemed to be caged in some cone-shaped structures made of yellow plastic cords. I was told that these were to protect the pines from heavy snows. Kanazawa is situated in the north of Japan's island of Honshu and there can be heavy snow in winter. I have never seen tall pines protected in this manner elsewhere in Japan.

A sign indicating the Ishikawa Prefecture Museum caught my eye and I wasted no time in entering. While paying the admission fee, to my great surprise I noticed inside a glass case some postcards for sale, one of which was a painting of the West Lake of Hangchow in Chekiang Province by the Japanese monk-painter Sesshu (1420–1506). I bought one and asked where I could see the original of the painting. The girl attendant told me that it was not on show at the moment. I tried hard to make her understand that I had come a long way, from America, and would like to take this opportunity to see it. She telephoned to the main office three times but nothing could be done. I was very disappointed, for this is the one painting that has never been reproduced in the many books on Sesshu's work published in Japan and the Western world. As far as I could judge from the postcard, the brush strokes, the ink treatment, and the composition were definitely by Sesshu's hand. Sesshu spent a year in China from 1467 to 1468 and first landed at Hangchow, spending six months in Chekiang Province before he went up north to Peking. This painting of the West Lake could have been one of the first paintings he did in China and could be dated the latter part of 1467. However, this painting of West Lake did not give me an impression that Sesshu had made any sketch of the scene on the spot. He composed the painting from what he saw in his head. He put the two famous peaks—the Northern High Peak and the Southern High Peak—much too close to one another and seemed to have dwarfed the whole place with the lake much too small in size. I could not find a record that the long banks built by Po Chü-i and also by Su Tung-p'o were made of bricks as Sesshu painted. Nevertheless, I wish I could have seen the original for a careful examination.

From the museum I went to the nearby Shinto shrine of Kanazawa-jinsha at the south corner of the garden. A rather big rock with an ox's head carved on it had a nice shape as a whole and I soon made a rough sketch of it. Quite close to the Shinto shrine was the Seison-kaku, a two-story Japanese structure said to have been erected as the residence of the wife of one of the daimio of Kanazawa. The building was noted for its fine architecture and Emperor Meiji and the present emperor Hirohito had both been here. Both emperors' photographs were hung on the wall.

Returning to the hotel for dinner, I had a talk with the clerk at the desk who could speak some English. I told him that I had seen some good pieces of Kutani porcelains and also some Kanazawa lacquerware, the principal industries of the city. But he replied that Kanazawa silk textiles, metal foils, and weaving machines were also major products here.

I saw much lotus growing outside of Kanazawa so I wrote to Kanazawa Municipal Office about it. After a good while a most interesting letter came to me from Mr. Isamu Matsuhira, officer, General Affairs Section, Kanazawa Municipal Office, as follows:

> The lotus roots have been cultivated mainly at Kosaka District in the suburbs of Kanazawa. The soil suitable for the lotus roots is found at the place, which can be plowed deeply in the damp rice field. Both the *Ishikawa Prefecture Chronicle* and *Kahoku County Chronicle* tell us that the first lotus-cultivated place is in and around Kosaka District of the northern suburbs of Kanazawa. There were two conditions necessary for cultivation of the lotus roots in the feudal age. First, it needed a place where the natural fertilizers such as sewage, garbage, or dirt were always thrown and abundant, and secondly it had to be the specific rice field where the rice bore almost no crop only to grow higher needlessly owing to scarce sunlight, located for a rice field to be permitted for cultivation of the lotus roots because in the feudal days growing other than rice was prohibited. As a place meeting with these two conditions, the damp rice field district around Ohimachi area was chosen and cultivated as the first place of the lotus root production. It is said that this cultivation has since moved and expanded to the adjacent Kosaka District and formed the present production area.
>
> Lotus flowers, as mentioned in the history, were used in the old days for offering to the Buddha as the flower symbolizing Buddhism, and they are still used now for the same purpose and also for appreciation. . . .
>
> Lotus roots were used as food in old times by the temples and some upper-class military families, but along with the increase of the demand, plant breedings have been made with introduction of new kinds. And now the roots, used as food in side dishes, are one of the principal vegetables produced in Kanazawa.
>
> Nowadays, the lotus roots are cultivated by groups of farmers on a wholesale business basis. They form the lotus roots production associations to do sale at the market.

Mr. Isamu Matsuhira also added that "in comparison with the income of the rice production, the lotus roots cultivation in the same rice field area can increase the proceeds by at least double to four times at the most. Also, lotus growing has an attractiveness in that the cultivation can be made at a poor rice field where no increase of rice harvest is expected." It is extremely interesting that from my casual look at the many lotus ponds on my way to Kanazawa, I now know that lotus roots can be traded on a wholesale business basis. And I was even more interested to know that in the Japanese feudal days no other crop besides rice was allowed to be cultivated. This must be due to the limited cultivating area that Japan has.

A carved dreaming ox

XXXIII

Lacquerware in Wajima

THE JNR's EXPRESS train took me from Kanazawa to Wajima on Noto Peninsula and I reached the Hosenkaku Inn in the still bright light of late afternoon. Mr. Masaaki Nakaguchi, the proprietor of the inn, received me with a broad smile, speaking some English. I wanted to see the evening market and he suggested taking me there in his car. The market was held in the front court of Sumiyoshi Shrine, one of the important Shinto shrines in Japan. Most of the goods, chiefly vegetables, fruits, and fish, were displayed in baskets, on low wooden stands, or on the ground and the sellers were nearly all women. They all had white or colored handkerchiefs wrapped around their heads and some of them were chopping the fish and even cooking them on the spot for the customers who ate there too. I thought the Japanese preferred eating fish raw, but this was not always so. I was told that this was one of the few evening markets still remaining in Japan. I wondered why people should

Evening market in Sumiyoshi Shrine

Massive boulders by Tsukumo Bay

flock here to buy things in the evening, though they could get most of the stuff in the shops on the main streets. Sumiyoshi Shrine has been in existence in Wajima for the past three hundred years. Mr. Nakaguchi thought the evening markets, or *Amamachi* in Japanese, probably went back about three hundred years too, though there was no exact date on their origin. Later Mr. Nakaguchi motored me to see the seacoast at Tsukumo Bay, where massive big boulders looked like a group of lions lying there enjoying the sea breeze. A legend tells that some three hundred years ago, a very powerful warrior named Uesugi Kenshin launched an attack on this part of the coast. The fishermen of the area put on masks representing ghosts and devils of hell and appeared to the accompaniment of drums and so frightened the invaders that they were driven from gaining control of the Noto area. A new road along the coast to the tip of Noto Peninsula was pointed out to me, which was specially built when the present emperor Hirohito came on a tour inspecting industries in 1958. A row of fishermen's houses was later shown to me. Fishing is one of the industries of Wajima and the fishermen are divided into two groups; one, the native born, the other, men from Kyushu. Though they were divided, they never had any friction over their work.

It is a rare case that a proprietor of an inn or hotel would take so much interest in his customers as Mr. Nakaguchi. One of the interesting

Evening market

things he did for me was to take me to the famous Inachu Lacquer Company. Miss Toshiko Inagaki received us graciously, offering us tea and, as a present for me, two pairs of chopsticks, products of the company. Many of the company's fine products were displayed in glass cases and on the walls. Most were articles for daily life, such as small boxes, flower vases, baskets, eating and drinking bowls, trays of different sizes, and various types of low tables. All of them were beautifully varnished in pleasing forms with good taste. A number of large lacquer panels on the walls attracted my attention greatly. They were in the modern manner with abstract and even cubist and nonobjective designs. Miss Inagaki remarked that since about 1935 a few designers had tried out modern abstract designs on their lacquer work and after the war, since about 1950, the lacquer workers in Wajima did not want their products to be left behind the times and took up modern abstract designs. "The lacquerware of Wajima," Miss Inagaki said, "has a tradition of almost eight hundred years. We recognize the great merit of the past and follow the tradition with what we can do in our modern achievement. We have been trying to improve our work year by year in order to produce new and interesting designs which will be in harmony with the already established shapes and color schemes. We were formerly handicapped by selling our wares with the old shapes and old designs and using the old methods. But now we can compete with many others."

While we were talking, the owner of the Inachu Lacquer Company came in and was introduced to me. He had been working for this company for more than forty years and looked very contented with the result. I was told there were about fifty people working here, but it was about dusk and too late for us to see them at work. The modern abstract designs on the few large panels were smoothly worked, but not by brush. However, this Western invasion is limited to the designs, and the shapes or forms of the Japanese bowls, vases, trays, tools, baskets, boxes, and cabinets all remain typically Japanese. Miss Inagaki later gave me a printed circular about the general historical development of Wajima's lacquerware with the additional remarks: "Wajima's lacquerware became famous because the Wajima lacquer works possessed a special technique and produced the best eating and drinking utensils for daily life. The land of Wajima has a special soil that is rich in silicon, which is most useful for lacquer production because of its absorbent and adhesive qualities. The workmanship of Wajima's lacquer is best from the fact that it does not peel readily."

Mr. Saburo Egami wrote me the following:

It is believed that the lacquer trees were first transplanted to Japan from China; however, the date is unknown. The legend says that in the middle of the third century Prince Yamato Takeruno-Mikoto discovered a clump of lacquer trees in Akiyama, Yamato, now in the Nara Prefecture. The pieces of lacquer work which seem to have been produced in the late Jomon period were unearthed in the Tohoku area.

During the period when Buddhism first flourished in Japan the art of making lacquerware developed rapidly, especially after the Asuka period (A.D. 552–645).

After the promulgation of the code of laws known as the Taiho Ritsuryo in A.D. 720, the farmers in the country were ordered to grow lacquer trees. Then, the cultivation of lacquer trees was carried on throughout the country under government patronage. Today, the lacquer trees grow more in Tohoku and Hokkaido than other areas.

Lacquerware is produced in various places in Japan. Wajima ware, one of the famous wares, is noted for its solid quality made by using a special base powder called Wajima base powder. For decoration the chinkin (sunken gold) is often applied with beautiful result.

It is told that one of the priests of the Negoroji Temple in Wakayama, which is famous as the cradle of the Negoro-nuri ware, came to Wajima in the early part of the fifteenth century and introduced the art of making the lacquerware to the people of Wajima.

Wajima ware is widely used for table utensils in daily use because it is durable and resists dampness.

I suppose the Wajima base powder to be the special Wajima soil rich in silicon that Miss Inagaki mentioned. I am interested in this connection with the local soil though I do not know whether any Chinese soil is rich in silicon or not. Actually the lacquer tree has long been known in China. The sap of this tree, *Rhus verniciferas*, may be used in its natural state after the removal of impurities and excessive moisture. The tree is very much like the poison oak and is indigenous to China. My friend Dr. Teh-k'un Cheng, reader in Far Eastern Art and Archaeology in the University of Cambridge, England, and author of eight volumes of *Archaeology in China*, wrote:

> The Chinese lacquer is a peculiar material. The sap is grayish white and about the consistency of treacle or molasses. On exposure to the air it turns yellowish brown and finally black. After being strained through a sheet of hempen cloth to remove the impurities, it is stirred gently to give the required uniform fluidity. It is then heated over a very low fire or in the sun and stirred again to evaporate the excess moisture. The liquid is finally stored in an air-tight vessel for use. It has a mysterious property, known as lacqueral, which is responsible for the fact that it sets hard in moisture. In its fluid form it is weak and easily acted on by a small quantity of salt, vinegar, oil or the weakest acid, but when hardened, it is insoluble in all solvents and becomes most resistant to salt and strong acid and can be preserved underground and in water for thousands of years. It is insulator of both heat and electricity. It is a convenient material to handle, for it can be worked for as long as it is necessary and will not harden until it is subject to moisture. Although it is a slightly irritant poison, workers in the industry soon become immune to it. The use of this mysterious tree sap that hardens with moisture and changes into a substance of great hardness and durability was a marvelous discovery.

Nevertheless, no record of the first discovery of this material and of its property is known in the long history of China. From archaeological excavations, it has been learned that lacquered objects were quite common in the Shang-Yin era (1523 B.C.–c. 1028 B.C.). They became more popular after the beginning of the Chou era (c. 1027 B.C.–256 B.C.), particularly in the Warring States period (403 B.C.–221 B.C.). Much of the lacquerware of the Warring States period, bearing many interesting natural and geometric designs, has been recently excavated. Lacquerware was carried to its highest peak in the Sung (A.D. 960–1279) and Ming (1368–1644) periods. There are two types of Chinese lacquer work, one with painted designs and the other with chiseled or engraved ones. The Japanese lacquerware on the whole have designs painted by brush or embossed and they show very fine workmanship. Though the Chinese first discovered the lacquer trees, which were later transplanted to Japan, the Japanese have continuously improved their technique while the Chinese stuck to the traditional method. Several Chinese lacquer workers from Chekiang Province went to learn lacquering in Japan in the later sixteenth century, particularly two brothers of a Ch'en family, who brought the technique back and started a fashion of Japanese-type lacquering in China. This was a good case of mutual exchange.

The next morning was finer than the day I arrived. I asked Mr. Nakaguchi if I could get to Hekurajima Island, which was so conspicuous standing off the extremity of the Noto Peninsula. It is an island 3.7 miles in circumference, completely uninhabited; it seems to have been directly connected with the mainland by a long sandy bar. Mr. Nakaguchi told me that it took a four-hour ferry trip to go there from Wajima, but the season for the ferry had not yet begun. Every summer about seven hundred families, fishing folk from Wajima, would go over there to gather shellfish and seaweed for making jelly. They carry out a definite system with schoolmasters, priests, and physicians, as well as police, and they work there for the summer months and return home in the beginning of autumn. Their forefathers must have found the summer months to be good for the gathering of shellfish and seaweed there. I was interested in the sense of system of these Wajima families in going there summer after summer.

Later Mr. Nakaguchi booked a taxi to take me around to a number of places nearby. First the driver took me to see the morning market, where many vendors spread their goods on the pavements in front of some shops—not so interesting as the evening market. After a look along the street where fishing families lived, I asked the driver to take me to see an ancient temple, Sojiji-Betsuin Temple, though I had no idea how far away it was, nor did I know anything about it. The road seemed endless and the scenery varied village after village, mountain after mountain, rice field after rice field. The sun was bright and the air

Entrance of Sojiji-Betsuin Temple

balmy. At long last an impressive temple gate of two stories beyond a red-painted bridge came in sight and I was surprised to see so few visitors at this important national treasure place. No sooner had this thought crossed my mind than a heavily loaded bus arrived at the entrance. None of the occupants looked foreign but were all Japanese. I could not follow them because they had a Japanese guide, so I strolled slowly here and there and found the architecture of the temples, all in wood, was similar to the temple Enkyoji on Mt. Shosha near Himeji. According to the printed information this temple was built in 1321, as the headquarters of the Sodo sect of Zen Buddhism, ranking with Eiheiji Temple in Fukui. In 1898, this temple burned down and the headquarters was moved to Tsuruni in Yokohama City. Then the present temple became the branch temple of Sojiji in Yokohama. The unpainted wooden architecture in the midst of many fine, old pine trees with their glossy dark green needles under the bright sunshine breathed an unusual quietness. In the center of the main hall I saw three statues: in the middle Sakyamuni, on the right Bodhidharma, and on the left Bodhisattva. This was the first time that I saw Bodhidharma placed in the main trinity arrangement. The transmitting lamp hall was one of the few original buildings that remained intact after the fire which the temple suffered in 1898. I closely examined a statue inside the Hall of the Scripture, for it looked so different from any other statue that I had seen in Japanese Buddhist temples. The statue had his hair clustered together on the top of his head with a small pin going through it and wore a red-lacquered robe and had some whiskers on a face like a Chinese Taoist deity. Though many people wrote that the Japanese had taken Confucianism and Ch'an Buddhism from China, little was said concerning Chinese Taoism, whether philosophy or religion. This red-robed Taoist deity in the Sodo temple astonished me greatly. Professor Yoshito Hakeda, an expert on Japanese Buddhism, once told me that the Sodo sect is one of the most popular in Japan, for it teaches Zen Buddhism and has a large following of Japanese farmers, while the Rinzai sect has followers among the samurai and scholars. The Sodo Zen had incorporated many local and native beliefs. This is probably why it had a statue dressed in a red robe. I could not help feeling amused by this new find in Japan. This recalls to my mind Basusennin (Vasu), one of the twenty-eight spirits subordinated to Kwannon, in Sanjusangendo in Kyoto. In Chinese pronunciation Basusennin is Po-su-hsien-jen, and its last two characters "hsien-jen" mean "an immortal in Chinese Taoist paradise." The statue is labeled as a hermit and looked like an Indian holy man. Except for the Chinese Pu-tai-ho-shang, who became Japanese Hotei Osho, and the Chinese Star of Longevity, or Shou-hsing, who became Japanese Jurojin, as I discussed in the chapter on Kamakura, very few other Chinese

Inside the Hall of the Scripture

The temple ground of Sojiji-Betsuin

native deities came to Japan. I was also interested to find that a wooden statue of Sheng-lung, Chinese originator of agriculture and medicine from time immemorial, in a small Gyokanji temple not far from Doga-shima on Izu Peninsula was worshiped with much incense burning by the local people. To my knowledge, nowhere in China was Sheng-lung carved as a wooden statue to be worshiped.

Tsukumo Bay

XXXIV

Bon Odori on Sado Island

AT KANAZAWA station I changed to a train for Niigata. The countryside scenery gradually became a seascape by the time Naoetsu was reached, where many people were bathing by a pebbly shore. As soon as it reached Niigata I caught a taxi for the Ryotsu Ferry, which was packed with people. There were no fixed seats for passengers on the boat and I followed the crowd into a large room fitted with tatami to the very edges of the room. Nearly every space was occupied and most people were either sitting or lying down. A great opportunity for life study, I thought. I looked around in the hope of finding somewhere to squeeze in. After a while I succeeded and managed to lay my body between two young men. Much talking and gossiping went on and on. A few people stood up, moving in and out to buy drinks and things to eat. The whole atmosphere was amicable and pleasant with no shouting, as if everybody belonged to one big family.

Upon reaching Ryotsu Bay I noticed a man holding a small flag with the words "Hagetu Hotel," which was where I was going to spend the night, and he soon conducted me there. No one in the hotel could understand me but I managed to make an arrangement for a bus trip to the other side of Sado Island the following day.

In the early morning I found the hotel was backed by Lake Kamo—a most placid stretch of water with a clear reflection of the majestic peaks of the Kimpoku Range to the north. There were a large number of fishing boats lying in the middle of the lake in complete stillness. Yet some movement was visible on one of the short lines; it was a fisherman who seemed to adjust his fishing net there in the distance. Presently a bird flew up from one of the boats toward the mountainside. It did not look like a crow nor a wild duck, for it had a longish body as well as a long neck; when it was against the grayish blue mountain its body looked white. Could it be a Japanese crested ibis? I wondered; if so, I could be regarded as very lucky to have seen it, for this heronlike bird of the Japanese species is only found on Sado Island and only about a dozen of them remain. They are considered a special national treasure.

When I was dining with a few Japanese friends in Tokyo I mentioned that I would be going to see Sado Island, and they told me that it was a romantic place in Japanese history full of well-known exiles and a home of the Okesa ballad songs. I was told that the channel between Sado and the west coast of Japan could be very rough and choppy, except in the summer. No one knows when the Japanese people began to populate the island, but a legend relates that the first travellers to Sado were a fox and a badger, who transformed themselves into an umbrella and a pair of slippers and then attached themselves to a human traveller to make the crossing to the island. "Well, the human traveller must be regarded as the first one, too," I remarked and all laughed. Our conversation soon concentrated on foxes and badgers. I told my friends that from my earliest childhood I had heard stories concerning ghosts or spirits and foxes, but I never heard a story about the badger in China.

One of my friends told me that the emperor Juntoku (1197–1242), who attempted to overthrow the Kamakura shogunate but was defeated by the regent Yoshitoki Hojo, was exiled to Sado. I found no parallel in the history of China. Another famous exile on Sado, I was told, was the

An ancient pure-land temple near Hagetu Hotel

great Buddhist priest Nichiren, who foretold the coming of the kamikaze, or divine wind, to shatter the Mongolian fleets under Kublai Khan, who invaded Japan in the thirteenth century, as I mentioned in the chapter on the Mongols and Hakata.

Remembering these stories, I set out from Kamo Lake to find how I could get to see the unhewn-timber palace at Izumi, but there was not enough time to go before I had to catch the bus for Aikawa. I took myself for a good walk along the main street, up one side and down the other, making a purchase of a small dish supposed to be the famous local product of red porcelain called Mumyoi-Yaki.

A man from the Hagetu Hotel directed me to the bus for Aikawa, some twenty-six miles away from Ryotsu. After leaving Ryotsu the bus moved up a continuous succession of gradually ascending slopes, rather narrow and perilous with rocky outcrops. From a prominent point I looked back on the country the bus had traversed. Multitudinous clouds spun out in feathery softness, mingled with innumerable hilltops. Presently a simple squarish-looking building called Hakuunso, or White-cloud ranch, on the top of Mt. Kimpoku was reached, where food could be had and local gifts were for sale. It was a beautiful spot and I only wished the building could have been more artistic and perhaps in typical Japanese style to enhance its surroundings. It was a hostel where one could spend the night at a very reasonable price. White clouds had gradually engulfed all the surroundings with only a few yards of land visible. The summer morning air on a peak a thousand feet above the sea was extremely fresh and invigorating, even in the clouds. I suddenly remembered the hut on Mt. Kimpoku where Nichiren had stayed, but no one, not even the bus conductor, could tell me where it was.

On our way down, the bus stopped by a small group of houses. They were the local museum, containing the relics of gold and silver mines which had been worked there. I learned that the gold mine had been discovered in 1601. After having seen the gold mine and the museum, the bus ride down was as full of interesting sights and surprises as had been the ascent.

All the way along the mountain road many pine trees and bamboos grew abundantly. There were many small camellia trees, too, for which

Rocks round Senkakuwan Bay

Sado is famous. Shortly we came to a big open ground where many busses had drawn up. We all got down to embark on a small steamer which cruises round Senkakuwan Bay. The bay water was deep indigo blue against the brownish or orange white rocky islets dotting the coast-line. As the boat steamed along steadily, one beautiful scene succeeded another. Occasionally a hawk emerged to circle in the air. Sometimes it flapped along and passed over us without even noticing us. Nothing seemed to be growing on those rocky islets, unlike those in Matsushima Bay. When the sun illuminated them every precipitous part and crag showed up and the water became azure and the sky above looked pale. Later the steamer passed close to the shore and moved through a big gap between two rather large islands, one of which was joined to the mainland. Both were linked together by a suspension bridge. We could hear some chattering high above! Apparently some people were standing there to gaze at the bay. While returning, the steamer moved close to the shore and we could see a number of rocky caves, one of which had a

A maid welcoming guests to Hotel Osado

semicircular entrance where the water continued to rush in and out. Another cave was guarded by two high steep rocks standing on either side, like pillars for a gate.

Meoto-iwa

After we landed, the bus took us to a nearby rocky beach, Nanaura Kaigan, where two big rocks stood out among a large number of small ones. These two rocks were called Meoto-iwa, or husband and wife rocks. All looked like ancient lava that had erupted from a nearby volcano years ago. I had already seen a famous pair of wedded rocks not far from Hiroshima and could not help wondering why the Japanese loved to call two rocks standing together husband and wife. Nobody could give me the reason.

Finally the bus stopped near the porch of the Hotel Osado to let me off. I was the only one to alight, but shortly afterward two fully loaded busses arrived and soon a large crowd streamed inside to fill the lobby. After a good bath in a hot spring, I went outdoors to the observation platform in the hotel grounds. Not far from the platform a long wooden pole stuck in the ground carried the notice "The Monument of the Hara-kiri Suicide of Ooka Genzaburo." No one could tell me the meaning of this, but later on Miss Matsu Nishino, introduced to me through a friend, wrote to tell me the following:

After the Sekigahara battle, many daimio (chiefs of castles) were discarded, and so the number of lordless samurai grew. There were no more battles, so they had no position and nothing to do; they flocked to the capital of Edo and lived in poverty. At the time of the death of Iyemitsu and when the Iyetsuna became the shogun, both lordless Shosetsu Yui and Chuya Marubashi planned to rebel together with many other lordless samurai. Chuya aimed at taking Edo and Shosetsu, becoming the head of the rebellion, was set to attack Sunpu and then Kyoto and Osaka in 1651 (Keian 4th). Unfortunately their secret leaked out and Chuya was caught at Hongo, Edo, and Shosetsu at Sunpu [now Shizuoka], where he committed suicide. This was called the Keian Case, the biggest event in the Edo period. Gen'emon Ooka and his elder son Genzaburo had a training center in the capital, for they were noted as great spear experts. The father loaned the map of the compound of the Edo Castle to Shosetsu and Chuya, and for this act they were exiled to Sado. In those days exiled people were permitted to make a living any way they could. So the father and son opened the spear training quarter at Suwamachi, Aikawa of Sado, and called their Marubashi system with many pupils. Among them were mountain workers, mountain chiefs as well as land officers, etc. But the young Genzaburo was an ambitious person and could not stand the dull teaching life for long, so he committed hara-kiri on the spot where the wooden pole stood. His father soon also died from illness.

There are many famous exiles in Japanese history. Both Oki and Sado islands were well-known places for exiles. Both islands were not easy to get to owing to their being in a choppy sea, hard to cross in those early days. As mentioned before, Oki Island received the two emperors, Go-Toba and Go-Daigo, within a hundred years. Sado Island still has the Kuroki Gosho, or unhewn-timber palace at Izumi, where the banished emperor Juntoku lived for twenty-two years. I was told his tomb was at Mano on the Ryotsu side, where a Mano Shrine stood nearby. Not far from the shrine was the Myosenji Temple, in which the exiled Hino Suketomo, a courtier of the emperor Go-Daigo (1288–1339), was buried when he was executed by the governor. Hino Suketomo's son was not allowed to see his father before the execution but in the end the son managed to kill the governor and escape from the island. Later came the Ooka father and son.

It is interesting how common was the practice of exile as a form of punishment in the early history of almost every country in the world. All countries tried to send their unwanted persons to remote and inaccessible places where life was not easy. But nowadays there is not a place which is not accessible.

Among all the visitors staying in the Hotel Osado, I was the only one who could not speak Japanese. While I was having difficulty in finding answers to my questions, a young man walked up to the desk in order to help. He could speak some English and we managed to make ourselves understood to some extent. I learned that there were two parallel mountain chains, one on the northwest of Sado Island where Mt. Kimpoku, about four thousand feet high, was the highest peak, and the other on the southeast. In between the two was a flat plateau where the soil was very fertile and good for growing rice. He told me that the quantity of rice produced each year, apart from being of the best quality, was not only sufficient to feed all on the island but much was shipped to other places on the Japanese mainland. There is an interesting story about how rice started to be grown on Sado Island, though no exact date was known. Hundreds of years ago a young boy of Shikoku Island went fishing with his stepfather in a small boat. They met an unusually heavy storm, were tossed and blown adrift for many days and eventually grounded on one of the beaches of Sado Island. The boy's mother had died and his stepfather never showed any love for him. As soon as the storm ceased, the stepfather sent the boy into the hills to gather some firewood for cooking. When he returned with a bundle of broken branches, his stepfather had set off in the boat and disappeared. Obviously the boy was abandoned on purpose, but he did not realize it. So he raised his voice and for hours shouted for his stepfather to come back but by dusk there was no sign of the boat. The boy wept hard, longing for his mother and became terrified when darkness came. He decided to kill himself by jumping into the sea. He was about to take off his clothes when he felt some grains which had been sewn inside the sleeves by his mother, who had told him to sow them in case he was in difficulty about making a living. This caused hope in his mind and he soon started to tear off the sleeves for the grains and resolved to plant them on the ground where he was standing. He looked after the rice plants with great care, the first crops were good and his method soon spread to all who lived on the island. The boy's name was Sansuke and a shrine was built for him at Matsugasaki on the island, where he is worshiped till the present day. Young children are universally known to be badly treated by their stepmothers, but Sansuke's treatment by his stepfather must be a rare case. However, it proved to be the good fortune of all the islanders!

Though Sado Island is only 330 square miles in area, it produces a number of distinctive things. Apart from the best quality rice, and the toki, or Japanese crested ibis, as mentioned before, the sea around the island is full of fish called tai, or sea bream, which the Japanese believe to be the best and noblest fish, and it is used on all festive occasions. Sado Island also produces the tanuki, an animal that resembles a fox though much smaller in size. It has short legs and cannot run very well or fast. Many people on the island keep them as pets and there are many stories about them. Camellias also grow abundantly on Sado Island and a very interesting story about them was told me.

Once upon a time there were two peddlers of Echigo Province on the Inland Sea who together sold their goods from house to house. On a hot day they felt tired after their midday meal and rested by the roadside. One of them fell asleep and the other kept watching his sleeping companion with interest. To his surprise he saw a horsefly dart out of his companion's nostril toward Sado Island and then fly back into his nostril again. Afterward the sleeper woke up and told his companion about a strange dream he had had. He had gone to see a beautiful garden belonging to a rich man on Sado Island, where many white camellias were in full bloom. A horsefly flew out from the roots of those white camellias and told him that he should dig round the roots and he would soon find an earthen jar full of gold coins. The other peddler listened to this dream intently and asked the dreamer to sell him his dream. A contract of the transaction was successfully concluded. Later they went home each taking his own way. The one who bought the dream went to Sado Island without telling his companion and sought service as a gardener with the rich man who owned the camellias. He got the job and waited for the camellias to bloom in the spring. But all the camellias that came into flower were red, not a single one was white. So he patiently waited for another year's blooms. Indeed, all the camellias were white the next spring. Again he waited patiently till the night fell and then went into the garden and dug the ground under the camellia trees, where he found the large earthen jar filled with gold coins. He then hid the jar and continued his work as gardener for another six months before he asked to return home. He eventually became a rich man on Echigo. What a lucky idea to have bought the dream!

After supper nearly everyone in the hotel changed into a kimono provided by the hotel as if all were in a kind of uniform for some special purpose. I felt sorry that I was the only one to be different, not that I did not care to change, but I had difficulty in walking with clogs. I was then invited to join the rest for a bus ride to a local theater where a series of typical local dances would be performed. The young man who could speak some English came to sit by me in the bus, explaining to me that this was the season for the Bon dance and Sado Islanders were particularly good at this dance. The theater was small and cozy. Many seats were already occupied but everyone from our bus, including myself, found a place also. The young man sat by my side and kept telling me to watch the graceful movement of the hands, arms, and legs of each dancer while he raised his own hands to give a demonstration. I appreciated his help and friendliness. He then told me that all the dancers on the stage were men, and that the song the musician sang was the famous Okesa ballad. After a pause a new dance and new song were presented. The difference between one dance and another as well as from one song to another must be very subtle, for I could not easily distinguish between them. On returning to the hotel, I found a squarish wooden structure in the center of the hotel grounds with many lanterns lit up all around. Many people were already dancing around the structure while music played through a loudspeaker. I was urged to join the dance but could not, so the young man went in himself. Though the Bon festival has its origin from Indian Buddhism, no one knows whether it came to China as a Buddhist All Souls'. It must then have been introduced to Japan from China via Korea. It has gradually become a merrymaking holiday for all Japanese.

Bon dance at the hotel grounds

XXXV

Mito and Chu Shun-shui of Ming China

SOMETIME IN 1954, when I started teaching at Columbia University, I had the great pleasure of meeting Dr. Daisetz T. Suzuki for the second time in New York. Our first meeting was at the London School of Oriental and African Studies in 1936 where I was then teaching. We were living quite close to one another in adjoining blocks. I used to visit Dr. Suzuki for some talk on Zen terminology in Chinese characters and he once gave me a book called *Jugyuzu*, or *Ten Oxen Pictures*, which had ten poems each attached to a picture, written and drawn by Chu Shun-shui (1600–1682). This book was published by Shindo Kaikan in the eleventh year of the Showa reign with a brief biographical account of Chu Shun-shui at the end, whom I came to know as a great Chinese scholar who spent nearly twenty-five of his eighty-two years in Japan. Later I read an account of Chu Shun-shui written by Dr. Shunzo Saka-maki in *Eminent Chinese of the Ch'ing Period*. Recently I read a book in Chinese entitled *Chu Shun-shui*, written by my friend Kuo Yuan of Taiwan. I had wondered why I did not know of this scholar before and why so little had been written about him in China, though I must have missed what Liang Chi-chao wrote about him in his *Yin-ping Shih Wen-chi* in 1915. Chu Shun-shui was unknown to the Chinese for more than two hundred years. For all I read about Chu Shun-shui he was known in Japan as a Confucian scholar. His calligraphy and drawings for the book *Jugyuzu* seemed to be the work of what was for him a mere hobby, for his association with Zen Buddhism was not mentioned any-where else.

While I was travelling in Japan for the third time I decided to pay homage to his grave at Mito. On a fine morning after having reached Mito by train I took a taxi to the Kikuya Hotel—a beautifully quiet spot with a small garden and tiny stream flowing underneath a red-painted bridge, which just fitted into the space left between the lounge and the other hotel rooms. The ingenuity of the Japanese in making use of any small space for an arrangement of trees and rocks in a miniature style is admirable. The manager of the hotel was most helpful and planned care-fully my trip to Zuiryusan after lunch. First he sent a person to take me to the bus stop for Hitachi-Ota, who in turn asked two young girls at the bus stop to tell me where to get a taxi for my destination at Hitachi-Ota. All worked out well. The road to Zuiryusan was flat and rather dusty with little traffic; on both sides there were crops about to turn yellow, for it was near the end of July.

Mr. Nishino, keeper of the Tokugawa family cemetery, was waiting for me at the main entrance. We greeted each other with a bow but no words. Mr. Nishino then led me through a well-shaded footpath with tall trees, centuries old, on both sides. The stillness of the summer afternoon, with sunshine penetrating through the leaves from above while some cicadas chirped their song incessantly, was a great contrast to the hustle and bustle of Tokyo. Making a turn to the left, I saw some ivylike creepers spreading their green leaves over the rocky surface of the lower slope of the hill. Between the clusters of green leaves emerged some reddish wildflowers with their petals half unfolded as if smiling. Soon a squarish enclosure appeared at the bottom of the hill and Mr. Nishino went to open the wooden gate to let me in. In the center of the enclosure was a cone-shaped tomb behind a three-foot-tall stone tablet bearing seven Chinese characters "Ming Chen-chun-tzu Chu Tzu Mu," or Tomb of Mr. Chu—a scholar gentleman of Ming, written by the Prince of Mito, Tokugawa Mitsukuni (1628–1700), the great patron of Chu

Tomb of Mr. Chu

DAITO, OR GREAT PAGODA, KOYASAN

THE SCENIC SPOT OF AMA-NO-HASHIDATE

Shun-shui during his years in Japan. I stood and bowed slowly in front of the tablet. Having moved round the enclosure, I was surprised at its cleanliness and made a gesture about it. Mr. Nishino understood and nodded with pride. Then he led me back toward the house, where I found a small wooden shrine with a carved wooden statue of Chu Shun-shui, wearing a Ming style cap and robe. It did not seem to have been the work of a master carver, so I doubted its likeness. However, I again made a bow to the statue before I sketched it roughly. It was a pity neither Mr. Nishino spoke English nor I Japanese, or I could have found out something of the history of the place, at least in the Tokugawa days. I read that Lord Mitsukuni retired to Zuiryusan to devote his time to writing the great Japanese history, or *Dai Nihon Shi,* as well as establishing the Mito school of thought in Japan. It is said that he followed the Chinese tradition and made a will which provided for an annual ceremonial service at Chu Shun-shui's tomb, which still takes place each year round the Chinese Ch'ing-ming Festival time—a time when the Chinese would take their families to visit their ancestral tombs with the customary offerings of food and paper money. It is amazing that this ceremony has been carried on since 1682.

Chu Shun-shui was born in the declining period of the Ming dynasty. At forty his great learning and ability became known to the court but he refused to serve with all the other wrongdoing ministers. His ambition was to restore power to the ruling emperor of the Ming house at the time, so he travelled to Annam, Siam, and Japan to seek possible military help but to no avail. The Ming house was already falling into Manchurian hands. He then returned to Japan to live in Nagasaki in 1659. In 1665, after repeated invitations from Lord Mitsukuni to serve on his historical commission, he accepted and stayed in Mito until his death in 1682. He did request to be allowed to resign and return to Nagasaki when he reached seventy years of age, but the leave was not given. Lord Mitsukuni treated Chu with greatest respect and revered him in the highest degree according to Confucius's code of rites. But it needed Mitsukuni's sincerity and loyalty to put Chu's teaching into practice. And it is really amazing that his loyalty to Chu should be preserved till the present day, as I had witnessed at Chu's tomb.

Apart from his staunch loyalty to the house of Ming, I admire Chu Shun-shui for his all-round scholarship. As Dr. Shunzo Sakamaki wrote in *Eminent Chinese of the Ch'ing Period*:

> Besides discussing history, philosophy, poetry, and politics with the Prince, he drew plans and made models of stone bridges and mausolea, wrote inscriptions on tombs and bells, made patterns of Chinese court dresses and sample costumes worn by different classes of Chinese people during the Ming dynasty. At Mitsukuni's request he

prepared in 1670 a detailed description of the Confucian State worship of China, together with wooden models of Confucian temples, schools and ceremonial utensils. In 1672, under Chu's instruction, the spring and autumn ceremonies to Confucius were first carried out in Japan.

Thus Chu was not merely a scholar just reading books and pondering their contents but he kept his eyes wide open to learn everything he could. From memory he could work out plans for buildings, design dresses, and make models for utensils. It is known that he designed the Koishikawa Korakuen Gardens in Tokyo and that the Confucian temple near Ochanomizu was built from his model. How could he have learned so much to be an architect, a dress designer, a model maker, potter, and also a ritual performer in his years in China before he arrived in Japan for the sixth time in 1659? Few Chinese scholars nowadays know much beyond the single subject they specialize in.

After having seen the small wooden shrine, a young lady, presumably Mr. Nishino's daughter, produced tea and local-made cakes. Then Mr. Nishino bade me good-by at the main entrance and I was soon driven back to Hitachi-Ota to catch a bus for the city. The sun was still high in a blue sky and I found my way to the site of Mito Castle, which was almost destroyed during the conflict at the 1868 Restoration and again by an air raid in 1945. The castle was not rebuilt.

Later I visited Mito Park to have a look round the well-known educational institution, the Kodokan—a building established by Tokugawa Nariaki (1800–1860) and the headquarters of the Mito school of thought of Japan. There is a well-kept library with many old editions of Japanese books. Behind the Kodokan, two shrines were pointed out, one dedicated to Kashima-Myojin, who represents Japanese military culture, and the other to Confucius for civil culture. It clearly indicates that Mitoism is a combination of military and civil cultures.

A taxi also took me to Tokiwa Park, or Kairakuen—one of the three most celebrated gardens in Japan. Originally it was designed for Nariaki, ninth Lord of Mito, as a retreat from the cares of office, but after his death it became a public park. It covers a large piece of ground and is reputed to have ten thousand ume trees. Kairakuen Garden, unlike Korakuen in Okayama or Kenrokuen in Kanazawa, has little sign of being artificially planned but relies chiefly on the natural formation of the land. There is an unusual naturalness in it as a whole; that is its charm.

I came to a cottage called Kobuntei, where Lord Nariaki used to gather men of letters for parties to compose poems. Before I left the garden I waited for a while by a big stone called Togykusen which has a beautiful meaning in Chinese, t'u-yü-chüan, which means "Spring of

spilling jade." A big hole was cut out of the stone to let the water gush
out from time to time. I was told that the stone was set up when the
Kairakuen Garden was built to provide cool drinking water which
sprang naturally from underground. The water did not gush out while I
was there.

After supper I lay in bed trying to revisualize what I saw in Mito. I
must say that it is interesting to see how the Confucian political theory
of China worked even better there than in China. This must be due to
the Japanese historical conventions and the social and geographical conditions of the land. Japan is less than one-fiftieth the size of China and
her people live with a system more easily controlled. But in the old days
China was too vast to exercise an effective system of control. That is
why China suffered dynastic revolutions from time to time. Government
in Japan by a powerful man, such as Tokugawa Bakufu, was "essentially
a military government which ruled by virtue of sheer force rather than
by a universally recognized right of sovereignty," as Professor Herschel
Webb told me. But they kept the Japanese emperor or empress still as
their legitimate head. Herschel also explained to me the Japanese
expression "Sonno Keifu," meaning "Revere the emperor, respect
Bakufu." Chinese Confucian theory comes into the first part of the
expression, while China never had a *Bakufu*—really powerful man—to
enforce the second part. Since the Second World War Japan has adopted
a democratic system.

Carved statue of Mr. Chu

XXXVI

Date's Sendai and Basho's Matsushima

AFTER SETTLING down in the Sendai Hotel for lunch, I telephoned Mr. Tamakake of Tohoku University. He is the assistant of Professor Ishida, Director of the Institute of Japanese Thought, who has written much about the society of the Tokugawa period and the connection with the Chinese Chu Hsi school of neo-Confucianism, and who was then working in Germany. When I arrived at Mr. Tamakake's office, he took me to the Department of Japanese Literature where seven scholars including two women proceeded to give me the names of Japanese writers and poets who were natives of Sendai, such as Shimazaki Toson, who published a collection of his poems, *Wakanashu*, or *Young Herbs Collection*; Tokutomi Roka, whose work *Yadorigi*, or *The wood with its parasites* is well known; Mayama Seika, whose novel *Minami Koizumimura* is highly recommended; and Doi Bansui. None of these works have been translated into English or Chinese. Owing to my inability to speak Japanese and as none of the scholars could speak English, we conversed through kanji writings, rather unsatisfactorily.

Mr. Tamakake had specially kept this afternoon free to show me round Sendai and I was touched by his kindness. At first we went to the site of the old Sendai Castle high up on a hill called Aoba, or Greenleaf, so the castle was also named Aoba-jo, or Green-leaf Castle. The castle, originally built in 1600, was no more except for a small part of its foundations, for it was completely destroyed by bombs in 1944. However it has an interesting history. Masamune Date (1566–1636) was born the heir of a petty chieftain. At eighteen he displayed his heroic spirit in avenging the assassination of his father. Gradually he asserted his power over the border warriors and became the most powerful daimio in the northeast of Japan, in deviation from the supremacy of Toyotomi Hideyoshi. Later he had to submit to Hideyoshi at Odawara in 1590. However, Hideyoshi was a shrewd warrior-statesman and did not pursue his personal grudge. Date even accompanied Hideyoshi on the conquest of Korea. Eventually Date was granted the whole territory with the castle as his residence. When the second Tokugawa shogun persecuted Christian converts at Edo, Date asked for the release of the

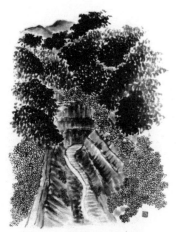

The river Hirosegawa far
down below

Franciscan, Padre F. Luis Sotelo, from whom he learned about the outside world. His interest in Christianity increased and it was at this time that he began to send his own ambassador to Spain and Rome. It could have been due to his personal interest that there have been a good number of Christian churches in the Sendai area till the present day. Though Date even gave permission to Sotelo to preach in his territory during the persecution days, the latter was executed at Nagasaki in 1624. Date did not die until twelve years later: why did he not try to save Sotelo's life?

Presently Mr. Tamakake called my attention to a stone monument with a Japanese poem or song written in beautiful hiragana engraved on it. He explained that this was the famous poem, "Moon over the Ruined Castle," written by Doi Bansui shortly after World War II.

We had to walk down a good way, for there was no bus or taxi, and came to a stone bridge over the river Hirosegawa. It was very high above the deep gorge. The bridge had red-painted railings on both sides and was quite conspicuous in the area surrounded by massive woods and hills. Mr. Tamakake exclaimed that this bridge was known as the Suicide Bridge of Sendai. I asked, "Do you mean this is a bridge where life ends or the life-ending bridge?" He nodded and continued, "Many have jumped over the railings to die here." I supposed that people would not come to die in the same way nowadays. Mr. Tamakake broke into a smile, saying that only a few months ago a man rode here in a taxi to jump down into the river. Actually there was no water in the river when we looked at it.

Still finding no taxi, we walked down to the main road. I told my companion that I saw a stone statue of a lady called Masaoka in the Shogakuji Temple in Meguro, Tokyo, who, I was told, was connected with Sendai. Mr. Tamakake nodded and said that this concerned a very popular classical Japanese play. The characters in this play had been performed by many famous actors. Lady Masaoka, or Sendai-Hagi or Bush-clover of Sendai, was a very loyal person who took the young son of Lord Date into her care and protected the boy in every way possible against the sinister plots of his father's enemy to kill him in order to overthrow the clan. She gave the boy no food but what she had cooked herself. She also taught her own son Senmatsu to be loyal to the prince, even to die for him. One day another lady of the court, who sided with the enemy, brought some sweets as a gift from the shogun to the prince. Though Lady Masaoka tried hard to prevent the prince from eating them, the other court lady pressed her not to act against the wish of the shogun, who was higher in position. Just at the critical moment her own son, Senmatsu, came to snatch the sweets and gulped them all down at once. The guilty lady and her attendants feared the plot would be dis-

Monument of Lord Date at
Sendai Castle

covered and tried to stab Senmatsu, but he had already died. Lady Masaoka clasped the cold body of her own son, praying for the safe passage of his spirit to heaven, for he had died a noble death.

Next Mr. Tamakake took me to see the famous Osaki Hachiman Shrine created by the great architect Gongen Zukusi. It was built in 1606 and is now counted as one of the most important cultural properties of Japan. We had to climb up a large number of stone steps. Unfortunately the shrine was being repainted and was covered with scaffolding so I could not get a view of it as a whole.

In the evening Mrs. Ishida and Mr. Tamakake came to dine with me on some Chinese dishes at the hotel. Mrs. Ishida told me that Sendai was often called Mori No Miyako, which means a "Metropolis of Woods," for there are many dense groves of trees on the surrounding hills. I also learned that on the night of January 14, all the pine trees and straw festoons used in the New Year decorations of most city houses would be brought together and piled in the courtyard of the Osaki Hachiman Shrine to be lit into a big bonfire, which was a most spectacular event and attracted a large crowd.

It was raining before I left Sendai and it rained still harder as I reached Matsushima. A heavy mist lay over the tall pine trees in front of the Park Hotel, where I was to stay. My eyes felt heavy and I thought what a dark and dull morning I had chosen to come to see one of the three most-renowned scenic spots of Japan. The mysterious look of the bay water seemed to call me out for a look despite the wet weather. As I came to the hall, the manager of the hotel greeted me in English, for he had done some work with the American army directly after the war. He kindly offered to take me out for a drive. A generous gesture could hardly be refused, so I got into his car and up a muddy, hilly road we went. He wanted to show me where Basho used to sit and gaze at the distant north where lies a strange little island called Kinkazan, or Gold Flower Island. Basho regarded it as an isolated paradise because the glittering yellowish mica that powdered the rocky face of the island looked like a cluster of gold flowers. Unfortunately everything was engulfed in dense fog and rain. The manager kept apologizing to me for the unexpected raw weather and insisted that it was not always like this in August. On our way down the hill, he observed that it was Basho who had made Matsushima even more famous and that in his kind of business he felt grateful to Basho. I wish Basho could have heard this! A poet's work does not always enter the head of a hotel manager.

Back at the hotel the manager gave me a colored umbrella and directions for a walk to see the old Zuinganji Temple founded in 828 and belonging to the Myoshinji school of the Rinzai sect of Zen Buddhism. At the entrance I found a large group of Japanese men and women, some in kimonos, each holding an umbrella rather like mine but in a different color. I soon realized that each hotel had a stock of umbrellas made for their guests' use and that rain must not be a rare visitor to this area. Inside the entrance two rows of tall upright Japanese cryptomeria trees lined the central path, looking serene and antique. Following the crowd walking through the main avenue, I noticed on the left a rather large stone tablet and left the crowd to go there to examine the design. It was a copy of a drawing of Kwannon by the T'ang master, Wu Tao-tzu, copied by a local artist, Denji Koike. There are two big, old mei trees, one on each side of the Nakamon, or central gate, with the respective names "red dragon mei" and "white dragon mei," for one must have white flowers and the other red.

I rejoined the other visitors to walk through the Kondo (Main Hall), and the Kairo (galleries), and the Peacock Room where I saw an interesting carved wood portrait of Lord Date, who had only one eye. He lost the other eye in one of his early campaigns. The temple was reconstructed by Lord Date in 1609 after the original building was destroyed by fire. Another good portrait in wood was of Heishiro, the lord abbot of the temple. Over the door was a woodcarving of a tiger among bamboos and on the window was one of a squirrel among grapes, both works by the famous carver, Hidari Jingoro. Later we came to a corridor with many blue tablets on each side of a wooden statue of Kwannon, on which a number of names of retainers were inscribed, for they all committed hara-kiri when their Lord Date died. This Japanese custom, com-

Caves inside the main entrance of Zuinganji Temple

mitting suicide by hara-kiri, is unique in the history of mankind. In many ancient cultures, such as the Egyptians and Assyrians, the servants or closest relations were buried alive with their dead rulers. In Confucius's days the Chinese began to carve wooden effigies for burial with the dead instead of real men; Confucius even did not agree to this, for he condemned harshly the inhuman practice of burying persons alive. Hara-kiri illustrates the Japanese conception of personal devotion and faith. It is not practiced now, I was told.

I returned to the tall cryptomeria avenue outside the central gate. On the left were many caves, dug out of the rocks, some of two stories. All were yellow and darkened from the burning of incense. It was said that they had been carved out for the wandering priests to stay in and meditate. I thought they might be similar to the Chinese Buddhist grottoes, such as the Lung Men or the Yün Kang caves in north China. But when I moved near them, I found they were shallow, both large and small, with one or two roughly carved Buddha-like figures here and there. I felt rather disappointed. However, though not old, there was a small statue, a beautifully carved Kwannon in granite seated on a rock not far from the central gate, of which I made a sketch. Then I came to the last and biggest cave near the main entrance to the bay and I learned that it was called Hosshin-kutsu, or Hosshin's Cave, for it was here that the abbot Hosshin used to sit for long meditation after he returned from China in the thirteenth century. Before Hosshin was appointed the abbot to the Zuinganji Temple, something interesting happened here. In this big cave there was a poorly carved bust of a Buddha set on a large stone, underneath which was said to have been deposited the hair of Hojo Tokiyori of Kamakura, who, though a former regent of the Kamakura shogunate and later a Zen priest, was not allowed to spend a night in the temple when he visited it, for at that time this temple belonged to the Tendai sect. So he spent the hours of darkness inside this cave. Upon his return to Kamakura he persuaded his successor, the new regent, to convert this temple to the Zen sect. Therefore, Hosshin was appointed the abbot of this temple. This episode interested me because I had never heard of any Buddhist monks being turned away from any monastery despite their belonging to different sects; as a rule in China any Buddhist monastery would provide shelter and food to any wandering monk.

Coming out of the Zuinganji Temple, I walked straight to the bay, where a large steamboat was moored. It was still raining hard and many groups of people were strolling about under different-colored umbrellas. A very unusual sight for me. I bought a ticket and went on board the boat, which presently moved away from the shore. The raindrops hit the window very hard. Nothing came in sight and there was a wild wind howling outside. Gradually a number of faint gray masses were floating

Carved Kwannon in granite

Matushima in rain

toward us and becoming darker with each moment. Some young children jumped down from their seats and shouted, "Shima, shima!"
("Island, island!"). A commotion started and all the youngsters jostled
against each other to get close to the front windows. I opened the door
and stood outside to face the lashing of the rain. Oh, how vigorous and
noisy were the raindrops that came to play with me! Fortunately it was
not a cold time of the year. I could not see the shapes of the different
islands distinctly.

Shortly the boat reached Shiogama and I realized my mistake in getting on the boat which was not for cruising round the bay. Many people
got off and ran in the rain for a bus which had just stopped by the main
road. I was the only one left in the empty shelter by the shore and felt
helpless. A few minutes later an elderly fellow approached me and I
showed him a map and indicated the Shiogama Shrine that I wanted to
see before returning to Matsushima. He seemed to understand what I
meant and ran off without hesitation. After ten minutes or so, he beckoned me to where he was standing in the rain, for he had found someone with a van who was willing to take me for the trip. There were no

Matsushima from Kanrantai

other visitors at Shiogama Shrine. This was the only empty shrine I visited. Nor did it look like a place much visited by sightseers. I ran up a few flights of stairs and made a good round of the place. Afterward I returned to Matsushima in the van.

The rain now stopped; it was fresh, with no wind; cool for an August afternoon, but not cold. My next activity was to take myself to the front yard of Kanrantai, or Wave-viewing House, built on the top of a rocky hill right above the bay. The building was said to have been a gift from Toyotomi Hideyoshi of Osaka Castle to Lord Date near the end of the sixteenth century. There was a famous screen, painted by Kano Sanraku (1559–1635), used only by members of the imperial family when visiting Matsushima. A young woman who was cleaning the floor advised me to stand in the center of the building for a good view. It was a picturesque confusion of pine trees and many islands in the distance. I then proceeded to the local museum. A poem on Matsushima by the English poet Edmund Blunden was written on a wall in large print, together with its Japanese translation; also a number of other poems in kanji by various Japanese poets. All gave the highest praise to the beauty of this noted scenic spot. In a number of glass cases were many colorful shells found on the shores of Matsushima.

Afterward I crossed over a red-painted bridge, called Togetsu-kyo, or Moon-crossing Bridge, which joined the mainland to Oshima Island. Passing through a few caves chiseled out of the rocks, I came out on a promontory. A youth of sixteen or seventeen was sitting on a wooden bench gazing at the water intently. I asked if he knew where the Basho monument was. It was on this island, Oshima, that Basho landed for the first time when he came to see Matsushima and I knew a monument had been erected to him here. The youth led me down a few steps and showed me not only the large stone with Basho's writing engraved on it, but many other stones engraved with the writings of other poets. The boy went back to his seat and I continued my walk along the footpath for a round of the island.

The following passage, taken from *The Narrow Road to the Deep North*, written by Basho, translated by Nobuyuki Yuasa, gives the poet's impression of that beautiful complex of islands.

After two miles or so on the sea, I landed on the sandy beach of Ojima (Oshima) Island. Much praise had already been lavished upon the wonders of the islands of Matsushima. Yet if further praise is possible, I would like to say that here is the most beautiful spot in the whole country of Japan, and that the beauty of these islands is not the least inferior to the beauty of Lake Dotei (Tungting Hu) or Lake Seiko (West Lake) in China. The islands are situated in a bay about three miles wide in every direction and open to the sea through a narrow mouth on the southeast side. Just as the river Sekko (Chien-t'ang River) in China is made full at each swell of the tide, so is this bay filled with the brimming water of the ocean, and innumerable islands are scattered over it from one end to the other. Tall islands point to the sky and level ones prostrate themselves before the surges of water. Islands are piled above islands, and islands are joined to islands, so that they look exactly like parents caressing their children or walking with them arm in arm. The pines are of the freshest green, and their branches are curved in exquisite lines, bent by the wind constantly blowing through them. Indeed, the beauty of the entire scene can only be compared to the most divinely endowed of feminine countenances, for who else could have created such beauty but the great god of nature himself? My pen strove in vain to equal the superb creation of divine artifice.

Basho may have read much about Tungting Hu, West Lake, and Chien-t'ang River in Chinese or in Japanese, but I don't think he had actually seen these three places which he alluded to in his description of Matsushima, for he was not known to have visited China. I know Tungting Hu—an immense lake far inland in central China, which is so big that standing on one side one is unable to see the opposite shore. There are only a few islands in that lake but they are not grouped so closely together as the islands in Matsushima.

Having seen the Basho monument, I went up to where I had first found the youth and there he was, still gazing at the bay. I remarked to him that he must be very fond of the sea. He understood and tried hard to answer me in English, but though he scratched his head again and again, he could not get out the right words. So he jumped up and took off his woolen jacket to show me the back of his shirt which had four

Godaigo Temple

words in English: Sendai Fukai Yacht Club. He then asked me to follow
him to the garage where his boat was kept, and there he made as if to
take his boat out and invite me for a ride with him. His friendly and
kind thought overwhelmed me, but it was rather late in the day, so I
thanked him and said good-by. He repeated the words with a big smile.

The next day I woke up to see the sun shining on me with all its
might. Directly after breakfast I walked along the bay shore up to
Godaigo Islet for a look at the small temple surrounded by many pine
trees; it was joined to the mainland by two short red-painted bridges.
Near the first bridge there was a middle-aged peddler with a basket full
of hermit crabs, which crawled all over the container, and a wooden
tank full of small green-shelled turtles for sale. I had never seen a hermit
crab before, which looked most comic, for it did not have a shelter of its
own but carried a snail shell on its back after having eaten the snail
inside. It looked neither a snail nor a crab, but walked like the hunch-
back of Notre Dame. I then went to the top of Godaigo and had a deep
breath of the fresh morning sea air. Having seen a bigger island called
Fukushima joined to the mainland by a long red bridge, I hurried down
there. I paid a small charge to walk over to the big island. Numerous tall
pine trees grew healthily all over Fukushima and the air was extraordinarily fresh and stimulating. The sun's rays penetrated through the long
pine needles as if they had been singled out by most skillful jade carvers
and made into emerald-jade needles. Following the footpath right down
to the edge of the island I was surprised to find a young couple already
there enjoying the morning glory of Matsushima Bay. A few other
islands are quite close to Fukushima on the side where I was standing
and I felt that I could even count the pine trees on each of them. How
beautiful and sublime they looked with their stately brownish trunks and

their fresh green needles blending with the opalescent waters of the bay and the delicate blue of the sky!

After a simple lunch at a small restaurant I decided to take a motor-boat cruise around the islands in the bay. There was a strong wind over the surface and I was sitting in a small motorboat while the boatman tried to show how fast the little engine could go. At first I felt myself greatly agitated by the swinging movement of the boat and was unable to fix my eyes on the various islands that passed by so quickly; later it seemed to me that it was the islands themselves that rushed ahead one after another. Many of the islands were quite small.

Presently I asked the boatman to slow the speed of the boat, but he did not understand. However, he steered the boat so as to give me a closer look at Yoroishima, Kabuto-shima, Futago-shima, and a few others before we passed through the open arch of Zaimoku-shima. The boatman told me the names but I found it difficult to catch his words clearly. He also told me that there were several hundred islands on the bay and that many of them were so close to one another that there would be no room for two boats to pass one another between them. Nearly every one of the islands had some interesting pine trees growing on them. A few islands had only a single pine standing on the edge of the rock in a most picturesque pose. Three of the islands caught my fancy more than others. Juniri-shima means "twelve consorts of the emperor," for it has twelve nicely shaped pines lined up in a row on the top of it. They were not of the same height, just like twelve different beauties parading together. Next came Nio-shima, which means "the god-guardian Nio," standing on the top of a tipped-up pedestal on guard against any unlawful happening over the whole bay. The third was Horai-shima; "Horai," or "Peng-lai" in Chinese, which has long been described in early Chinese literature as an imaginary, mysterious paradise lying somewhere in the eastern China Sea—a Chinese utopia where the inhabitants are all fairies or immortals free from any human entanglements and also free from the daily necessities for life, such as eating and drinking, and free from illness. Most Chinese had longed to find this place to live ever since the early days of Chinese history.

Someone on the road told me that I could get a much better view of all the islands from the top of Mt. Tomi-yama. I immediately took a taxi up Tomi-yama, or Rich Mountain. I got as far as the Daigyoji Temple, which was founded by the priest Dosui between the years of 1661 and 1673. The fine view of the whole Matsushima Bay outside the temple entrance attracted me so strongly that I forgot to go inside for a look. Indeed, it was a most impressive and unforgettable sight, having all the islands in view. Another footpath by the temple side led me to the summit. I drew a deep breath, telling myself how lucky I was to see so much and so beautiful a panorama in so short a stay. I could not forget

Basho while in Matsushima and wondered if he, in the sixteenth century, had been where I was now. The whole Matsushima Bay now became a sizable lake with large and small dark gray patches here and there in the center under the clearest and bluest sky. Suddenly the sun had lowered itself like a crimson disk hanging in the air to warm everybody near and far. No, it was not a disk but a red ball which someone had kicked into the air and which bounced onto several of the islands in the bay and gradually sank lower and lower. It was eventually lost to sight. What glorious moments I had watching the sun's ball spinning slowly while I held my breath tightly. Nature was a great artist to have produced such a splendid effect. How beautiful, how mild and soft, how harmonious, how rich! Had Basho ever seen this exquisite display of nature up Tomi-yama some three hundred years ago? I wondered.

Dinner tasted unusually good that evening. I went up to my room for a rest in bed. Before I knew it, two hours later the bright moon was shining through the window. I became restless, for I never like to miss anything in my travels. I got up about nine o'clock and walked over the little red-painted bridge to the Godaigo Temple. Nobody was there at that hour of the night and the whole ground seemed to belong to me. I moved round the little temple in order to get the best site to gaze at the moon. The moon was waning, though its clear light was still powerful enough to light up the neighboring islands and water. I was standing between tall pine trees with their lovely shaped trunks and their boughs constantly swaying gently in the evening breeze. There was a vibrating image of a not-too-round moon reflected in the water. The unusual, perfect silence of this tiny islet, the cold silvery light of the moon, contrasting with the broad shadows across the buildings on the bay shore, all combined to make the scene romantic and impressive. Suddenly I remembered the poem "Chinese Moon Festival," written by Po Chü-i, which ends with the line: "This night the pure light is stronger here." I borrowed this line to open my little verse as follows:

今夜清光此處多
我遊松島幸如何
五大堂前涼似水
雙松月下影婆娑

Tonight this place enjoys more of the pure light.
How lucky has been my journey to Matsushima!
Standing before Godaigo in the evening cool as water,
A pair of tall pines share my joy dancing happily under the moon!

Again, I asked myself if Basho had enjoyed a moonlit night on Godaigo as I did then?

My friend and colleague Professor Arthur Danto described his feeling about Basho as follows:

When I think of him [Basho], what comes characteristically to mind is the marvelous advice he gave a fellow poet: do not follow in the footsteps of the masters—seek what they sought. This statement has the qualities of the poetry it has generated: quiet, condensed, of a diamantine clarity and chill power, a silent exposition of sudden comprehension. There is only artistic nirvana, but very many paths to reach it by. One may arrive only on one's own path, so each must eke out his own artistic salvation, though salvation is the same for all. So one's own person is logically complicated in the attainment of an art which extrudes individuality completely, and one finds oneself just to the degree that he loses himself. Basho, as a man, lived in that space between personality and its obliteration in oneness with reality, not quite in the world but not quite out of it either; like a bat, as he wryly put it, neither mouse nor bird, but a hybrid transitional creature *between* states of being. I am always moved by his travel writings. These are emblems of his restlessness in being. He always sets forth with the sense and perhaps the hope of finality, not intending to return, seeking some ultimate escape only to find that escaping as such is its own fulfillment, salvation consisting in the attempt to find it, more than in any state one might have believed it led to. So one transcends reality precisely by remaining in it; which is a deep teaching of Zen; and reality, all the while remaining what it is, is spiritualized and intensified, rotated back onto itself through some special dimension. Perhaps never completely back onto itself. There is always enough discrepancy to feed his restlessness, driving him out again and into another journey. And at critical points, he fuses with the masters; in an act of poetry (and poetry is at once action and substance, as his theory requires), pausing before some celebrated views or a famous tree which one of his predecessors had lifted into art before, and which he had to reclaim for his own art, and bring into a new unity with himself and the art of the past. The travels are artistic and religious pilgrimages, but Basho is always *sec*, a mixture of irony and faith, shrewd and witty, with a kind of crooked saintliness, aware of his limits as only one who has found beyond them could be. His life is one of the exemplary lives, one I would like to have lived. But we must not follow the footsteps of the masters if we are to find what they sought.

Arthur Danto has been a professor of philosophy for many years and author of many books on philosophy. I must admit that I have not studied Basho as Arthur did. What has interested me chiefly in Basho is his extremely economical use of words to express a profound thought in his haiku. This is his great achievement and no other haiku poet was ever able to surpass him. I don't know if Basho would be regarded as one of the originators of haiku in Japan, but his haiku have actually raised Japanese poetry to world appreciation. His great follower Buson, a poet as well as a painter, emphasized the importance of the haiku poet's standing above worldly matters in order to avoid vulgarization of the haiku. I have not been able to read much of Buson's poems, for very few of them were translated into English. However, this is one translated by R. H. Blyth:

> Coming out of the box,
> This pair of dolls,
> How could I forget their faces?

In Buson's landscape painting he followed Sesshu in some ways, but his work was far from reaching the standard of Sesshu's. He did not even dare to try the *Haboku* style.

The rules of haiku must be strictly complied with, only seventeen syllables in each poem, and the poet must have the ability to select words in the most concentrated way. Basho's ingenuity was in daring to say what others would not say and also paradoxically to turn what people most commonly say into a poem, for instance:

> O! Matsushima!
> O! O! Matsushima, O!
> O! Matsushima!

Whoever came to see Matsushima, his first words might easily be "O! Matsushima!" Basho repeated this three times and added two more "O's" to make the poem into exactly seventeen syllables. Several Western poets discarded this poem as absurd. Of course, they could write this type of childish poem themselves, but it was Basho who started to write it first. Matsushima's beauty is really beyond words' description, let alone a few words with so limited a number of syllables. If one tried to write in the same way about the other two Japanese special beauty spots—Itsukushima or Ama-no-hashidate—in a poem of only seventeen syllables, a good result would not be easily achieved. Basho's poem on Matsushima has its greatness in the sound and feeling within the narrow restriction. A good poem gains much of its beauty from the feeling of the words conveyed by their actual sound, not obviously from their meaning. It just so happens that only *Matsushima* fitted into the number of syllables for the haiku. Basho did not make another attempt to write a similar poem.

XXXVII

Lake Towada and Jesus

I CAUGHT AN early train from Morioka station for Towada-Minami, then
changed to a bus for Lake Towada. After about an hour's drive the bus
stopped at Hakka Pass and all the passengers got down to have a look at
the scenery of the lake down below. Upon arriving at Wainai, I was the
only one to get off the bus. I took my handbags and walked toward the
village, which consisted of only a few houses, and showed my card at
the local inn. The maid in the main hall cleaning the tatami could not
understand me. A young man then came in and pointed out to me that
this was not the inn I had booked for my stay and telephoned for a car
to come to take me to the Towada Hotel. It was a rather long ride. The
road rose gradually until the car stopped at the porch of the hotel. It was
situated on a prominent mound beside a slope of the mountain and
faced a part of the lake with no buildings nearby. The manager could
speak some English and he provided me with a Western lunch. Afterward he called the hotel car to take me down to Yasumiya for a boat
trip on the lake.

There were a good many buildings in Yasumiya, most of which were
gift shops and eating places, a number of Japanese inns and a small
museum too. I found my way to the boat for the trip to Nenokuchi. The
sun had gone behind the clouds, but it was bright enough to see everything all round. Lake Towada is said to be the largest crater lake in
Japan and has been compared with the famous Crater Lake in America.
All around the lake shore were healthy woodlands with two promonto-

Rocks along Nakayama Peninsula

ries, Nakayama Peninsula and Mikura Peninsula, dividing the lake into three parts: East Lake, Central Lake, and West Lake. The motorboat started from East Lake, rounded first Nakayama Peninsula and then Mikura Peninsula, and passed many interesting rocky islands along the way, many of which had pines growing on them. The whole lake has a circumference of about twenty-six miles, about five times as large as Lake Chuzenji at Nikko. It is stocked with salmon trout and the best time for fishing is from June to the end of July when the fish become so numerous even amateur anglers can catch a lot.

There are many noted rocks standing out of the thick woods on the Nakayama Promontory, which are called Jigomori-iwa ("Self-secluding Rock"). A legend says that in the latter part of the ninth century a Shinto priest Nansobo, who used to live at Toga in Aomori Prefecture, was presented by the deity Gongen with a pair of iron sandals, with the instruction that he should end his pilgrimage at the place where the sandals broke. This was at Lake Towada. Nansobo spent many years in seclusion on Nakayama Promontory and one day he threw himself in the water and was killed. In the lake there lived a dragon transformed from a woodman of gigantic stature and great strength named Hachiro-Taro from Kusaka in the Akita Prefecture, who became thirsty and drank from a brook, and eventually he converted the valley into a lake for his

A small island along the shore walk of Yasumiya

dwelling. When Nansobo threw himself into the lake there was a struggle between him and Hachiro-Taro as to who should have the possession of the lake, but Nansobo won in the end. So there Nansobo has been established with a granite statue of himself, which could be regarded as the first stone sculpture in Japan.

On the east side of Nakayama Promontory there was a place called Ouranaiba, which means place of divination or place of fortunetelling. It is said that from ancient times many country people came here to place bronze coins on pieces of paper in the water to test whether their prayers would be answered. If the coin sank immediately or if the paper stood erect the prayer was considered answered. A good many years ago a Shinto priest hired a diver to recover the coins from the bottom and the value of 2,000 yen were said to have been salvaged at the time.

It took an hour and a half to reach Nenokuchi, a very small place which has only two or three gift shops and a place where bus tickets were sold and a big bench to rest while waiting for the bus to Yasumiya. While waiting for the bus I felt that Nenokuchi was very quiet. A few young boys and girls running about hardly seemed to stir the air but even enhanced its stillness. The bus ride to Yasumiya took about thirty minutes. Now the place was thronged with more people than when I went on board the motorboat. They were wandering about the gift shops or walking along the wide footpath by the lake shore. I moved toward Nakayama Peninsula with the thick wooded shore on my right and on my left the lake. The air was fresh and cool. In the distance I saw two small islets, one of them having a tiny shrine on it. The scenery became more and more rustic, increasing in beauty. However, the air became somewhat disquieted round two nude figures standing on a stone pedestal—a creation of a modern Japanese sculptor. They seemed to be a great attraction for many visitors and everyone came to take photographs of the statue—called the Maidens of Towada—from all angles. The faces of the nude women were somewhat Japanese, but the proportions of their bodies were quite European. Both were stout and buxom. The whole setting did not seem to me to be an appropriate one. However, this statue, like similar nude sculpture in other cities, indicates clearly that Japanese artists are very selfconscious of their own body structures. Suddenly the motorboat returned from Nenokuchi as if arguing with me that the motorboat was not traditionally Japanese and yet suited the run around the lake quite well. Well, the motorboat is not an art creation!

Maidens of Towada

Two busloads of visitors were pouring into the hotel porch when I arrived; apparently the Hotel Towada is well known. The Japanese system of co-ordination between the hotel management and the trans-

portation authorities is really admirable. I had had a full day and went
to rest directly after the evening meal.

When I woke early the next morning, the thunder growled, the wind
howled, the rain fell in hissing torrents, and impenetrable darkness still
covered the earth. I knew that I was lying in bed high up a mountainside
with a deep lake far down below, but I had never been in such alarming
surroundings before. Gradually the first moment of day broke through
with a faint dull light and the rain, like showers of steel, beat against the
windows. After breakfast the downpour became more violent than ever
and the wind was rising through the trees with an extraordinary sound.
Some of the tall and long branches as I saw them through the window
looked like judo wrestlers trying to throw one another down. Usually I
could enjoy scenery in all kinds of weather conditions, but now a succession of uneasy emotions had crept up inside me. I had been told that
Japan's coastal cities were exposed to summer typhoons and that
Typhoon Number Nine was then moving northward. I began to wonder
if this disturbing storm would prevent me from going farther on my
journey the next day as planned. As long as it lasted, I had to confine
myself entirely within the walls of the small room, lying on the tatami all
the while with nothing to read and in no mood to retouch my sketches
which I had made the day before. The howling noise outside made me
feel quite miserable for the first time in all my travels. The storm raged
on and on till late afternoon. Thoughts of what to do the next day worried me, for I did not know Japanese nor where to ask for help if the
typhoon actually came this way. Fortunately Mr. Tadao Hibino of the
Hankyu Express in Tokyo, who had arranged the itinerary for my trip,
kindly called me long-distance to say that the typhoon would not reach
this area and that the storm would probably soon abate. A most com-
forting message and I felt rather relieved. As the night approached,
darkness closed in. The gales came on to blow harder and harder and
showed no sign of abating while I ate my dinner halfheartedly. They
blew on till late at night. Suddenly the following lines from "Tao Tê
Ching" by Lao-Tzu came into my mind: "No squall lasts all the morning; neither does torrential rain fall the whole day." Apparently Lao-Tzu,
who lived in the northern part of China, had not experienced the kind of
weather which I was having by Lake Towada.

At what time early in the morning the storm stopped I had no idea,
but the sun shone into my room so brightly all I had thought the day
before vanished with no trace. I caught an early bus from Yasumiya for
Aomori through the Oirase Valley. It moved slowly in order to let us
have a glimpse between the trees of the rapids and waterfalls along the
Oirase River. The murmuring of the streams could be heard all the way.
I could not help composing the following lines:

Yesterday the rain teemed but today it is fine;
The sound of running water escorts me all the
    way.
A myriad trees and a thousand hills pass by as if
    flying,
The air becomes fresher and purer beyond Lake
    Towada.

Presently the bus emerged onto the top of the hill range, with a wide
expanse all round. The grandeur of the whole countryside took my
breath away. The farthest cluster of houses was my destination—the city
of Aomori. There used to be a special custom in Aomori which was
called "night harvesting," or *yotagari* in Japanese. In the early feudal
days most of the farmers' wives had no means of their own, but they
were given small pieces of land by their husbands where they could cul-
tivate and grow something for sale in their spare time. They generally
did their work at night. This came to my mind when I saw women washing their husbands' cars at night in Japanese cities. I think Japanese
women are the most hard-working lot in the world.

During the stormy day by Lake Towada, I was ready to go to see
Jesus's tomb near Towada. I heard about it from Lee Chia. Very few
Japanese know about it. Mr. Lee told me that he made a special trip to
Lake Towada to see what was rumored to be Jesus's tomb and had also
written an article about it, which was published in a Chinese newspaper.
After having read a book entitled *Jesus Died in Japan* by the great Shin-
toist Miss Yamane, he decided to follow the Chinese proverb "To hear
about something a hundred times is not like seeing it once" and went to
investigate for himself. Arriving at Lake Towada, he drove deep into the
mountains for two hours until he reached a small paved lane with a
board inscribed in Japanese: "Entrance to Jesus's Tomb." Walking a
few yards up the narrow path, he came on another wooden board with
the words "Divine Spring of Jesus." At the end of another thirty or forty
yards he came upon some level ground where two small tomb mounds
stood side by side with a wooden cross on one and a wooden board on
the other. Not far from the tombs stood two large wooden boards, one
with a description in Japanese and the other in English. Professor
Burton Watson made a new translation of the description from a photograph which Mr. Lee had given me.

Jesus Christ came to Japan at the age of twenty-one and for the following twelve years studied theology here. At the age of thirty-four, he returned to Judah and worked to spread the teaching of God, but the Jews of that time would not accept the teachings of Christ, on the contrary they arrested him and were about to execute him on the cross. It so happened however, that Jesus's younger brother Isukiri took his brother's place and died on the cross. Meanwhile, Jesus himself, fleeing from execution on the cross, made his way with great difficulty back to Japan, where he settled down in the village of Herai, lived to a great old age, and died here. In this holy spot, the spirit of Jesus is worshiped at the Torai Grave on the right, and that of his brother Isukiri is worshiped at Toshiro Grave on the left. The above account is said to be based upon the last will and testament of Jesus Christ.

Mr. Lee told me that the original name of the place, Herai, sounds like Hebrew. He had some photographs of the place and of the wooden boards, and gave me a set of them. In his article Mr. Lee says that this legend did not actually start in Towada itself, but was found in an old record in his family archives by Motomaro, the head of the feudal family of the Takeuchi. In 1935 the great historian Toriya Banzann left his home in the Akita Prefecture to come to this out-of-the-way place Herai in order to investigate the tombs described in the Takeuchi archives. (The Takeuchi archives were destroyed in 1945 by American bombs.) The archives said that after Jesus's birth His mother was persecuted by the Jews and had to run for her life. Therefore Jesus left home at the age of twelve, going first to India, where He received instruction from a heavenly saint in the Himalayan mountains. He then proceeded gradually eastward and reached Japan at the age of twenty-one. He next went to the port of Hoodatsu of Kanezawa, studying Shintoism under Prince Takeuchi Yutin, head of the shrine of Kooso Koodaijingu, for a number of years, and mastered more than fifty different kinds of magic, and healed the sick by divine power, and learned to become invisible. He left Japan at the age of twenty-five and taught first along the Italian coast and then proceeded over the European continent. At the eleventh hour He escaped the suffering on the cross, for His young brother came to die for Him. Taking with Him a lock of His brother's hair He bade farewell to His disciples for the last time on the Mount of Olives. Jesus reached Aomori Prefecture at the age of forty and lived near Lake Towada till His death at 106. It is said that with the publication of Miss Yamane's book, *Jesus Died in Japan*, the legend became widespread not only in Japan but also in Germany and Italy where Hitler and Mussolini were interested. Though many might have much to question about this legend, I wish I could have gone to see the tomb for myself as Mr. Lee did. Mr. Lee also told me that in that little village where the tombs were, there was a local popular song with words incomprehensible to the Japanese, which has been studied and translated by Dr. Kawashuda Eiji, a Japanese theologian:

> Praise your glorious name:
> You have driven away the hairy people!
> Praise your glorious name!

The words of this song are said to sound like Hebrew. Regarding this legend I can only say that I have never heard of Jesus's brother Isukiri before. I also wonder why there was no single sign of any connection with Jesus in Towada by those ardent Christians in Shimabara and Amakusa during the Christian persecution in Japan!

Entrance to Jesus's Tomb

XXXVIII

The Planned Undersea Tunnel

AFTER A WHOLE day of torrential rain, a bright sunny morning was most welcome on my way to Aomori. After a good, long bus ride the city came in sight. The sun was quite high in the sky and there was a quaint and wild fragrance from the rice fields in the air. It was near harvest time. I left the bus and made for the wharf and joined the throng waiting to go on board the ferry.

It was a much bigger and better ferryboat than those I went on to Okishima and to Sado Island. I had a window seat, comfortable and with plenty of room to walk about between rows of seats. The invigorating and pleasant sea air came in through the half-open window. Changeable and vast, sublime in all its forms was the sea, when the wind blew, its surface and its color changed underneath clouds and sun with shadow after shadow running over it. At first the sky was limpid blue and cloudless; now groups of clouds floated over the horizon. Cloud was the visible breathing, the suspended breath of earth. There was much activity on the surface of the running waves, which moved joyously across a glorious tossing wilderness of blue and white. Though joy-intoxicated, I was curious as to why I saw no screeching sea gulls overhead in the Sea of Japan, or in the strait between Aomori and Hakodate. Around the British Isles, and among all the Greek islands I had seen countless noisy sea gulls. I was told that the Japanese are the greatest fish-consuming people in the world and that they had eaten up most of the fish around the Japanese coast and left little for the sea gulls! Hakodate is known as the great fishing center of Japan, and it is little wonder that few sea gulls were seen over this stretch of water.

Presently land appeared and then a larger promontory, which could be Mt. Hakodate. The crossing took four hours and I enjoyed being on the sea again!

After having a meal in the hotel I took a taxi to Hakodate Park, where I had a quick look at the Fisheries Museum. I should never have imagined that so many different fish have been caught for human consumption! I also had a look at the archaeological museum. After that I went to see the Goryokaku Fort, built by Takeda Hisaburo, a Dutch

A stone monument of Takeda
Hisaburo

scholar, in 1855. My friend Mr. Saburo Aratake, director and manager of the Kenkyusha Publishing Company, Tokyo, was born in Hakodate and told me that at Goryokaku Fort the naval force led by Enomoto Buyo (1836–1908) made its last stand in support of the Tokugawa shogunate but was eventually overwhelmed by the Meiji might. The grass growing around the fort was tall and thick, apparently not in use for a long time, and I found it difficult to get a complete view of it. Near a row of lovely tall pine trees stood a stone monument to the builder of the fort.

A bronze statue of Takuboku

Later the driver found for me the stone monument of the young poet Takuboku by the seashore. It was a bronze statue probably with good likeness, sitting absolutely alone as if to indicate that the poet's short life had been stormy at times, for a high tide could have come to the foot of its pedestal. In recent years I took interest in reading some translations of Japanese poetry, chiefly by Professor Donald Keene and Professor Burton Watson. The following is a short poem by Takuboku translated by Watson:

> Those seaside roses
> On dune
> Of a northern shore
> Surf-scented
> Will they bloom again
> This year?

Professor Mason Gentzler told me that in his class on Chinese and Japanese poetry many students showed great liking for Takuboku's work, for the poet was young and the subjects he wrote about seemed to be what was needed by the young Americans. Later I was introduced to a specialist, Miss Imai Yasuko, on Takuboku's poetry, who told me that Takuboku died at twenty-six years of age and had a rather unhappy life, for he had failed in love affairs. The young poet was very much interested in the countryside and in nature, which can be detected from his work. I thought Takuboku might be a Japanese Robert Burns, but such a comparison seemed unjustifiable, for Burns was a farmer-poet while Takuboku was not.

I also had a quick look at the Trappist monastery from a distance, as I knew that no man would be allowed to go there without introduction. Dr. Gregg M. Sinclair, President Emeritus of the University of Hawaii, had told me about his visit there:

> It was in 1913 that my friend Bill Sutherland and I spent a little time at the Trappist monastery in Hokkaido, and what a wonderful time we had! I corresponded for years with one of the Belgian priests, Brother Tarcisius; later he returned to Belgium, and we lost track of each other. All the brothers were gracious to us, perhaps because we

were introduced by Father Villon, of Hagi, Japan, who had left
France after the debacle in 1870, had become a chaplain on an
American war vessel and learned English in six months, landed in
Japan shortly thereafter and stayed there all his life. A superior per-
son, with a rare sense of humor—in English.

That was more than fifty years ago. Hakodate has changed much in the
meantime but I doubt if either the Trappist convent or the Trappist
monastery has changed. There are one hundred nuns, Japanese and foreign, in the convent and sixty men in the monastery. Both the men and
the women vowed not to speak before they came.

It was still summer, but Hakodate was much cooler than Tokyo. I
decided to walk along the seashore for a while as there was still good
light. Many deep-sea fishing boats were anchored by the wharf. Soon a
streetcar stopped not far from where I was and I got on it to be taken up
to the top of Mt. Hakodate. The magnificent view of the beauty of the
country around the city as well as the wide expanse of the sea all came
in sight. Gradually darkness crept in from every corner. The mystery of
the long lingering of the twilight over the sea, the hills, and the city in
the slow process of making the seen into the unseen could only be felt
on that very spot at that very moment.

The Tsugaru Strait between Hakodate and Aomori is 113 kilometers
long and the water could be very rough at times. In the early days many
had encountered terrible storms unexpectedly while crossing in the old-
fashioned boats of wood and many shipwrecks and much loss of life
occurred. This might be the reason why there had not been much interest shown in Hokkaido in early Japanese history. Since the running of a
modern steamer-ferry at the later part of the nineteenth century, the
communication between Hokkaido and the main island, Honshu, grew
more frequent. I went to Hakodate during the centennial of the development of Hokkaido. A project of building the Seikan Undersea Tunnel
has been under study for some twenty years. Mr. Saburo Egami wrote to
me:

> The excavation for the investigation of the undersea tunnel between
> Hakodate and Aomori was started in May, 1964. But the date of the
> commencement of construction and the completion are not yet an-
> nounced officially. It is said that the government expects that the tun-
> nel will be completed in1975.

He also sent me a folder including the information that the total length
of the proposed Seikan Undersea Tunnel is 36.4 kilometers, undersea
distance 22.0 kilometers, maximum depth of water 140 meters, depth
below the sea bed 100 meters. Its geology would be Miocene sedimen-
tary rocks and volcanic rocks and about ten faults are expected. It

would comprise two single-track tunnels or one double-track tunnel. There would be electric trains running through it.

Hakodate must have new city plans to meet its forthcoming development when the Seikan Undersea Tunnel is completed. This, the longest undersea tunnel under construction, can be regarded as a colossal engineering feat. When the Seikan Undersea Tunnel is completed, Japan will have added a new wonder to the already existing wonders of the world.

I had several kinds of fish for dinner, a piece or two of each, though I could not identify them by name, apart from the *wakasaki*, or pond smelt fried; a tiny piece of salmon broiled; two small white o-sashimi which I took to be carp; and two other kinds which I had not tasted before. It must be most common to have many fish for dinner in Hakodate. The yearly catch of this city alone, generally for ten months only, amounts to half of the tonnage caught in the whole of Japan. According to the statistics, the 1964 Japanese fishing industry production aggregated 6,350,000 tons, ahead of the Soviet Union and the United States but, in terms of tonnage, second to Peru (9,130,000 tons). But the Peru catch included many small species which were used for fertilizer and animal feed. Yet almost 90 per cent of the Japanese catch was consumed as human food and was thus of more monetary value than Peru's. The Japanese have the reputation of being the world's biggest fish eaters. Fish is included in every meal. Thus Japan has developed the finest fish cuisine known the whole world over. Fish has been part of the Japanese way of life since ancient days. Many Japanese family names are derived from those of fish, or else are connected with fishing or fishing instruments such as the net. If the Japanese did not actually go deep-sea fishing they all knew about it. At least, many Japanese are very fond of angling; they love to catch fish as well as eat them. The Japanese language and culture are full of images and allusions related to fish and fishing. A red fish, *tai*, or sea bream, must be served whole to each person, for *tai* symbolizes happiness—to cut it means separation, a bad omen for marriage. A boiled lobster, called *ebi* in Japanese, means long life, for the Japanese lobster has long whiskers like an old man and is indispensable for the New Year Festival. It is interesting that the Japanese lobster has no large claws in the drawings or photographs of it. And the Fugu-Chochin, or lantern made of the swollen globefish, are kept as ornaments. There is a well-known Japanese phrase, Ebi-Tai, which means to use ebi, a prawn, as bait to catch tai, in the sense of venturing for a big profit from a small investment. I knew that in London one could easily open a conversation with any Londoner by simply mentioning the weather. It seems to me that in Japan one could begin a conversation with any Japanese just by mentioning fish, for then the Japanese face would beam.

Fish have long been depicted in Japanese paintings and carvings. But early in the Meiji era (1868–1912) a Japanese technique called gyotaku for faithfully and artistically preserving the image of a fish was perfected. They look like a kind of ink rubbing of Chinese calligraphy. But these fish rubbings need more skill, for the fish body is not flat like a stone engraving.

It was quite natural for the Japanese emperor to choose fish as the subject for his New Year Poetry Party in 1967. Forty-three thousand tanka, an ancient Japanese poetry form involving thirty-one syllables linked to heighten the imagery, were submitted, evoking the subject in its natural river, lake, or sea and also singing of their delicious taste after being cooked or merely sliced, as well as their sizes and species. Only thirty-four were chosen as the winning tanka. The Japanese not only eat the poisonous *fugu*, or globefish; but also *tako*, or octopus; and *ika*, or cuttlefish; and *same*, or sharks. I had not realized that sharks were edible, for sharks are man-eaters! In Japan there is *kamaboko*, commonly called fish sausage, which is considered a delicacy, and is a necessary item for ceremonial occasions. The fish used for making kamaboko consist of sea bream, cod, flatfish, shark, and others.

In popular folklore Japanese *unagi*, or eels, and *iwana*, or bull trout, could transform themselves into human beings. The Japanese rivers, lakes, and ponds seem to be full of unagi and the Japanese have many fine ways of cooking the eels to make them tender and delicious; cooked eels are even for sale freely like candies. The Japanese revere eels as sacred creatures possessing all the virtues of protecting and giving fortune to those who believe in them. There is a legend that when Damo Hideyuki intended to throw poison into the river Tadami in 1611, an enormous eel transformed itself into a monk as Nushi, or master of the river, and came to prevent Damo Hideyuki from doing so in order to save the lives of all the fish living in the river.

Endless legends and stories about fish of one kind or another could be related for pages and pages. Catfish are closely related with earthquakes, as described in the chapter on Hakone. The most interesting thing to me is that the Japanese, having been so much connected with fish and shellfish, have often used them for artistic designs. For instance, the ultra-modern architectural design of the famous swimming pool for the 1966 Tokyo Olympics by Kenzo Tange is a giant shell of a type of shellfish! Dr. Tange might have not been conscious of it when he designed the building. He is one of the outstanding modern architects of the world today, but he is Japanese so he designed this shellfishlike swimming pool, which a man of another nationality might not have done.

I feel happy to have gone to the source from which all the fish that the Japanese eat are supplied—Hakodate.

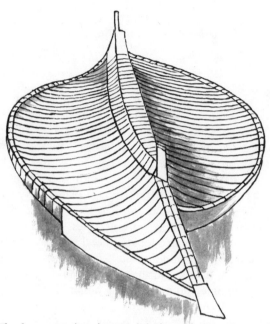

The famous swimming pool designed by Dr. Kenzo Tange

XXXIX

Mt. Showa Shinzan and Lake Toya

IT TOOK A little more than three hours on an express train to get from Hakodate to Toya station. The Hotel Manseikaku is not at the station but by Lake Toya. A taxi took me on a most picturesque road, one lovely panorama succeeding another all the way. In about twenty minutes we came to a pleasant valley with a large number of houses and great patches of dark green trees. Gazing into the distance, I caught sight of the lake far away and the faint image of the lofty Mt. Yotei, a delightful sight. Presently we came down to the level street, which was quite long and lined with gift shops on both sides. After a short left turn I entered a most modern Western-looking hotel with an enormous lobby facing the lake. This was an addition built in 1952 to the original typically Japanese building. I was told that the old building was always full, and its adjacent building could house seven hundred school students and two hundred guests. I just could not imagine how there could be so much business in this rather out-of-the-way place. Not a single European or American face could I see on my arrival. Indeed, the Japanese are always travelling; it is they themselves who keep the hotels going all over the country. How do they manage to have so much free time, let alone the means?

Later I rested in a luxurious armchair in the lounge enjoying the tranquil scenery over the lake. A number of motorboats were cruising in all directions but no sound of their engines could be heard, for the large glass windows were closed. An obliging young man, Mr. Hoka, at the front desk, informed me that I had enough time to make a boat trip to the central island and back before dinner, and that next day I could see the still-active volcano and the Ainu village. I followed his suggestion immediately and soon found the landing stage to wait for the boat.

It was a mild August afternoon. It would have been very hot in Tokyo, but Toya lies far to the north and does not have the heat even in midsummer, especially when pleasant breezes blow over the spacious lake, which is over twenty-four miles in circumference. All round, the lake shore was thickly wooded. The central island, Nakanoshima, looked like hot buns in the soft misty light with many hues all melted together in great harmony.

Our boat was moving steadily toward it as if we were all standing ceremoniously to meet a beauty. Even the speedboats that occasionally came near ours did not seem to cause any disturbance. But the absence of a single screeching sea gull over this enormous lake marked something very strange in my experience. This was probably due to its having been formed by the upheaval of Mt. Shiribeshi and consequently there were few fish in it to attract the birds. However, the unexpected appearance of an eagle circling in the air, together with the small white dot of a swan close by the shore of the island, visible as our boat drew nearer and nearer, enlivened the scene. A small red-painted Japanese pagoda emerged from the lake water adding a picturesque note to the whole setting. I remember the English lines:

> The eagle he is lord,
> The swan is lord below!

How fortunate to have both appearing at the same time!

Soon we landed on the island and went round the museum, which has all kinds of tree specimens on display. One specimen labeled "Shina" was pointed out to me as a wood which was used for carving the bears. But I could not identify this tree as one that also grows in China. Apart from the museum there was little else for visitors to explore, for the island was so thickly covered with lofty trees that there was hardly space to walk. We did not linger long before we returned to the boat for the voyage back. When we were a little distance away from the central island I suddenly noticed that at the northeast a high mountain stood out clearly, which must be Mt. Shiribeshi (Yotei), or Ezo-Fuji, for it had a graceful cone shape like Mt. Fuji and had snow on its top as well. Ezo is the old name for Hokkaido so Ezo-Fuji is the Mt. Fuji of Hokkaido.

After dinner I went out for a walk along the main street, gazing at the local gifts in one shop after another. The gifts sold in Toya are different from those I saw on Honshu or Kyushu, for here they sold well-polished local stones in different colors, chiefly dark green and soy red, and fox furs and furs of other animals like mink and otter, and carvings of bears, and the most prominent items of all, statues of Ainu people. I also saw carvers in two shops working on a piece of wood by removing the unwanted wood with a knife. Both carvers used similar-sized pieces of wood and also carved similarly so that their finished products were almost identical. I could see that they had been trained by the same master, or else their hands had become like machines. The human hand could become a tool like a piece of machinery if the mind does not play its part. This is what distinguishes a craftsman's work from an artistic creation: craftsmanship merely shows dexterity of hand while an art creation displays the combined efforts of hand and mind.

Bear carver

It was a delicious morning when I woke the next day—bright sunshine, light summer air, a sky almost cloudless, and a fresh yet delicate verdure on the trees. Mr. Hoka sent a young man to escort me to the bus for Showa Shinzan, the new volcanic mountain. After a fifteen-the neighborhood. We gazed up at the rocky mountain, only 1,337 feet in height, where a few wisps of white smoke puffed up from time to minute drive we got down at a row of gift shops—the only buildings in time, indicating that the volcano was still active. Japan's Official Guide says about Showa Shinzan:

> On and after December 18, 1944, several earthquakes were felt daily in this locality, and the ground, which was at the time covered with vegetable fields, rose at a rate of 7.8 inches a day. On July 23, 1945, there was a severe eruption, followed by several others, and by February, 1946, a new active volcano was formally recognized. As this was a phenomenon, the government named it a "National Treasure" and now grants it special protection.

The interesting part is that it was named as a "National Treasure" and was officially called New Mountain of Showa Reign. This is an example of the Japanese mind trying to turn everything to advantage. The eruption of a volcano would generally be regarded as a great disaster to

THE WATERFALL AT SOUNKYO, HOKKAIDO

RED-CRESTED CRANES IN KUSHIRO, HOKKAIDO

Showa Shinzan

society and might cause much suffering to the people. If the Chinese met this kind of situation, they would simply say, "Mei yu fa tzu," or "There is nothing to be done," and would just leave the situation as it was and endure it. But the Japanese would try to make the best of the disaster. Showa Shinzan is now the most important and new attraction for people visiting Toya, which has therefore become a more prosperous place than ever. I watched many people climbing the rather steep slope so as to approach the holes where the white smoke was puffing upward. Directly against the white smoke each figure, though very small, stood out clearly, reminding me of the eighteenth-century European miniature silhouettes cut from black paper. Very few trees could grow on this volcanic mountain, but there were some green patches of grass. The surface of the top part of the mountain looked rocky with its brown and yellow colors, and some purple tints appeared when the bright sun shone directly on it from the spotless azure sky. There was a stunning color scheme in the whole scene which could work out a good composition for a painting.

Directly opposite Showa Shinzan is another volcano, Usu, which erupted violently in 1910, not at its summit but at the sides, where four large cones formed at the time and are still noticeable. A ropeway is built here to bring people up for a grand view of Showa Shinzan and I joined many others to ride to the top. The round top of Showa Shinzan now became a rather large red brass caldron with white smoke rising all the time as if some interesting food were being prepared there for all the hungry travellers. Later I saw a notice board pointing to a place called

Silver Pond and I began to walk in that direction along a footpath with thick growth on both sides. Thistles, wild roses, and many other weed-like flowers grew undisturbed along the way. I met no other person. Near the end of the path, I was suddenly confronted with a small pond directly facing the bright sun, glittering brilliantly, as if it were a sheet of silver. It looked like a perfect little jewel.

When the ropeway brought me back to the row of gift shops I followed a large crowd toward the Ainu village. Though no student of anthropology or linguistics, I have tried to meet the Australian aborigines in Alice Springs, New Guineans in Paupua, the sea Dyaks and land Dyaks in Borneo, and a few others during my travels. My interest in the Ainus was roused by the word *white* to qualify the word *aborigines*, for many scholars thought that the ancient Ainu people came from Caucasia, so that they were Caucasians belonging to the Assyrian type. In early Chinese books, the Ainu people were called Hsia Yi and lived in the northern part of Japan. I was amazed that some of them were still in existence. After having paid an admission fee, I chuckled to myself that I was wrong in saying there were no real hippies in Japan, for we Orientals, or so I thought, could not grow much of a mustache or beard. The Ainu men I saw had bushy mustaches and long beards. This is why they were called hairy people. A young Japanese guide invited each of his group to put on an Ainu robe and to wear an Ainu wreath on their head for a group photograph. I watched the event with a strange feeling inside me. This Ainu village—the first in my visit to Hokkaido—seemed to me very similar to an Indian reservation in the American West, but even the money-minded Americans had not worked such a device for providing Indian dresses for the visitors to be photographed in. The ingenuity of the Japanese mind went a step further and I could not help admiring their cleverness in exploiting the natural vanity of human nature! The Ainu men wore a different robe from that of the women, but when the large crowd was told to stand for a group photograph, they all—men and women, boys and girls—put on the type of robe worn only by Ainu women. Besides, only the Ainu men could have wreaths of straw on their heads, but all the visitors put them on for the photograph: a laughable display! After the photograph of the first group was taken, the second group followed—about thirty in each. Then we all sat in a circle while a white-mustached and -bearded Ainu with a straw wreath and a red jacket over a black robe with white-line-and-circle design stepped into the center of the ground and murmured a few words in prayer while he made some motions with a rod over a black-lacquered bowl which he held in his left hand. Then he stepped back and seated himself beside an Ainu woman who was sitting near the entrance to a thatched hut. There was a black ring round the woman's lips, which I realized was their ancient custom of having the lips tattooed before marriage. Dr. Sakuzaemon Kodama, in his study on the tattooing of the Ainus, says that "when an Ainu girl becomes thirteen, her upper lip is tattooed, and when she reaches fifteen her lower lip is also tattooed." Not many of the young Ainu women follow this custom now. Later six young Ainu girls and women, all nontattooed, in similar black robes but with different designs began to dance in the middle of the circle, with movements entirely unlike any Western dance and not quite Japanese. After this dance a big stone mortar was shifted into the center and four young females, each holding a long pole, began pounding in the mortar, suggesting their ancient way of pounding grain, while they danced round again and again. This reminded me of the scenes I saw of many African villages in the modern movies. There was a famous painting by Emperor Hui Tsung of the twelfth century in the Boston Museum of Fine Arts, which depicted four women pounding silk in a similar manner. Finally the two guides led their groups away, while I followed a few remaining visitors to have a look round the village huts, in one of which I saw a number of ancient lacquered boxes piled together by the walls and in another an Ainu woman was weaving a piece of cloth in a very similar manner to that of the sea Dyaks whom I saw weaving in North Borneo. An elderly Ainu with bushy white mustache and beard was sharpening his knife on a stone. However, I did not catch any sight of bears, though I have read much about the Ainus' association with the bear, which they worshiped as their kami, or god. From Dr. Kindaichi's translation from the Ainu language of *A Small Tradition of Oina*, the following story of the love affair between Oinakami and a lovely female kami tells much about the Ainu people.

She (the female kami of Horobetsu) had an elder sister and an elder brother. When she became old enough to wear Mo-ur (the dress of a grown woman) and be tattooed, her brother instructed her to move into a new house. This exemplified the old Ainu custom which allows suitors to visit the prospective bride in her own dwelling. There she serves a bowl of food of her own cooking to each young man. The young visitor, after eating half of the food, was to return the bowl to the young hostess. If she accepted it and ate the remaining food, it signified that she complied. If not, it was a sign of disapproval.

Later I told Mr. Hoka what I saw in the Ainu village at Showa Shinzan, and he agreed with my assumption that nearly every one of the Ainu people now spoke Japanese and that there have been many mixed marriages. The present number of twenty-three hundred pure Ainu people, he said, was decreasing rapidly. But he could not tell whether the Ainu village was in existence before the eruption of Showa Shinzan in 1945. I thought they had been moved here to add another attraction for the visitors who came to see Showa Shinzan, for I noticed that the thatched huts looked quite new!

XL

The Bear Ranch in Noboribetsu

Changing shoes

IT WAS A pleasant ride from Lake Toya to Noboribetsu Spa, but I noticed that pine trees were not so conspicuous in the Hokkaido landscape as they are on Honshu and Kyushu. Someone had told me that it was only a few minutes' walk from the bus station to the hotel Daiichi Takimotokan. I walked along together with the whole busload and another busload followed us. I was surprised to see all these people going to the same hotel. I wondered what could have attracted so many people to come here. Inside the entrance of the hotel hundreds of pairs of slippers were arranged in row upon row. We were all busy changing into them and several men and women stood round to collect our shoes. So far this was my first experience of entering a hotel at the same time with hundreds of other people, and I found the sight of us all changing shoes together very comic and tried to make a rough sketch in my head as this could be regarded as one of the typical sights of Japan, not to be seen in any city in Europe or America.

A maid came to take me to my room and afterward she gave me a bag and a small towel, showing me the way to the bath. Already a crowd of nude figures was in the hot spring and some were sitting close by the wall each facing a small mirror. I had not been in a big bath before but I could not very well withdraw and had to follow suit. Actually nobody bothered about anybody else. Suddenly a number of nude figures stood up on their toes and two elderly ones burst into laughter. I felt that I was facing the fresco in the Chapel of St. Brizic in which a large number of nude figures was standing in the picture of the Resurrection of the Body at Orvieto, Italy. Or better still, I was studying Hieronymus Bosch's bizarre masterpiece *The Garden of Delights*, painted more than four hundred years ago, which was brilliantly described, "A crowd of naked people stands around. . . . Others ride aimlessly in circles. . . . Still others swim languidly. . . . A few black men and women mingle with the white groups, peacefully accepted. . . ." Though the last quoted line may not be quite appropriate, I soon realized that I was in the picture, peacefully accepted. Those who were standing on their toes were trying to look over the low wall beyond

which lay the big bath for women. I did not know how many bathing
pools were in this large hotel. Several nude men were walking over to
the women's pools. I was told that the mixed baths were discontinued in
Japan after the Second World War but Hokkaido observes this change
halfheartedly. Would this be the reason for so many people coming to
this hotel, I wondered.

After I had dressed and left the changing room I lost the way back to
my room, for there were many long corridors and they all looked alike.
The inside of the Daiichi Takimotokan was really enòrmous. Then came
the evening meal with many small dishes of Japanese food brought in by
the maid. I ate quite a bit and went out in the hotel-provided kimono for
a better look at the main street. Many dressed like me and did the same,
but no one could have guessed that I was born in China. Nearly all the
shops sold similar wood carvings of bears and of a bearded Ainu man
and his wife, like those I saw at Lake Toya. They also had polished
stone jewelry, typical Hokkaido products.

The maid woke me about seven o'clock for breakfast. When I entered
the dining hall the sight of two or three hundred people breakfasting
together gave my steps a check. Many maids were busy serving food
and there was much activity all the while.

After breakfast I walked over to see Jigokudani, or the Valley of
Hell, the sound of which reminded me of those few hells I saw in Beppu.
It was a short walk behind the hotel to a stone bridge where a number
of people were already leaning on the low parapet watching the heavy
white steam rising continuously in big balls at several places in the
ravine. Actually it was a huge crater with rounded mounds of cinders of
a reddish brown color amid clouds of steam from the water bubbling out
of some hidden caves. From the roadside by the hill on my left I walked
and saw tiny figures in black silhouetted against the white vapor, for
some had walked very close to the sulphurous steam. I then followed a
few descending into the ravine and found that most of the conical rocks
were either brownish yellow or yellow white. Hardly any plants had survived, though some scanty grass tried hard to live. We approached a
bubbling pool where clouds of sulphurous steam rose, though it was still
a good way from where I was standing. It was evil looking yet awe
inspiring. It made me feel I had lost touch with reality. It was hard to
believe that we could actually stand on the very edge of a madly boiling
caldron. At moments I thought I could even hear underground echoes of
my footfalls. The earth's shell seemed thin enough. Yet we men did not
have any fear of this thin shell being broken one day. Hardest of all to
understand was that the ground on which we stood was reddish brown,
light in shade, whereas the pools of mud, whose level was only a few
feet below that of the dry, hard earth surrounding them, were dark,

almost black. Could it be possible for us to stand on the red-hot thin shell, without feeling burned at all? Endlessly the thick-walled bubbles rose, took hemispherical form, ruptured, formed, ruptured, formed, plopping, slumping, plopping, slumping, sinking back into the scalding fluid matrix whence they continued to rise. This reminded me of many mud pools which I saw in Rotorua, the weird thermal region of New Zealand. I wonder if the Ainus, whose ancestors first lived in Nobori-betsu, would have some legends about the Valley of Hell. The geometric designs on the Ainus' robes did not seem to have been inspired by the mud pools. The Jigokudani is a full mile in circumference and about four hundred feet deep. Even if the five hells in Beppu were put together they would not be more than one-fourth of its size. The term *Hell*, in Chinese "to yu," which means "prison underneath the earth," is derived from the importation of Indian Buddhism to China. In most Chinese monasteries a special hell would be erected to contain a large number of small figu-rines made of clay or stone depicting the activities of the ten hell deities, or ten Yamas. The principle of Buddhism centers on two words, *cause* and *effect*. A good cause brings good effect and bad ones bad. After death, the spirit of the deceased had to stand the judgment of the ten Yamas, the rulers of purgatory, one by one. Up to the last Yama, a deci-sion for reincarnation was made whether he or she should be a human being or animal in the next life depending on what course, good or bad, he had taken while living. All these clay or stone figurines were horri-ble-looking demons to serve as a warning to all people to do good during their lives. These ten rulers of hell were imitated by the Chinese Taoist temples. In China the Chinese did not like to mention this term

Bear ranch

"ti yu" in public. But the Japanese seem not to mind it at all. I never imagined that I would actually come to stand right inside a Valley of Hell.

A young man at the desk of the hotel who could speak some English told me that there was a bear ranch nearby and that I should go and see it before I left Noboribetsu. A cable car took me up to it in less than twenty minutes. The sun was shining brightly and the first thing to come in sight was an enclosure marked "Bear Kindergarten," in which some ten young bear cubs were playing with all kinds of toys—rubber balls, baby carts, wooden stairs, chunks of wood, and so forth. It sounded appropriate, though there was no teacher. Their antics and pranks usually detain visitors as they pass by, and I lingered there myself for a good while. Hokkaido is notable for its bears, as it is close to Siberia and Russia, but much development has occurred on Hokkaido and the bear population has been decreasing for many years. Perhaps this bear ranch has been established for the breeding of bears. From the carved bears I saw in Lake Toya and Noboribetsu Spa, they were fish-eating animals, for most carved bears had fish in their mouths. This was new to me, for I had always believed that bears were specially fond of honey, fruits, and vegetables. Several carved marble bears have recently been excavated from ancient tombs in China of some two or three thousand years ago. A number of Chinese carved jade bears and also a number of bronze bears are on display in some public museums of Europe and America. Bears must have been a common animal in north China in the early days. Not a single wild bear has now been seen in the Chinese mountains or countryside. I was surprised to read in the Japanese newspaper that in 1967 a forty-seven-year-old woman was injured when a bear attacked her in the bush at Osaka, Yonezawa City, Yamagata Prefecture, northern Japan, and that a month earlier a man was attacked by a bear on a mountain path.

Presently I reached the upper enclosure along the hill slope where some twelve or more fully grown bears were kept. They were playful too, but somehow, they did not arouse the same amusement. It was interesting to see one of two bears stand up, resting its whole body on its two hind legs, and walk like a man. The other did likewise immediately and they engaged in a sort of hand-to-hand combat, not fighting really. It resembled a Japanese sumo match in some aspects, for both bears were well fed and the heaviness of the lower part of their bodies made them unable to walk with feet together, so they had to spread their legs wide apart.

Bears are found in almost every portion of the earth's surface. A Scandinavian aphorism that the bear "has the strength of ten men and the sense of twelve" means that the bear is not only very strong but very intelligent.

XLI

The Shiraoi Ainu Village and Lake Shikotsu

I WAS TOLD that Shiraoi was the most popular Ainu village on Hokkaido, so I felt a pleasant expectation as the bus rolled steadily on under a bright sun in unusually soft and fair weather for late August, particularly in the northernmost part of Japan. After about thirty minutes the bus came to a halt and a number of the passengers got down and I followed them. A long row of gift shops had goods similar to those I saw at Lake Toya and at Noboribetsu—the small polished stones, the furs, the wooden bears, and small carved wooden rings and charms, and so on. There was neither a live bear to be seen in the village, nor a display of Ainu dances like those I saw in the first Ainu village by Showa Shinzan. But most of the thatched huts, better built, had their doors open for visitors. I entered one of them and found many people kneeling round a big fire of small blocks of wood burning on the hearth, a well-cut square on the floor, with well-laid tatami all round it. A rosy-faced Ainu elder with white hair, white eyebrows, white bushy mustache and beard in his robe with black-and-white designs, a bright red jacket, and a wreath of yellow straw on his head, was holding a black lacquered bowl in his left hand and a short stick in his right with which he made strange motions over the bowl, while murmuring to himself. Then he talked to all around him in Japanese as if explaining everything in detail. I began moving round the spacious room to look at the large lacquered boxes stacked along the walls. They were their treasures and heirlooms. According to Professor Takakura Shinichiro's essay "A Short History of Japanese Policy for Ainu—from contact to assimilation," the northern part of Ou region was the dwelling of the Ainu settlement in the eighth century. At that time the Japanese government set up Sendai and its environs as the base of operations and built the fortress between Akita and the southern part of Iwate for the purpose of making a defense against the rebellion of the natives and with the idea of assimilating the natives who were living near there at the same time. In other words, before the eighth century, most of the people who lived on Hokkaido, including the small place now called Shiraoi, were the Ainus. These lacquer boxes which I now saw could have been handed down from those early days, though they

A burning fire and an elder Ainu

did not in fact look so old. Though the designs on the lacquer boxes varied from one to another, they employed many curves, circles, spirals, squares, and angles in the intricate geometric patterns. I wished I could have stayed there longer for a study of them.

I returned to stand behind the sitting crowd while the fire of charcoal and wood was burning brilliantly with lively flames spiraling upward. The pinkish face of the elder Ainu glowed and his eyes glittered on all those surrounding him. The yellow straw wreath on his head and the white lines of the designs on his robe seemed to have all turned to gold and silver and his white eyebrows, mustache, and beard into silver strings. One object startled me somewhat: it was a rather big gold wrist-watch which was visible when he raised his arm from time to time. I realized that I was still in modern Japan.

In one of the other huts I found an elderly Ainu woman weaving cloth, sitting upright with her legs stretched underneath a piece of hemp fiber which was tied to a short pole stuck into the floor. I then noticed two or three small huts constructed on high poles to serve as granaries where the Ainus kept their foodstuffs dry.

Presently I was standing together with a few others when one of the Ainu chiefs came to talk to me in rapid Japanese of which I could not understand one word. Apparently he mistook me for a Japanese and asked me why I did not try to approach him and talk to him. A young

Japanese tried to explain this to me, saying that the old chief would like to have his photograph taken with me. The mystery was solved and I naturally felt happy to be photographed with him on my left and an Ainu woman, probably his wife, on my right, with another long-bearded Ainu in an Ainu robe behind me. Then we all shook hands cheerfully. Both Ainu chiefs and the elderly Ainu woman spoke to me in a most courteous manner after they knew that I came from China, though unfortunately the young Japanese student could not translate their remarks clearly to me. The Ainus have long been known as a peace-loving people and there was little organized resistance recorded in Japanese history when the Japanese tried to colonize them. During all the time I was in Shiraoi, I heard not one word of the ancient Ainu language spoken. Professor Jiro Ikegami of Hokkaido University says in his lecture "A brief introduction to the Ainu language":

> As for the number of speakers of Ainu it is already very small today. With some exceptions, only old men and women of about seventy years of age or more speak Ainu. But they are bilingual and speak Japanese rather than Ainu. Younger people speak only Japanese. Ainu is likely to be forgotten even by old men and women. Contrary to common belief, Ainu is not yet a dead language. But we can say it is quite near extinction. The field study of Ainu is an urgent work.

Linguists will have their own theory about preserving the Ainu language as well as many other ancient languages. But one thing is clear—all the ancient languages, if put into written form for printed records, would

An elderly woman weaving cloth

An Ainu village at Shiraoi

preserve themselves. The languages which are only used orally will sooner or later disappear.

On my way to the Shiraoi Folk Museum I heard the young Japanese student explain to an American lady that in 1881 Emperor Meiji came to Hokkaido to witness the bear festival and dancing as demonstrated by the Ainus from Shiraoi. This soon became widely known all over Japan and in other parts of the world. The killing of a live bear for the bear festival aroused a great deal of controversy among the Japanese themselves, and the practice was later stopped. In the museum, which was opened in 1967, a number of exhibits representing the old customs and relics for fishing, hunting, weaving, and worshiping were displayed in models. There were some original fur shoes and dresses from the skins of deer, bear, fox, and other animals, but there was nothing to show how the bear festival was performed.

A number of Japanese women, not Ainus, were sitting round the entrance gate, selling small bundles of young plants, which looked to be cedar or cypress shoots which could be planted out of doors or in pots. I suppose they were locally grown and sold to the visitors as souvenirs. I took out my handbags from the cloakroom and asked where I could find the bus stop for Tomakomai. A young man with short whiskers and a beard, who appeared to be one of the new generation of Ainus, stood up and took the bags from my hands saying, "Let's go!" He was apparently familiar with the Americans after the war and I obediently followed him. He put my bags down by a lamppost and told me that there would be a ten-minute wait for the next bus. I was greatly surprised at his friendly gesture and thanked him gratefully.

After reaching Tomakomai I had to change to another bus for Shikot-suko, which took about an hour. It had begun to rain, and a rather cold wind blew across the bus stop carrying with it the sound of the massive, tall pines like the roaring of waves. I looked around for the Shikotsuko Grand Hotel, where I was to stay for the night. Nowhere was the hotel. Eventually someone appeared and directed me down some stone steps to the landing stage for the steamer to cross to the other side of Lake Shikotsu. While crossing the lake in the late afternoon, the rain fell more and more creating a crystal curtain between me and the surrounding high mountains, Mt. Eniwa and Mt. Tarumae. I was told that these two mountains were still active volcanoes but there was no sign of their activity to be seen from the boat. The lake looked bigger than it had seemed at my first glance, for the rain had obscured its edges. Our boat was the only one on the lake.

At the second landing stage a young maid was waiting for me and she took my handbags and led me to the hotel. It was a very secluded modern building backed by a high mountain and half circled with luxuriant trees. An ideal hermitage for anyone with Chinese Taoistic inclinations. I was surprised to find every modern convenience inside like those of a modern hotel in Tokyo or New York. I was served Western food, though I asked for the local speciality of Zari-Gani, a rare special dish of crayfish. It was not forthcoming. Nevertheless, with my hunger appeased I felt content and rested after a full day of activity. None of the hotel staff could understand English, though I wished I could find out something about the neighborhood. After a short doze I found the rain had stopped. The hotel was not big and no other visitors had arrived yet. I went to stroll round by the lake side. It was a delicious evening, not cold but fresh with the still twilight air so tranquil and I could even hear a leaf turning in the breeze. But the wind must have been stronger in the far distance, for when I lifted my head I could see the white, fleecy clouds driven vigorously along—now veiling, and now exposing the dazzling full moon that had risen above the faraway hills. A beautiful sky at that moment! In spite of the growing chilliness, a beautiful world! Nature is a great artist; her pictures are forever displayed around us, but the picture I was witnessing at the moment could not be imitated by human hand. I had never imagined I would have come to such a remote, secluded, and tranquil place for the night!

When I came down next morning a young couple, apparently newly married, was already at breakfast. This hotel would be an ideal place for honeymooning. After breakfast I set out for a morning walk along the left-hand footpath. It had evidently been cut out of the lower slope of the mountain long ago and might have been a hunting trail of the Ainus, who must have lived here in the past. I walked down to the lake shore as long as I could set my feet on the big pebbles among the tall weeds, but did not realize that I had intruded into the domain of a crow colony, and scores of them flew up all at once with a loud noise of flapping wings and cawing as if telling me to get off their land. I stood still and watched them flying in such disorder, yet with some order traceable in their circling formation. They did not intend to leave their domain. While watching the flight of their jet black bodies against the shimmering lake surface, I also noticed the delightful effect of the early sun's disappearing above a woody hill in the distance: it just seemed, as Shakespeare said, to "stand tiptoe upon the misty mountain's top." It darted its diverging rays through the rising vapor from the lake surface and its radiance caught the tops of the trees. One of the choicest appearances of nature!

Presently I reached the inn by the first landing stage, where the boat had stopped the day before. I later learned from Mr. T. Sawa, manager of the Shikotsuko Grand Hotel, that it was called Okotan-So. *Okotan* means "Village beside the river mouth" in the Ainu language. *So* is a Japanese word for a cottage or inn. As there was no more footpath, I retraced my steps. My eyes were becoming preoccupied with a maze of tall and short trees, many of which I could not name, when unexpectedly I saw a notice on a tree trunk with the kanji words "The claw marks of a bear" and I thought the marks rather new. According to Mr. Sarashina Genzo's book *Customs of the Ainu People*, the bear is the Ainu's god and each bear would leave some claw marks on tree trunks to indicate the boundary of its own domain, which no other bear should enter. If that was the case, the claw marks of each bear must be different from one another. So I moved closer to examine the claw marks carefully in the expectation of finding another, but I found no more. Then I reached some open ground after passing by a number of summer bungalows which lay in the front of another hotel in Japanese style, bigger than Okotan-So and also the one where I was staying. Mr. Sawa had told me that this hotel, the Marukoma Ryokan, was usually frequented by fishermen from the towns around Lake Shikotsu during the summer for the fishing season of *himemasu* (a kind of trout). There were two cars parked side by side near the edge of the lake shore. Three workmen were repairing the banks while a woman was gathering some plants. Suddenly a number of wild ducks appeared from the long weeds, quacked insistently for a while, and then rose up, flew over the treetops along the lake shore, and disappeared. Their quacking was the only sound that stirred the morning air and enhanced the unusual freshness and tranquillity. I was about to return to the Grand Hotel when four young men rushed out of Marukoma Ryokan roaring with laughter. One of them addressed me but I could not answer. Another who could speak some English came to ease the situation. They were all university students, natural and friendly, full of interest and curiosity about the American students' demonstrations as soon as they learned that I came from New York. One of them remarked that very few foreigners, particularly Americans, thought of coming to this quiet place, for they all rushed to visit the more famous spots, such as the great temples in Kyoto. I explained to them that I was born in China, at which they all exclaimed in surprise. The one who talked about Americans actually came from Kyoto to study in Hokkaido, for there are good departments of agriculture and fishery in the University of Sapporo. Though we could not converse in long sentences, nor could I explain the student demonstrations at Columbia University very well to them, we managed to chat for a good while. I liked the naturalness and friendly manner of these four young men. The one who spoke some English after looking at his wrist watch suggested I might join them for a ride, saying that they would take me back, for they were staying at Marukoma Ryokan. I was most touched by their unusual kindness and I accepted without hesitation. We all got into the car and began to go down a road with high mountains on both sides. There was much chattering and laughter inside the car, in which I could take no part. Every turn opened a new view, a fresh combination of green, red soil, dark tree trunks, white clouds, and bright sunshine. The car made a few turns and then stopped at a place which the young men had come to see and which they wanted me to see as well. We were actually at the entrance to a narrow lane flanked by lofty slabs of enormous rocks. Both rocks were joined with many groups of similar ones zigzagging their way all along, though I could only see a short distance. The path ahead was only partly visible and shrouded in mystery. All the surfaces of the rocks were covered with short, fine mosses, soft, beautiful, and in all shades of green; they were velvetlike carpets as if some heavenly maid had laid them out on the rocks for airing. One of the young men told me that this path would lead us to Mossy Cave. It was difficult to walk on the volcanic ashes all along the way but the sight of so many silky velvet carpets hanging on both sides had taken my breath away, so that I did not notice anything else. The rocks and the mosses had many forms and many hues, some of which stood in the full glare of sunshine and some untouched by the rays, but all melted together in harmony. I don't remember seeing this kind of scenery anywhere else in all my travels. An interesting feature was that the rocks on both sides were originally one solid piece which had been split in two when the volcanic mountain erupted thousands of years ago. Not being far from the lake and the region having much rain and snow in winter had helped the mosses to grow evenly all over the surface. I was happy to have come to see it on a sunny day, for I imagined this path to the cave must have often been sealed off by thick clouds and mists. On our return trip I felt deeply grateful to the young men who had suggested taking me here with them. The friendly gesture to me was something to remember as was the experience of walking to the mossy cave.

Mossy Cave

XLII

The Second Tokyo in Future Sapporo

IT HAD BEGUN to rain after I crossed Lake Shikotsu to catch a Chuo bus for Sapporo. Though a cold wind blew all the way, it was not really cold, for at the end of August it was still summer in this far north area. I was told that this was the best time to see Hokkaido, for most of the holiday makers had returned home. I arrived at the Sapporo Grand Hotel and I found that I could only stay for one night, for it was fully booked by many who came to attend the Eighth International Congress of Anthropological and Ethnological Sciences, which would begin the next morning.

I had thought that since Hokkaido lies in the northernmost area of Japan it could not be very modern. I was completely wrong. According to Mr. Sjizuyuki Ken's writing Hokkaido, formerly called Ezo and inhabited by the Ainus, started to be developed in a grand scale during the Meiji Restoration. In the second year of Meiji, the new Meiji government set up the Hokkaido Commissioner General's office and Kiyotaka Kuroda, just returned from abroad, as the first commissioner.

> At the request of the commissioner general, the U. S. Government sent General Horace Capron, director of the Agricultural Bureau, and his assistants to Hokkaido in the fourth year. . . . He later recommended the government to invite Dr. William Smith Clark to Sapporo to teach.

It is little wonder that Sapporo has long been systematically developed in a Western manner.

The hotel was quite close to the center of the city and I noticed an Eiffel Tower-like structure in the distance. I walked toward the tower and to my great surprise saw a big bronze sculpture group of three naked women dancing back to back on the center of a round pedestal. None of the three women gave the slightest illusion of being Japanese. They looked healthy and buxom as well as quite tall in comparison with women walking in the street. I bought a ticket to go to the top of the tower. The distant hills were hardly visible in the rain and mist. Many people were on the top and many business activities were going on. These towers seem to be an indispensible item in any modern Japanese city and they have become the gift centers. Oh, how the Japanese love to buy gifts and toys!

Afterward I got down to the streets to walk around. Again and again I met a sidewalk vendor with his steaming cart of hot corn on the cob for sale and many Japanese bought and ate them, nibbling on their way. Surely this used not to be a Japanese fashion. Did Dr. William S. Clark introduce it when he became the president of the Agricultural College in Sapporo in 1876? I read that Indian corn or maize had been introduced to Japan in 1655 by the Portuguese from Fukien Province of China, not from America directly. Of course the two hundred years' isolation of Japan in the Tokugawa era might account for its slow development. Nothing like nibbling the corn on the cob from steaming carts could be seen in the streets of Tokyo, Osaka, or any other big cities of Japan.

There is no Sapporo Castle, nor any Buddhist temple noticeable in the neighborhood. Even Shintoism came to Sapporo rather late, for there is a Sapporo Shrine more than two miles away from the center of the city on a hill called Maruyama. This shrine is dedicated, as I read in Japan's Official Guide, to three Shinto deities who are believed to have undertaken a meritorious service for the development of this northernmost land of Japan.

Dr. Jukichi Suzuki

No sooner had I got back to the hotel than I had a telephone call from Dr. Jukichi Suzuki, professor of English Literature at Hokkaido University, introduced to me by Mr. Saburo Aratake, a Hakodate-born friend of mine. He thought I should see Sapporo with a good guide. Professor Suzuki came to dine with me at the hotel at eight o'clock and I found that he had been educated at Harvard University and knew Professor I. A. Richards there. We had a good talk about Cambridge and Boston and then set out to see what real Sapporo night life looked like. It was raining hard again and I could not see where we were going. We came to the old quarter of Sapporo, though I could not see much before I was led up a few steps and entered a *shuan*, a kind of old Hokkaido wine restaurant where food was also served. The room was not very big and a middle-aged woman sat behind an L-shaped counter by a big barrel-like stove, which contained a fresh charcoal fire. On the strong wooden beams hung a number of oddities, including pans and bottles and many other things of which I could not tell the names. Two low-ampere electric lamps kept the room rather dim. We were the only visitors at the time, between nine and ten o'clock, and I was led to sit by the end of the counter near the wall. Professor Suzuki ordered a number of small fish, called shishemo, shaped like a willow leaf, which I was told were a special delicacy only found in East Sapporo and nowhere else. This fish is very famous in Tokyo and Osaka. The woman behind the counter took the fish and baked them on an iron plate over the open fire.

We drank the famous Sapporo beer to go with the fish, which tasted very tender and had a fine texture. I was happy to have tasted it in Sapporo.

Presently a young couple came in, both about twenty years of age, and ordered the same fish as we. They whispered to each other. Soon another couple followed and the room then became livelier than before, though still very quiet. Professor Suzuki said that Sapporo, being in the far north and in a cold region, had more contact with nature than the warm places and had not been corrupted by civilization. I remarked that the proposed construction of the undersea tunnel between Aomori and Hakodate could change Sapporo in particular and Hokkaido in general into a very modern area. "Though I don't wish to see Sapporo become another Tokyo," continued Professor Suzuki, "I am afraid Hokkaido may become the center of future Japan, for all efforts have been concentrated to develop this area."

Monument in Sapporo station

The second place we went to was a *nomiya*, a Japanese type of public bar, though not quite "public," for it was exclusive in its own way. It was inside a rather tall house, which was divided into a number of rooms, each of which was a nomiya. I was led up three flights of stairs to a very small room where two young women received us with smiles. Apparently Professor Suzuki has been a customer here before. There were only two small tables with four seats. With the two women moving about and a good-sized counter, there seemed to be little space for others to come to it. Professor Suzuki had much to talk about to the women, cracking jokes in Japanese as well. The younger of the two told us that she had been taken to live in Manchuria when she was only three years old and then returned to live in Tokyo when she was ten. Now she had been in Hokkaido for ten years. I asked if she knew a few words of Chinese but she did not. Later she put on a gramophone record and danced with Professor Suzuki in the narrow space left for walking. We two were the only visitors for the whole evening and the two women seemed to be quite happy with their occupation. On our way out I inquired how they could make a living in such a small place with so few customers. I got the answer that all the small nomiya in the house were like that, and that was the Japanese type of bar with its regular customers. I got back to the hotel at half past twelve and Professor Suzuki promised to come to take me out the next morning.

A nude statue in the main street of Sapporo

He arrived on time, for he wanted to take me to the opening of the Eighth International Congress of Anthropological and Ethnological Sciences. He knew all the Japanese participants, many of whom were his colleagues. We reached the assembly room before the Emeritus Professor of Hokkaido University, Dr. Tetsuo Inukai, started to make "Some Ethnological Remarks on the Ainu People," saying that the ancestors of the Japanese Ainus could have come from Central Asia—they were Stone Age Caucasians travelling through Asia Minor to Hokkaido. He illustrated his talk with a number of color slides showing some stones from excavations different from those found in Hokkaido and also with one slide of an old Ainu woman and a man with a long black beard, both of whom I had actually seen in Shiraoi three days ago. I was happy to recognize them. The whole lecture was conducted in English and gave me a great deal of insight into many things that I saw in Shiraoi and also in the small Ainu village near Showa Shinzan. Professor Sakuzaemon Kodama, who is known to have a fabulous collection of things Ainu of every description, gave an opening speech as the chairman. There were several other good lectures and I could not listen to them all.

Poplar avenue

Afterward, Suzuki drove me to see a number of things in Sapporo and then we went to Hokkaido University for lunch. After having seen different departments of the university, he took me to the famous poplar avenue, which was planted by Dr. William Clark in 1876. It has now become one of the landmarks for sightseeing in Sapporo. I have seen many poplars in Europe, particularly in Italy, but no poplars were to be seen anywhere in Japan except in Sapporo. Rarity becomes precious, as the Chinese proverb says; so people came to Sapporo to see poplars. I smilingly said to Professor Suzuki that poplars represent the Occidental civilization—clear-cut and straightforward, while the crooked pines the Oriental civilization. Dr. Clark made a great name in Hokkaido as if he had lived here for many years, although he only stayed for eight months.

Suzuki had already made arrangements with a young colleague, Professor Yoichi Hitachi, to wait for me outside the Botanical Gardens to show me round a small museum there, half of it devoted to the development of modern Hokkaido and half to Ainu artifacts. The Botanical Garden, like many others in the world, contains many thousands of plants, but the size is rather limited. I was told that there were many interesting Alpine plants specially growing on Hokkaido Island and this garden was rich in them. After having examined a number of the Ainu artifacts in the museum, we went for a stroll round the garden. Later we had a look at an exhibition of *The Late Artists*—works by local artists who had died within the past thirty years or so.

In the course of our conversation we touched on some of the more notable international topics such as the student unrest in America, the landing on the moon, and heart transplants. Professor Hitachi's eyes beamed as he told me that he had just heard from the wireless before he left his house that there had been a successful heart transplant operation in Sapporo Hospital the night before. He also mentioned that the broadcaster had expressed his surprise that most of these operations on hearts were done in rather provincial towns like Cape Town, Houston, and

Sapporo, rather than in the major capital cities of the world. This remark led me to ask how to define the term "provincial towns." A town with the most modern equipment for heart transplant could not be regarded as provincial. It so happened that I had a good talk on heart transplants in Oklahoma City with Dr. Stewart Wolf, director of the Oklahoma Medical Research Foundation, before I came to Japan, so the topic interested me much. I told Professor Hitachi that Dr. Wolf thought everybody knows the heart itself has nothing to do with a person's behavior or attitude toward others. But whether heart transplant is desirable and feasible will raise a lot of practical problems. The chief one would be the enormous cost of the operation. Dr. Wolf continued to say that death was a normal part of every life and that he believed the words of his friend Dr. Robert Page, "the doctor's job is to add life to years, not just years to life," were quite right. Professor Hitachi joined me in agreement with Dr. Wolf.

Professor Hitachi came to have coffee with me in the hotel and soon afterward left for his evening class of English. About 7 P.M., Suzuki telephoned that he was coming to see me with a great specialist on Ainu customs and life. The Ainu specialist Mr. Sarashina Genzo gave a broadcast on Ainu life and customs before he came that evening. We three had a good talk over Sapporo beer, since both preferred it to sake, and some white sashimi. I must admit that I knew very little about the Ainu people. Mr. Sarashina had Suzuki as his interpreter, saying that most of Hokkaido popular folk songs came from Honshu except the Ainus' own songs. Hokkaido used to have masses of herring and all the local fishermen sang all kinds of herring songs. One could hear them in almost every eating place where the fishermen gathered for meals and sake. But in recent years no herring were caught round Hokkaido and none were for sale in the fish market and no one knew the reason for this sudden disappearance. Therefore fishermen sang no more herring songs in this city. The Ainu people have the same belief as the Japanese that the sun is a goddess because it gives warmth like woman, while the moon is cold like man. I said that someone in Lake Toya told me that the Ainu people had more wet wax in their ears than other races. Mr. Sarashina did not know this. But again he said that the Ainu believed those who have long ear lobes would live long. He then looked at my rather long ear lobes and laughed, saying that I could have some relation with the Ainu race. Another legend I learned was that there once was a beautiful goddess called Kunou, whose father wanted her to marry the god of the earth, for he was brave and strong. But she refused and ran away. When her father eventually found her hiding behind tall grass, he scolded her and finally changed her into a plant with a yellow flower called Fukuju-So. Mr. Sarashina said that Fukuju-So is the only plant

Mr. Sarashina Genzo

which attracted the attention of the Ainu, who as a hunting and fishing tribe showed little interest in plants. They called this flower Chirai-apappo (a flower which tells the coming up of *Chirai*, a fish that looks like a small salmon). Some Ainus in southwest Hokkaido called this flower Knau-nono (flower of Kna). Fukuju-So is the Japanese New Year flower, to be seen in many homes on that special occasion, for it symbolizes happiness. Then I asked about the Fupope Cave near Yoichi. Mr. Sarashina said that in this cave some symbols looking like birds and fish and boats are carved on the walls. Some unknown prehistoric race was said to have lived there, but nothing was known about them.

Professor Suzuki told me that Mr. Sarashina was also a poet, having written much about Hokkaido in a book published some time ago, and he translated one of them as follows:

> Excited surf distinguishing outline of this island;
> The voices of the sea birds flying along the white beach
> Mingle into a chorus with the songs by men challenging the sea.
> Mornings and evenings were only on the silver scales (fish)
> But the inland kept all silent darkly,
> And only the wind and wild animals passed there now and then.

Mr. Sarashina, with a great love for nature, prefers to spend his time in the country among hills and trees and is seldom to be found in the city. Suzuki remarked that it was my luck to meet him when he came down to do the broadcast. Before Mr. Sarashina left the hotel with Suzuki, he gave me a specially inscribed copy of his recently published book, *Customs and Life of the Ainus*.

The next morning I tried to arrange a trip to Yoichi to see the Fupope Cave but could not work it in with my time schedule for other places. So I went to Jozankei instead. The sun was shining brightly and there was not much traffic on the well-paved road. The bus driver dropped me not far from the hotel where I was to stay. It is said that Jozankei is one of the most popular spas in Hokkaido, for it is easy to get there from Sapporo. I asked at the reception desk about seeing Choshiguchi Cliff. A clerk came out to show me the way himself. We turned toward a red-painted bridge, under which the water was flowing rather rapidly. The Toyohira River is not very deep but is very clear. I stood in the middle of the bridge facing the high cliff on my right. Two big rocks stood between the cliff and a small hill covered with green trees on my left, with a tiny wooden shrine on the top of the bigger rock, among a number of dwarf trees with the river valley twisting round behind as if some mysteriously beautiful scenery were there. I was the only person there. Crossing the bridge, I found a small Jozankei Kwannon temple built with its back close to the hill slope. In front of it stood

Choshiguchi Cliff

a wooden board with a short history of Jozankei Spa. It seems that the spa was discovered in 1858–1866 and that the springs are alkaline and carbonate, unlike many other hot springs on Honshu or Kyushu.

Afterward I crossed over the main road and noticed a stone carved with three kanji words, "Jozanji," so I climbed up the steps for a look. It was a rather new temple belonging to the Sodo sect. No one was about and I could not go in to see the main hall and other things. I also found a Jozankei Shrine which was also quite new, indicating that both Shintoism and Buddhism were newcomers to this part of Japan. Perhaps the visitors to the hotels and inns at Jozankei had time only for taking hot-spring baths and could not contribute anything to the temples and shrines. On my way back to the main road, I heard a number of youngsters playing ball in the school. A boy of six or seven saw me coming, got down from his bicycle, gave me a deep bow with a smile, and then rode past me. I was astonished at his being so polite at such a tender age.

After passing the school I did not go back to the hotel but made a right turn and walked along a footpath with tall shrubs and small trees shading me. The murmuring of the running water in the river beyond the shrubs on my right was most pleasant to hear. There was a spirit of tenderness, a burst of freshness and delicate feeling that possessed me on my way. At one moment the wind stealthily lifted its long wings from leaf to leaf. At another two or three sparrows flew in front of me and then, perched on a nearby branch, tilted their heads this way and that to scrutinize me. From here I saw the river Toyohira had several curves in its course with many small pebbles lying on the shore, shining brightly against the sun.

Jozankei is not big and the few hotels, inns, and other houses all cling together by the river Toyohira, surrounded by tall hills and mountains. Yet it lies close by a main highway. Perhaps the peak season for visitors was over, for I did not see many while I was there. After a sumptuous meal in the hotel with a few types of fish dishes and then a good bath in the hot springs, I had not felt more relaxed and contented since I came to Hokkaido.

But nature was playing a game with me. Next morning a heavy mist covered the sky and rain was falling incessantly. I had intended going to see the Nakayama Pass for an immense panoramic view of the land, but mists and clouds seemed to gather round the road so I returned to Sapporo earlier than I had planned. This time I went to stay at the Yamagataya, a Japanese-style inn. Despite the rain, now just drizzling, I went out to find some books about old Hokkaido. But in three old bookshops nothing came to be what I searched for. However I saw in Sapporo, as in most Japanese cities, more people in bookshops than in other types of

A monument for the horse soul near Jozankei Shrine

shops. If my judgment is correct, I think the reading public in Japan has a very high percentage of the population. With almost no illiterates, the spread of culture and knowledge would be easy through the modern means of communication. I have travelled in most parts of the globe and can confidently say that Japan's culture is a remarkably homogeneous one reaching to every possible corner of its territory and is far more homogeneous than that of any other land that I have seen. Within the past hundred years Hokkaido has caught up with Japan's other three islands.

Presently I was on the verge of the main boulevard in the center of the city but could not move into the center, for both sides were thickly lined with people in their new, clean clothes with the Japanese national flags in their hands—all looking happy and smiling when the drizzle stopped. Both the emperor and empress had arrived in Sapporo that day to initiate the celebration of Hokkaido's Centenary, and the people were all out to welcome the royal pair by waving the national flag as they passed by. This reminded me of the great English Jubilee celebration when all the London streets were packed with people waiting to see King George V and Queen Mary go by. Many, many English saved money to have new clothes made for the special occasion. I don't know if some of the Sapporo women did the same. When I got back to the inn, soon Professor Katayama Atsushi, another teacher of English at Hokkaido University, came to see me at the suggestion of Professor Suzuki. He was kind enough to take me to the station for my ticket to Asahikawa the next day. After that we went to a popular dining place for a meal. A friend of his, Mr. Kikuo Fujioka, came to join us an hour later. Mr. Fujioka was a teacher of Chinese history in a Sapporo high school, with great interest in the years of the Chinese revolution of 1911 under the leadership of Dr. Sun Yat-sen, who changed imperial China into a republic. He wanted to know something about two important figures of those days, Yüan Shih-k'ai and Chang Chien, and also hoped to get a copy of a Chinese translation of the book entitled *The Empress Dowager, Tzu Hsi,* by an Englishman, J. O. Bland, published in London in 1912. We communicated by means of writing Chinese characters and most of the important names in those days of Chinese revolution I mentioned he knew. He was delighted to have met a Chinese who could tell him something he wanted to know. I was a young boy during those revolution years, though I admit to be no historian. What interested me about him in this meeting was that he could have known so much about China and that a Japanese high school even in the far north could have someone like him to teach Chinese history while China's high schools never had anyone teaching Japanese history. This humiliated me more when I thought of no special courses on Japanese history and culture in any Chinese universities.

After the meal Mr. Fujioka insisted on having me visit his house. His wife soon had tea ready and both his daughter and son were in college and knew some English. It was most unfortunate that I could not converse with them in Japanese, otherwise I might have found something about the young Japanese point of view toward the present day developments and activities. I then bade them good night and the son drove me back to the inn in his father's car. It was another memorable, happy moment that I had in Sapporo.

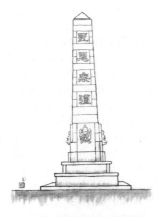

A monument dedicated to
imperial kindness

XLIII

Asahikawa and Kamui-kotan

AFTER THE train left the city of Sapporo for Asahikawa I noticed the countryside was quite flat for a long way with blue hills far in the distance. The fields, not rice fields, but pasture for cattle and sheep, presented a Western type of countryside scene. In addition there were a number of big cylindrical silos rising by the side of farmhouses here and there, similar to those seen in the countryside of New England. The train made two or three short stops before it finally reached my destination. The Rev. Rudolph Kuyten was already on the platform to meet me and take me to his home. Rudolph and I met at Columbia University several years before, when he took a few courses there. He told me one day that his missionary area was in Hokkaido, where there were many beautiful places to see and that I should make an effort to go there for a look in the future. So an arrangement was made when I decided to include Hokkaido in my third trip to Japan. I nearly missed him, for he now had a handsome black mustache on his upper lip, which was not there before. However, it would be difficult to miss him among all Japanese faces. Rudolph was born in Holland, educated in America, and has been doing missionary work in Japan for the past six years or so. It took no time for him to drive home and I was well received by Mrs. Kuyten, Trina, with their two sons, Daniel, six, and Jonathan, two. Unlike many other missionary workers, Rudolph has great interest in artistic activities: he paints in oils and also does woodcarving and sculpture. Besides, he loves nature and goes everywhere he can to fish.

The Kuytens have been living in Asahikawa for more than five years. After a good meal, Rudolph suggested motoring me around the locality. He took me first to the Ainu village in Chikabumi. Before we entered the village, the head Ainu, named Konosa, stopped him and with a big smile, told him that his daughter had given birth to a son that very morning. Rudolph congratulated him with a hearty handshake. They had a short conversation and Rudolph told him who I was. The Ainu chief then told Rudolph that he had worked in the coal mines in Shantung for seven years, and that he liked the Chinese but had little love for the Japanese. This unusual statement astonished Rudolph, for he had not heard it before. It surprised me too; it was as if he did not consider himself to be a Japanese. On our way into the village Rudolph explained to me that Chikabumi is the Ainu term meaning "the home of the birds." It was the third Ainu village that I had come to see. Many shops were selling the same kinds of Ainu gifts, such as the carved bears, the Ainu totem designs for charms, and animal furs. Rudolph knew everybody in this village and everyone wanted to have a word with him. An Ainu couple in their late thirties approached him, needing his help with something. The man had no beard, which was unusual for an Ainu. Rudolph soon told me that he had to work among the Japanese. He was a quiet fellow, but the woman not: she had a great deal to say and laughed and gesticulated often. Rudolph explained that she told him she was a hairy woman! She had a sense of humor; she laughed when she said it. All the Ainus of both sexes were known to have more hair than other races: men always wore long beards and older women had their lips tattooed black, although not many tattooed women were to be seen in the three villages that I visited. When we came out of this village, the Ainu chief, Konosa, who was still doing some repairing on the gate, told Rudolph that he wanted to learn some English in the winter. Rudolph knew that he was seventy-seven years of age and we could not help admiring his young spirit for learning.

Then we went to see Mr. Kiyoshi Kawasaki, the editor and proprietor of a local magazine entitled *Asahigawai Karu-aki*. Rudolph admired him very much, for he used to be a journalist for an Asahikawa newspaper, had retired recently, and started the magazine single-handedly, running everything himself. I was interested to know how he could manage to make both ends meet. He remarked that it was very difficult at the start but now it paid its way, for each issue sold four or five thousand copies. Such a sale could bring many advertisements from local companies. Though Asahikawa was a modern city, most of the population was engaged in three occupations—making sake and paper pulps and catering the armies. Mr. Kawasaki gave me a copy of the latest issue of his magazine, which contains most of the local happenings.

After a cup of tea at his mission's coffee center Rudolph drove me to the place where he had been learning judo. It was on the top floor of the tall, modern building of the city police force. On each flight of the stairs, some officer still sitting in his office would voice greetings to Rudolph. There were about twenty people in the judo room, mostly between twenty and thirty years of age. Nearly everyone was barefoot and had changed into the white working tunic and white trousers. They were all practicing, two in a set. Just before starting, they bowed to one another, then one would try to shoulder the other up onto his back and throw him down on the floor with a big bang. After he got up, the fallen one

would bow again to his opponent and start again and another big bang
followed. The noise of these big bangs, following one after another while
many were practicing, was great. Rudolph was almost double the size of
many of those in the practicing room. The younger ones smiled whenever they looked at Rudolph. I asked Rudolph if he had ever been
thrown to the floor with a big bang. "Many a time," he said. Rudolph's
courage was admirable. "Judo is a healthy practice," continued
Rudolph, "and a very useful technique for life, too."

One day Rudolph had to go to Sapporo for a conference, and Trina
suggested taking her husband's place and accompanying me to Kamui-
kotan on an excursion. Kamui-kotan is a place of Ainu legend not far
from Asahikawa, but she had not yet been there. She then started to
make inquiries about the place from Mr. Sumio Sakata and asked if he
could join us. Mr. Sakata was a schoolteacher whom I had met three
days before. Later he telephoned to say that he found someone to teach
for him so he could go with us. Trina also found someone to look after
the children. All worked out well.

We went by train. The morning sun lit up every rock along the shore
of the river Ishikari. Some of them must have been washed and battered
by the water for years to become so well polished with shiny, translucent
surfaces like black jade. Mr. Sakata told me that people used to come
from many places to collect these rocks for gardens and even for table
ornaments. In recent years the local government had set up laws to protect them from being taken away. The river Ishikari has never been
known to dry up, though it has less water in summer than in winter. The
river bed became narrow at points and curved when some delightful
gorge scenery could be detected now and then. There were small rapids,
too, and though the tumultuous surges could not be heard owing to the
noise of the train, we could see the ceaseless spray against the rocks and
the gleaming crystals against the sun.

Coming out of the station, I walked straight to the edge of the river to
have a good look at the rocks. They were clustered together beautifully.
Sakata pointed to an enormous round rock like a crag head a little distance away from the station, saying that was what we were going to see.
That crag head among a massive growth of many tall trees seemed to be
frowning down on us with the air of a tyrant. Sakata led the way and
Trina and I followed. We came first to a small garden with a pond in the
center. Thistles, wild roses, and other weedlike, wayside flowers grew all
round. The pond was full of water-lily leaves but no flowers. We then
moved along a narrow footpath with masses of dwarf bamboos growing
all around. Sakata said that they were called Kuma-Zasa, or bear bush,
for bears used to be coming in and out of them. According to Mr. W. J.
Bean, Curator of London's Kew Gardens, this dwarf bamboo, named *B*.

Judo exercise

Disticha, Mitford, is a native of Japan, with stems 1 to 2½ feet high, most of them about as thick as a lady's hatpin, and zigzagged; the joints are ½ to 3½ inches apart, bearing solitary branches. The leaves are arranged in two opposite rows; they measure ¾ to 2½ inches long and 1/6 to ⅓ inches wide; and are rounded at the base and pointed, bright green above but slightly glaucous beneath. The leaf sheaths are hairy on the edges. They spread quite extensively. More and more bear bushes appeared as we moved on. The footpath seemed to be endless. We then saw some big mushrooms growing on the tree bark, which, we were told, were called Monkey Seats on account of their looks. Sakata bent down to pick another kind of mushroom, like a small ball, and when he squeezed it it emitted a white smoke; he said that this was called Bomb Mushroom. What a good place for botanists this would be!

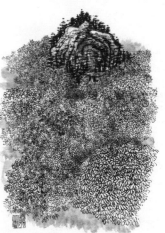

Kamui-kotan Rock

We were now standing by a large rugged-faced rock with sharp edges. It seemed to have been slashed into pieces with a sword. Few people seemed to have come here before us. But presently two young people, a boy and girl of about eighteen, walked past us, and Sakata urged us to move on, too. We had to pick our way through even thicker bear bushes. There was no more footpath to follow. Sakata tried to ascend blindly ahead of us. Trina and I had to set our feet wherever we could, step by step, and grasp either a small tree or some root nearby. The soil under my feet suddenly gave way and I fell down to find myself sitting on a tiny rock. I felt that I need not go up any further, yet I could not get down either. At the same time my curiosity held up my spirits, for I wanted to see what could really be up there. Sakata knew nothing about it either, but he was exploring, saying jokingly that there is a Japanese proverb, "Only smoke and fools love a high place." Trina and I laughed. We were actually in a sort of jungle surrounded by trees and shrubs in their free growth. While we were struggling upward, Sakata quoted another Japanese expression, "One has to sweat to enjoy." Going right up through the twisted and moss-covered branches with loose soil and broken stones under our feet, we three looked like good mountaineers and continued our climb. After twenty minutes ascending over a narrow and most irregular path that we created ourselves, climbing over some small boulders, and crawling underneath the trunks of fallen trees, we finally came to the top of the rock. Nothing, neither a small shrine nor a stone tablet, was to be seen. The space we were standing on was flat, but very small, with trees on three sides and only one side left open. By this open side our eyes were well repaid for our hardships in coming up. The lovely winding Ishikari River below us stretched away to infinity. On the other side of the river and far beyond lay a wide expanse of several low hills—I mean low when seen from the higher ground—lofty mountains by the horizon, and green fields with patches of yellowed crops here and there veiled by a thin haze in the bright morning sun—all looked soft and beguiling. Many tiny beetlelike cars moving on the few thin string-like roads did not disturb the stillness of the air but added life to the entrancing scene. The grandeur of the scenery almost took my breath away.

Sakata began to tell us the legend about the huge rock on which we were standing. It was believed to be the body of an evil god or demon called Nichine-Kamui, who lived on this upper reach of the Ishikari River. The water of this river was the life line of the Ainus who lived down below in the valleys of the Ishikari and Kamikawa rivers. In the deeper part of the Ishikari River near Kamui-kotan—where we were now—lived a fish called Cho-same—a kind of shark—but the Ainus called it Shame-Kamui and worshiped it as the patron god of the river. They made an offering of the first salmon or trout they caught each year. Whenever the Ainus rowed upstream, they would tap their canoes in order to let the god know that they were his own people, so that they could pass over his dwelling in safety. Otherwise their canoes would not be able to move farther and would capsize. This was why the place was called Kamui-kotan, meaning "the village where gods live." This patron god had many lovable children who liked to play near their home. But one spring a large amount of snow melted farther up river and caused a big flood, with the banks of the Ishikari River overflowing everywhere. Some of the god's children floated down with the rapid torrent, so the god laid himself across the narrow part of the river in order to prevent his children from being carried even farther away to the sea.

While telling the story, Sakata pointed to the narrow part of the river that our eyes could just reach. One day the demon Nichine-Kamui decided to destroy the Ainus in the lower valley by filling up the narrow gap with an enormous rock in order to stop the water flowing any farther down for the Ainus' use. This proved to be very effective. But the Ainus' most-worshiped mountain god, the bear called Nupuri-Kamui, saw this and soon removed a part of the rock to let the water flow again. This angered the demon terribly and he attacked the bear with all his might. The culture god, Samaikuru, had a sister Operiperi, who happened to see the fierce fight being waged between the demon and the bear and she went to her brother to ask help for the bear. Samaikuru dashed down immediately and, guarding the bear with his back, shouted, "You, evil demon, deserve a great punishment!" He then kicked the enormous rock off the river and drew his sword against the demon. The latter was not his match and soon lost ground, falling into the mud. Samaikuru tried to stab the demon, missed his head but hit his body. To this day we could see the sword cuts on the rock. These were known as Emushikesi—*Emushi* meaning "the sword" and *Keshi*, "the trace."

Eventually the head of the demon was called Nichine-Reyusa. This we saw in the river on our way here. But the body of the demon became this enormous rock on which we were standing. I remarked that nothing gave an indication that many people were ever here before us. The way down was a little less trying than the ascent, for we knew our path better.

After crossing the rail line we walked over a long bridge across the Ishikari River and gazed back at the rock that we had just come from. The rock did not look so enormous, but the mass of growth around it was really formidable. We later crossed the road to have lunch at the only restaurant near the bus stop. The bus soon came and we returned along a route which was different from the railroad.

We did not go back home straightway, for Sakata suggested showing us the famous forest Sutorobu-Matsubayashi, which was chosen as the background for the novel *Hyōten*, or *Freezing Point*, by Mrs. Miura Ayako. This novel had an immediate success, not only had it won the first prize in the fiction contest sponsored by a great Japanese daily newspaper *Asahi Shimbun*, but also had more than twenty printings within five months and was made into a movie and a TV serial. It was said that each time the TV show was about to start, most housewives and many other people would not even answer important telephone calls for they had to see the show. It was a phenomenal and sensational success at the time and this forest became even more famous.

Sutorobu-Matsubayashi has thousands of tall pine trees and many different species from foreign countries. They were systematically planted in rows with well-paved footpaths left for walks between them. The trees have no lower branches and it is good for walking, cool and pleasant. The forest is divided into two parts with an open space between, where I suppose the waters of the Biei River would flow over when in flood. At the time we were there there was no water, so we crossed the gap to the other part. Standing by the edge of the forest, we could see far away where the river flowed over a wide expanse. It could be a natural reservoir when the river was high or it became a big skating rink when frozen. Sakata pointed out to us that somewhere along the river shore was the scene of a murder committed in the novel. The young heroine, supposed to be the daughter of the murderer, lived quite close to the forest, and used to come here in the morning to read the Japanese translation of Emily Brontë's *Wuthering Heights*. This intrigued me, for I know the background of *Wuthering Heights*, which is an expansive moor of Haworth in West Riding of Yorkshire and I had been in Haworth on several occasions when I lived in England. So I wanted to read this novel, but Sakata did not know whether *Freezing Point* had been translated into English. Both Trina and I enjoyed the day's excursion and I felt particularly good for the additional find of a Japanese lady novelist in Asahikawa.

Hyōten haunted me for days and months. I asked my English and American publishers if they could locate a translation of it, but to no avail. Almost a year later, to my great surprise, my friend and colleague, Professor C. T. Hsia, author of *The Classic Chinese Novel* and other books, showed me a copy of the Chinese translation by Hsü Pai of *Freezing Point*, published in Taiwan in 1966. I asked him to lend it to me to read. I was surprised to find this Chinese translation had also gone into several reprintings. This indicates that there was something moving in the novel, otherwise the Japanese would not have made so much fuss over it, nor would the Chinese in Taiwan spend the time to read it. However, the quality of a great piece of work needs to be judged through the discrimination of years. So I eagerly read the thick translation right through with scarcely a break. After I had read it, I began to question why English or American translators had not yet done this one.

The novel described a family of four, the father named Keizo, director of the local hospital; the mother, Natsue, a noted beauty of the city of Asahikawa who had an uncertain affection for one of the hospital doctors named Murai; the son, Tokru, a high school student; and a three-year-old daughter, Ruriko. One afternoon Ruriko was sent out to play and was later found out to have been murdered by the shore of the Biei River. The mother longed for the dead daughter and so a baby girl was adopted from a local orphanage and she happened to be the murderer's daughter. Dr. Keizo knew of this but decided to adopt her, for he was interested in the Christian teaching of "love thine enemy." (This is the Japanese interpretation.) However, he did not tell his wife Natsue about it. The long-kept secret came out in the end. And the adopted girl, the heroine Yohiko, turned out to be not the murderer's daughter.

The principal plot of the novel was extremely unusual and many of the intertwining intrigues and frustrations were well knit together and cleverly arranged, which won my admiration. All these could have counted for the immediate success of the novel, but the unusual point is the authoress's ingeniousness in having picked up that line from the Bible, "to love thine enemy as thy self." Though Dr. Keizo wanted to put this into practice, he never tried to tell his wife about their adopted baby's parentage and to persuade her to practice the same Christian principle. Why and why not? Apparently he felt that his wife could not take it, for it was not humanly possible. And here and there in the novel were passages that indicated Dr. Keizo's secretly not liking his wife's association with the other doctor. This might have been the actual motive for the adoption. If so, this impure motive could be regarded as something betraying the important sense of the Christian principle. Western readers might question this point as I do.

Nevertheless, it would be most interesting to find how the Bible's line "love thine enemy" could have entered the Japanese lady writer's head in working out a novel. I am absolutely positive that despite all its possible success in name and wealth, this could have never induced a Chinese writer to devote his energy to a lengthy piece of work, because Chinese minds have been so deep-rooted and steeped in the teachings of Confucian moralists. The Chinese are a very pragmatic people with deadly practical minds.

The Chinese can say "love thine enemy," but could not easily suppress his instinctive passion to care daily for the daughter of the man who had murdered his own daughter In the feudal days of Japan there were endless stories about revenge by filial sons, by members of the clan, by retainers, and by noted samurai. But the Meiji Restoration led to a thorough change of the Japanese people in daily conduct from the old ways. Therefore, the theme described in *Freezing Point* could be possible; thus a great success. But I cannot understand why the translation of this novel in Chinese had a success, too, in Taiwan.

From my reading of *Freezing Point* it has aroused my usual wonderment why in recent years Japan has produced many notable novelists while China has very few. I don't mean that China has not had any good novels published in the past fifty years or so, but none, in my way of thinking, could win international approval and understanding. So far very few modern Chinese novels have been translated into any Western language. I have often discussed this matter with Professor C. T. Hsia, whose book *The Classic Chinese Novel* deals chiefly with the six famous Chinese novels: *The Romance of the Three Kingdoms, The Water Margin, Journey to the West, Chin P'ing Mei, The Scholars*, and *The Dream of the Red Chamber*. All of these have been translated into a number of Western languages and each has successful sale in the Western book market. But they were all old publications and the last of the six was first published in 1792. Though Professor Hsia has also written a book on *A History of Modern Chinese Fiction*, he agreed with me that few could prove greatly successful in translation. I would like to find out why we have not had many good novels published like those in Japan in recent years. The reason could easily be the nature of Chinese written language, which is concise and so makes it difficult to write lengthy pieces of work. Those six famous Chinese novels were not all written in Chinese classical language, but the classical expressions appeared here and there all the way. It is true that writing in vernacular language has now been well established in China since 1917. Still it needs a great hand to write the vernacular expressions well. The Japanese have no difficulty in expressing themselves vernacularly and they have been writing fiction freely from Lady Murasaki's days. Besides, Japan has been Westernized since 1855 and in recent years the way of life in Japan, particularly in the big cities like Tokyo, Kyoto, Osaka, and Sapporo, shows little difference from that in the Western cities. Most Japanese behave almost like Westerners. Though China has been catching up in Westernization, the whole social structure of the Chinese way of life has not yet been modeled on the West. Besides, many Japanese words are polysyllables instead of monosyllables like Chinese. The Japanese can easily incorporate many Western expressions into their own language such as *milk, miruku* in Japanese; *hotel, hoteru* in Japanese; *restaurant, lesutolanto* in Japanese; and so forth. This may be why their novels can be easily translated for Western readers, for they express themselves in almost similar manner. This is not so in Chinese. The greatest stumbling block preventing the Chinese from producing great modern novels still lies in the deep-rooted Confucian moralists' teaching of the clear cut between man and woman. No matter how advanced the Westernization of Chinese life may be, modern, well-educated Chinese men and women cannot conduct a lengthy conversation together, intimately or not. Without good dialogue between men and women the novel cannot become great. For instance, the great success of the six famous Chinese classical novels did not rely on their good dialogues between men and women. *The Romance of the Three Kingdoms* dealt entirely with political intrigue and military arrangements, with no women taking part at all; *The Water Margin* concerned many Robin Hood–type characters, and none of them was a woman; *Journey to the West* solely described the supernatural world of demons, spirits, and the Buddhistic paradise; *The Scholars* showed more pedantic men than women attacking the civil service examination of the time; *Chin P'ing Mei* removed the Confucian coat of Chinese life by describing its erotic side in minute detail and included very little conversation and discussion of life between men and women in general; and *The Dream of the Red Chamber* centered on a young hero among many, many women; but if he were not effeminate, he could not have been there. In other words, the last of the six dealt with women entirely but little conversation between men and women. The writers of these six famous classical novels, who could produce great works without good dialogue between men and women, were really admirable. We modern writers of China must struggle to overcome that stumbling block. Only then will there be a great modern Chinese novel in circulation!

A memorial monument of the
eruption of a volcano

XLIV

The Waterfalls at Tenninkyo and Sounkyo

As LONG promised, Rudolph Kuyten decided to show me what he considered the most beautiful spots in Hokkaido. On the road we met little traffic.

There seemed to be some promise of rain; and it soon rained quite heavily. A cold wind blew across the hills when we entered a side road, carrying with it the sound of a waterfall. At first it was a gentle, intermittent splashing, but it soon became a mighty roar above the river. The water of the river rushed down swiftly, jumping at places when obstructed by large rocks. Crossing a cement bridge, Rudolph parked the car in the front of a nice-looking hotel. No other house was in sight. Smilingly Rudolph led the way by a cliff up a wet road and then some rather slippery steps. There we stood against a metal railing, facing directly opposite the middle of a lovely waterfall. The upper part of the fall came through the dense morning rain-mist, which still covered the treetops on both sides. As a rather large rock obstructed the center, the water divided to run down on both sides as though a big sheet of white satin was being split around a beauty's neck and then joined together at the waistline. There were a good many rocks of different sizes down below, over which the water splashed with much foam and pearly sparks shooting all round. There was infinite variety and clarity combined. Never was water more exquisitely tricky—now pouring down in a big volume like a silky rope, now darting over the large and small rocks, flashing amid the rain-washed greens with drumming and bubbling music at the same time, and now disappearing yet once more appearing. It was a beautiful spot. We were the only two gazing at the falls intently and I was completely absorbed in the enchantment of the scene when the rain-mist gradually disappeared to expose the upper part of the fall. Rudolph smilingly said: "This is the beautiful waterfall of Tenninkyo!"

Tenninkyo Waterfall

We then walked back to the hotel and before lunch we went for a hot-spring bath. Rudolph remarked that the greatest attraction of Japan for him was the hot-spring bath and he would never miss it whenever he came near one. The attraction of this hotel established in this secluded spot is its three hot-spring baths. Each one came from a different spring and each contained different mineral ingredients. One of the baths was outdoors. Rudolph tried all three, taking a dip in each. Directly after I left the bath, four undressed ladies entered as if it were a daily occurrence for them. After lunch we strolled along the lower part of the river and crossed a small bridge to walk along the narrow bank, for Rudolph, the keen fisherman, wondered if he would see any mountain trout, which are said to be abundant there.

Later Rudolph asked me to have a look at the village at Memambetsu, which had suffered much damage from an eruption of a nearby volcano several years ago. No trace of the destruction was to be seen. We then stopped at the local university building where Rudolph teaches English, and he fished out two pieces of water plant to be taken back for his fish tank. He told me to feel the water in a small pond. It was quite warm and yet many small goldfish lived in it swimming gracefully and happily. This was where I learned for the first time that fish could live in warm water.

After my expressed enjoyment at Tenninkyo, Rudolph wanted to take me to see an even better and more beautiful spot the next day. Moving through delicious air under bright sunshine in a sky almost cloudless, we were soon in the wide-open country with fields on both sides. Far away to the right a small hill was pointed out to me, called Doroboyama, or Burglars' Hill. It has a big cave with iciclelike formations. In the cave there used to be amassed piles of articles stolen from the Tokugawa's samurai who had escaped persecution from the island of Honshu. Burglars' Hill is close to the city of Tomakomai, which is now the great center for all Japanese newsprint.

The road we drove along was not particularly quiet. The combined trilling of many cicadas in the roadside trees was formidable. Unlike Honshu, Shikoku, and Kyushu, Hokkaido has few pine trees.

Presently we entered the Daisetsuzan National Park and the scenery changed from flat fields to high mountains. The valley was flanked by fifty-foot-high rocky walls. A number of rocky peaks looked unusually interesting, and I asked Rudolph to stop for a rest. No sooner had we got out of the car in the small town called Sounkyo Spa than we met unexpectedly Mr. Kiyoshi Kawasaki and his young assistant. They had come to Sounkyo Spa from Asahikawa the night before, for Emperor Hirohito and Empress Nagako were to come from Sapporo that afternoon. The emperor is interested in marine biology and the empress is very fond of collecting wildflowers. Hokkaido is unique in Japan for its Alpine flora, and it was thought that the imperial couple might stay for a few days. Mr. Kawasaki came to collect material for his paper. We wished him good luck before we went for a quick lunch.

Next we took a ride on the cable car to the top of Mt. Kurodake. An observation stand was erected on a promontory. We were now looking out over hundreds of mountaintops, blue, purple, violet, and fresh green, for the sun was shining straight on some and aslant on others, and on others still not at all. A moment later, the sun's rays shifted and the bright illuminated peaks grew dim and partly lit ones grew in brilliance. Clouds like furry balls were rolling incessantly, though slowly, intensifying the glory to the eye as well as to the mind; I was entranced in admiration.

Seldom had I seen a more sublime or more beautiful panoramic view, leading me to conceive at each moment some heaven beyond. A revelation in my mind was the immensity and breadth of nature, the exquisite color scheme of dark green with patches of lighter green intermittently separated by reddish and purple volcanic ranges. I could not say how much of the whole area of 573,000 acres which composed Daisetsuzan National Park, the largest of all national parks in Japan, could be seen from that point. Reflecting how majestic and beautiful these mountains were under the fine September weather, I wondered what they would look like in a Hokkaido winter when the terrible snowdrifts piled up and leveled every gap between the ranges into an enormous flat white world.

As we motored out of Sounkyo Spa, the scenery became even more spectacular than on our arrival. It was a delight to see how the rocky cliffs rose straight from the river in columns and pinnacles in a series of almost hexagonal pillars, though many were hidden behind the tall trees. We got out of the car and Rudolph led me through a gap in the trees to the riverside. A loud exclamation from someone: "Oh, what a beautiful waterfall." This was called Ryusei-no-Taki, or Shooting Star Falls in kanji translation, indicating the speed with which the water shot its way downward. It was guarded on either side by two lofty and sharp-edged cliffs, covered by lovely and colorful foliage, some yellow and a few turning red. What charm, what classic beauty, and what a setting for a painting! My mind formed the following poem on the spot:

日上聽濤潺
對此驚奇蹟
靜境益特章
舞態炫人目
輕盈似雪仙
閃爍洒銀沫
似瀉幾何年
白練飛崖巔

A sheet of white silk flies over the cliff,
How many years have you been falling like this?
Glittering as you scatter silver foam,
Your supple movement resembles a snowy fairy.

Your dancing steps dazzling human eyes,
This tranquil scene engenders passion.
Facing the unusual sight with astonishment,
I wish to listen to your whispering day after day.

After a short walk along the river from the Shooting Star Falls we came to another waterfall, known in Japanese as Ginga-no-Taki, or Milky Way Falls. We Chinese call the Milky Way Silver River, as do the Japanese in kanji. It is an appropriate name for the falls, for it did not rush down as full as the Shooting Star but splashed all the way down, producing a cloud of misty vapor which veiled the treetops to give the whole area an ethereal beauty, visible yet unattainable. There are a few more waterfalls all along the Sounkyo Gorge but the Shooting Star and the Milky Way are the two best. While we were moving on slowly I remembered a legend told me by Mr. Sumio Sakata about the Ishikari River. Up the river in Kamikawa lived a special race of the Tokachi Ainu people, who differed from other Ainus nearby. One day the Ainus in Kamikawa found a large amount of rhubarb leaves floating down while they were fishing in the Ishikari River a little way off, near the Sounkyo Gorge. The large rhubarb leaves, growing abundantly everywhere in Hokkaido, were used by the Ainus as drinking containers. When they saw so many rhubarb leaves, the chief of the Kamikawa Ainus thought that the Tokachi Ainus must have been massing up the river ready to attack the Kamikawa Ainus, so he told his people to be ready to meet the onslaught. He knew that they would come to attack, for they wanted to take over the rich and peaceful village at Kamikawa, but he feared that his people were not numerous enough to oppose them and worried terribly. His guess was not wrong and no sooner had he ordered his people to stand by than thousands of his enemies rushed down the river in many canoes. They steered by the winding rapids under the towering cliffs. Suddenly all the steersmen ceased to guide the

A Massachusetts silo in Hokkaido

canoes, for all those Tokachi Ainus noticed a number of beautiful girls, naked, dancing on the top of the cliffs and became so enraptured that they continued to gaze at them till they forgot what they came for. While they gazed at the naked dancing girls so intently, an unexpected torrent poured down and drowned them all. Thus the Kamikawa Ainus were saved. The explanation was that the naked dancing girls were the beautiful high waterfalls, which deceived their eyes when they approached the Sounkyo Gorge at dusk. I thought this was the most ingenious story about waterfalls that had ever come to my knowledge.

After the Milky Way Fall we moved slowly to see the few smaller falls on the way. Then both sides of the gorge became more exposed with large walls of unusual rocky columns and pinnacles, actually presenting on the sharp face of the promontory the appearance of a magnificent gallery, or colonnade, upward of a hundred feet in height. The enormous wall on the left side, which we were facing, Rudolph called God's Cathedral, which was a good term for the imposing natural construction. I also thought those columns, arranged so neatly side by side, appeared to be like huge organ pipes. They also reminded me of those lofty and massive basalt columns, rising to the height of 315 feet, which were known as the Giant's Loom near Port Noffer in Ireland. I saw them years ago when I lived in Europe. But the Giant's Loom was formed by the sea and had no trees growing round it, unlike this wall of basalt columns in Sounkyo.

The rocky cliffs formed of basalt columns with sharp edges became more prominent when we drove out of the gorge and into the open of Daisetsuzan National Park. Close to the exit were the charming scenic spots, Kobako ("small box") and Obako ("big box"). They looked like two different boxes, for both had rocky cliffs which looked like corrugated walls. Some of the cliffs were lit up by a blaze of bright sunshine, revealing them in reddish yellow color with a number of small trees growing out of the cleft between the rocks. The mellow tints of the cliffs and the fresh green leaves, some of which were turning red, reflected in the rushing water of the Ishikari River, and the bright green of the grass on the river's margin were most tempting to an artistic hand.

Rudolph used to come to this area to fish. It was along the upper part of the Ishikari River a little way from Obako. The river bed was quiet and there were no rocky cliffs on either side. Rudolph put on his long rubber boots to wade in by the edge of the thick reed bush. He was the lonely fisherman in the picture of a massive river moving under a bright sunny sky. I stepped onto one rock after another amidst the running water, which was clear to the bottom and which seemed to be passing by so hastily. I remembered the Tokachi Ainus, who must have passed this part of the river to go to attack the Kamikawa Ainus down the Sounkyo

Gorge. It could have been very noisy then when all the war canoes rushed by together. But now it was unusually tranquil in the balmy air!

No trout were caught. On our way back home I thought of Sounkyo Gorge, which was formed when the upper Ishikari River eroded the lava congelation in the north side of Mt. Daisetsuzan thousands of years ago. I wonder who was the first person to discover it. No doubt one of the early Ainus. Though the Sounkyo Gorge is not so extensive and curious an assemblage of basalt columns as the Irish Giant's Loom, which covers one thousand square miles, it is still a wondrous creation of nature. I composed the following verse:

God's work, spirit's axes, cut out the Sounkyo Gorge,
Flying falls, hanging cliffs, also a world's wonder.
Am I the guest of the Peach-blossom Spring?
This secluded, beautiful spot should be known to all.

The Peace-blossom Spring refers to an ancient Chinese Taoist utopia which every Chinese longed to visit as a guest.

A Hokkaido farmhouse with a Massachusetts silo, near Asahikawa

XLV

Ainus, Marimos, and Lake Akan

THE DAWN was softly, slowly breaking; we left for the long journey to Daisetsuzan National Park and then on to Lake Akan for a few days' stay. There were a number of trees tinged with crimson, faint and fine, for autumn appears in the far north earlier than in the south. Far ahead of our car two hawks were spirally ascending the skies, in a glorious graceful manner, which enhanced the stillness of the air. The sun was not yet out when we entered Sounkyo Gorge. We stopped to have a look at Kobako and Obako.

Less than an hour later, rain poured down heavily and everywhere was overcast. It became dark. Upon our arrival at Sekihoku-toge, we stopped and entered a small hut which sold things to eat and drink. Rudolph knew the shopkeeper and had a baked squid—dried and salted—which seemed to be a popular food on sale almost everywhere in Japan. I had a hot corn on the cob with a bottle of milk. The rain did not stop and we had to move on. It was a downhill drive and the peaks rolled backward one after another and were soon lost in the dense clouds. Hills on both sides looked like a sea of mountains with pale, bluish waves moving away from us. A sight of beauty and mystery!

Seller of squids

After another two hours we reached Kitami—quite a good-sized city. Rudolph wanted to introduce me to a Catholic priest, a Dutchman, who had spent two or three years in China, but he was not in his church. On the wall there was a good painting of a Dutch ship in color, apparently painted by a Japanese artist in the early Nagasaki days when only Dutch ships could put into port there.

Afterward we had a good lunch and also a look round the shops. I found a beautiful rock on a handsome stand in a rock shop which was much to my liking but too heavy to take back to New York with me by air.

By the time we reached Bihoro, the rain had stopped. Rudolph drove on and on, ascending a promontory where a number of huts joined in a row had gifts and souvenirs for sale. Oh, what a beautiful lake—Lake Kutcharo—surrounded with blue hills, lay below before our eyes! The calm, overcast, soft afternoon with its light mist obscured not only all

Ainus of Bihoro-Toge

the strong tints of nature but all the smaller variations of forms, for the hills were lost. A little island called Nakazima was in the center. It seemed to be a general mass of mellow harmony, well composed with gleaming water all around, and sober coloring, unmarked by any strength of effect. The place was called Bihoro-Toge. A peculiarly beautiful sight! It was also a strategic spot! I wondered if any important historical event had ever taken place here, for this was an ancient Ainu living center. I was later told that nothing had happened here before. This made me realize that the Ainu people, so unlike the American Indians, never staged any resistance against the Japanese encroachment.

It was rather late in the day and we were the only passers-by. A young girl in a bright red jumper was propelling a pushcart with hot corn on the cob and baked octopus and squids for sale. As soon as she saw Rudolph she exclaimed in surprise and begain to talk to him rapidly. She must have seen him many times before. As we came up to her pushcart she spoke to me in Japanese. Rudolph explained that she was making a complimentary remark about me and that she thought I looked like a scholar. How worldly this girl was! My travels with Rudolph have confused many people who always took me as a guide for Rudolph but never thought it was the other way round. The girl was about twenty and quite good looking. She was very lively, talking to Rudolph and laughing all the while. Then we went to the edge of the promontory, where a few Ainu people in their costumes were standing.

A girl propelling a pushcart

Two bearded Ainu men and one Ainu woman asked Rudolph to sit with them for a photograph and then I sat with them for another photograph. It had become windy from the lake and chilly too. A few big trucks arrived and most of the small stores were dismantled and the goods packed up for home. The Ainu people, with their young bear sitting on the top of the truck, left for home too. Rudolph then drove down around Lake Kutcharo and onto a small peninsula called Wakoto Peninsula. We entered a small wood for a cup of hot coffee, which Trina had prepared for us. Later we strolled along the lake shore. Some autumnal tints could be detected on some trees nearby. The water surface became wrinkled by the evening wind and Rudolph told me to keep a good watch on the water for some tiny green duckweed balls which might be washed up on the shore. These green duckweed balls were a special product only to be found in Lake Akan. They were called marimo. An old Ainu man offered a few brownish-colored duckweed balls, and Rudolph bought two. These were not real marimo, for the real one, Rudolph told me, was now prohibited by law to be collected privately. This sounded rather mysterious and I began to be anxious to see the real marimo! None was washed ashore!

Dusk had already crept in. Rudolph said that he loved driving at night, for night had eyes. This was a new theory to me; he thought one should try to see more clearly at night. After three hours our destination, Hotel Ichikawa, was reached. Rudolph remarked that the season to visit Lake Akan was nearly over and there would soon be heavy snow all around. After a good hot bath and a substantial dinner, Rudolph took me to see a few friends of his. First we went to see a young sculptor, Tadao Nishiyama, whose medium was wood and who had made a good name around Lake Akan. He was born in Tokyo but had now settled down at Lake Akan. Many of his woodcarvings were shown to me and I found he had a good technique and interesting ideas. He had not only made a good name for himself in the area, but also made a good, regular income from an invention of his derived from the following legend:

The Rev. Mr. Kuyten and Mr. Nishiyama

> Long, long ago, the bitterly cold weather had lasted for many days at the Kotan or village of Ainus, and food was running short. When people were suffering from hunger, they found some food almost every morning which was brought to them during the night by unknown people from the neighborhood. So, as tradition says, Ainu people escaped starving to death. Afterward, as they came to know it was Koropokkurus, or dwarfs, who lived under the leaves of giant butterburs, that had done them such a great favor, they began to worship them as their gods or saviors.

Mr. Nishiyama created a small woodcarving in the style of an Ainu totem pole as a gift for sale, quite original yet peculiar to the Akan Ainus. It was sold to the summer visitors and he had to employ two or three helpers to turn out as many little dwarf gifts as they could day by day. A most profitable enterprise! At the same time, he kept up his creative activities and produced a number of works each year to be shown in the big cities. Most of his big carvings were in bas-relief, breathing an air of local Ainu life, which could be the main source of his great success. Some of his bigger works were hanging in the restaurants and also in the local library and assembly place. I found him a very agreeable, friendly young man, and it was a great pity that I could not converse with him in order to discuss his ideas.

Nishiyama then went with us to a local coffee club run by Madame Ikeda. We all drank Sapporo beer. There was a small band playing Western music. A few young people came in for drinks and then left. Afterward, the young singer came to sit with us and I was told that she was quite well known in the big cities. Later Mrs. Nishiyama joined us for a moment and I was interested in her face, which I recognized from examples of her husband's work. She was his model.

Afterward Rudolph took me to see the Ainu village not far from the hotel. Except for two or three totem poles erected outside the entrance, the shops and living quarters of the Ainus were similar to those I saw in other places. We came to a shop where stood an elderly Ainu man with

pure white beard who knew Rudolph and talked to him happily. He
found out where I came from and said that he had been to China via
Russia some fifty years ago but he could not remember much now. I
never knew why many of the Ainu people went to China. He was a jolly
fellow and expressed his opinion about the world that everyone should
live like brothers with no quarrel whatsoever. Rudolph promised we
would come back again.

The next day we spent in Kushiro. On the third morning, Rudolph
drove me to see Mr. Nishiyama's shop again and asked him to go with
us to see two small lakes, Lake Panke and Lake Penke, as the Ainus
called them. Both lakes were secluded in a dense wooded area with
masses of tall trees growing thickly round the lake shores and we had
difficulty finding a little opening to get down to the edge of the water.
We stood by each lake for a while and the effect was very lovely when
the sun rose in unsullied brightness, diffusing its ruddy light over the
upper part of the trees, which contrasted with the deeper shadow below
while the center of the lake suddenly began to gleam like a mirror!

When we came up to the road again, Nishiyama pointed out a tree
called shina that he used for his carvings and he also told me that most
of the wood carvings of bears and Ainu folks were made of this tree. He
also said that the well-knit texture of this wood could withstand heat.
Mr. Egami of the Tokyo Information Center told me that the shina tree
(*Tulid japonica*) is indigenous to Japan and has never been transplanted
to any other part of the world, and that this tree is best suited to carving
because it is soft and resists fissure. This would explain why Japan produced many fine wooden Buddhist statues.

I then asked Rudolph about seeing the real marimo. Nishiyama sug-

Marimo preservation place

gested taking us to the place on the lake shore where a guard was stationed to protect the marimo from being stolen. Marimo, or *Glad Ophora Sauteri*, is a singular spherical green ball in various sizes, found only in Lake Akan. This rare water plant usually measures from half an inch to eight inches in diameter and floats and sinks according to weather conditions. It is said that marimo comes up to the surface to release oxygen at rather regular intervals and then sinks to the depths of the lake when it has absorbed enough oxygen to weigh it down. Owing to marimo's peculiar and unusually velvetlike appearance, many people came to Lake Akan specially to collect it to take home and keep in glass bowls indoors. Even the imperial family kept some. Gradually there were no more marimos to be seen in Lake Akan so a law was passed to protect them, and people were asked to return to the lake all marimos they had. Five came back from the imperial family; so no one could keep marimo privately. As it has since become one of the great attractions of Lake Akan, stories of people trying to steal marimo were not few. A conservation area was established. After a five-minute drive, we found the place. An elderly man was standing close to an opening between two long metal pipes closing off the shores of the lake. It was here that the marimo used to be pushed ashore. The old man would not move a step from where he was standing to exchange a word with our friend; then his old wife came out from the only house nearby—the one specially built for the old couple to live in. The wife was very amicable and told us that they had taken the job some five years ago. She said that a marimo of more than six inches' diameter would be about two hundred years old; those of more than a foot diameter would be nearly five hundred years old, though she did not tell how she knew this to be so. I admired their being so faithful to their duty. Nishiyama thought that so far nobody could explain why the marimo formed itself into a round ball. He also said that a lake in Sakhalin, Russia, and a lake in Switzerland have similar kinds of marimos, but no one had made any comparison with the ones found in Lake Akan.

A great fuss has been made over the marimo of Lake Akan. There was a love story attached to it which Mr. Sumio Sakata told me;

Setona was a beautiful daughter of a chief. She loved a servant named Manibe. He was handsome, strong, and clever. They played together picking flowers in the fields, paddling a canoe, and playing the reed flute. Thus they spent happy days together. But these happy days did not last long. On Setona's sixteenth birthday, her future husband was to be chosen. Setona wanted to marry Manibe, but against her will Menika, son of the vice-chief, was chosen. Menika knew that his beautiful wife loved the servant. He was jealous and angry and decided to murder him. One night he waylaid and suddenly attacked

Manibe with a sword. But Manibe fought back and instead gave him a serious wound from which Menika died. Manibe knew that he would have to die, for he had killed his master's son-in-law. As he could not excuse himself even though it was in self-defense, he went to Lake Akan in a canoe and drowned himself in the center of the lake. Days passed by, and Setona had been in tears day and night. One night she heard a familiar tune from the lake. It was Manibe's reed flute. She paddled a canoe to the center of the lake. She never returned. Later people found a pair of green weed balls floating side by side that then disappeared. Later they reappeared. So marimo represents their spirits.

now become very popular, and almost everyone at Lake Akan and those who come to see it know it.

Mizumo o wataru kaze samishi	Wind blowing over the surface of lake lonely
Akan no yama no mizu-umi ni	On the lake of Mt. Akan.
Ukabu Marimo yo, Nani omou	Oh, floating Marimo, what is in your mind?
Marimo yo, Marimo, Midori no Marimo	Oh, Marimo, Marimo, You Marimo of green.

Ever since the discovery of the marimos, which have become a great topic in Japan, many poems have been written about them. My friend Burton Watson has made a number of translations of them:

(I)   When it's fair weather, floating on top of the water,
      When it's cloudy, sinking down to the bottom.
      Love is sad! We agree with a sigh,
      Marimo, marimo, tears of Marimo!
                                        Anonymous

(II) Wind across the water comes blowing sad:
      What do you think of as you float on the lake of Mount Akan,
      Marimo, marimo, emerald marimo?
                                        Anonymous

(III) An inn in winter—
      Marimo of Akan
      The only green thing.
                  Yamaguchi Seison

Gradually a Marimo Festival developed—a Shinto priest leads a procession, and two Ainu elders in their costumes, holding a beautiful green marimo, row a boat to the center of the lake in order to put this marimo back into the water. This festival has been staged annually for the past few years. Only the Japanese with an innate sense for organization and for festival could have done it so well!

We had arranged to go to the Hotel O-Akan for lunch and Madame Ikeda and her daughter were already there waiting for us. This hotel was situated a little way from the city of Akan down the road to Kushiro and used to be the best one in this area. No one was staying there at the time. The five of us had the whole dining hall to ourselves and the meats were cooked in the Genghis Khan manner, but there was far too much for us to eat. Madame Ikeda once lived in Peking and she prepared the food very well. There was a beautiful brook below the window of the dining hall and we all went for a look. Nothing could be more pleasing than listening to the murmurs of the running brook and watching water running over stones and being caught in the sun to turn silvery. Rudolph went down to walk by the brook in order to see if there were any trout.

Nishiyama had booked a motorboat to take himself, Rudolph, and me around Lake Akan. The two ladies would not join us. We started while the sun was still high. The lake is quite big, 16.5 miles in circumference and is surrounded by dense woods and hills with Mt. Me-Akan on its west side and Mt. O-Akan on the east. The wind over the water was not too strong. The boatman seemed to want to take us to the little island to see the marimos quickly; the boat pitched up and down as it was shooting its way through the waves. That which but an hour before was calm, now became a scene of sublime and chaotic uproar! Our destination was finally reached and we followed a big throng from the sightseeing boat which must have arrived a little earlier. The small island was thickly wooded and we walked along a narrow footpath and came to an open place with two small ponds of clear water in which were a number of green velvetlike balls. Most of them were about two or three inches in diameter and four big ones looked to be five or six inches in diameter. Apart from the marimos in the two ponds, nothing could be seen on the

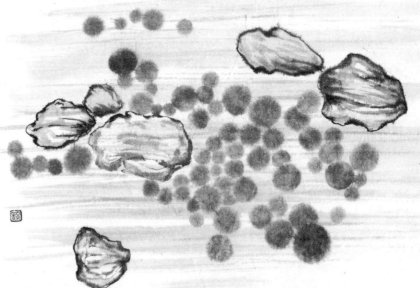

A number of marimos in the pond

little island. I was very happy to have seen the real marimo, though they were lying motionless. The island was almost in the eastern part of Lake Akan. Through an opening between the trees I could see the blue hills on the other shore, behind which was Mt. Me-Akan with clouds of white steam on the top of it, for it was still volcanically active. The Ainu people seemed to be interested in sex for they even so designate the mountains! Mt. Me-Akan is the female and Mt. O-Akan is the male.

Afterward our motorboat took us around the lake, and the steersman was told not to go as fast as before. The air was fresh but cold, for the sun was about to sink in the west; I enjoyed the changing beauty of the scene, and the contrast between splendor while the sun was still high, and the obscurity when the sun was setting. The varied tints of the autumnal leaves on some of the trees glowed under the parting rays in particularly soft colors.

Presently our boat shot into a narrow waterway between dense trees. Suddenly hundreds of black crows flew into the air as if they were a big force to drive us away. Nishiyama burst out laughing, saying there were too many crows in Lake Akan and the Ainus did not like them, for they thought the crows were devils. I remembered that according to an Ainu legend the ancestor of the crow dived into the mouth of a demon to prevent him from swallowing the sun and that was why we have daytime now. Nishiyama said also that the Ainu people regarded the eagle as god of day and the owl god of the night. When our boat came out of the waterway the crows flew into the air again. I was interested in watching them in flight.

While walking later, Nishiyama pointed out a kind of grass plant with ball-like flowers. It was called sakasafuji; its root was poisonous and the Ainu people used it to kill the bear for bear festivals. Wild rhubarb growing along the roadside seemed to be one of the most common plants everywhere, particularly in Hokkaido.

After a good dinner at our hotel, Rudolph took me to the Buraku village where we saw the white-bearded old Ainu man again. He told us that there would be a Bear Festival taking place in an hour or so. We stopped at several shops and in one of them Rudolph asked to see Mr. Araki Mitsuo. We were told to go upstairs. After greetings, Mr. Araki and I exchanged visiting cards and on his I found four titles, one of which was President of the Buraku Association, indicating that he is the leader of the Ainus in the area of Lake Akan. There was a fire in the small stove in the center of the room, for it was quite chilly outside that evening. Mrs. Araki prepared tea for us, somewhat in the Chinese manner rather than like the Japanese tea ceremony. I asked a few questions concerning Ainu customs and Mr. Araki gave me a small booklet about them in Japanese. At last I asked if they ate bears and if they would eat the bear's palms or the forepaws. Mr. Araki stood up saying, "Oh, yes; that was a delicacy! We ate bear's palm. The bear's paws are eaten only by the chief and the rest eat the meat." This made me most happy, for I had asked this question at several places after my arrival in Hokkaido but no one could give me an answer. I had a purpose in asking this question. Mencius (fourth century B.C.), the pupil of Confucius's grandson, once said, "I like fish, and I also like bear's paws. If I cannot have the two together, I will let the fish go, and take bear's paws" (translated by Professor James Legge). This means that bear's paws were regarded as a delicacy in China in the fourth century B.C. In those early days in north China bears could have been among the common wild animals seen about. Bears were mentioned in the first Chinese anthology of poetry, or Book of Songs, dating back to the twelfth century B.C., if not earlier. Mencius was not the only one who loved eating bear's paw. Though bears were common in ancient China, nothing about a cult such as a Bear Festival was ever recorded in ancient Chinese books.

Something was making a noise outside like the sound of Chinese fire-crackers exploding from time to time. We went down and saw a fire on the woodpile which we had noticed when we came in. The Bear Festival was on. A good many people were standing on each side of the central square where the festival was taking place. Dry wood bars were piled up in the shape of a squarish box in which a young bear was supposed to be kept for the special occasion, but this festival was not a first rate one and therefore no bear took part. Most of the Ainu people of the village came to join the show in their local costumes. The old man with white eyebrows and long white beard whom we had met twice before was the chief performer in a colorful costume with red lining and a yellow straw ring round his head above his brows. He held a stick called Saishu Bashi in his right hand and a lacquered cup in the left and was murmuring a prayer in Ainu. After that, the Ainu people gathered together dancing and singing in the center—the song being similar to those that I heard in other Ainu villages. This was followed by two young Ainu men dancing with a dagger or sword in the right hand of each, while two young girls danced in partnership. At the end all the Ainu people joined together for a last dance. But the chilly autumn wind blew hard toward the center of the square and most of the spectators felt cold and moved out of the village quickly. Thus the festival was over. Two young bears were tied up in the front of two gift shops but played no part. I was told that this Bear Festival took place only once a year and I felt lucky to have seen it.

However, it differed greatly from the Ainu Bear Festival, or *Iyomante*, that Dr. Joseph M. Kitagawa wrote about.

Hepere—a bear cub

Little needs to be said about the long period of preparation that precedes the festival itself. The bear's cub (Hepere) is given the utmost courtesy and affection. It is fed with dried fish and millet. . . . The present writer participated in *Iyomante* on August 3, 1935, at Piratori. The whole series of rites usually lasts for three days. The Ainus are careful that the intoxicant should not attract evil spirits, and for this purpose the Inau of Kotan Kor Kami (the kami of the village, that is, the owl) is placed on top of the barrel. The main part of *Iyomante* takes place on the second day. The Hepere is led around the sacred ground several times. . . . People shoot Hepere-ai (arrows for the cub) at the visitors. The Hepere-ai are offered to the departing visitor as a souvenir, and people can take them home as good luck charms.

Dr. John Batchelor writes: "The shouting now becomes deafening, and the bear sometimes furious. But the wilder the bear becomes, the more delighted the people get. While being so dragged, two young men rushed forward and seized him (bear) by the face and ears and others catch hold of his fore and hind legs. He is thus taken to two poles lying on the ground, having had an Inau wood thrust into his mouth at which he bites hard. In some places an arrow is shot into his heart and all the places and all the blood carefully caught in a vessel and drunk warm by the elders. However, the creature is not given the *coup de grâce* by the arrow till after the throttling has commenced."

At Piratori, arrows were used to dispatch the Hepere, not once but two or three times. The blood was caught carefully and drunk. Those who drink fresh bear's blood at *Iyomante* have to stay away from women until the coming of the new moon. If they do not do so, it is believed that they will die. For this reason, only the elders are urged to drink the bear's blood warm.

From the above description, the bear was the chief object of the festival and it had to be killed in the end. This explained to me, too, why I saw always one or two young bears chained in front of a gift shop in all the Ainu villages that I visited in Hokkaido. The most paradoxical point is that the Ainus respected the bear as their god of the mountains where they lived, yet their god provided them with flesh to keep them alive. There are wood-carved bears in Hokkaido everywhere and the bear is therefore the symbol of the land. Dr. Kitagawa continued:

> In a real sense, *Iyomante* is the supreme religious act of the Ainu community in that it embodies all the essential features of symbol, ritual, and myth through which and by which the Ainus have formed a cosmic significance of their existence throughout the ages. . . . Since the turn of this century, the Ainus have come under the impact of modern Japanese civilization to the extent that the latter tends to undercut the foundations of traditional Ainu life and culture. An increasing number of Ainus have adopted the Japanese language and culture and way of life, discarding their ancestral traditions. It has been pointed out that the number of Ainus who are well versed in the epics (Yukar) and religious practices is rapidly decreasing, and even the observance of *Iyomante* might soon become a thing of the past. . . . The full scale celebration has not been held since 1935. The Japanese Press in the summer of 1958 engaged in a heated controversy regarding the justification for killing a bear even in a sacred religious rite . . . *Iyomante* was a long ritual; there was a gradual heightening of religious feeling among those who watched and those who took part. . . . The ecstatic expressions of those who participated in the singing, dancing, and praying gave one every reason to believe that for the Ainus, at any rate, the memorable experience of their ancestors had become real again in the performance of *Iyomante*.

I enjoyed reading Dr. Kitagawa's description, which was recommended to me by Professor Alex Wayman, but I must admit that I was not induced to wish to have been a witness at Piratori's *Iyomante*. Being no student of religion nor of anthropology, I am interested to know what had been done in the past, but do not wish some of the things the ancient people did to be carried on to the present day.

I feel fortunate to live in this era and still be able to meet some of the Ainu people in their own villages. But I doubt if there will be many Ainus left to live up to their traditions some years from now, for Hokkaido is being rapidly modernized. There will be more mixed marriages between Ainus and Japanese, particularly if the Ainu children receive

Sakata said that this was not an Ainu legend, but one created by a shrewd bus company to entertain the passengers on their way to Lake Akan. A song about marimo was composed at the same time and it has the same kind of education as the Japanese. They would want to have TV in their homes, go to the movies, enjoy themselves in the nightclubs, and dance the modern dances, as well as live in modern homes and eat modern foods. They would resent being called a backward race.

According to Hsin T'ang Shu, or the New History of the T'ang Dynasty (618–960), China already knew of the existence of the Ainu people in Japan, as Professor Carrington Goodrich and Dr. Ryusaku Tsunoda recorded: "The beards of the Ainus were four feet long. They carried arrows on the neck, and without ever missing would shoot a gourd held on the head of a person standing several tens of steps away." What good shots they must have been! It is interesting that when the empress Saimei sent Sakabe-no-Muraji-Iwashiki as the Japanese ambassador to the court of T'ang, two Ainus (a man and a woman) were included in the diplomatic mission. This would mean that in those early days the Ainu people were on the same footing as the Japanese. Why have the Ainu people never taken any active part in the Japanese political development since then? The compiler of the Nihon-Shoki also said that the T'ang emperor was most curious about the Ainus and asked many questions about them. The Japanese ambassador explained to the Chinese emperor that the Ainus lived in the northernmost region of Japan. He also remarked that the Ainus did not grow the five grains but ate meat as a regular diet and they lived in the mountains and not in houses. What a great pity it was that this particular Japanese ambassador did not find out, as I did, that the Ainus considered the bear's paws a delicacy! The T'ang emperor would have become more interested in the Ainus, for he must have read about Mencius's remark on fish and bear's paws! The saddest part was that the T'ang emperor never thought of asking a court painter to make a painting of those two Ainus who came to his court; otherwise we should have something on which to base our study of the modern Ainus in Hokkaido.

A country sight in Hokkaido

XLVI

Red-crested Cranes in Kushiro

AFTER A GOOD night beside Lake Akan, Rudolph suggested taking me to see a hot waterfall. This intrigued me, for I have never heard of a hot waterfall. It was a dry morning, quite mild, though sunless. We stopped first at Bogakudai, or Terrace for gazing at Mt. O-Akan, but could see nothing, for it was hidden by moving clouds. We then came to an unfrequented yellowish brown earth road by the side of a small lake. The water of the lake was extraordinarily clear with hardly anything in it. The Ainu people called this lake Oneto, Rudolph told me. Bubbles of sulphuric gas kept rising. Suddenly a sound was heard from somewhere like a monk in a temple beating his wooden fish and reciting the sutra at the same time. There was no Buddhist temple anywhere. Rudolph took out his field glasses and discovered a big woodpecker having a morning meal.

Gradually we reached a point where we could see some flying water sparkling ahead against the sunshine; it was Takinoyu, or Soup Waterfall. It was not a tumultuous surge between grassy banks but many silvery lines of water sprinkling down among oddly arranged rocks. I walked to the lower part and dipped my right hand into the water; it was quite warm. Rudolph walked up the rocks to the top in order to see if he could find some dried snake skins for me. While he was up on the highest part, two Japanese men and four women in kimonos arrived. The older of the two men was attracted by Rudolph's effort in climbing so high up and walked up there too.

A wandering monk from
Shimonoseki

Rudolph returned empty-handed but he explained why he wanted to find some snake skins. On one occasion he gave a snake skin to a young Ainu girl who was delighted with it and put the skin in her handbag as soon as she received it, saying that it would bring her luck, as the Ainus believed that it symbolized wealth.

Japan seems to have more snakes than many other lands. According to the report of the Tokyo Metropolitan Police, thousands of snakes are purchased every week in Tokyo alone. The *Shima-Hebi,* or striped snake, is in great demand, for it is believed to have special medicinal value. About 80 per cent of the snakes sold are charred and powdered or dried and pulverized and made into pills and capsules to be used as medicine. About 20 per cent go to the table, boiled, baked, or roasted. Dozens of licensed snake dealers in Tokyo, constituting the Snake Dealers' Guild, maintain groups of professional snake catchers in several parts of the country. The best snake-hunting district is reported to be in Shimane Prefecture and around Lake Biwa, although there are numerous other noted snake regions throughout Japan. I used to hear people joking about the Cantonese eating snakes. Now I learned something about snake-eating in Japan and the hot waterfall as well. (A year later I saw the Maruonotaki Waterfall in Kirishima National Park, the water of which was a hot downpour.)

On our way back to lunch, we met a Buddhist priest with a bamboo basketlike hat covering his head, begging alms from house to house. Rudolph explained to me that he was a komuso (*komu*, a kind of coarse straw matting, *so*, a priest). Originally priests of a branch of the Zen sect playing the *shakuhachi*—a vertical flute—would go through the streets begging. The straw matting eventually evolved into the basket-shaped hat. The basket hat was once used by spies disguised as komuso while endeavoring to discover military and political secrets and by criminals as a means of concealment. Asked where he came from, the priest answered, "Shimonoseki"—the southernmost tip of Honshu and very far away from Lake Akan.

In the afternoon the weather changed. There was a bright sun high above. I proposed to Rudolph that we go to Kushiro to see the red-crested cranes while it was fine. The red-crested crane is called tancho-zuru, or simply tancho. There is a Tanchozuru National Park recently established between Kushiro and Lake Akan. The birds were first observed to come to nest in the marshland of Kushiro in 1924, and gradually the Kushiro district was known as the only natural habitat of these cranes. The wild ones flew over from Siberia every October and November and stayed till March and April. Since the establishment of this national park a number of cranes have been kept and tamed under a special custodian.

This particular bird has long been an important object in the history of Chinese literature and art. When I heard of this crane park in Hokkaido I was determined to see it. Rudolph took me willingly. On our way out of the town of Lake Akan, I saw a woman selling hot Hokkaido crabs with beautiful red shells with long legs like those of spiders, quite large in size, in front of a shop and I bought a couple of them for the trip.

There was little traffic on the road. The trees on both sides of the road were still in their fullest dress in early September. We were going down the hills which stretched far to the seashore, where the city of

Mr. Ryoji Takahashi

Kushiro lies. Presently we saw a horizontal wooden board with the words "Tanchozuru National Park." Rudolph parked the car near the high wire enclosure. We walked close to the enclosure but could see little inside, for the trees and grass were quite tall. Unexpectedly we heard a cry like the chirping of a sparrow, but louder, from a young bird in a gray brown coat with wings sparsely feathered. A notice hanging on the wire told us that this young bird, called Roro, was hatched on May 15, 1968. Then we saw another one in the next enclosure, hatched a month later. Far, far away inside the big enclosure among masses of grass walked two little white birds, and we knew that they must be the parents. But we could not see them properly. Suddenly Rudolph got a bright idea; he asked me to give him a visiting card and walked straight to the office to ask if he could have a key for us to go inside for a closer look at the bigger birds. He thought he could show my card to prove I had come all the way from New York to see this bird and it would be a pity not to be able to see it properly. After a few minutes Rudolph came back without a key but the custodian, Mr. Ryoji Takahashi, came along with him. Mr. Takahashi told us that we need not go inside the enclosure, for he could call the birds to come near the netting. So he called out something in Japanese quite loudly and all the white-bodied birds, four in number, began to walk back toward us. Again, Mr. Takahashi called out, louder than before, which Rudolph interpreted to mean "Hurry up; we want to see you." Indeed the four white-bodied cranes with black tips on their wings dashed along near the wire. There was a young just-matured one among the four, though it still had a yellowish brown coat. Each one had a red spot on the top of its head as expected. I felt satisfied to see them so close at hand. Each had a long strip of black feathers round a good part of its neck. They walked and pecked the grass elegantly and slowly, unlike the gluttonous pigeons, and they moved in a stately manner. Presently Mr. Takahashi said that he would tell the cranes to sing for us. No sooner had he called than all four cranes stretched their long, long necks straight upward with their beaks pointing to the sky and sang as loud as they could. The voices were resonant and trumpetlike. They reminded me of a line from the ancient Confucius classic *Book of Songs*:

Ho ming ju chiu kao,   The crane cries in the ninth pool of the marsh,
Sheng wen ju t'ien.   And her voice is heard in the sky.

Indeed, their song is meant to be heard across the sky. Confucius lived in the sixth century B.C. That means cranes appeared in China in the sixth century B.C., if not earlier. For the first time I heard birds which could be told to sing and obeyed. Even a well-trained dog could not be more obedient than that. One of Confucius's disciples, Kung Yeh-ch'ang was known to understand bird language, but had not the reputation of being able to ask the bird to sing. How Mr. Takahashi managed to train the cranes to understand what he said to them is really a great mystery.

Mr. Takahashi then told us that they had tried to rear baby cranes in brooders, but none of them lived. When he came here to take the post as custodian, he decided to raise the baby cranes in a natural environment. He made a great success of the first baby, Roro. When it was first hatched, he took it to his bed and fed it with water and rice like his own child. As baby birds are accustomed to hide their heads under their mother's wings, this baby crane would put its head under his arm for the whole night. "For forty-five days," he continued, "the baby crane never dirtied my bed." Mr. Takahashi remarked that his wife gave him much careful cooperation in the success. The baby crane developed an affection for him; it would touch his mouth with its beak as if kissing. The baby crane would always cry for him whenever he was near, as it was crying when we were standing with him. It would take three years for the baby crane to grow a red crest on the top of its head, and in the fourth year, it would become fully mature. When winter starts in October, many wild cranes would migrate to Kushiro from Siberia and the newly matured cranes might fly away with the rest when they migrated back to Siberia in the spring. I asked if he had had to do something to their wings so that they would not fly away. He said no and that the cranes could fly anywhere they liked but they would always come back when he called. He told us also that his cranes could recognize his voice from ten kilometers away, but an ordinary dog would answer his master's call within one kilometer only. This gave proof to many ancient Chinese stories of how some Chinese poets or men of letters or Taoist hermits loved to keep the red-crested cranes as pets in their gardens and used to set them free to fly away in the morning and they would usually return in the evening. An instance is the passage written by the poet-painter-statesman, Su Tung-p'o (1036–1101):

> Chang kept two cranes and they were carefully trained by him. Every morning Chang would release the cranes westward through a gap to fly away and alight in the marshy land below, or soar aloft in the clouds at the birds' own will. They would return at nightfall with the utmost regularity. And so he named his abode the Chalet of Crane.

There were a good many famous buildings in China with the word *ho*, or *crane*, in their names. This bird was known as the Manchurian crane, or *Grus montignosia*, for it was hatched in the northern tip of Manchuria. Chinese masters since the Sung period, if not earlier, loved to paint this bird, simply because of its pure white body plumage and black wing tips and neck which suit the Chinese brush strokes very well indeed. Many good examples of the masterpieces on this bird are still in existence. One instance is the famous painting of a crane by the Zen monk-painter Mu Ch'i of the Sung period (960–1270) in the treasure house of Daito-kuji, Kyoto.

This red-crested crane has long been used in Japanese artistic designs for woodcarvings and textiles as well as for screen paintings. The crane was represented by a good many Japanese artists such as Kano Motonobu (1476–1559), Masanobu (1434–1530), and Okyo (1733–1795). Perhaps Sesshu Toyo (1420–1506), who painted three big screen paintings with cranes in each, could be regarded as the first one to paint this bird in Japan, but he seemed to have been influenced by Chinese work. Dr. Yoshimaro Yamashina listed this bird in his book, *Birds in Japan,* as *Grus japonesis,* or Japanese Crane, Tancho. Mr. Saburo Egami told me that the Japanese generally believe the crane lives for one thousand years and the tortoise for ten thousand years—hence both are motifs in Japanese art symbolizing longevity and therefore happiness. He also told me two interesting Japanese expressions. One is "Tsuru No Hito Koe," meaning "the cry of the crane," which denotes the voice of one in authority, for the crane has been regarded as a bird that lords over other birds. The other saying is "Semba-Zuru," or a thousand cranes, meaning a large flock of cranes. Cranes are a symbol of good luck and are often found in the designs of dresses. The Nobel Prize winner for literature, Yasunari Kawabata, chose the title *Thousand Cranes* for his novel with such an implication as Semba-Zuru for "good luck."

Mr. Takahashi told us that it was ten years ago when he first took on the post as the custodian of the Tanchozuru National Park; he was thirty-five when we met him. He had many disappointments in tackling his task; after the first five years he said that he began to despair and intended to quit the work. However, his patience and determination kept him going a little longer. Gradually the matured cranes grew confident, began to respond to his calls willingly, and eventually became friends with him. Now he wants to raise more and more baby cranes. Before we parted we congratulated Mr. Takahashi on his great success and hoped his wish would come true. With his patience and iron will he had achieved an apparently impossible task. He could no doubt make a success of anything he wanted to undertake.

In the evening Rudolph asked the proprietor of the hotel to lend us the movies he took when the mass of wild cranes gathered in the park of Kushiro one winter. The movie lasted about twenty minutes and showed hundreds of wild cranes on the marshy park, some walking in a stately manner on their two tall, slender legs with elegant movement, some pecking in the grass in various poses, and many dancing and chasing

each other round. These movements were clearly connected with music
playing at the same time, for the proprietor had cleverly asked a composer to work the music out for him. The cranes showed perfect rhythm.
The quick movement of the cranes and the swift turning of their tall,
slender legs coincided with the rhythm of the music while they flapped
their large wings as they seemed to spread their enormous skirts in swirling round. They were most interesting to watch and indeed the cranes
could dance and danced well. I asked Rudolph to repeat the show
twice—most unforgettable!

In China, Pao Chao (421–465), a well-known poet of the time,
wrote a long rhymed prose piece on "Dancing Cranes," or "Wu-ho Fu,"
describing the movement and performance in beautiful phrases. In the
Cleveland Museum of Art, there is a long scroll painting in color, entitled *The Land of Immortals* (*Hsien-shan t'u*) by Ch'en Ju-yen (active
fourteenth century), a section of which depicts a hermit or an immortal
watching two cranes dancing as if they had been taught by a teacher.
When I saw the cranes in Kushiro and the movie of them dancing in
that park I began to admire our forefathers' keen observation of nature
and the characteristics of nature's creatures.

From *The Land of Immortals*

XLVII

Epilogue

TIME HAS COME for me to end my observations on my silent travelling, though I have still left untouched a few places that I visited. And, of course, there are still many more interesting places in Japan that I have not yet visited. Nothing in the world comes to a perfect completion but there is always another time and another hope. The ancient Chinese philosopher Chuang-tzu wrote that "life has a limit, knowledge none." I can only try to understand whatever I can.

As I wrote in the prologue, this volume, unlike others in the series of Silent Traveller books, deals with many more than a single city. The reason is that I did not manage to stay in any Japanese city for any length of time and since I have no ability to read and speak the Japanese language my observations of a place were somewhat limited. However, my impression of each place was fresh, genuine, and uninfluenced by others, though many people might have wished me to stay longer in their cities to see additional interesting spots. I know that I may have missed much, but, if I am not too presumptuous, I believe that I have been able to see many more places than most of those who go to this east Asian corner from other lands.

I don't know if the Chinese were the first foreigners to go to Japan, since they were the closest neighbors. It is a tradition that in the beginning of the third century B.C. the first emperor of Ch'in sent one Hsü Fu, in charge of thousands of unmarried boys and girls across the China Sea in search of an immortal paradise, but they never returned. I wrote that when I was passing through the industrial city of Shingu on my way to Kii-Katsuura I was told about a new temple for the worship of Hsü Fu that had been built there. Apparently the Japanese believed that this was where Hsü Fu and his thousand unmarried boys and girls landed. Even now there are many Japanese with the surname of Ch'in living there. The remote ancestors of these Ch'in families could have been the first foreigners who came to Japan. Later, in the seventh century A.D., Japan sent many scholars and learned monks to China, but very few Chinese were known to have gone to Japan at that time. When the Mongolian ruler of China invaded Japan in the thirteenth century A.D. many

Chinese went as soldiers. Though most of them perished in the great storm that wrecked the entire Chinese fleet, some could have survived and stayed on in Japan. During the Tokugawa period in the seventeenth century only the Chinese and Dutch were allowed to live in Nagasaki and many Chinese must have continued to arrive from China. At the end of the Ming period many Chinese scholars and monks who refused to live under the Manchurian rule took refuge in Japan. When the first revolution took place and after China became a republic, many more Chinese, particularly young students, went to study modern science in Japan. The number of Chinese who have come to live in Japan since the early days must therefore be considerable. In spite of such numbers of Chinese who lived in Japan, very few of them appear to have written about or painted what they saw there. Many of them, of course, were merchants and did not write or paint. It is amazing that very few books on the history and culture of Japan were written and published in China, while for several hundred years Japanese scholars turned out books on every aspect of China. I must not forget that Huang Tsun-hsien (1848–1905), counselor to the Chinese legation in Tokyo in 1877, did compile a forty-volume history of Japan which was published in China, but it never had any popular circulation and has long disappeared from the Chinese book market.

Years ago when I lived in England I bought a set of Japanese books, six volumes in all, entitled *T'ang t'u ming sheng t'u hui* in Chinese, or *Todo meisho zue* in Japanese, meaning *Illustrations of famous places of the land of T'ang*. It was compiled by Okada Syokue, illustrated by Oka Yugaku and Ohara Minsei, and published in Osaka in 1805. It covered every beautiful and famous place in Peking and elsewhere in the whole province of Chihli (now called Hopei). There were five more sets, each about another province in China, including one for my own province, Kiangsi, and my native city, Kiukiang. I tried to buy this set but none was obtainable. Though they were published about a hundred and fifty years ago, they clearly showed that the Japanese had long been interested in describing every corner of China, not only in words but in pictures and maps. This induced me to think of going to Japan to do something similar. Indeed, I should have gone to see Japan before I went to England, for Japan is much closer to China than England is, but there were reasons for my not having done so. In my younger days I knew nothing of Japan, except that she had done a great wrong to China, which made her much disliked by the Chinese. I was born only a few years after Japan had crushed China in the Sino-Japanese war of 1895. The Japanese militaristic government then took great pride in its victory over the two big nations, Russia and China, and began a program of expansion. Having already colonized Korea and Formosa, she continued her political intrigues to gain more land from China and caused continuous troubles for the Chinese government from that time until 1945, when Japan capitulated at the end of the Second World War. In my elementary school days I read accounts in our school books of the Japanese wrongs to the Chinese, which instilled much hatred toward Japan and the Japanese in my young mind. When I went to high school and later to college I took part again and again in the nationwide students' strikes against Japan and joined the demonstrations to boycott Japanese goods. Naturally I then had no desire to go and see that unimaginably hateful land. Even if I had wanted to, the elders of my family would not have allowed me to do so. In those days most of the youngsters born in my generation were under strict parental control.

Then in 1928 Japanese troops for no apparent reason came to occupy Tsi-nan Fu in Shantung Province. The newly established Chinese Nationalist Government in Nanking was fully absorbed in dealing with the remnants of the Chinese warlords. China's indignation was aroused, calling for the immediate withdrawal of the Japanese troops from Chinese soil. But the commander of the Japanese army with orders from his military government demanded face-to-face talks with the head of the Chinese Nationalist Government. This could not be done, for it was improper for the head of a nation to talk with a mere troop commander of another country. So the National Government in Nanking sent a team of negotiators under the leadership of Tsai Kung-shih, who happened to be my great-uncle on my mother's side. At that time my elder brother, Chiang Chi (alias Chiang Ta-chuan), was working as the chief secretary to the military governor of Shanghai, and I was then teaching in Shanghai Chi-nan University, having just finished my own studies. Great-uncle Tsai came immediately from Nanking to Shanghai to have a talk with my brother and to ask if I would go with him as his assistant. I could not very well leave without permission from the president of my university, so my brother advised him that I would catch the next train for Tsi-nan in the north, the following day. Early next morning, however, we were informed that as soon as my great-uncle and his staff reached the outskirts of their destination, twelve of them were at once disposed of, not a single trace of their bodies was to be found! The men had been murdered. I think the Japanese army had been ordered not to settle the incident locally (it is now called the Tsi-nan incident in history books), for fear of its becoming a local issue, and so that the commander could say that he never knew of the delegation's arrival and could still demand an interview with the head of the Chinese Central Government.

From all the trouble China suffered from Japan there seemed to be an unwritten taboo everywhere in China against discussing Japan, as well as against going to see that country. This may account for so few books on Japan being written and published in China.

Well, I have grown older since then and have seen so many things outside China, and have also read more views on life by the great Eastern and Western thinkers. The idea has also grown in me that although hatred is one of seven inevitable human passions, which would arise within anyone who had been wronged by another, a modern man ought to think rationally enough that it would not be correct to extend his hatred to someone who had not actually wronged him, nor to those who had played no part in the wrong. It is an ineradicable fact that China was wronged by Japan again and again in the past, but the present people of Japan cannot be held responsible for their predecessors. I have always had the belief that not every inhabitant of a country could be involved in its wrongdoing and that human nature, as Confucius believed, is the same everywhere.

While I was teaching in the London School of Oriental and African Studies, I met the late Dr. D. T. Suzuki when he came to introduce Zen Buddhism to the West. I found him most scholarly and refined in character. Later we met several times again at Columbia University, where I made friends with other Japanese scholars and also with my colleagues who are specialists in Japanese literature and art. I began to read more books on many aspects of things Japanese and my interest grew continually, so that I wanted to see the country for myself. The result is that I went there not only once, but four times. I was always treated very kindly and courteously everywhere I went as I have described in this book. My great faith in human nature being alike everywhere has been strengthened. I have come to the conclusion that if there is no personal conflict stemming from some sophisticated notion such as nationalism, or patriotism, or race, people everywhere can be thoroughly congenial and kind when they meet one another. But once somebody becomes strongly conscious of belonging to a particular nation, race, religious sect, or ideology, that person's attitude becomes distorted and he loses his original congeniality and kindness. Thus troubles, arguments, and wars have ensued. During the last war I remember reading in England about two brothers of the same parentage, one of whom lived in Germany and the other in England, and from these circumstances they were obliged to fight one another. Of course they had no reason to fight but every reason not to. The only hope I can see for the peace of the world is that in the very near future the name of a nation should become a mere geographical label; for instance, when Japan is simply thought of as an area of the earth which includes Kyoto, Tokyo, and all the other cities, while the United States becomes New York or San Francisco, and

China, Peking or Nanking, and so forth. This will by-pass all differences of nationality, race, religion, and even ideology. There would then be no quarrels and wars. For this reason I decided to write this book about a nation, Japan, in the same way as I wrote about a single city in my other Silent Traveller books.

This book of mine may be regarded as the work of a very odd Chinese who managed to see more places in Japan than even most of the Japanese themselves and who believes, as Confucius did, that humans are alike everywhere on the globe. If my thought could win some sympathetic support for abolishing the names of nations for distinguishing between peoples and substituting for them the names of places in which live people who are just like other people all over the earth, my humble effort to encourage world peace will not be too futile.

Incidentally, had I managed to go with my great-uncle to the north of China in 1928, I, too, might have disappeared from this world that night. No book then.

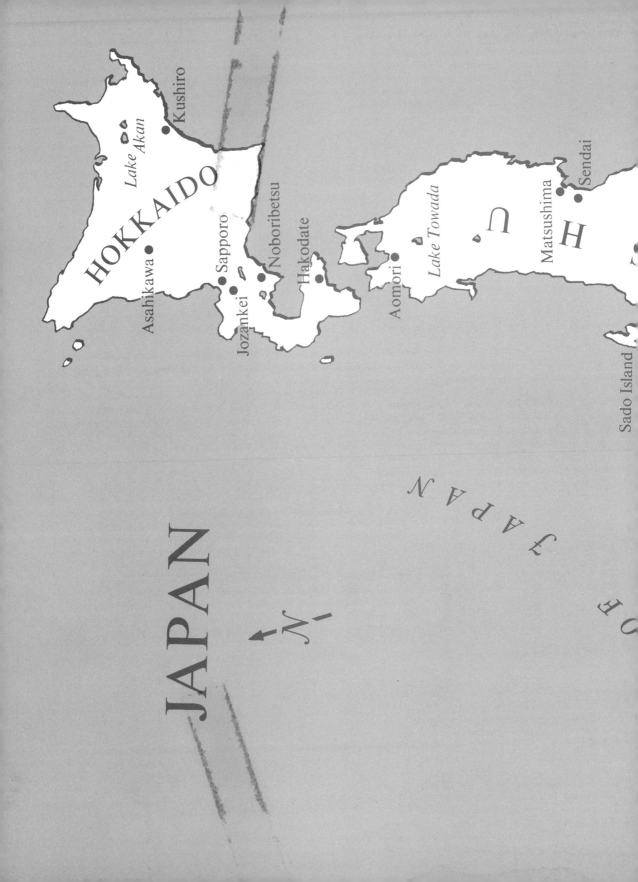